Lord Charles Cavendish Fulke Greville, of a famous English family of poets and politicians, moved in the high inner circles of politics and society during the turbulent years in England and Europe, 1814-1860, when the highbred continental world gave way to a triumphant bourgeois one. His early resolve to record for history what actually happened amounted to, at his death, eight volumes of *Memoirs,* so telling that Queen Victoria exploded over their first publication, even though they then extended only to William IV's death, and, as Louis Kronenberger relates in his introduction, "they then omitted what would have most made her explode."

For this edition of Greville's *Memoirs,* Louis Kronenberger has extracted the cream of the chronicles: the most telling incidents, the episodes and intrigues that best illuminate the character and influence of such prominent English and continental figures as Wellington, Melbourne, Louis Philippe, Talleyrand, Napoleon—and their self: George IV, William IV, and Victoria.

His comments and anecdotes range from the first intimation of Byron's homosexuality to Louis Philippe's reaction to his fall in the Revolution of 1848; from Melbourne's skillful management of the young and willful Queen Victoria to Disraeli's mangling of Peel in the struggle over the corn laws; from the conditions in a debtors' prison to the strange ethics of two doctors who performed an operation on a young boy. All these amount to an intimate tour through fifty of the most important years of English—and European—history.

THE GREAT WORLD

THE
GREAT WORLD

Portraits and Scenes
from Greville's Memoirs

(1814-1860)

EDITED

WITH AN INTRODUCTION BY

Louis Kronenberger

1963

Garden City, New York

DOUBLEDAY & COMPANY, INC.

LIBRARY OF CONGRESS CATALOG CARD NUMBER 63–7703
COPYRIGHT © 1963 BY LOUIS KRONENBERGER
ALL RIGHTS RESERVED
PRINTED IN THE UNITED STATES OF AMERICA
FIRST EDITION

Table of Contents

Introduction   vii

Bibliographical Note   xvii

The English Royal Family   xix

Biographical Data   xxi

The Reign of King George IV   1

The Reign of King William IV   35

The Reign of Queen Victoria   117

Index   347

Introduction

English history is rich in men—Greville is one of the most notable —who from their writing tables looked out upon English history and turned back to chronicle it. Now in letters and despatches, now in diaries and journals, they set down the eloquent moments that revivify the past, or the scraps of firsthand knowledge or unfiltered gossip that help illuminate it. Thanks to such letters and diaries and memoirs, we know just how one man, or many men, or all of England felt about a prince's marriage or a nobleman's murder, a naval disaster or a maiden speech. Thanks too, we are informed as to what *actually* happened; or why things so abruptly went wrong; or who was behind it all; or on whom the dread decision really rested; or round whom the storm clouds finally broke. For by virtue of such chroniclers we look not only out the window but also behind the door, we not just hear men speak but intercept their nods and glances, we not just marvel at the calm they maintain or the front they put up, but see them crazed with fury or crumpled in despair.

Such men have been invaluable chroniclers of events from being indefatigable connoisseurs of news. What they could not witness themselves they sought accounts of from people who did. And since to be privy to so much that went on in high places, and often behind closed doors, one usually had to be high-placed oneself, it is no accident that almost all these chroniclers were members of the great world, were influential bishops like Burnet

or sinuous peers like Hervey or sons of Prime Ministers like Walpole or adventurous patricians like Scawen Blunt; or were
temporarily courted and cosseted like Swift, or annually country-
housed and fed like Creevey. You had to be sure of a place in
the sun to learn all that went on in the shade and the darkness;
had to know the right people to hear all about the wrong deeds.
Yours was often a secondary, a so to speak sedentary role, but it
meant getting quick tidings of primary matters: if, so to speak,
Rothschild was the first man in England with the news of Waterloo, you were to be first with the news of Rothschild.

In that sense Charles Cavendish Fulke Greville was most splendidly placed. We need only pause over his name to see how much
history, poetry, aristocracy it encompassed. His remote ancestor
was Sir Philip Sidney's friend and fellow-poet Fulke Greville,
and his Greville relations were the Earls of Warwick. His
mother's father, the Duke of Portland, was twice Prime Minister
and almost the grandest of Whig grandees, who had furthermore
married the daughter of one equally grand, the Duke of Devonshire. And when Greville was a child, his grandfather obtained
for him the reversion of two very pretty posts—the Secretaryship
of Jamaica, an island he would never set eyes on, and a Clerkship
of the Privy Council, a politically neutral place where he sat,
throughout four decades, with ranking statesmen and reigning
ministers. When a young man, Greville, from his interest in racing, came to manage the stables of the Duke of York who, but
for dying betimes, would have succeeded his brother George IV
as King of England. It was not during working hours alone, however, that Greville met the richest, the royalest, the most powerful and brilliant people in England. During his leisure hours he
had the run of the very best clubs and country houses; and, never
marrying, he everlastingly dined out, at dinner tables that might
in a pinch have converted themselves into Cabinet meetings. But
as one side of him diverged from politics to racing, another
turned toward letters and intellect. He had, too, a taste for travel;
as a young man he paid a lengthy visit to Italy, on other occasions
he went to Ireland and Germany, and a number of times to Paris.

His access to political affairs at home was not without consequences: he became well acquainted with successive editors of
the London *Times*,[1] feeding them news and occasional articles
and in turn being fed by them plums for his diaries. And he is
linked to letters as well as to journalism. His Jamaican sinecure
bore a certain fruit through Greville's publishing that minor classic of Jamaican life, Monk Lewis's *Journal of a West India Pro-
prietor*.

But Greville's own Journal is his passport to becoming a great
minor classic himself, as one of the very few *indispensable* English memoir-writers. He is indispensable because no one writing
of English (and at times Continental) history between 1820 and
1860 can possibly ignore him or easily not quote from him; he can
be disagreed with and occasionally discredited, but as a "source"
he simply cannot be done without. His was indeed a privileged
place, and during a period of momentous transition when political designs kept tilting with historical forces. Politics was something Greville didn't just *happen* to chronicle; he made it his
life's business. His work is not, like Hervey's, primarily a description of life at Court; he did not, like Walpole, excel at turning
gossip into an art: Greville's is chiefly a concern with the internal
and subterranean life of Parliament, with the life (and death) of
administrations. From much else he turned away. "If I . . . chose
to insert all the trash of diurnal occurrences," he writes, "the
squabbles of the Jockey Club, and things which had better be
forgotten . . . I might fill books full in no time, but I can't and
won't." In general, he disdained gossip for gossip's sake; and
though the result, in general, was to save his *Memoirs* from nasti-
ness and triviality, it robbed them at times of lightness and fizz.
Gossip usually had to crystallize into scandal (as with the Lady
Flora Hastings *crise*) or shed light on events for Greville to grant
it entry; and on those scores it gained fairly frequent entry and
proves both salt and leaven to the *Memoirs* as a whole. Gossip
of a different kind, *political* gossip, with all that it entailed of

[1] The second of them, Henry Reeve, became after Greville's death the
editor of these *Memoirs*.

prognostication and hearsay, is of course the very essence of his
Journals. Just as Greville disdained repeating boudoir anecdotes
and stable-yard squabbling, he refused to repeat what anyone
could come upon in the public press. Indeed his object, with
regard to posterity, was to supplement the public press; to jot
down things that never got into the papers or were designedly
kept out of them. And so, for posthumous publication, he queried
and harried and "interviewed" statesmen and M.P.s, Cabinet
Ministers and diplomats, and their sisters and their cousins and
their aunts. What resulted was an immense mass of speculation
before the event, of discussion at the time of it, and of interpretation afterwards, much of it confidential and extremely revealing,
some of it comically wishful or astigmatic, where fears loom large
and come to nothing, or prophecies rumble and come to even less.

All this recording of political measures and talk and tactics concerns, as I have said, so great an age of transition as to constitute
a period of transformation. Beginning his Journal in 1814, in a
highbred Regency world, Greville wound it up in 1860, in a
triumphant bourgeois one. Betweenwhiles, along with the clam-
orous problems of India and Ireland, there were such great issues
at home as Catholic Emancipation, the first Reform Bill, Chart-
ism, the Corn Laws and Free Trade, and the agitation over a
second Reform Bill. As for men, the list begins with Castlereagh
and Canning, embraces Wellington, Liverpool, Grey, Huskisson,
Peel, Palmerston, Melbourne, Lord John Russell, Derby, Clarendon, Sidney Herbert, to conclude with Cobden and Bright, Disraeli and Gladstone. In many instances Greville records the chops
and changes, the shifts and soundings, over days, weeks, months
and even years. Almost always he records something not found
elsewhere, or a version unlike all others, or a version unlike his
own of two days before. With its comments on issues and events,
and its comments on other commentators, the whole thing approaches a political round game, a hare-and-hounds of opinion,
till the chronicle takes on as many voices as changes of key.

The countless footnotes to history that Greville's *Memoirs* supply have provided thousands of actual footnotes for later histo-

rians; this side of the *Memoirs* is priceless source material. All the
same, it is the side that has chiefly benefited specialists and later
writers. It is not, I think, the side that has most nourished Greville's own readers, who will find more engrossing accounts of the
Corn Laws agitation or the Crimean War in other books—in books
that *drew on* Greville. For often matters are duller, and far more
long-winded, behind the scenes than before the footlights. Hence
I have scamped the Great-Issues-and-Events side of the *Memoirs*.
The endless day-by-day entries on, say, the first Reform Bill are
such that no single day seems altogether sufficient. We must in
any case distinguish between the Greville who chiefly provides
others with information and the Greville who constantly provides
us with pleasure. The pleasure he gives is of a front-seat view, or
of a backstage glimpse, at just the moment when we shall see
and hear something vital yet particularly special, historical yet
wonderfully human. And in distinguishing between the two Grev-
illes, we must glance at what distinguishes the man himself: at
what he brought to his opportunities and how, at times, he contrived them; at what manner of man he was along with what kind
of aristocrat; how perceptive was his eye along with how patient
his ear; and, finally, how well he could write up what he wrote
down.

Born in 1794 and dying in 1865, he not unnaturally belonged by
temperament to the age he came out of. The new order of things
he confronted in middle life created an inner conflict for him and
a lag in sympathy. He shares, however, the best patrician impulses of the earlier age—he caught and kept what was most enlightened and humane in the great eighteenth-century tradition.
He believed in an unobstreperous progress; he deprecated selfish
upper-class abuses; he desired a better life for the poor. Indeed,
he was for every reform that would not discommode his own welfare. (This is no cynical sneer but only what he half-admitted
himself.) As he got older, he grew more set. He remained a Whig
when the Whigs themselves had changed their name to Liberals;
and what by then he often found most alarming were not the
palpable diseases of society but the projected cures. Yet he was

never a real fossil as he was never a fool. He had, for one thing, that perhaps best gift in the old Whig heritage, a certain balance and love of balance, a certain fairmindedness and effort at fairmindedness, so that it is toward the irresponsible and the intemperate that he seems most severe, and no less when they are ultra-Tory than ultra-radical. He is as outraged, again, by a Palmerston's high-handed methods as by any socialist's beliefs, and as incensed by royalty's attempts to usurp power as by agitators' to undermine it. He shared the old grandee-Whig dislike of the Royal Family, he had the disdain of the great country houses for the Court; and though he had a Court connection by way of the Duke of York, that never prevented his calling the Duke's elder brother, George IV, a pig and the worst of Kings; or his younger brother, William IV, a clown and quite scandalously unroyal; or his niece, Victoria, far more willful than wise. Small wonder that Queen Victoria exploded over the publication of his *Memoirs*, even though they then extended only to William IV's death, even though they then omitted what would have most made her explode.

But toward royal personages, as toward almost everyone else, he was always fair enough to admit his bias or explain his bile; and in the end he did ample justice to their good points, to George's aristocratic tastes or William's democratic ways, and to what was conscientious and judicious in Victoria and Albert. If no brilliant psychologist of men, or notable critic of arts and societies, he was marvelously conversant with the high life of his times, and sagaciously curious about its methods and motive power. As a privileged worldling, he was seldom taken in by noble assertions and professions in high places, he knew every *cui bono* and *sauve-qui-peut* of the ambitious and the powerful; and anything he knew was always the starting-point for finding out what he didn't. There were, to be sure, people about whom he was constantly shifting ground, some even—like the Duke of Wellington—about whom he conspicuously changed his opinion; and about certain people there were things he never apprehended. But as people lived on, or more particularly as they died off, he wrote solid, cogent, perceptive, remarkably unbiased—or admittedly quite biased—summations of their character and summaries of their careers. These seem to me, indeed, perhaps the best things he did, and among the best things that anyone has done of that sort. He is, to be sure, no Saint-Simon; he seldom summons people to life with a gesture or a phrase, or makes them completely visible, audible, unique. It is rather the opposite: he is a sovereign writer of obituaries, with just enough sense of occasion not to be waspish or petty, but with not so much as to be muzzled by a *De mortuis*. He not just means to tell the truth, he manages to. But, as against composing epitaphs at people's deaths, he is constantly recounting episodes in their lives, portraying his man as bully or buffoon, as taunting the Lords or taming the Commons. As is hardly surprising, he oftener does better with men he dislikes than with men he admires—partly, of course, because he can be more biting, but partly because they themselves are apt to have more bite. Peel and Palmerston are among his decided successes.

In the end, however, Greville wasn't deeply interested in people as people. He was interested, rather, in people as representative figures—the great landowner, the indomitable Tory, the successful whipper-in; or, again, as quite *un*representative figures, whether celebrities like Wellington or prodigies like Macaulay. And he was most of all interested in men of affairs, in those who pulled the strings or ran the show, who established harmony or fomented uproar, who won votes or delivered them. Greville spent his life in clubs and country houses, yet he gives us little, in the end, that mirrors club or country-house life. To his own way of thinking, he misspent his life on the racecourse, and as so great a *bon vivant* that he was forever laid up with gout. Yet of this side of things we are given hardly a pungent anecdote; what we have instead, and in abundance, is self-depreciatory lament and self-recriminatory confession, all of it only saved from being cant by his saying frankly that it is too late for him to reform; and by no means all of it saved from being comic.

But—to resume—his concern with people rests largely on what

they know or think, and even then in terms of current issues and crises. Or of what once were issues and crises, for next to inside news Greville most values illuminating reminiscence. And about such things his curiosity is immense. In his own fashion he was a good deal of a Boswell, which is to say a good deal of a busybody. Again and again we get peeps into how industrious he could be: "I had the curiosity," he says of Lord William Russell's murderer, "to go . . . to Tothill Fields prison to see the man"; adding two days later: "Just after writing the above, I went to the house in Norfolk Street, to look at the premises, and the places where the watch and other things were found hidden." And every so often we find him not just examining the premises, but determinedly stalking his prey: "After looking for him for several mornings in the Park, through which he walks in his way to the Courts, I fell in with Thessinger." And the calls he paid on men whose knowledge he sought cannot always, however well he knew the men themselves, have been welcomed. He was forever asking people to talk, as it were, for posthumous publication. And his deafness, at such times, cannot have been very endearing, while his disposition could at moments be "crosser than any pair of tongs." But if a good deal of a busybody, and as hard to escape from in parks as at clubs, he was almost as often Johnson as Boswell, almost as often sought out for his opinions as he sought others out for theirs. If he contrived to meddle, he was yet very frequently asked to mediate; if he panted after leaks, he neatly patched up differences; and by way of his *Times* connection, was often a very valuable go-between. And finally, the examiner of premises and the stalker of prey was laboring so steadily—and dextrously—at his vocation, that on its own terms and for its own time the result remains unparalleled.

Greville's "serious" interests went, however, far beyond political issues, just as his leisure extended far beyond the racecourse and the social round. He came from a world whose commanding figures were cultivated men who delighted in elegance and wit and not least in ideas; a world of lineage that sufficiently prized intellect to constantly break bread with it. Even as the nineteenth century advanced, men of birth continued to be men of background. Matthew Arnold, looking back to the eighteenth century, was moved to cite—as part of its highbred aura—Lord Granville quoting Homer on his deathbed. But in Arnold's own century Melbourne and Disraeli, Prime Ministers both, are but the best-known of cultivated men of affairs. Lord Derby, also a Prime Minister, did a famous translation of Homer; Greville's politico brother-in-law, Lord Ellesmere, did a translation of *Faust;* of Lord Harrowby, who refused to be Prime Minister, Madame de Stael said that he "knows our literature a little better than we ourselves do." In a society that not only made recondite Latin allusions one was expected to identify, but good Latin puns one was expected to laugh at; a society that still went on a version of the Grand Tour, and still paid its visits to the ranking salons; a society that could hold the table at dinner no less than the House at midnight, Greville—to maintain his place—had to be more than a duke's grandson. He had to be, as he was, well-read; and well-read in fairly back-breaking writers. His Whiggishness, moreover, made him an habitué of Holland House, with its wheelchair Lord and whipcracking Lady, where fell the showers of Sydney Smith's wit and rolled the torrents of Macaulay's learning, and where too, along with distinguished foreigners, came Melbourne and Palmerston and the ineffable Brougham of whom Macaulay said: "He half-knows everything." On the Continent too, particularly in Paris, Greville encountered the best brains along with the best blood. Birth he could take for granted; and though, when Reform seemed to stride too fast, or his sinecures were endangered, he might dwindle into an aristocrat, he was never a foolish snob and could berate not just his own class but his own cousins. The Bentincks were "insolent, overbearing worshippers of each other, and inflated with notions of their own consequence and right."

At moments Greville might have displayed a more robust comic sense, though his very indignation over Palmerston or the Royal Family helps double the fun. At moments too we might wish for Macaulay's sense of theatre or Walpole's knack for phrase —yet Greville could aptly enough describe Wellington in old age as a kind of "secular Pope" or Holland House as "the house of all Europe." And Macaulay indulged his gift for theatre at some cost to truth, as Walpole achieved his gift for phrase with some help from malice. One of Greville's greatest virtues is his feeling for truth: even his misstatements were never dishonestly actuated and were, as soon as known, avowed. His own definition of what a Journal should be strikes me as notably sound: "To be good, true and interesting, [it] should be written without the slightest reference to publication, but without any fear of it." And it seems to me that he steadfastly followed his rule and richly fulfilled his aim.

Bibliographical Note

The present text is based upon the following:

1. *The Greville Memoirs*. Edited by Henry Reeve.

   A Journal of the Reign of King George IV and King William IV.
   3 vols. London: Longmans, Green & Co. 1874.

   A Journal of the Reign of Queen Victoria: 1837–52.
   3 vols. Longmans. 1885.

   A Journal of the Reign of Queen Victoria: 1852–60.
   2 vols. Longmans. 1887.

2. *The Greville Memoirs*. Edited by Lytton Strachey and Roger Fulford. 8 vols. London: Macmillan & Co. 1938.

The English Royal Family

GEORGE III (1738–1820)
m. Charlotte of Mecklenburg-Strelitz

His sons:

GEORGE IV (1762–1830) m. Caroline of Brunswick
his daughter Charlotte, d. 1817; married to
Leopold of Saxe-Coburg, later King of the
Belgians and uncle of Queen Victoria

FREDERICK, Duke of York (1763–1827)

WILLIAM, Duke of Clarence, later WILLIAM IV
(1765–1837)

EDWARD, Duke of Kent (1767–1820), father of
Queen Victoria

ERNEST, Duke of Cumberland, afterwards King of
Hanover (1771–1851)

AUGUSTUS, Duke of Sussex (1773–1843)

ADOLPHUS, Duke of Cambridge (1774–1850)

His granddaughter:

QUEEN VICTORIA, (1819–1901) d. of the Duke of Kent
and Princess Victoria of Saxe-Coburg
m. Prince Albert of Saxe-Coburg (her first cousin).

Biographical Data

These entries aim at providing a few salient facts in the careers of such contemporaries of Greville's as command attention in these pages. Omitted, as needing no identification, have been the very famous—Victoria and Albert, Disraeli and Gladstone, Wellington and Macaulay. Allotted briefer notice than they might otherwise have received are those whose obituaries by Greville himself are to be found in the text: these have an asterisk before their names.

ABERDEEN, GEORGE HAMILTON GORDON, 4th Earl of (1784–1860), Tory statesman; Secretary at War, twice Foreign Secretary, Prime Minister during the Crimean War; as Foreign Secretary terminated controversy over NW boundaries of the U.S. and Canada.

*ALVANLEY, WILLIAM ARDEN, 2nd Baron (1789–1849).

ASHBURTON, ALEXANDER BARING, 1st Baron (1774–1848), head of the great Baring banking house for 18 years; for 29 years an anti-Reform M.P., shifting from the Whig to the Tory side; Ambassador (1842) to the U.S.

BEAUVALE, FREDERICK LAMB, Lord (1782–1853); diplomat; English Ambassador to Austria 1831–41; married daughter of the

Prussian Minister to Austria; younger brother of Lord Melbourne, to whose title he succeeded.

BROUGHAM, HENRY, Baron (1778–1868), leading contributor to the *Edinburgh Review*, popular defender of Queen Caroline, advocate of Reform; M.P., Lord Chancellor—able, energetic and eloquent; over-confident, eccentric and ill-behaved.

CANNING, GEORGE (1770–1827), statesman; entered Parliament 1794, as a follower of Pitt; co-author of the satirical *Anti-Jacobin;* Foreign Minister during Napoleonic Wars; differed with Castlereagh and dueled with him; about to become Viceroy to India when, on Castlereagh's death, he succeeded him at the Foreign Office and eventually became Prime Minister. Still remembered for some witty verses.

CLARENDON, GEORGE W. F. VILLIERS, 8th Earl of (1800–70), liberal statesman, early entered the diplomatic service (St. Petersburg, Madrid); later Lord-Lieutenant of Ireland and three times Foreign Secretary. Espoused peace and civilization; refused many honors, including the Governor-Generalship of India.

COBBETT, WILLIAM (1762–1835), in early life a solicitor's clerk, British Army private, Philadelphia bookseller. Back in England, first supported Pitt, then vehemently opposed the Tories; prosecuted and imprisoned for remarks on military flogging. Tried unsuccessfully to enter Parliament; made political tours, published in the well-known *Rural Rides;* prosecuted for an inflammatory libel (jury disagreeing); entered the reformed Parliament in 1832. A political Radical, he survives as a vigorous writer and journalist on many subjects.

CONYNGHAM, Lady (1769–1861), born Elizabeth Denison, married a Tory Irish peer who became 1st Marquis Conyngham, was mistress of George IV as Prince Regent and King. She and her husband always lived at Court where she was heaped with presents and where, to the day of George IV's death, her influence was immense.

CREEVEY, THOMAS (1768–1838), Whig M.P.; almost without income became a great society favorite who moved from country house to country house and whose well-known "Papers" are a mine of gossip, anecdote, and social history.

*CROKER, JOHN WILSON (1780–1857), Tory political and literary man, notorious for his scathing review of Keats's *Endymion;* edited Boswell's *Johnson;* his posthumous *Papers* provide interesting political pictures and sidelights.

DERBY, EDWARD, 14th Earl of (earlier, Lord Stanley) (1799–1869), entered Parliament 1822; advocate of Reform, Catholic Emancipation and Free Trade; later left Whigs to become in time leader of the Tories; Prime Minister in 1852 and 1858, headed the party that passed the 2nd Reform Bill; in 1868 surrendered its leadership to Disraeli.

* D'ORSAY, ALFRED (1801–52), Frenchman who came to London in his youth and became famous as an artist and dandy. The lover of Lady Blessington, he was part of the literary and artistic society that she long entertained at Gore House.

EGERTON, FRANCIS, 1st Earl of Ellesmere (1800–57), son of 1st Duke of Sutherland, husband of Greville's sister, entered Parliament 1822, successively Under-Secretary for the Colonies, Chief Secretary for Ireland, Secretary at War. Immensely rich, he did much writing and translating, including a successful version of Dumas at Covent Garden.

ELDON, JOHN SCOTT, 1st Earl (1751–1838), lawyer, M.P., supporter of Pitt, successively solicitor-general, attorney-general, chief justice, and for 25 years Lord Chancellor. Instituted office of vice-chancellor; strongly anti-Whig, strongly against Catholic Emancipation.

ELLESMERE, Earl of. *See Francis Egerton.*

GRAHAM, SIR JAMES (1792–1861), Whig statesman, long-term M.P., Home Secretary and twice First Lord of the Admiralty.

GRANVILLE, GEORGE LEVESON-GOWER, 1st Earl (1773–1846), diplomat; successively English Ambassador to Russia, to the Netherlands, and for many years to France.

GREY, CHARLES, 2nd Earl (1764–1845), Whig statesman who became a party leader from his maiden speech on; follower of Fox and bitter opponent of Pitt, who came out of retirement in 1830 to head the ministry that pushed through the great Reform Bill. He resigned soon after over the Irish Tithe Bill, ending his political career.

GUIZOT, FRANÇOIS (1787–1874), French statesman and historian; variously Minister of the Interior, of Public Instruction, and of Foreign Affairs; Ambassador to England, 1840; Prime Minister whose conservative policy was a decisive cause of the Revolution of 1848. A leading historian of his time, he is perhaps best known today for his *Histoire de la Civilization en Europe.*

HARDY, SIR THOMAS MASTERMAN (1769–1839), British admiral, Nelson's flag captain, later 1st Sea Lord; of the same family as the novelist.

HASTINGS, LADY FLORA (1806–39), daughter of 1st Marquis of Hastings; appointed lady of the bedchamber to Victoria's mother, the Duchess of Kent; unmarried, she was rumored pregnant, causing a Court scandal; examined and certified not to be; died soon after of enlargement of the liver; a "graceful volume" of her poems and translations published in 1841.

* HOLLAND, ELIZABETH VASSALL FOX, Lady (1770–1845), married Sir Godfrey Webster who divorced her for adultery with Lord Holland, whom she then married; the hostess of Holland House who, for all her tyrannical and ill-mannered ways, made it one of the most illustrious gathering places in English history.

* HOLLAND, HENRY FOX, 3rd Baron (1773–1840), brought up by his uncle, Charles James Fox; became an active and liberal Whig in Parliament; Lord Privy Seal in the ministry "of All the Talents"; Chancellor of the Duchy of Lancaster under Grey and Melbourne; scholarly dilettante, friend of writers, married to the great hostess of Holland House (*see above*).

LAMB, FREDERICK. *See Lord Beauvale.*

LEHZEN, LOUISE (d. 1870), a German clergyman's daughter, governess to Queen Victoria's half-sister on her mother's side, Princess Féodore, before becoming governess to Victoria; created a Hanoverian baroness in 1827; retired to Hanover in 1842.

LEWIS, MATTHEW GREGORY ("Monk"), (1775–1818), verse writer and dramatist whose nickname and popular place in literature derive from his indecent Gothic novel, *The Monk.* His West Indian *Journal,* however (*see Introduction*), if far less well known, has perhaps higher claims.

* LIEVEN, DOROTHEA CHRISTOPHOROVNA, Princess de (1785–1857), wife of the Russian Ambassador to Berlin and to London; mistress of Metternich, salonnière and friend of the great, well-known letter writer and diarist.

* LUTTRELL, HENRY (1765?–1851), natural son of a nobleman, a famous wit and diner-out, remembered for some light verse and as a great talker, "the most epigrammatic conversationalist" that Byron had ever met.

* MELBOURNE, WILLIAM LAMB, 2nd Viscount (1779–1848), Whig statesman; entered Parliament 1806; Chief Secretary for Ireland; twice Prime Minister; a man of much personal distinction; adored adviser of the young Queen Victoria; husband of Byron's inamorata, Lady Caroline Lamb.

MOORE, THOMAS, (1779–1852), Irish poet best known for some short lyrics and lighter pieces and for *Lalla Rookh;* close friend of Byron's, whose life he wrote and whose Memoirs, bequeathed to him, he destroyed.

* O'CONNELL, DANIEL (1775–1847), Irish politician and patriot, ardent fighter for Catholic rights before Emancipation. Afterwards he sat in the House of Commons where he and his followers, through holding the balance between Whigs and Tories, gained a good deal of power. He was arrested in 1843 and found guilty of conspiracy, but the English House of Lords reversed the decision; in Catholic Ireland he became, through his eloquence and enthusiasm, the great political figure of his day.

PALMERSTON, HENRY JOHN TEMPLE, 3rd Viscount (1784–1865), entered the House of Commons (his peerage was Irish) 1807; Lord of the Admiralty 1807; Secretary at War through successive Governments 1809–28; twice Foreign Secretary; Home Secretary; twice Prime Minister (1855–58; 1859–65). First a liberal Tory, later a Whig, he was essentially an Independent who "pledged himself to no party but judged every question on its merits." At the Foreign Office he vitally affected the current history of Europe and did much to raise

England's prestige; tenacious of purpose and often tyrannical in method, he created crises and made enemies, but was
often a popular hero, and was personally a good-humored
man.

* PEEL, SIR ROBERT (1788–1850), entered Parliament 1809; after
various offices became Home Secretary, 1822; vigorously opposed the Reform Bill. Briefly a Conservative Prime Minister
in 1834; in 1839 refused to form a ministry because of the
"Bedchamber crisis." Prime Minister from 1841 to 1846 when,
by supporting what he had long opposed, he achieved the
repeal of the Corn Laws, and so much lost Tory support as
to resign. On domestic matters, thereafter, he backed the
Whigs.

RAGLAN, Lord (1788–1855), son of the 5th Duke of Beaufort,
served in the Peninsular War, lost an arm at Waterloo, for
many years military secretary at the Horse Guards, later
master-general of ordnance, and field marshal. On the outbreak of the Crimean War made commander-in-chief of the
British Army; perturbed by his men's sufferings and in failing
health, died of cholera.

RANKE, LEOPOLD VON (1795–1886), distinguished German historian, world-famous (and still well known) for his *History of
the Popes;* among his other works, *History of the Reforma-
tion in Germany; History of England;* when over 80 began
a history of the world which had extended to nine volumes
at his death.

* ROGERS, SAMUEL (1763–1855), a man of much wealth and mild
poetic talent who in his own day enjoyed a high place in
letters and in literary society; offered the Laureateship on
Wordsworth's death but declined it. Unlike his poetry, his
Table Talk still has interest.

RUSSELL, LORD JOHN (1792–1878), son of 6th Duke of Bedford; liberal statesman; entered Parliament 1813. In 1830 became Paymaster of the Forces under Lord Grey; presented the Reform Bill to the House, helped with great ability to pass it, and when the Whigs soon after went out, was recognized as Opposition leader. After serving in several administrations, became Prime Minister, 1846–52; headed the Foreign Office under Palmerston, after whose death he again became Prime Minister. Defeated, 1866 on the 2nd Reform Bill, he resigned and never again held office.

SMITH, SYDNEY (1771–1845), Anglican minister, co-founder of the *Edinburgh Review*, habitué of Holland House, eventually a Canon of St. Paul's. One of the great wits of his era, in both his talk and his writings, he survives in many remarks that still seem witty.

SPENCER, FREDERIC, 4th Earl (1798–1857), successively Lord Chamberlain and Lord Steward of the Household to Queen Victoria; inherited and enriched his bibliomaniac father's great library.

STANLEY, LORD. *See Earl of Derby.*

* TALLEYRAND, CHARLES MAURICE [de Talleyrand-Périgord], (1754–1838), French diplomat and wit; excommunicated bishop; Foreign Minister under the Directory, under Napoleon, under Louis XVIII; Ambassador to England under Louis-Philippe.

TAYLOR, SIR HENRY (1800–86), served for some 50 years in the Colonial Office while writing numerous verse dramas, of which *Philip van Artevelde* was most famous. Some of his prose aphorisms still seem striking.

THIERS, LOUIS-ADOLPHE (1797–1877), French statesman; at various
times Minister of Commerce, of the Interior, Foreign Secretary and Prime Minister; arrested during the 1851 *coup
d'état* and expelled from France; returned to become Prime
Minister at the time of the Franco-Prussian War, and President of the Republic.

NOTE

Bracketed footnotes in regular type are by the first editor of Greville's *Memoirs*, Henry Reeve.

Bracketed footnotes in italics are by the editor of the present volume.

All others are Greville's own.

The Reign
of
King George IV*

* He was, of course, Regent until 1820.

September 16*th*, 1814. It has been doubted whether Buonaparte was ever much addicted to women: Sir Charles Stuart who is just arrived from Paris, and who relates many interesting anecdotes which he has picked up there, avers that he was, and that at Berlin and other places He used to intrigue with women, going about incognito as King of Westphalia, or some such title, his grandeur being such that he went about incognito as a King!

October 27*th*. When the Commissioners who are appointed to examine into the state of the King's health, are introduced into his apartment for that purpose, it is usual for the Physicians to engage him in conversation, in order to satisfy themselves of the real state of his disorder. The King has always avoided talking of publick affairs, nor have the Physicians ever informed him of any passing events. Sir Henry Halford, however, resolved (upon a recent examination by the Commissioners) to acquaint him with the great events which had taken place in Europe. Upon entering the Apartment, the King said as usual 'What news is there, Sir Henry?' 'Very great news, Sir,' he replied. 'Indeed'; said the King, 'but before you tell me the news, tell me how Lord Westmoreland does.' 'He is very well, Sir,' replied Sir Henry, 'and constantly asks after Your Majesty with the greatest affection.' 'Indeed'; said the King, 'after me still?' and he leant back and cried like a child; then said 'He is a rough man, but has an excellent heart at bottom'—'but come,' he added 'what is the news?' 'Sir,' said Sir Henry, 'the Emperors of Austria and Russia, and the King of Prussia are at the head of their Armies in the heart of France.' 'Indeed'; cried the King with great emotion. 'Yes, Sir,' said Sir Henry, 'and Your Majesty's Army is in France also.' At this intelligence the King appeared greatly agitated, and eagerly asked 'Who commands?' 'Lord Wellington, Sir' replied Sir Henry. 'That's a damned lie,' said the King 'He was shot two years ago'—and then he began to talk incoherently. It is curious to observe these first glimmerings of reason thro' the darkness of his understanding, and the momentary interest excited in his mind by such intelligence.

Wednesday, March 29th, 1815. I dined at Chiswick and heard from Tierney the story which has been hinted at in the Newspapers, of the man who offered to communicate to Govt. much information concerning Buonaparte, for a sum of money, £500 I believe. The story is this:—He was an Upholsterer, and was employed to put up some curtains in Buonaparte's House at Elba. Whilst he was mounted on his ladder arranging the furniture, he observed the Emperor (who was in the Room) occupied with much earnestness and attention about some papers which covered the Table. Upon Napoleon's going out of the room shortly afterwards, he descended from his occupation and examined the papers. He found a great deal of interesting matter and carried off a part containing Buonaparte's cypher, his proclamation, and other documents relating to his late invasion. These papers he brought over here and offered to Govt. for a sum of money, but he was not attended to by anyone. The papers are now at Stockdale's Shop in Pall Mall, and Mr. Stockdale says that many Persons have seen them, although they are not to be shown any more.

August 4th, 1818. I went to Oatlands[1] on Saturday. We played at whist till four in the morning. On Sunday we amused ourselves with eating fruit in the garden, and shooting at a mark with pistols, and playing with the monkeys. I bathed in the cold bath in the grotto, which is as clear as crystal and as cold as ice. Oatlands is the worst managed establishment in England; there are a great many servants, and nobody waits on you; a vast number of horses, and none to ride or drive.

August 15th. The parties at Oatlands take place every Saturday, and the guests go away on Monday morning. These parties begin as soon as the Duchess leaves London, and last till the October meetings. During the Egham races there is a large party which remains there from the Saturday before the races till the Monday se'nnight following; this is called the Duchess's party, and she invites the guests. The Duke is only there himself from Saturday to Monday. There are almost always the same people, sometimes more, sometimes less. We dine at eight, and sit at table till eleven. In about a quarter of an hour after we leave the dining-room the Duke sits down to play at whist, and never stirs from the table as long as anybody will play with him. When anybody gives any hint of being tired he will leave off, but if he sees no signs of weariness in others he will never stop himself. He is equally well amused whether the play is high or low, but the stake he prefers is fives and ponies.[2] The Duchess generally plays also at half-crown whist. The Duke always gets up very early, whatever time he may go to bed. On Sunday morning he goes to church, returns to a breakfast of tea and cold meat, and afterwards rides or walks till the evening. On Monday morning he always sets off to London at nine o'clock. He sleeps equally well in a bed or in a carriage. The Duchess seldom goes to bed, or,

---

[1] [Oatlands Park, Weybridge, at that time the residence of the Duke of York.]

[2] [Five-pound points and twenty-five pounds on the rubber.]

if she does, only for an hour or two; she sleeps dressed upon a couch, sometimes in one room, sometimes in another. She frequently walks out very late at night, or rather early in the morning, and she always sleeps with open windows. She dresses and breakfasts at three o'clock, afterwards walks out with all her dogs, and seldom appears before dinner-time. At night, when she cannot sleep, she has women to read to her. The Duchess of York[3] is clever and well-informed; she likes society and dislikes all form and ceremony, but in the midst of the most familiar intercourse she always preserves a certain dignity of manner. Those who are in the habit of going to Oatlands are perfectly at their ease with her, and talk with as much freedom as they would to any other woman, but always with great respect. Her mind is not perhaps the most delicate; she shows no dislike to coarseness of sentiment or language, and I have seen her very much amused with jokes, stories, and allusions which would shock a very nice person. But her own conversation is never polluted with anything the least indelicate or unbecoming. She is very sensible to little attentions, and is annoyed if anybody appears to keep aloof from her or to shun conversing with her. Her dogs are her greatest interest and amusement, and she has at least forty of various kinds. She is delighted when anybody gives her a dog, or a monkey, or a parrot, of all of which she has a vast number; it is impossible to offend her or annoy her more than by ill-using any of her dogs, and if she were to see anybody beat or kick any one of them she would never forgive it. She has always lived on good terms with the Royal Family, but is intimate with none of them, and goes as little as possible to Court. The Regent dislikes her, and she him. With the Princess Charlotte she was latterly very intimate, spent a great deal of time at Claremont, and felt her death very severely. The Duchess has no taste for splendour or magnificence, and likes to live the life of a private individual as much as possible.

The Duke of York is not clever, but he has a justness of under-

---

[3] [The Duchess of York was born Princess Royal of Prussia; she married the Duke of York in 1791, and died on the 6th of August, 1820.]

standing, which enables him to avoid the errors into which most of his brothers have fallen, and which have made them so contemptible and unpopular. Although his talents are not rated high, and in public life he has never been honourably distinguished, the Duke of York is loved and respected. He is the only one of the Princes who has the feelings of an English gentleman; his amiable disposition and excellent temper have conciliated for him the esteem and regard of men of all parties, and he has endeared himself to his friends by the warmth and steadiness of his attachments, and from the implicit confidence they all have in his truth, straightforwardness, and sincerity. He delights in the society of men of the world and in a life of gaiety and pleasure. He is very easily amused, and particularly with jokes full of coarseness and indelicacy; the men with whom he lives most are *très-polissons,* and *la polissonnerie* is the *ton* of his society. But his aides-de-camp and friends, while they do not scruple to say everything before and to him, always treat him with attention and respect. The Duke and the Duchess live upon the best terms; their manner to one another is cordial, and while full of mutual respect and attention, they follow separately their own occupations and amusements without interfering with one another. Their friends are common to both, and those who are most attached to the Duke are equally so to the Duchess. One of her few foibles is an extreme tenaciousness of her authority at Oatlands; one way in which this is shown is in the stable, where, although there are always eight or ten carriage-horses which seldom do any work, it is impossible ever to procure a horse to ride or drive, because the Duchess appropriates them all to herself. The other day one of the aides-de-camp (Cooke) wanted to drive Burrell (who was there) to Hampton Court; he spoke of this at breakfast, and the Duke hearing it, desired he would take the curricle and two Spanish horses which had been given to him. The Duchess, however, chose to call these horses hers and to consider them as her own. The curricle came to the door, and just as they were going to mount it a servant came from the Duchess (who had heard of it) and told the coachman that her Royal Highness knew nothing of it, had not ordered it, and that the curricle must go home, which it accordingly did.

February 4th, 1820. I returned to Woburn on Sunday. We shot the whole week and killed an immense quantity of game. On Sunday last arrived the news of the King's death. The new King has been desperately ill. He had a bad cold at Brighton, for which he lost 80 ounces of blood; yet he afterward had a severe oppression, amounting almost to suffocation, on his chest. Yesterday afternoon he was materially better for the first time.

February 20th. The Ministers had resigned last week because the King would not hear reason on the subject of the Princess. It is said that he treated Lord Liverpool very coarsely, and ordered him out of the room. The King, they say, asked him 'if he knew to whom he was speaking.' He replied, 'Sir, I know that I am speaking to my Sovereign, and I believe I am addressing him as it becomes a loyal subject to do.' To the Chancellor he said, 'My Lord, I know your conscience always interferes except where your interest is concerned.' The King afterwards sent for Lord Liverpool, who refused at first to go; but afterwards, on the message being reiterated, he went, and the King said, 'We have both been too hasty.' This is probably all false, but it is very true that they offered to resign.

July 14th. Read 'Les Liaisons Dangereuses.' Much has been said about the dangerous tendency of certain books, and probably this would be considered as one pregnant with mischief. I consider this a mere jargon, and although I would never recommend this book (because it is so grossly indecent) I should never apprehend the smallest danger to the most inexperienced mind or the warmest passions from its immoral tendency. The principle upon which books of this description are considered pernicious is the notion that they represent vice in such glowing and attractive colours as to make us lose sight of its deformity and fill our imagination with the idea of its pleasures. No one who has any feeling or a spark of generosity or humanity in his breast can read this book without being moved with compassion for Madame de Tourval and with horror and disgust towards Valmont and Madame de Merteuil. It raised in my mind a detestation of such cold-blooded, inhuman profligacy, and I felt that I would rather every pleasure that can flow from the intercourse of women were debarred me than run such a course. The moral effect upon my mind was stronger than any which ever resulted from the most didactic work, and if anyone wants to excite remorse in the most vicious mind I would recommend him to make use of 'Les Liaisons Dangereuses' for the purpose.

May 2nd, 1821. Lady Conyngham[4] lives in one of the houses in Marlborough Row. All the members of her family are continually there, and are supplied with horses, carriages, &c., from the King's stables. She rides out with her daughter, but never with the King, who always rides with one of his gentlemen. They never appear in public together. She dines there every day. Before the King comes into the room she and Lady Elizabeth join him in another room, and he always walks in with one on each arm. She comports herself entirely as mistress of the house, but never suffers her daughter to leave her. She has received magnificent presents, and Lady Elizabeth the same; particularly the mother has strings of pearls of enormous value. Madame de Lieven said she had seen the pearls of the Grand Duchesses and the Prussian Princesses, but had never seen any nearly so fine as Lady Conyngham's. The other night Lady Bath was coming to the Pavilion. After dinner Lady Conyngham called to Sir William Keppel and said, 'Sir William, do desire them to light up the saloon' (this saloon is lit by hundreds of candles). When the King came in she said to him, 'Sir, I told them to light up the saloon, as Lady Bath is coming this evening.' The King seized her arm and said with the greatest tenderness, 'Thank you, thank you, my

---

[4] [George IV's mistress]

dear; you always do what is right; you cannot please me so much as by doing everything you please, everything to show that you are mistress here.'

January 2nd, 1828. M'Gregor told me the other day that not one of the physicians and surgeons who attended the Duke of York through his long and painful illness had ever received the smallest remuneration, although their names and services had been laid before the King. He told me in addition that during sixteen years that he attended the Duke and his whole family he never received one guinea by way of fee or any payment whatever.

About three weeks ago I passed a few days at Panshanger, where I met Brougham; he came from Saturday till Monday morning, and from the hour of his arrival to that of his departure he never ceased talking. The party was agreeable enough— Luttrell, Rogers, &c.—but it was comical to see how the latter was provoked at Brougham's engrossing all the talk, though he could not help listening with pleasure. Brougham is certainly one of the most remarkable men I ever met; to say nothing of what he is in the world, his almost childish gaiety and animal spirits, his humour mixed with sarcasm, but not ill-natured, his wonderful information, and the facility with which he handles every subject, from the most grave and severe to the most trifling, displaying a mind full of varied and extensive information and a memory which has suffered nothing to escape it, I never saw any man whose conversation impressed me with such an idea of his superiority over all others. As Rogers said the morning of his departure, 'this morning Solon, Lycurgus, Demosthenes, Archimedes, Sir Isaac Newton, Lord Chesterfield, and a great many more went away in one post chaise.'

London, January 19th. Canning's industry was such that he never left a moment unemployed, and such was the clearness of his head that he could address himself almost at the same time to several different subjects with perfect precision and without the least embarrassment. He wrote very fast, but not fast enough for his mind, composing much quicker than he could commit his ideas to paper. He could not bear to dictate, because nobody could write fast enough for him; but on one occasion, when he had the gout in his hand and could not write, he stood by the fire and dictated at the same time a despatch on Greek affairs to George Bentinck and one on South American politics to Howard de Walden, each writing as fast as he could, while he turned from one to the other without hesitation or embarrassment.

January 28th. All the Ministers (old and new) were at Windsor the other day; but it was contrived that they should not meet, the *ins* being in one room and Landsdowne and Carlisle in another, and it was afterwards discovered that in a third room by himself was Goderich.

June 29th. I dined yesterday with the King at St. James's—his Jockey Club dinner. There were about thirty people, several not being invited whom he did not fancy. The Duke of Leeds told me a much greater list had been made out, but he had scratched several out of it. We assembled in the Throne Room, and found him already there, looking very well and walking about. He soon, however, sat down, and desired everybody else to do so. Nobody spoke, and he laughed and said, 'This is more like a Quaker than a Jockey Club meeting.' We soon went to dinner, which was in the Great Supper Room and very magnificent. He sat in the middle, with the Dukes of Richmond and Grafton on each side of him. I sat opposite to him, and he was particularly gracious to me, talking to me across the table and recommending all the good things; he made me (after eating a quantity of turtle) eat a dish of crawfish soup, till I thought I should have burst. After dinner the Duke of Leeds, who sat at the head of the table, gave 'The King.' We all stood up, when his Majesty thanked us, and said he hoped this would be the first of annual meetings of the sort to take place, there or elsewhere under his roof. He then ordered paper, pens, &c., and they began making matches and stakes; the most perfect ease was estab-

lished, just as much as if we had been dining with the Duke of
York, and he seemed delighted. He made one or two little
speeches, one recommending that a stop should be put to the
exportation of horses. He twice gave 'The Turf,' and at the end
the Duke of Richmond asked his leave to give a toast, and again
gave 'The King.'

August 6th. I brought Adair[5] back to town, and he told me a
great many things about Burke, and Fox, and Fitzpatrick, and
all the eminent men of that time with whom he lived when he
was young. Burke's conversation was delightful, so luminous and
instructive. He was very passionate, and Adair said that the first
time he ever saw him he unluckily asked him some question
about the wild parts of Ireland, when Burke broke out, 'You are a
fool and a blockhead; there are no wild parts in Ireland.' He was
extremely terrified, but afterwards Burke was very civil to him,
and he knew him very well.

He told me a great deal about the quarrel between Fox and
Burke. Fox never ceased to entertain a regard for Burke, and at
no time would suffer him to be abused in his presence. There was
an attempt made to bring about a reconciliation, and a meeting
for that purpose took place of all the leading men at Burlington
House. Burke was on the point of yielding when his son suddenly
made his appearance unbidden, and on being told what was going on said, 'My father shall be no party to such a compromise,'
took Burke aside and persuaded him to reject the overtures. That
son Adair described as the most disagreeable, violent, and wrong-
headed of men, but the idol of his father, who used to say that
he united all his own talents and acquirements with those of Fox
and everybody else. After the death of Richard Burke, Fox and
Burke met behind the throne of the House of Lords one day,
when Fox went up to Burke and put out both his hands to him.
Burke was almost surprised into meeting this cordiality in the

---

[5] [Right Hon. Sir Robert Adair, the friend of Fox, formerly ambassador
at Constantinople and Vienna. It was he whom Canning once called 'Boba-
dare-a-dool-fowla.']

same spirit, but the momentary impulse passed away, and he doggedly dropped his hands and left the House.

January 12th, 1829 [*Lord Mount Charles*] talked to me about Knighton, whom the King abhors with a detestation that could hardly be described. He is afraid of him, and that is the reason he hates him so bitterly. When alone with him he is more civil, but when others are present (the family, for instance) he delights in saying the most mortifying and disagreeable things to him. He would give the world to get rid of him, and to have either Taylor or Mount Charles instead, to whom he has offered the place over and over again, but Mount Charles not only would not hear of it, but often took Knighton's part with the King. He says that his language about Knighton is sometimes of the most unmeasured violence—wishes he was dead, and one day when the door was open, so that the pages could hear, he said, 'I wish to God somebody would assassinate Knighton.' In this way he always speaks of him and uses him. Knighton is greatly annoyed at it, and is very seldom there. Still it appears there is some secret chain which binds them together, and which compels the King to submit to the presence of a man whom he detests, and induces Knighton to remain in spite of so much hatred and ill-usage. The King's indolence is so great that it is next to impossible to get him to do even the most ordinary business, and Knighton is still the only man who can prevail on him to sign papers, &c. His greatest delight is to make those who have business to transact with him, or to lay papers before him, wait in his anteroom while he is lounging with Mount Charles or anybody, talking of horses or any trivial matter; and when he is told, 'Sir, there is Watson waiting,' &c., he replies, 'Damn Watson; let him wait.' He does it on purpose, and likes it.

This account corresponds with all I have before heard, and confirms the opinion I have long had that a more contemptible, cowardly, selfish, unfeeling dog does not exist than this King, on whom such flattery is constantly lavished. He has a sort of capricious good-nature, arising however out of no good principle or good feeling, but which is of use to him, as it cancels in a moment and at small cost a long score of misconduct. Princes have only to behave with common decency and prudence, and they are sure to be popular, for there is a great and general disposition to pay court to them. I do not know anybody who is proof against their seductions when they think fit to use them in the shape of civility and condescension. The great consolation in all this is the proof that, so far from deriving happiness from their grandeur, they are the most miserable of all mankind. The contrast between their apparent authority and the contradictions which they practically meet with must be peculiarly galling, more especially to men whose minds are seldom regulated, as other men's are, by the beneficial discipline of education and early collision with their equals. There have been good and wise kings, but not many of them. Take them one with another they are of an inferior character, and this I believe to be one of the worst of the kind. The littleness of his character prevents his displaying the dangerous faults that belong to great minds, but with vices and weaknesses of the lowest and most contemptible order it would be difficult to find a disposition more abundantly furnished.

February 26th. The debate on Monday night in the House of Lords was very amusing. It was understood the Duke of Clarence was to speak, and there was a good deal of curiosity to hear him. Lord Bathurst was in a great fright lest he should be violent and foolish. He made a very tolerable speech, of course with a good deal of stuff in it, but such as it was it has exceedingly disconcerted the other party. The three royal Dukes Clarence, Cumberland, and Sussex got up one after another, and attacked each other (that is, Clarence and Sussex attacked Cumberland, and he them) very vehemently, and they used towards each other language that nobody else could have ventured to employ; so it was a very droll scene. The Duke of Clarence said the attacks on the Duke [of Wellington] had been *infamous;* the Duke of Cumberland took this to himself, but when he began to answer it could not recollect the expression, which the Duke of Clarence directly supplied. 'I said "infamous."' The Duke of Sussex said that the Duke of Clarence had not intended to apply the word to the Duke of Cumberland, but if he chose to take it to himself he might. Then the Duke of Clarence said that the Duke of Cumberland had lived so long abroad that he had forgotten there was such a thing as freedom of debate.

March 8th. [*Lord Harrowby*] talked a great deal of Fox and Pitt, and said that the natural disposition of the former was to arbitrary power and that of the latter to be a reformer, so that circumstances drove each into the course the other was intended for by nature. Lord North's letter to Fox when he dismissed him in 1776 was, 'The King has ordered a new commission of the Treasury to be made out, in which I do not see your name.' How dear this cost him, and what an influence that note may have had on the affairs of the country and on Fox's subsequent life!

March 16th.—17th. I received a message from the King, to tell me that he was sorry I had not dined with him the last time I was at Windsor, that he had intended to ask me, but finding that all the Ministers dined there except Ellenborough, he had let me go, that Ellenborough might not be the only man not invited, and 'he would be damned if Ellenborough ever should dine in his house.' I asked Lord Bathurst afterwards, to whom I told this, why he hated Ellenborough, and he said that something he had said during the Queen's trial had given the King mortal offence, and he never forgave it. The King complains that he is tired to death of all the people about him. He is less violent about the Catholic question, tired of that too, and does not wish to hear any more about it. He leads a most extraordinary life—never gets up till six in the afternoon. They come to him and open the window curtains at six or seven o'clock in the morning; he breakfasts in bed, does whatever business he can be brought to transact in bed too, he reads every newspaper quite through, dozes three or four hours, gets up in time for dinner, and goes to bed between ten and eleven. He sleeps very ill, and rings his bell forty times in the night; if he wants to know the hour, though a watch hangs close to him, he will have his *valet de chambre* down rather than turn his head to look at it. The same thing if he wants a glass of water; he won't stretch out his hand to get it. His valets are nearly destroyed, and at last Lady Conyngham prevailed on him to agree to an arrangement by which they wait on him on alternate days. The service is still most severe, as on the days they are in waiting their labours are incessant, and they cannot take off their clothes at night, and hardly lie down.

18*th.*   I was at Windsor for the Council and the Recorder's report. We waited above two hours; of course his Majesty did not get up till we were all there. A small attendance in Council—the Duke, Bathurst, Aberdeen, Melville, and I think no other Cabinet Minister. I sent for Batchelor, the King's *valet de chambre,* and had a pretty long conversation with him; he talked as if the walls had ears, but was anxious to tell me everything. He confirmed all I had before heard of the King's life, and said he was nearly dead of it, that he was in high favour, and the King had given him apartments in the Lodge and some presents. His Majesty has been worried to death, and has not yet made up his mind to the Catholic Bill (this man knows, I'll be bound). But what he most dwelt on was Sir William Knighton. I said to him that the King was afraid of the Duke. He replied he thought not; he thought he was afraid of nobody but of Knighton, that he hated him, but that his influence and authority were without any limit, that he could do anything, and without him nothing could be done; that after him Lady Conyngham was all-powerful, but in entire subserviency to him; that she did not dare have anybody to dine there without previously ascertaining that Knighton would not disapprove of it; that he knew everything, and nobody dared say or do a thing of any sort without his permission. There was a sort of mysterious awe with which he spoke of Knighton, mixed with dislike, which was curious.

March 21st, at night.   This morning the Duke [*of Wellington*] fought a duel with Lord Winchelsea. Nothing could equal the astonishment caused by this event. Everybody of course sees the matter in a different light; all blame Lord W., but they are divided as to whether the Duke ought to have fought or not.

Lord W.'s letter appeared last Monday, and certainly from that time to this it never entered into anybody's head that the Duke ought to or would take it up, though the expressions in it were very impertinent. But Lord Winchelsea is such a maniac, and has so lost his head that everybody imagined the Duke would treat what he said with silent contempt. He thought otherwise, however, and without saying a word to any of his colleagues or to anybody but Hardinge, his second, he wrote and demanded an apology. After many letters and messages between the parties (Lord Falmouth being Lord Winchelsea's second) Lord Winchelsea declined making any apology, and they met. The letters on the Duke's part are very creditable, so free from arrogance or an assuming tone; those on Lord Winchelsea's not so, for one of them is a senseless repetition of the offence, in which he says that if the Duke will deny that his allegations are true he will apologise. They met at Wimbledon at eight o'clock. There were many people about, who saw what passed. They stood at a distance of fifteen paces. Before they began Hardinge went up to Lords Winchelsea and Falmouth, and said he must protest against the proceeding, and declare that their conduct in refusing an apology when Lord Winchelsea was so much in the wrong filled him with disgust. The Duke fired and missed, and then Winchelsea fired in the air. He immediately pulled out of his pocket the paper which has since appeared, but in which the word 'apology' was omitted. The Duke read it and said it would not do. Lord Falmouth said he was not come there to quibble about words, and that he was ready to make the apology in whatever terms would be satisfactory, and the word 'apology' was inserted on the ground. The Duke then touched his hat, said 'Good morning, my Lords,' mounted his horse, and rode off. Hume was there, without knowing on whose behalf till he got to the ground. Hardinge asked him to attend, and told him where he would find a chaise, into which he got. He found there pistols, which told him the errand he was on, but he had still no notion the Duke was concerned; when he saw him he was ready to drop. The Duke went to Mrs. Arbuthnot's as soon as he got back, and at eleven o'clock she wrote a note to Lord Bathurst, telling him of it, which he received at the Council board and put into my hands. So little idea had he of Lord Winchelsea's letter leading to anything serious that when on Wednesday, at the Council at Windsor, I asked him if he had read it, he said, laughing, 'Yes, and it is a very clever letter, much the wisest thing he ever did; *he has got back his money.* I wish I could find some such pretext to get back mine.' At twelve o'clock the Duke went to Windsor to tell the King what had happened. Winchelsea is abused for not having made an apology when it was first required; but I think, having committed the folly of writing so outrageous a letter, he did the only thing a man of honour could do in going out and receiving a shot and then making an apology, which he was all this time prepared to do, for he had it ready written in his pocket. I think the Duke ought not to have challenged him; it was very juvenile, and he stands in far too high a position, and his life is so much *publica cura* that he should have treated him and his letter with the contempt they merited; it lowered him, and was more or less ridiculous. Lord Jersey met him coming from Windsor, and spoke to him. He said, 'I could not do otherwise, could I?'

April 5th. The question [*on Catholic Emancipation*] was put at a little before twelve last night, and carried by 105—217 to 112 (a greater majority than the most sanguine expected)—after a splendid speech from Lord Grey and a very good one from Lord Plunket. Old Eldon was completely beat, and could make no fight at all; his speech was wretched, they say, for I did not hear it. This tremendous defeat will probably put an end to anything like serious opposition; they will hardly rally again.

April 13th. I went on Friday morning to the Old Bailey to hear the trials, particularly that of the women for the murder of the apprentices; the mother was found guilty, and will be hanged to-day—has been by this time.[6] The case exhibited a shocking

---

[6] [Two wretched women named Hibner were tried, and one of them convicted for the murder of a parish apprentice named Francis Colepitts by savage ill-treatment. The elder prisoner was found guilty and executed on the 13th of April.]

scene of wretchedness and poverty, such as ought not to exist in any community, especially in one which pretends to be so flourishing and happy as this is. It is, I suppose, one case of many which may be found in this town, graduating through various stages of misery and vice. These wretched beings were described to be in the lowest state of moral and physical degradation, with scarcely rags to cover them, food barely sufficient to keep them alive, and working eighteen or nineteen hours a day, without being permitted any relaxation, or even the privilege of going to church on Sunday. I never heard more disgusting details than this trial elicited, or a case which calls more loudly for an investigation into the law and the system under which such proceedings are possible. Poverty, and vice, and misery must always be found in a community like ours, but such frightful contrasts between the excess of luxury and splendour and these scenes of starvation and brutality ought not to be possible; but I am afraid there is more vice, more misery and penury in this country than in any other, and at the same time greater wealth.

July 10*th.* I dined with the Duke of Wellington yesterday; a very large party for Mesdames the Duchesse d'Escars and Madame du Cayla; the first is the widow of the Duc d'Escars, who was Premier Maître d'Hôtel of Louis XVIII., and who was said to have died of one of the King's good dinners, and the joke was, 'Hier sa Majesté a eu une indigestion, dont M. le Duc d'Escars est mort.' Madame du Cayla[7] is come over to prosecute some claim upon this Government, which the Duke has discovered to be unfounded, and he had the bluntness to tell her so as they were going to dinner. She must have been good-looking in her youth; her countenance is lively, her eyes are piercing, clear complexion, and very handsome hands and arms; but the best part about her seemed to be the magnificent pearls she wore, though these are not so fine as Lady Conyngham's. All king's mis-

[7] [Madame du Cayla had been the *soi-disant* mistress of Louis XVIII., or rather the favourite of his declining years. It is curious that in 1829 the last mistress of a King of France should have visited London under the reign of the last mistress of a King of England.]

tresses seem to have a rage for pearls; I remember Madame Narischkin's were splendid. Madame du Cayla is said to be very rich and clever.

After dinner the Duke talked to me for a long time about the King and the Duke of Cumberland, and his quarrel with the latter. He began about the King's making Lord Aberdeen stay at the Cottage the other day when he had engaged all the foreign Ambassadors to dine with him in London. Aberdeen represented this to him, but his Majesty said 'it did not matter, he should stay, and the Ambassadors should for once see that he was King of England.' 'He has no idea,' said the Duke, 'of what a King of England ought to do, or he would have known that he ought to have made Aberdeen go and receive them, instead of keeping him there.' He said the King was very clever and amusing, but that with a surprising memory he was very inaccurate, and constantly told stories the details of which all his auditors must know to be false. One day he was talking of the late King, and asserted that George III. had said to himself, 'Of all the men I have ever known you are the one on whom I have the greatest dependence, and you are the most perfect gentleman.' Another day he said 'that he recollected the old Lord Chesterfield, who once said to him, "Sir, you are the fourth Prince of Wales I have known, and I must give your Royal Highness one piece of advice: stick to your father; as long as you adhere to your father you will be a great and a happy man, but if you separate yourself from him you will be nothing and an unhappy one;" and, by God (added the King), I never forgot that advice, and acted upon it all my life.' 'We all,' said the Duke, 'looked at one another with astonishment. He is extremely clever and particularly ingenious in turning the conversation from any subject he does not like to discuss.

'I,' added the Duke of Wellington, 'remember calling upon him the day he received the news of the battle of Navarino. I was not a Minister, but Commander-in-Chief, and after having told me the news he asked me what I thought of it. I said that I knew nothing about it, was ignorant of the instructions that had been given to the admiral, and could not give any opinion; but "one thing is clear to me, that your Majesty's ships have suffered very much, and that you ought to reinforce your fleet directly, for whenever you have a maritime force yours ought to be superior to all others." This advice he did not like; I saw this, and he said, "Oh, the Emperor of Russia is a man of honour," and then he began talking, and went on to Venice, Toulon, St. Petersburg, all over the Continent, and from one place and one subject to another, till he brought me to Windsor Castle. I make it a rule never to interrupt him, and when in this way he tries to get rid of a subject in the way of business which he does not like, I let him talk himself out, and then quietly put before him the matter in question, so that he cannot escape from it. I remember when the Duke of Newcastle was going to Windsor with a mob at his heels to present a petition (during the late discussions) I went down to him and showed him the petition, and told him that they ought to be prevented from coming. He went off and talked upon every subject but that which I had come about, for an hour and a half. I let him go on till he was tired, and then I said, "But the petition, sir; here it is, and an answer must be sent. I had better write to the Duke of Newcastle and tell him your Majesty will receive it through the Secretary of State; and, if you please, I will write the letter before I leave the house." This I did, finished my business in five minutes, and went away with the letter in my pocket. I know him so well that I can deal with him easily, but anybody who does not know him, and who is afraid of him, would have the greatest difficulty in getting on with him. One extraordinary peculiarity about him is, that the only thing he fears is ridicule. He is afraid of nothing which is hazardous, perilous, or uncertain; on the contrary, he is all for braving difficulties; but he dreads ridicule, and this is the reason why the Duke of Cumberland, whose sarcasms he dreads, has such power over him, and Lord Anglesey likewise; both of them he hates in proportion as he fears them.' I said I was very much surprised to hear this, as neither of these men were wits, or likely to make him ridiculous; that if he had been afraid of Sefton or Alvanley it could have been understood. 'But,' rejoined the Duke, 'he never sees these

men, and he does not mind anybody he does not see; but the
Duke of Cumberland and Lord Anglesey he cannot avoid seeing,
and the fear he has of what they may say to him, as well as of
him, keeps him in awe of them. No man, however, knows the
Duke of Cumberland better than he does; indeed, all I know of
the Duke of Cumberland I know from him, and so I told him
one day. I remember asking him why the Duke of Cumberland
was so unpopular, and he said, "Because there never was a father
well with his son, or husband with his wife, or lover with his mistress, or a friend with his friend, that he did not try to make mischief between them." And yet he suffers this man to have constant access to him, to say what he will to him, and often acts
under his influence.' I said, 'You and the Duke of Cumberland
speak now, don't you?' 'Yes, we speak. The King spoke to me
about it, and wanted me to make him an apology. I told him it
was quite impossible, "Why," said he, "you did not mean to offend
the Duke of Cumberland, I am sure." "No, sir," said I; "I did not
wish to offend him, but I did not say a word that I did not mean.
When we meet the Royal Family in society, they are our superiors, and we owe them all respect, and I should readily apologise
for anything I might have said offensive to the Duke; but in the
House of Lords we are their peers, and for what I say there I am
responsible to the House alone." "But," said the King, "he said
you turned on him as if you meant to address yourself to him
personally." "I did mean it, sir," said I, "and I did so because I
knew that he had been here, that he had heard things from your
Majesty which he had gone and misrepresented and misstated in
other quarters, and knowing that, I meant to show him that I was
aware of it. I am sorry that the Duke is offended, but I cannot
help it, and I cannot make him an apology."'

September 5*th.* Yesterday I went with Amyot to his house,
where he showed me a part of Windham's diary. In Windham's
diary are several Johnsoniana, after the manner of Boswell. I was
much struck with his criticisms on Virgil, whom he seems to have
held in great contempt, and to have regarded as inferior to Ovid.
He says, 'Take away his imitation of Homer, and what do you

leave him?' Of Homer his admiration was unbounded, although he says that he never read the whole of the 'Odyssey' in the original, but that everything which is most admirable in poetry is to be found in Homer.

Windham told Johnson that he regretted having omitted to talk to him of the most important of all subjects on which he had often doubted. Johnson said, 'You mean natural and revealed religion,' and added that the historical evidences of Christianity were so strong that it was not possible to doubt its truth, that we had not so much evidence that Cæsar died in the Capitol as that Christ died in the manner related in the Bible. It has always appeared to me questionable whether Johnson was a believer (I mean whether his clear and unbiassed judgment was satisfied) in Christianity; he evidently dreaded and disliked the subject, and though he would have been indignant had anybody hinted that he had doubts, his nervous irritation at any religious discussion betokened a mind ill at ease on the subject. I learnt one thing from Windham's diary which I put into immediate practice, and that is, to write mine on one side only, and leave the other for other matters connected with the text; it is more convenient certainly.

September 16th. I have been living at Fulham at Lord Wharncliffe's Villa for six or seven weeks (keeping a girl, of whom although she has good looks, good manners, and is not ill disposed I am getting tired, and I doubt if ever I shall take one to live with me again. Henry de Ros, who is the grand purveyor of women to all his friends, gave her to me).

The King has nearly lost his eyesight, and is to be couched as soon as his eyes are in a proper state for the operation. He is in a great fright with his father's fate before him, and indeed nothing is more probable than that he will become blind and mad too; he is already a little of both.

September 23rd. Old Creevey is rather an extraordinary character. I know nothing of the early part of his history, but I believe he was an attorney or barrister; he married a widow, who died a few years ago; she had something, he nothing; he got into Parlia-

ment, belonged to the Whigs, displayed a good deal of shrewd-
ness and humour, and was for some time very troublesome to the
Tory Government by continually attacking abuses. After some
time he lost his seat, and went to live at Brussels, where he became intimate with the Duke of Wellington. Then his wife died,
upon which event he was thrown upon the world with about
200*l.* a year or less, no home, few connections, a great many acquaintance, a good constitution, and extraordinary spirits. He
possesses nothing but his clothes, no property of any sort; he leads
a vagrant life, visiting a number of people who are delighted to
have him, and sometimes roving about to various places, as fancy
happens to direct, and staying till he has spent what money he
has in his pocket. He has no servant, no home, no creditors; he
buys everything as he wants it at the place he is at; he has no ties
upon him, and has his time entirely at his own disposal and that
of his friends. He is certainly a living proof that a man may be
perfectly happy and exceedingly poor, or rather without riches,
for he suffers none of the privations of poverty and enjoys many
of the advantages of wealth. I think he is the only man I know in
society who possesses nothing.

November 9th.　Dined to-day with Byng and met Tom Moore,
who was very agreeable; he told us a great deal about his forthcoming 'Life of Byron.' He is nervous about it; he is employed in
conjunction with Scott and Mackintosh to write a history of England for one of the new publications like the Family Library.
Scott is to write Scotland, Mackintosh England, and Moore Ireland; and they get 1,000*l.* apiece; but Scott could not compress
his share into one volume, so he is to have 1,500*l.* The republication of Scott's works will produce him an enormous fortune; he
he has already paid off 30,000*l.* of the Constable bankruptcy
debt, and he is to pay the remaining 30,000*l.* very soon. A new
class of readers is produced by the Bell and Lancaster schools,
and this is the cause of the prodigious and extensive sale of cheap
publications. Moore had received a letter from Madame de
Guiccioli to-day; he says she is not handsome. Byron's exploits,
especially at Venice, seem to have been marvellous. He used to

go to the Ridotto every night, and afterwards take home with him five or six women of the commonest sort with whom he had an orgy. Henry de Ros heard of him at Venice and says he left a great name there in that line. Moore *said* he did not believe in the stories of his fancy for Boys, but it looked as if he does believe it from his manner. Moore said he wrote with extraordinary rapidity, but his corrections were frequent and laborious. When he wrote the address for the opening of Drury Lane Theatre, he corrected it repeatedly.

I saw Miss Fanny Kemble for the first time on Friday, and was disappointed. She is short, ill made, with large hands and feet, an expressive countenance, though not handsome, fine eyes, teeth, and hair, not devoid of grace, and with great energy and spirit, her voice good, though she has a little of the drawl of her family. She wants the pathos and tenderness of Miss O'Neill, and she excites no emotion; but she is very young, clever, and may become a very good, perhaps a fine actress. Mrs. Siddons was not so good at her age. She fills the house every night.

November 20th. Roehampton. Only Moore and myself; Washington Irving and Maclane, the American Minister, come to-morrow. Moore spoke in the highest terms of Luttrell, of his wit and information, and of his writings, to which he does not think the world does justice, particularly the 'Advice to Julia,' but he says Luttrell is too fearful of giving offence. Moore was very agreeable, told a story of Sir —— St. George in Ireland. He was to attend a meeting at which a great many Catholics were to be present (I forget where), got drunk and lost his hat, when he went into the room where they were assembled and said, 'Damnation to you all; I came to emancipate you, and you've stole my hat.' In the evening Moore sang, but the pianoforte was horrid, and he was not in good voice; still his singing 'va dritto al cuore,' for it produces an exceeding sadness, and brings to mind a thousand melancholy recollections, and generates many melancholy anticipations. He told me as we came along that with him it required no thought to write, but that there was no end to it; so many fancies on every subject crowded on his brain; that he often read what he had written as if it had been the composition of another, and was amused; that it was the greatest pleasure to him to compose those light and trifling pieces, humorous and satirical, which had been so often successful. He holds Voltaire to have been the most extraordinary genius that ever lived, on account of his universality and fertility; talked of Scott and his wonderful labour and power of composition, as well as the extent to which he has carried the art of book-making; besides writing this history of Scotland for Dr. Lardner's 'Encyclopædia,' he is working at the prefaces for the republication of the Waverley Novels, the 'Tales of a Grandfather,' and has still found time to review Tytler, which he has done out of the scraps and chips of his other works. A little while ago he had to correct some of the proofs of the history of Scotland, and, being dissatisfied with what was done, he nearly wrote it over again, and sent it up to the editor. Some time after finding another copy of the proofs, he forgot that he had corrected them before, and he rewrote these also and sent them up, and the editor is at this moment engaged in selecting from the two corrected copies the best parts of each.

November 21st. Washington Irving wants sprightliness and more refined manners. He was in Spain four years, at Madrid, Seville, and Grenada. While at the latter place he was lodged in the Alhambra, which is excellently preserved and very beautiful; he gives a deplorable description of the ignorance and backward state of the Spaniards. When he returned to France he was utterly uninformed of what had been passing in Europe while he was in Spain, and he says that he now constantly hears events alluded to of which he knows nothing.

December 1st. No Council yet; the King is employed in altering the uniforms of the Guards, and has pattern coats with various collars submitted to him every day. The Duke of Cumberland assists him, and this is his principal occupation; he sees much more of his tailor than he does of his Minister. The Duke of Cumberland's boy, who is at Kew, diverts himself with making the guard turn out several times in the course of the day to salute him.

January 17*th*, 1830. The two Grants (Charles and Robert) are always together, and both very forgetful and unpunctual. Somebody said that if you asked Charles to dine with you at six on Monday, you were very likely to have Robert at seven on Tuesday.

Genoa, March 18*th*. The Apennines are nothing after the Alps, but the descent to Genoa is very pretty, and Genoa itself exceeds everything I ever saw in point of beauty and magnificence.

I passed the whole day after I got here in looking into the palaces and gardens and admiring the prospect on every side. You are met at every turn by vestiges of the old Republic; in fact, the town has undergone very little alteration for hundreds of years. Genoa appears to be a city of palaces, and although many of the largest are now converted to humbler uses, and many fallen to decay, there are ample remains to show the former grandeur of the princely merchants who were once the lords of the ocean. The old palace of Andrew is now let for lodgings, and the Pamfili Doria live at Rome. The walls are covered with inscriptions, and I stopped to read two on stone slabs on the spot where the houses of malefactors had formerly stood, monuments of the vindictive laws of the Republic, which not only punished the criminal himself, but consigned his children to infamy and his habitation to destruction; though they stand together they are not of the same date.

Evening. Passed the whole day seeing sights. Called on Madame Durazzo, and went with her and her niece, Madame Ferrari, to the King's palace. Like the others, a fine house, full of painting and gilding, and with a terrace of black and white marble commanding a view of the sea. The finest picture is a Paul Veronese of a Magdalen with our Saviour. The King and Queen sleep together, and on each side of the royal bed there is an assortment of ivory palms, crucifixes, boxes for holy water, and other spiritual guards for their souls. For the comfort of their bodies he has had a machine made like a car, which is drawn up by a chain from the bottom to the top of the house; it holds about six people, who can be at pleasure elevated to any storey, and at each landing-place there is a contrivance to let them in and out. I saw the churches—San Stefano, Annunziata, the Duomo, San Ambrosio, San Cyro. The churches have a profusion of marble, and gilding, and frescoes; the Duomo is of black and white marble, of mixed architecture, and highly ornamented—all stinking to a degree that was perfectly intolerable, and the same thing whether empty or full; it is the smell of stale incense mixed with garlic and human odour, horrible combination of poisonous exhalations. I must say, as everybody has before remarked, that there is something highly edifying in the appearance of devotion which belongs to the Catholic religion; the churches are always open, and, go into them when you will, you see men and women kneeling and praying before this or that altar. This seems more accordant with the spirit and essence of religion than to have the churches, as ours are, opened like theatres at stated hours and days for the performance of a long service, at the end of which the audience is turned out and the doors are locked till the next representation. Then the Catholic religion makes no distinctions between poverty and wealth—no pews for the aristocracy well warmed and furnished, or seats set apart for the rich and well dressed; here the church is open to all, and the beggar in rags comes and takes his place by the side of the lady in silks.

Rome, April 4th. To the Farnesina: Raphael's frescoes, the famous Galatea, and the great head which Michael Angelo painted on the wall, as it is said as a hint to Raphael that he was too minute. There it is just as he left it. Here Raphael painted the Transfiguration, and here the Fornarina was shut up with him that he might not run away from his work. It might be thought that to shut up his mistress with him was not the way to keep him to his work. Be that as it may, the plan was a good one which produced these frescoes and the Transfiguration.

In the evening I went to St. Peter's, when I was amply recompensed for the disappointment and bore of the morning. The church was crowded; there was a Miserere in the chapel, which was divine, far more beautiful than anything I have heard in the Sistine, and it was the more effective because at the close it really was night. The lamps were extinguished at the shrine of the Apostle, but one altar—the altar of the Holy Sepulchre—was brilliantly illuminated. Presently the Grand Penitentiary, Cardinal Gregorio, with his train entered, went and paid his devotions at this shrine, and then seated himself on the chair of the Great Confessional, took a golden wand, and touched all those who knelt before him. Then came a procession of pilgrims bearing muffled crosses; penitents with faces covered, in white, with tapers and crosses; and one long procession of men headed by these muffled figures, and another of women accompanied by ladies, a lady walking between every two pilgrims. The cross in the procession of women was carried by the Princess Orsini, one of the greatest ladies in Rome. They attended them to the church (the Trinità delle Pellegrine) and washed their feet and fed them. A real washing of dirty feet. Both the men and the women seemed of the lowest class, but their appearance and dresses were very picturesque. These processions entered St. Peter's, walked all round the church, knelt at the altars, and retired in the same order, filing along the piazza till they were lost behind the arches of the colonnades. As the shades of night fell upon the vast expanse of this wonderful building it became really sublime; 'the dim religious light' glimmering from a distant altar, or cast by the passing torches of the procession, the voices of the choir as they sang the Miserere swelling from the chapel, which was veiled in dusk, and with no light but that of the high taper half hid behind the altar, with the crowds of figures assembled round the chapel moving about in the obscurity of the aisles and columns, produced the most striking effect I ever beheld. It was curious, interesting, and inspiring—little of mummery and much of solemnity. The night here brings out fresh beauties, but of the most majestic character. There is a colour in an Italian twilight that I have never seen in England, so soft, and beautiful, and grey, and the moon rises 'not as in northern climes obscurely bright,' but with far-spreading rays around her. The figures, costume, and attitudes that you see in the churches are wonderfully picturesque.

Naples, April 22nd. Yesterday to Pompeii, far better worth seeing than anything else in Italy. Who can look at other ruins after this? At Rome there are certain places consecrated by recollections, but the imagination must be stirred up to enjoy them; here you are actually in a Roman town. Shave off the upper storey of any town, take out windows, doors, and furniture, and it will be as Pompeii now is: it is marvellous.

This morning we went to an Ursuline convent to see two girls take the veil. The ceremony was neither imposing, nor interesting, nor affecting, nor such as I expected. I believe all this would have been the case had it been the black veil, but it was the white unfortunately. I thought they would be dressed splendidly, have their hair cut off in the church, be divested (in the convent) of their finery, and reappear to take leave of their relations in the habit of the order. Not at all. I went with A. Hill and Legge, who had got tickets from the brother of one of the *sposine;* we were admitted to the grating, an apartment about ten feet long by five wide, with a very thick double grating, behind which some of the nuns appeared and chattered. A turning box supplied coffee and cakes to the company. I went to the door of the parlour (which was open), but they would not admit me. There the ladies were received, and the nuns and novices were laughing and talking and doing the honours. Their dress was not ugly—black, white, and a yellow veil. The chapel was adorned with gold brocade, and blue and silver hangings, flowers, tapers; a good orchestra, and two or three tolerable voices. It was as full as it could hold, and soldiers were distributed about to keep order; even by the altar four stood with fixed bayonets, who when the Host was raised presented arms—a military salute to the Real Presence! The brother of one of the girls did the honours of the chapel, placing the ladies and bustling about for chairs, which all the time the ceremony was going on were handed over heads and bonnets, to the great danger of the latter. It was impossible not to be struck with this man's gaiety and *sang-froid* on the occasion, but he is used to it, for this was the fourth sister he has buried here. When the chapel was well crammed the *sposine* appeared, each with two *marraines*. A table and six chairs were placed opposite the altar; on the table were two trays, each containing a Prayer Book, a pocket-handkerchief, and a white veil. The girls (who were very young, and one of them rather pretty) were dressed in long black robes like dressing-gowns, their hair curled, hanging down their backs and slightly powdered. On the top of their heads were little crowns of blue, studded with silver or diamonds. The ladies attending them (one of whom was Princess Fondi and another Princess Bressano) were very smart, and all the people in the chapel were dressed as for a ball. There was a priest at the table to tell the girls what to do. High Mass was performed, then a long sermon was delivered by a priest who spoke very fluently, but with a strange twang and in a very odd style, continually apostrophising the two girls by name, comparing them to olives and other fruit, to *candelabri,* and desiring them to keep themselves pure that 'they might go as virgins into the chamber of their beloved.' When the Sacrament was administered the ladies took the crowns off the girls, who were like automata all the time, threw the white veils over them, and led them to the altar, where the Sacrament was administered to them; then they were led back to their seats, the veils taken off and the crowns replaced. After a short interval they were again led to the altar, where, on their knees, their profession was read to them; in this they are made to renounce the world and their parents; but at this part, which is at the end, a murmuring noise is made by the four ladies who kneel with them at the altar, that the words may not be heard, being thought too heart-rending to the parents; then they are led out and taken into the convent, and the ceremony ends. The girls did not seem the least affected, but very serious; the rest of the party appeared to consider it as a *fête,* and smirked and gossiped; only the father of one of them, an old man, looked as if he felt it. The brother told me his sister was eighteen; that she would be a nun, and that they had done all they could to dissuade her. It is a rigid order, but there is a still more rigid rule within the convent. Those nuns who embrace it are for ever cut off from any sort of communication with the world, and can never again see or correspond with their own family. They cannot enter into this last seclusion without the consent of their parents, which another of this man's four sisters is now soliciting.

Rome, May 31st. The process of saint-making is extremely curious. There are three grades of saintship: the first, for which I forget the name, requires irreproachable moral conduct; the second (beatification), two well-proved miracles; the third (sanctification), three. It costs an immense sum of money to effect the whole, in some cases as much as 100,000 piastres. The process begins by an application to the Pope, on the part of the relatives of the candidate, or on that of the confraternity, if they belong to a religious order. The Pope refers the question to a tribunal, and the claimants are obliged to appear with their proofs, which are severely scrutinised, and the miracles are only admitted upon the production of the most satisfactory evidence. Individuals continually subscribe for this purpose, particularly for members of religious orders, in order to increase the honour or glory of the society. These trials last many years, sometimes for centuries. There is a Princess of Sardinia, sister of the late King, who died lately, and they want to make a saint of her. The money (estimated at 100,000 piastres) is ready, but they cannot rout out a miracle by any means, so that they are at a dead standstill before the second step. Nobody can be sanctified till two hundred years after their death, but they may arrive at the previous grades before that, and the proofs may be adduced and registered.

June 1st. After dinner to the San Gregorio to see the frescoes, the 'Martyrdom of St. Andrew,' the rival frescoes of Guido and Domenichino, and afterwards drove about till dark, when we went to a most extraordinary performance—that of the Flagellants. I had heard of it, and had long been curious to assist at it.

The church was dimly lit by a few candles on the altar, the congregation not numerous. There was a service, the people making the responses, after which a priest, or one of the attendants of the church, went round with a bundle of whips of knotted cord, and gave one to each person who chose to take it. I took mine, but my companion laughed so at seeing me gravely accept the whip, that he was obliged to hide his face in his hands, and was passed over. In a few minutes the candles were extinguished, and we were left in total darkness. Then an invisible preacher began exhorting his hearers to whip themselves severely, and as he went on his vehemence and passion increased. Presently a loud smacking was heard all round the church, which continued a few minutes; then the preacher urged us to fresh exertions, and crack went the whips again louder and faster than before as he exhorted. The faithful flogged till a bell rang; the whips stopped, in a few minutes the candles were lit again, and the priest came round and collected his cords. I had squeezed mine in my hands, so that he did not see it, and I brought it away with me. As soon as the candles were extinguished the doors were locked, so that nobody could go out or come in till the discipline was over. I was rather nervous when we were locked up in total darkness, but nobody whipped me, and I certainly did not whip myself. A more extraordinary thing (for sight it can't be called) I never witnessed. I don't think the people stripped, nor, if they did, that the cords could have hurt them much.

Venice, June 16th. The Hall of the Council of Ten (the most powerful and the most abominable tribunal that ever existed) has been partly modernised. In the Chamber of the Inquisitors of State is still the hole in the wall which was called the 'Lion's Mouth,' through which written communications were made; and the box into which they fell, which the Inquisitors alone could open. There were 'Bocche di Lioni' in several places at the head of the Giant's Staircase, and in others. The mouths are gone, but the holes remain. Though the interior of the Ponte di Sospiri is no longer visible, the prisons are horrible places, twenty-four in number, besides three others under water which the French had closed up. They are about fourteen feet long, seven wide, and seven high, with one hole to admit air, a wooden bed, which was covered with straw, and a shelf. In one of the prisons are several inscriptions, scrawled on the wall and ceiling.

There are two places in which criminals, or prisoners, were secretly executed; they were strangled, and without seeing their executioner, for a cord was passed through an opening, which he twisted till the victim was dead. This was the mode pursued with the prisoners of the Inquisitors; those of the Council were often placed in a cell to which there was a thickly grated window, through which the executioner did his office, and if they resisted he stabbed them in the throat. The wall is still covered with the blood of those who have thus suffered. From the time of their erection, 800 years ago, to the destruction of the Republic nobody was ever allowed to see these prisons, till the French came and threw them open, when the people set fire to them and burnt all the woodwork; the stone was too solid to be destroyed. One or two escaped, and they remain as memorials of the horrors that were perpetrated in them.

The Reign
of
King William IV

London, July 16th, 1830. I returned here on the 6th of this month, and have waited these ten days to look about me and see and hear what is passing. The present King and his proceedings occupy all attention, and nobody thinks any more of the late King than if he had been dead fifty years, unless it be to abuse him and to rake up all his vices and misdeeds. Never was elevation like that of King William IV. His life has been hitherto passed in obscurity and neglect, in miserable poverty, surrounded by a numerous progeny of bastards, without consideration or friends, and he was ridiculous from his grotesque ways and little meddling curiosity. Nobody ever invited him into their house, or thought it necessary to honour him with any mark of attention or respect; and so he went on for above forty years, till Canning brought him into notice by making him Lord High Admiral at the time of his grand Ministerial schism. In that post he distinguished himself by making absurd speeches, by a morbid official activity, and by a general wildness which was thought to indicate incipient insanity, till shortly after Canning's death and the Duke's accession, as is well known, the latter dismissed him. He then dropped back into obscurity, but had become by this time somewhat more of a personage than he was before. His brief administration of the navy, the death of the Duke of York, which made him heir to the throne, his increased wealth and regular habits, had procured him more consideration, though not a great deal. Such was his position when George IV. broke all at once, and after three months of expectation William finds himself King.

July 18th. The new King began very well. Everybody expected he would keep the Ministers in office, but he threw himself into the arms of the Duke of Wellington with the strongest expressions of confidence and esteem. He proposed to all the Household, as well as to the members of Government, to keep their places, which they all did except Lord Conyngham and the Duke of Montrose. He soon after, however, dismissed most of the equerries, that he might fill their places with the members of his own family. Of course such a King wanted not due praise, and plenty of anecdotes were raked up of his former generosities and kindnesses. His first speech to the Council was well enough given, but his burlesque character began even then to show itself. Nobody expected from him much real grief, and he does not seem to know how to act it consistently; he spoke of his brother with all the semblance of feeling, and in a tone of voice properly softened and subdued, but just afterwards, when they gave him the pen to sign the declaration, he said, in his usual tone, 'This is a damned bad pen you have given me.' My worthy colleague Mr. James Buller began to swear Privy Councillors in the name of 'King George IV.—William, I mean,' to the great diversion of the Council.

A few days after my return I was sworn in, all the Ministers and some others being present. His Majesty presided very decently, and looked like a respectable old admiral. The Duke [of Wellington] told me he was delighted with him—'If I had been able to deal with my late master as I do with my present, I should have got on much better'—that he was so reasonable and tractable, and that he had done more business with him in ten minutes than with the other in as many days.

I met George Fitzclarence, afterwards Earl of Munster,[1] the

[1] [Eldest son of King William IV. by Mrs. Jordan, who was shortly after the accession created an earl by his father. The rank of 'marquis's younger

same day, and repeated what the Duke said, and he told me
how delighted his father was with the Duke, his entire confidence
in him, and that the Duke might as entirely depend upon the
King; that he had told his Majesty, when he was at Paris, that
Polignac and the Duke of Orleans had both asked him whether the
Duke of Clarence, when he became King, would keep the Duke
of Wellington as his Minister, and the King said, 'What did you
reply?' 'I replied that you certainly would; did not I do right?'
'Certainly, you did quite right.'

He began immediately to do good-natured things, to provide
for old friends and professional adherents, and he bestowed a
pension upon Tierney's widow. The great offices of Chamberlain
and Steward he abandoned to the Duke of Wellington. There
never was anything like the enthusiasm with which he was
greeted by all ranks; though he has trotted about both town and
country for sixty-four years, and nobody ever turned round to
look at him, he cannot stir now without a mob, patrician as well
as plebeian, at his heels. All the Park congregated round the gate
to see him drive into town the day before yesterday. But in the
midst of all this success and good conduct certain indications of
strangeness and oddness peep out which are not a little alarming,
and he promises to realise the fears of his Ministers that he will
do and say too much, though they flatter themselves that they
have muzzled him in his approaching progress by reminding him
that his words will be taken as his Ministers', and he must, there‑
fore, be chary of them.

At the late King's funeral he behaved with great indecency.
That ceremony was very well managed, and a fine sight, the
military part particularly, and the Guards were magnificent. The
attendance was not very numerous, and when they had all got

children' was conferred upon the rest of the family. The King had nine natural children by Mrs. Jordan: 1, George, a major-general in the army, afterwards Earl of Munster; 2, Frederick, also in the army; 3, Adolphus, a
rear-admiral; 4, Augustus, in holy orders; 5, Sophia, married to Lord de
l'Isle; 6, Mary, married to Colonel Fox; 7, Elizabeth, married to the Earl
of Errol; 8, Augusta, married first to the Hon. John Kennedy Erskine, and
secondly to Lord John Frederick Gordon; 9, Amelia, married to Viscount
Falkland.]

together in St. George's Hall a gayer company I never beheld; with the exception of Mount Charles, who was deeply affected, they were all as merry as grigs. The King was chief mourner, and, to my astonishment, as he entered the chapel directly behind the body, in a situation in which he should have been apparently, if not really, absorbed in the melancholy duty he was performing, he darted up to Strathaven, who was ranged on one side below the Dean's stall, shook him heartily by the hand, and then went on nodding to the right and left. He had previously gone as chief mourner to sit for an hour at the head of the body as it lay in state, and he walked in procession with his household to the apartment. I saw him pass from behind the screen. Lord Jersey had been in the morning to Bushy to kiss hands on being made Chamberlain, when he had received him very graciously, told him it was the Duke and not himself who had made him, but that he was delighted to have him. At Windsor, when he arrived, he gave Jersey the white wand, or rather took one from him he had provided for himself, and gave it him again with a little speech. When he went to sit in state, Jersey preceded him, and he said when all was ready, 'Go on to the body, Jersey; you will get your dress coat as soon as you can.' The morning after the funeral, having slept at Frogmore, he went all over the Castle, into every room in the house, which he had never seen before except when he came there as a guest; after which he received an address from the ecclesiastical bodies of Windsor and Eton, and returned an answer quite unpremeditated which they told me was excellent.

He is very well with all his family, particularly the Duke of Sussex, but he dislikes and seems to know the Duke of Cumberland, who is furious at his own discredit. The King has taken from him the Gold Stick, by means of which he had usurped the functions of all the other colonels of the regiments of the Guards, and put himself always about the late King. He says the Duke's rank is too high to perform those functions, and has put an end to his services. He has only put the Gold Sticks on their former footing, and they are all to take the duty in turn.

In the meantime the Duke of Cumberland has shown his teeth in another way. His horses have hitherto stood in the stables which are appropriated to the Queen, and the other day Lord Errol, her new Master of the Horse, went to her Majesty and asked her where she chose her horses should be; she said, of course, she knew nothing about it, but in the proper place. Errol then said the Duke of Cumberland's horses were in her stables, and could not be got out without an order from the King. The King was spoken to, and he commanded the Duke of Leeds to order them out. The Duke of Leeds took the order to the Duke of Cumberland, who said 'he would be damned if they should go,' when the Duke of Leeds said that he trusted he would have them taken out the following day, as unless he did so he should be under the necessity of ordering them to be removed by the King's grooms, when the Duke was obliged sulkily to give way. When the King gave the order to the Duke of Leeds, he sent for Taylor that he might be present, and said at the same time that he had a very bad opinion of the Duke of Cumberland, and he wished he would live out of the country.

The King's good-nature, simplicity, and affability to all about him are certainly very striking, and in his elevation he does not forget any of his old friends and companions. He was in no hurry to take upon himself the dignity of King, nor to throw off the habits and manners of a country gentleman. When Lord Chesterfield went to Bushy to kiss his hand, and be presented to the Queen, he found Sir John and Lady Gore there lunching, and when they went away the King called for their carriage, handed Lady Gore into it, and stood at the door to see them off. When Lord Howe came over from Twickenham to see him, he said the Queen was going out driving, and should 'drop him' at his own house. The Queen, they say, is by no means delighted at her elevation. She likes quiet and retirement and Bushy (of which the King has made her Ranger), and does not want to be a Queen. However, 'l'appétit viendra en mangeant.' He says he does not want luxury and magnificence, has slept in a cot, and he has dismissed the King's cooks, 'renversé la marmite.'

He keeps the stud (which is to be diminished) because he thinks he ought to support the turf. He has made Mount Charles a Lord of the Bedchamber, and given the Robes to Sir C. Pole, an admiral. Altogether he seems a kind-hearted, well-meaning, not stupid, burlesque, bustling old fellow, and if he doesn't go mad may make a very decent King, but he exhibits oddities. He would not have his servants in mourning—that is, not those of his own family and household—but he sent the Duke of Sussex to Mrs. Fitzherbert to desire she would put hers in mourning, and consequently so they are. The King and she have always been friends, as she has, in fact, been with all the Royal Family, but it was very strange. Yesterday morning he sent for the officer on guard, and ordered him to take all the muffles off the drums, the scarfs off the regimentals, and so to appear on parade, where he went himself. The colonel would have put the officer under arrest for doing this without his orders, but the King said he was commanding officer of his own guard, and forbade him. All odd, and people are frightened, but his wits will at least last till the new Parliament meets. I sent him a very respectful request through Taylor that he would pay 300l., all that remained due of the Duke of York's debts at Newmarket, which he assented to directly, as soon as the Privy Purse should be settled—very good-natured. In the meantime it is said that the bastards are dissatisfied that more is not done for them, but he cannot do much for them at once, and he must have time. He has done all he can; he has made Errol Master of the Horse, Sidney a Guelph and Equerry, George Fitzclarence the same and Adjutant-General, and doubtless they will all have their turn. Of course the stories told about the rapacity of the Conynghams have been innumerable. The King's will excited much astonishment, but as yet nothing is for certain known about the money, or what became of it, or what he gave away, and to whom, in his lifetime.

July 20th. At one there was to be a Council, I never saw so full a Court, so much nobility with academical tagrag and bobtail. When this mob could be got rid of the table was brought in and the Council held. I begged the King would, to expedite the business, dispense with kneeling, which he did, and so we got on rapidly enough; and I whispered to Jersey, who stood by me behind the King with his white wand, 'The farce is good, isn't it?' as they each kissed his hand. I told him their name or country, or both, and he had a civil word to say to everybody, inviting some to dinner, promising to visit others, reminding them of former visits, or something good-humoured; he asked Lord Egremont's *permission* to go and live in his county, at Brighton.

All this was very well; no great harm in it; more affable, less dignified than the late King; but when this was over, and he might very well have sat himself quietly down and rested, he must needs put on his plainer clothes and start on a ramble about the streets, alone too. In Pall Mall he met Watson Taylor, and took his arm and went up St. James's Street. There he was soon followed by a mob making an uproar, and when he got near White's a woman came up and kissed him. Belfast (who had been sworn in Privy Councillor in the morning), who saw this from White's, and Clinton thought it time to interfere, and came out to attend upon him. The mob increased, and, always holding W. Taylor's arm, and flanked by Clinton and Belfast, who got shoved and kicked about to their inexpressible wrath, he got back to the Palace amid shouting and bawling and applause. When he got home he asked them to go in and take a quiet walk in the garden, and said, 'Oh, never mind all this; when I have walked about a few times they will get used to it, and will take no notice.'

July 24th. In the meantime the King has had his levee, which was crowded beyond all precedent. He was very civil to the people, particularly to Sefton, who had quarrelled with the late King.

Yesterday he went to the House of Lords, and was admirably received. I can fancy nothing like his delight at finding himself in the state coach surrounded by all his pomp. He delivered the Speech very well, they say, for I did not go to hear him. He did not wear the crown, which was carried by Lord Hastings. Etiquette is a thing he cannot comprehend. He wanted to take the King of Würtemberg with him in his coach, till he was told it was out of the question. In his private carriage he continues to sit backwards, and when he goes with men makes one sit by him and not opposite to him. Yesterday, after the House of Lords, he drove all over the town in an open calèche with the Queen, Princess Augusta, and the King of Würtemberg, and coming home he set down the King (*dropped him,* as he calls it) at Grillon's Hotel. The King of England dropping another king at a tavern! It is impossible not to be struck with his extreme good-nature and simplicity, which he cannot or will not exchange for the dignity of his new situation and the trammels of etiquette; but he ought to be made to understand that his simplicity degenerates into vulgarity, and that without departing from his natural urbanity he may conduct himself so as not to lower the character with which he is invested, and which belongs not to him, but to the country.

At his dinner at St. James's the other day more people were invited than there was room for, and some half-dozen were forced to sit at a side table. He said to Lord Brownlow, 'Well, when you are flooded (he thinks Lincolnshire is all fen) you will come to us at Windsor.' To the Freemasons he was rather good. The Duke of Sussex wanted him to receive their address in a solemn audience, which he refused, and when they did come he said, 'Gentlemen, if my love for you equalled my ignorance of everything concerning you, it would be unbounded,' and then he added something good-humoured. The consequence of his trotting about, and saying the odd things he does, is that there are all sorts of stories about him which are not true, and he is always expected everywhere.

July 25th. The King continues very active; has immense dinners every day, and the same people two or three days running. He has dismissed the late King's band, and employs the bands of the Guards every night, who are ready to die of it, for they get no pay and are prevented earning money elsewhere. The other night the King had a party, and at eleven o'clock he dismissed them thus: 'Now, ladies and gentlemen, I wish you a good night. I will not detain you any longer from your amusements, and shall

go to my own, which is to go to bed; so come along, my Queen.'
The other day he was very angry because the guard did not
know him in his plain clothes and turn out for him—the first appearance of jealousy of his greatness he has shown—and he ordered them to be more on the alert for the future.

July 26th. Still the King; his adventures (for they are nothing
else) furnish matter of continual amusement and astonishment to
his liege subjects. Yesterday morning, or the evening before, he
announced to the Duke of Wellington that he should dine with
him yesterday; accordingly the Duke was obliged, in the midst
of preparations for his breakfast, to get a dinner ready for him. In
the morning he took the King of Würtemberg to Windsor, and
just at the hour when the Duke expected him to dinner he was
driving through Hyde Park back from Windsor—three barouches-
and-four, the horses dead knocked up, in the front the two Kings,
Jersey, and somebody else, all covered with dust. The whole mob
of carriages and horsemen assembled near Apsley House to see
him pass and to wait till he returned. The Duke, on hearing he
was there, rushed down without his hat and stood in his gate in
the middle of servants, mob, &c., to see him pass. He drove to
Grillon's 'to drop' the King of Würtemberg, and at a quarter past
eight he arrived at Apsley House. In the evening I went to Crockford's, where I found Matuscewitz, who gave me a whole account
of the dinner. The two Kings went out to dinner arm in arm, the
Duke followed; the King sat between the King of Würtemberg
and the Duke. After dinner his health was drunk, to which he
returned thanks, sitting, but briefly, and promised to say more
by-and-by when he should give a toast. In process of time he
desired Douro to go and tell the band to play the merriest waltz
they could for the toast he was about to give. He then gave 'The
Queen of Würtemberg,' with many eulogiums on her and on the
connubial felicity of her and the King; not a very agreeable theme
for his host, for conjugal fidelity is not his forte. At length he
desired Douro to go again to the band and order them to play
'See the conquering hero comes,' and then he rose. All the company rose with him, when he ordered everybody to sit down.

Still standing, he said that he had been so short a time on the throne that he did not know whether etiquette required that he should speak sitting or standing, but, however this might be, he had been long used to speak on his legs, and should do so now; he then proposed the Duke's health, but prefaced it with a long speech—instituted a comparison between him and the Duke of Marlborough; went back to the reign of Queen Anne, and talked of the great support the Duke of Marlborough had received from the Crown, and the little support the Duke of Wellington had had in the outset of his career, though after the battle of Vimeiro he had been backed by all the energies of the country; that, notwithstanding his difficulties, his career had been one continued course of victory over the armies of France; and then recollecting the presence of Laval, the French Ambassador, he said, 'Remember, Duc de Laval, when I talk of victories over the French armies, they were not the armies of my ally and friend the King of France, but of him who had usurped his throne, and against whom you yourself were combating;' then going back to the Duke's career, and again referring to the comparison between him and Marlborough, he gave to him his fullest and most cordial confidence. The Duke returned thanks. The whole company stood aghast at the King's extraordinary speech and declaration. Falck gave me a delightful account of the speech and of Laval. He thought, not understanding one word, that all the King was saying was complimentary to the King of France and the French nation, and he kept darting from his seat to make his acknowledgments, while Esterhazy held him down by the tail of his coat, and the King stopped him with his hand outstretched, all with great difficulty. He said it was very comical.

August 3rd. I went yesterday to the sale of the late King's wardrobe, which was numerous enough to fill Monmouth Street, and sufficiently various and splendid for the wardrobe of Drury Lane. He hardly ever gave away anything except his linen, which was distributed every year. These clothes are the perquisite of his pages, and will fetch a pretty sum. There are all the coats he has ever had for fifty years, 300 whips, canes without number, every sort of uniform, the costumes of all the orders in Europe, splendid furs, pelisses, hunting-coats and breeches, and among other things a dozen pair of corduroy breeches he had made to hunt in when Don Miguel was here. His profusion in these articles was unbounded, because he never paid for them, and his memory was so accurate that one of his pages told me he recollected every article of dress, no matter how old, and that they were always liable to be called on to produce some particular coat or other article of apparel of years gone by. It is difficult to say whether in great or little things that man was most odious and contemptible.

August 5th. Yesterday morning it appeared that the affair at Brussels was much more serious than Esterhazy had given me to understand; and, as far as can be judged from the unofficial statements which we have, it appears likely that Belgium will separate from Holland altogether, it being very doubtful whether the Belgian troops will support the King's Government.

In the event of such a revolution, it remains to be seen what part Prussia will take, and, if she marches an army to reduce Belgium to obedience, whether the Belgians will not make overtures to France, and in that case whether King Louis Philippe will be able to restrain the French from seizing such a golden opportunity of regaining their former frontier; and if they accept the offer, whether a general war in Europe will not ensue.

In these difficult circumstances, and in the midst of possibilities so tremendous, it is awful to reflect upon the very moderate portion of wisdom and sagacity which is allotted to those by whom our affairs are managed. I am by no means easy as to the Duke of Wellington's sufficiency to meet such difficulties; the habits of his mind are not those of patient investigation, profound knowledge of human nature, and cool, discriminating sagacity. He is exceedingly quick of apprehension, but deceived by his own quickness into thinking he knows more than he does. He has amazing confidence in himself, which is fostered by the deference of those around him and the long experience of his military successes. He is upon ordinary occasions right-headed and sensible, but he is beset by weaknesses and passions which must, and continually do, blind his judgment. Above all he wants that suavity of manner, that watchfulness of observation, that power of taking great and enlarged views of events and characters, and of weighing opposite interests and probabilities, which are essentially necessary in circumstances so delicate, and in which one false step, any hasty measure, or even incautious expression, may be attended with consequences of immense importance. I feel justified in this view of his political fitness by contemplating the whole course of his career, and the signal failure which has marked all his foreign policy. If Canning were now alive we might hope to steer through these difficulties, but if he had lived we should probably never have been in them. He was the only statesman who had sagacity to enter into and comprehend the spirit of the times, and to put himself at the head of that movement which was no longer to be arrested. The march of Liberalism (as it is called) would not be stopped, and this he knew, and he resolved to govern and lead instead of opposing it. The idiots who so rejoiced at the removal of this master mind (which alone could have saved them from the effects of their own folly) thought to stem the torrent in its course, and it has overwhelmed them. It is unquestionable that the Duke has too much participated in their sentiments and passions, and, though he never mixed himself with their proceedings, regarded them with a favourable eye, nor does he ever seem to have been aware of the immensity of the peril which they were incurring. The urgency of the danger will unquestionably increase the impatience of those who already think the present Government incapable of carrying on the public business, and now that we are placed in a situation the most intricate (since the French Revolution) it is by no means agreeable to think that such enormous interests are at the mercy of the Duke's awkward squad.

Sefton gave me an account of the dinner in St. George's Hall on the King's birthday, which was magnificent—excellent and well served. Bridge[2] came down with the plate, and was hid during the dinner behind the great wine-cooler, which weighs 7,000 ounces, and he told Sefton afterwards that the plate in the room was worth 200,000*l*. There is another service of gold plate, which was not used at all. The King has made it all over to the Crown. All this plate was ordered by the late King, and never used; his delight was ordering what the public had to pay for.

Newark, September 18th.   Came to town on Thursday, and in the afternoon heard the news of Huskisson's horrible accident, and yesterday morning got a letter from Henry with the details, which are pretty correctly given in the 'Times' newspaper. It is a very odd thing, but I had for days before a strong presentiment that some terrible accident would occur at this ceremony, and I told Lady Cowper so, and several other people. Nothing could exceed the horror of the few people in London at this event, or the despair of those who looked up to him politically. It seems to have happened in this way:—While the Duke's car was stopping to take in water, the people alighted and walked about the railroad; when suddenly another car, which was running on the adjoining level, came up. Everybody scrambled out of the way, and those who could got again into the first car. This Huskisson attempted to do, but he was slow and awkward; as he was getting in some part of the machinery of the other car struck the door of his, by which he was knocked down. He was taken up, and conveyed by Wilton and Mrs. Huskisson (who must have seen the accident happen) to the house of Mr. Blackburne, eight miles from Heaton. Wilton saved his life for a few hours by knowing how to tie up the artery; amputation was not possible, and he expired at ten o'clock that night. Wilton, Lord Granville, and Littleton were with him to the last. Mrs. Huskisson behaved with great courage. The Duke of Wellington was deeply affected, and it was with the greatest difficulty he could be induced to proceed upon the progress to Manchester, and at last he only yielded to the most pressing solicitations of the directors and others, and to

[2] [Of the house of Rundell and Bridge, the great silversmiths and jewellers of the day.]

a strong remonstrance that the mob might be dangerous if he did not appear. It is impossible to figure to one's self any event which could produce a greater sensation or be more striking to the imagination than this, happening at such a time and under such circumstances: the eminence of the man, the sudden conversion of a scene of gaiety and splendour into one of horror and dismay; the countless multitudes present, and the effect upon them—crushed to death in sight of his wife and at the feet (as it was) of his great political rival—all calculated to produce a deep and awful impression. The death of Huskisson cannot fail to have an important effect upon political events; it puts an end to his party as a party, but it leaves the survivors at liberty to join either the Opposition or the Government, while during his life there were great difficulties to their doing either, in consequence of the antipathy which many of the Whigs had to him on one side and the Duke of Wellington on the other. There is no use, however, in speculating on what will happen, which a very short time will show.

Agar Ellis told me yesterday morning that he had received a letter from Brougham a day or two ago, in which he said that he was going to Liverpool, and hoped there to sign a treaty with Huskisson, so that it is probable they would have joined to oppose the Government. As to the Duke of Wellington, a fatality attends him, and it is perilous to cross his path. There were perhaps 500,000 people present on this occasion, and probably not a soul besides hurt. One man only is killed, and that man is his most dangerous political opponent, the one from whom he had most to fear. It is the more remarkable because these great people are generally taken such care of, and put out of the chance of accidents. Canning had scarcely reached the zenith of his power when he was swept away, and the field was left open to the Duke, and no sooner is he reduced to a state of danger and difficulty than the ablest of his adversaries is removed by a chance beyond all power of calculation.

Huskisson was about sixty years old, tall, slouching, and ignoble-looking. In society he was extremely agreeable, without much animation, generally cheerful, with a great deal of humour, information, and anecdote, gentlemanlike, unassuming, slow in speech, and with a downcast look, as if he avoided meeting anybody's gaze. It is probably true that there is no man in Parliament, or perhaps out of it, so well versed in finance, commerce, trade, and colonial matters, and that he is therefore a very great and irreparable loss.

London, November 8th.   Parliament met, and a great clamour was raised against the King's Speech, without much reason; but it was immediately evident that the Government was in a very tottering condition, and the first night of this session the Duke of Wellington made a violent and uncalled-for declaration against Reform, which has without doubt sealed his fate. Never was there an act of more egregious folly, or one so universally condemned by friends and foes. The Chancellor said to Lady Lyndhurst after the first night's debate in the House of Lords, 'You have often asked me why the Duke did not take in Lord Grey; read these two speeches (Lord Grey's and the Duke's), and then you will see why. Do you think he would like to have a colleague under him, who should get up and make such a speech after such another as his?'

The effect produced by this declaration exceeds anything I ever saw, and it has at once destroyed what little popularity the Duke had left, and lowered him in public estimation so much that when he does go out of office, as most assuredly he must, he will leave it without any of the dignity and credit which might have accompanied his retirement. The sensation produced in the country has not yet been ascertained, but it is sure to be immense. I came to town last night, and found the town ringing with his imprudence and everybody expecting that a few days would produce his resignation.

November 9th.   Southey told an anecdote of Sir Massey Lopes, which is a good story of a miser. A man came to him and told him he was in great distress, and 200*l.* would save him. He gave him a draft for the money. 'Now,' says he, 'what will you do with this?' 'Go to the bankers and get it cashed.' 'Stop,' said he; 'I will cash it.' So he gave him the money, but first calculated and deducted the discount, thus at once exercising his benevolence and his avarice.

December 2nd. The Liverpool election, which is just over, was, considering the present state of things, a remarkable contest. It is said to have cost near 100,000*l.* to the two parties, and to have exhibited a scene of bribery and corruption perfectly unparalleled; no concealment or even semblance of decency was observed; the price of tallies and of votes rose, like stock, as the demand increased, and single votes fetched from 15*l.* to 100*l.* apiece. They voted by tallies; as each tally voted for one or the other candidate they were furnished with a receipt for their votes, with which they went to the committee, when through a hole in the wall the receipt was handed in, and through another the stipulated sum handed out; and this scene of iniquity has been exhibited at a period when the cry for Reform is echoed from one end of the country to the other.

December 5th. The Duke of Wellington's fall, if the causes of it are dispassionately traced and considered, affords a great political lesson. His is one of those mixed characters which it is difficult to praise or blame without the risk of doing them more or less than justice. He has talents which the event has proved to be sufficient to make him the second (and, now that Napoleon is gone, the first general) of the age, but which could not make him a tolerable Minister. Confident, presumptuous, and dictatorial, but frank, open, and good-humoured, he contrived to rule in the Cabinet without mortifying his colleagues, and he has brought it to ruin without forfeiting their regard. Choosing with a very slender stock of knowledge to take upon himself the sole direction of every department of Government, he completely sank under the burden. Originally imbued with the principles of Lord Castlereagh and the Holy Alliance, he brought all those predilections with him into office. Incapable of foreseeing the mighty events with which the future was big, and of comprehending the prodigious alterations which the moral character of Europe had undergone, he pitted himself against Canning in the Cabinet, and stood up as the assertor of maxims both of foreign and domestic policy which that great statesman saw were no longer fitted for the times we live in. With a flexibility which was more remarkably exhibited at subsequent periods, when he found that the cause he advocated was lost, the Duke turned suddenly round, and surrendered his opinions at discretion; but in his heart he never forgave Mr. Canning, and from that time jealousy of him had a material influence on his political conduct, and was the primary motive of many of his subsequent resolutions. This flexibility has been the cause of great benefits to the country, but ultimately of his own downfall, for it has always proceeded from the pressure of circumstances and considerations of convenience to himself, and not from a rational adaptation of his opinions and conduct to the necessities and variations of the times. He has not been thoroughly true to any principle or any party; he contrived to disgust and alienate his old friends and adherents without conciliating or attaching those whose measures he at the eleventh hour undertook to carry into execution. Through the whole course of his political conduct selfish considerations have never been out of sight. His opposition to Canning's Corn Bill was too gross to admit of excuse. It was the old spite bursting forth, sharpened by Canning's behaviour to him in forming his Administration, which, if it was not contumelious, certainly was not courteous. When at his death the Duke assumed the Government, his disclaiming speech was thrown in his teeth, but without much justice, for such expressions are never to be taken literally, and in the subsequent quarrel with Huskisson, though it is probably true that he was aiming at domination, he was persuaded that Huskisson and his party were endeavouring to form a cabal in the Cabinet, and his expulsion of them is not, therefore, altogether without excuse. On the question of the Test Act it was evident he was guided by no principle, probably by no opinion, and that he only thought of turning it as best he might to his own advantage. Throughout the Catholic question self was always apparent, not that he was careless of the safety, or indifferent to the prosperity of the country, but that he cared as much for his own credit and power, and never considered the first except in their connection with the second. The business of Emancipation he certainly conducted with considerable judgment, boldly trusting to the baseness of many of his old friends, and showing that he had not mistaken their characters; exercising that habitual influence he had acquired over the mind of the King; preserving impenetrable secrecy; using without scruple every artifice that could forward his object; and contriving to make tools or dupes of all his colleagues and adherents, and getting the whole merit to himself. From the passing of the Catholic question his conduct has exhibited a series of blunders which have at length terminated in his fall. The position in which he then stood was this:—He had a Government composed of men who were for the most part incompetent, but perfectly subservient to him. He had a considerable body of adherents in both Houses. The Whigs, whose support (enthusiastically given) had carried him triumphantly through the great contest, were willing to unite with him; the Tories, exasperated and indignant, feeling insulted and betrayed, vowed nothing but vengeance. Intoxicated with his victory, he was resolved to neglect the Whigs, to whom he was so much indebted, and to regain the affections of the Tories, whom he considered as his natural supporters, and whom he thought identity of opinion and interest would bring back to his standard. By all sorts of slights and affronting insinuations that they wanted place, but that he could do without them, he offended the Whigs, but none of his cajoleries and advances had the least effect on the sulky Tories. It was in vain that he endeavoured to adapt his foreign policy to their worst prejudices by opposing with undeviating hostility that of Mr. Canning (the great object of their detestation), and disseminating throughout all Europe the belief of his attachment to ultra-monarchical principles. He opposed the spirit of the age, he brought England into contempt, but he did not conciliate the Tories. Having succeeded in uniting two powerful parties (acting separately) in opposition to his Government, and having nobody but Peel to defend his measures in the House of Commons, and nobody in the House of Lords, he manifested his sense of his own weakness by overtures and negotiations, and evinced his obstinate tenacity of power by never offering terms which could be accepted, or extending his invitations to those whose authority he thought might cope with his own. With his Government falling every day in public opinion, and his enemies growing more numerous and confident, with questions of vast importance rising up with a vigour and celerity of growth which astonished the world, he met a new Parliament (constituted more unfavourably than the last, which he had found himself unable to manage) without any support but in his own confidence and the encouraging adulation of a little knot of devotees. There still lingered round him some of that popularity which had once been so great, and which the recollection of his victories would not suffer to be altogether extinguished. By a judicious accommodation of his conduct to that public opinion which was running with an uncontrollable tide, by a frank invitation to all who were well disposed to strengthen his Government, he might have raised those embers of popularity into a flame once more, have saved himself, and still done good service to the State; but it was decreed that he should fall. He appeared bereft of all judgment and discretion, and after a King's Speech which gave great, and I think unnecessary offence, he delivered the famous philippic against Reform which sealed his fate. From that moment it was not doubtful, and he was hurled from the seat of power amidst universal acclamations.

[*Memorandum added by Mr. Greville in April* 1850.]

N.B.—I leave this as it is, though it is unjust to the Duke of Wellington; but such as my impressions were at the time they shall remain, to be corrected afterwards when necessary. It would be very wrong to impute *selfishness* to him in the ordinary sense of the term. He coveted power, but he was perfectly disinterested, a great patriot if ever there was one, and he was always animated by a strong and abiding sense of duty. I have done him justice in other places, and there is after all a great deal of truth in what I have said here.

December 16th. There has been a desperate quarrel between the King and his sons. George Fitzclarence wanted to be made a Peer and have a pension; the King said he could not do it, so they struck work in a body, and George resigned his office of Deputy Adjutant-General and wrote the King a furious letter. The King sent for Lord Hill, and told him to try and bring him to his senses; but Lord Hill could do nothing, and then he sent for Brougham to talk to him about it. It is not yet made up, but one of them (Frederick, I believe) dined at the dinner the King gave the day before yesterday. They want to renew the days of Charles II., instead of waiting patiently and letting the King do what he can for them, and as he can.

February 12th, 1831. I saw the day before yesterday a curious letter from Southey to Brougham, which some day or other will probably appear. Taylor showed it me. Brougham had written to him to ask him what his opinion was as to the encouragement that could be given to literature, by rewarding or honouring literary men, and suggested (I did not see his letter) that the Guelphic Order should be bestowed upon them. Southey's reply was very courteous, but in a style of suppressed irony and forced politeness, and exhibited the marks of a chafed spirit, which was kept down by an effort. 'You, my Lord, are *now* on the Conservative side,' was one of his phrases, which implied that the Chancellor had not always been on that side. He suggested that it might be useful to establish a sort of lay fellowships; 10,000*l.* would give 10 of 500*l.* and 25 of 200*l.*; but he proposed them not to reward the meritorious, but as a means of silencing or hiring the mischievous. It was evident, however, that he laid no stress on this plan, or considered it practicable, and only proposed it because he thought he must suggest something. He said that honours might be desirable to scientific men, as they were so considered on the Continent, and Newton and Davy had been titled, but for himself, if a *Guelphic* distinction was adopted, 'he should be a *Ghibelline*.' He ended by saying that all he asked for was a repeal of the Copyright Act, which took from the families of literary men the only property they had to give them, and this 'I ask for with the earnestness of one who is conscious that he has laboured for posterity.' It is a remarkable letter.

February 25th. I am just come home from breakfasting with Henry Taylor to meet Wordsworth; the same party as when he had Southey—Mill, Elliot, Charles Villiers. Wordsworth may be bordering on sixty; hard-featured, brown, wrinkled, with prominent teeth and a few scattered grey hairs, but nevertheless not a disagreeable countenance; and very cheerful, merry, courteous, and talkative, much more so than I should have expected from the grave and didactic character of his writings. He held forth on poetry, painting, politics, and metaphysics, and with a great deal of eloquence; he is more conversible and with a greater flow of animal spirits than Southey. He mentioned that he never wrote down as he composed, but composed walking, riding, or in bed, and wrote down after; that Southey always composes at his desk.

March 2nd. The great day at length arrived, and yesterday Lord John Russell moved for leave to bring in his Reform Bill. To describe the curiosity, the intensity of the expectation and excitement, would be impossible, and the secret had been so well kept that not a soul knew what the measure was (though most people guessed pretty well) till they heard it. He rose at six o'clock, and spoke for two hours and a quarter—a sweeping measure indeed, much more so than anyone had imagined, because the Ministers had said it was one which would give *general* satisfaction, whereas this must dissatisfy all the moderate and will probably just stop short enough not to satisfy the Radicals. They say it was ludicrous to see the faces of the members for those places which are to be disfranchised as they were severally announced, and Wetherell, who began to take notes, as the plan was gradually developed, after sundry contortions and grimaces and flinging about his arms and legs, threw down his notes with a mixture of despair and ridicule and horror. Not many people spoke last night: Inglis followed John Russell, and Francis Leveson closed the debate in the best speech he has ever made, though rather too flowery. Everything is easy in these days, otherwise how Palmerston, Goderich, and Grant can have joined in a measure of this sweeping, violent, and speculative character it is difficult to conceive, they who were the disciples of Castlereagh and the adherents of Canning; but after the Duke of Wellington and Peel carrying the Catholic question, Canning's friends advocating Radical Reform, and Eldon living to see Brougham on the Woolsack, what may one not expect?

March 7th. Nothing talked of, thought of, dreamt of, but Reform. Every creature one meets asks, What is said now? How will it go? What is the last news? What do *you* think? and so it is from morning till night, in the streets, in the clubs, and in private houses.

March 11th. It is curious to see the change of opinion as to the passing of this Bill. The other day nobody would hear of the possibility of it, now everybody is beginning to think it will be carried. The tactics of the Opposition have been very bad, for they ought to have come to a division immediately, when I think Government would have been beaten, but it was pretty certain that if they gave time to the country to declare itself the meetings and addresses would fix the wavering and decide the doubtful. There certainly never was anything like the unanimity which pervades the country on the subject, and though I do not think they will break out into rebellion if it is lost, it is impossible not to see that the feeling for it (kept alive as it will be by every sort of excitement) must prevail, and that if this particular Bill is not carried some other must very like it, and which, if it is much short of this, will only leave a peg to hang fresh discussions upon.

March 23rd. The House divided at three o'clock this morning, and the second reading was carried by a majority of *one* in the fullest House that ever was known—303 to 302—both parties confident up to the moment of division; but the Opposition most so, and at last the Government expected to be beaten. I walked home, and found the streets swarming with members of Parliament coming from the House. My belief is (if they manage well and are active and determined) that the Bill will be lost in Committee, and then this will be the best thing that could have occurred.

March 24th. I met the Duke of Wellington, who owned to me that he thought this small majority for the Bill was on the whole the best thing that could have occurred, and that seems to be the opinion generally of its opponents.

A sort of repose from the cursed Bill for a moment, but it is said that many who opposed it before are going to support it in Committee; nobody knows. When the Speaker put the question, each party roared 'Aye' and 'No' *totis viribus.* He said he did not know, and put it again. After that he said, 'I am not sure, but I think the ayes have it.' Then the noes went out into the lobby, and the others thought they never would have done filing out, and the House looked so empty when they were gone that the Government was in despair. They say the excitement was beyond anything.

April 24th. At Newmarket all last week, and returned to town last night to hear from those who saw them the extraordinary scenes in both Houses of Parliament (the day before) which closed the eventful week. The Reform battle began again on Monday last. On Thursday the Ministers were again beaten in the House of Commons on a question of adjournment, and on Friday morning they got the King to go down and prorogue Parliament in person the same day. This *coup d'état* was so sudden that nobody was aware of it till within two or three hours of the time, and many not at all. They told him that the cream-coloured horses could not be got ready, when he said, 'Then I will go with anybody else's horses.' Somebody went off in a carriage to the Tower, to fetch the Crown, and they collected such attendants as they could find to go with his Majesty. The Houses met at one or two o'clock. In the House of Commons Sir R. Vyvyan made a furious speech, attacking the Government on every point, and (excited as he was) it was very well done. The Ministers made no reply, but Sir Francis Burdett and Tennyson endeavoured to interrupt with calls to order, and when the Speaker decided that

Vyvyan was not out of order Tennyson disputed his opinion, which enraged the Speaker, and soon after called up Peel, for whom he was resolved to procure a hearing. The scene then resembled that which took place on Lord North's resignation in 1782, for Althorp (I think) moved that Burdett should be heard, and the Speaker said that 'Peel was in possession of the House to speak on that motion.' He made a very violent speech, attacking the Government for their incompetence, folly, and recklessness, and treated them with the utmost asperity and contempt. In the midst of his speech the guns announced the arrival of the King, and at each explosion the Government gave a loud cheer, and Peel was still speaking in the midst of every sort of noise and tumult when the Usher of the Black Rod knocked at the door to summon the Commons to the House of Peers. There the proceedings were if possible still more violent and outrageous; those who were present tell me it resembled nothing but what we read of the 'Serment du Jeu de Paume,' and the whole scene was as much like the preparatory days of a revolution as can well be imagined. Wharncliffe was to have moved an address to the Crown against dissolving Parliament, and this motion the Ministers were resolved should not come on, but he contrived to bring it on so far as to get it put upon the Journals. The Duke of Richmond endeavoured to prevent any speaking by raising points of order, and moving that the Lords should take their regular places (in separate ranks), which, however, is impossible at a royal sitting, because the cross benches are removed; this put Lord Londonderry in such a fury that he rose, roared, gesticulated, held up his whip, and four or five Lords held him down by the tail of his coat to prevent his flying on somebody. Lord Lyndhurst was equally furious, and some sharp words passed which were not distinctly heard. In the midst of all the din Lord Mansfield rose and obtained a hearing. Wharncliffe said to him, 'For God's sake, Mansfield, take care what you are about, and don't disgrace us more in the state we are in.' 'Don't be afraid,' he said; 'I will say nothing that will alarm you;' and accordingly he pronounced a trimming philippic on the Government, which, delivered as it was in an imposing manner, attired in his robes, and with the greatest energy and excitation, was prodigiously effective. While he was still speaking, the King arrived, but he did not desist even while his Majesty was entering the House of Lords, nor till he approached the throne; and while the King was ascending the steps, the hoarse voice of Lord Londonderry was heard crying 'Hear, hear, hear!' The King from the robing-room heard the noise, and asked what it all meant. The conduct of the Chancellor was most extraordinary, skipping in and out of the House and making most extraordinary speeches. In the midst of the uproar he went out of the House, when Lord Shaftesbury was moved into the chair. In the middle of the debate Brougham again came in and said, 'it was most extraordinary that the King's undoubted right to dissolve Parliament should be questioned at a moment when the House of Commons had taken the unprecedented course of stopping the supplies,' and having so said (which was a lie) he flounced out of the House to receive the King on his arrival. The King ought not properly to have worn the Crown, never having been crowned; but when he was in the robing-room he said to Lord Hastings, 'Lord Hastings, I wear the Crown; where is it?' It was brought to him, and when Lord Hastings was going to put it on his head he said, 'Nobody shall put the Crown on my head but myself.' He put it on, and then turned to Lord Grey and said, 'Now, my Lord, the coronation is over.' George Villiers said that in his life he never saw such a scene, and as he looked at the King upon the throne with the Crown loose upon his head, and the tall, grim figure of Lord Grey close beside him with the sword of state in his hand, it was as if the King had got his executioner by his side, and the whole picture looked strikingly typical of his and our future destinies.

Such has been the termination of this Parliament and of the first act of the new Ministerial drama.

May 7th. Nothing could go on worse than the elections—Reformers returned everywhere, so much so that the contest is over, and we have only to await the event and see what the House of

Lords will do. In the House of Commons the Bill is already carried.

June 5th. All last week at Fern Hill for the Ascot races. The Royal Family came to the course the first day with a great *cortége* —eight coaches and four, two phaetons, pony sociables, and led horses—Munster riding on horseback behind the King's carriage, Augustus (the parson) and Frederick driving phaetons. The Duke of Richmond was in the King's calèche and Lord Grey in one of the coaches. The reception was strikingly cold and indifferent, not half so good as that which the late King used to receive. William was bored to death with the races, and his own horse broke down. On Wednesday he did not come; on Thursday they came again. Beautiful weather and unprecedented multitudes. The King was much more cheered than the first day, or the greater number of people made a greater noise. A few cheers were given to Lord Grey as he returned, which he just acknowledged and no more. On Friday we dined at the Castle; each day the King asked a crowd of people from the neighbourhood. We arrived at a little before seven; the Queen was only just come in from riding, so we had to wait till near eight. Above forty people at dinner, for which the room is not nearly large enough; the dinner was not bad, but the room insufferably hot. The Queen was taken out by the Duke of Richmond, and the King followed with the Duchess of Saxe Weimar, the Queen's sister. He drinks wine with everybody, asking seven or eight at a time. After dinner he drops asleep. We sat for a short time. Directly after coffee the band began to play; a good band, not numerous, and principally of violins and stringed instruments. The Queen and the whole party sat there all the evening, so that it was, in fact, a concert of instrumental music. The King took Lady Tavistock to St. George's Hall and the ball room, where we walked about, with two or three servants carrying lamps to show the proportions, for it was not lit up. The whole thing is exceedingly magnificent, and the manner of life does not appear to be very formal, and need not be disagreeable but for the bore of never dining without twenty strangers. The Castle holds very few people, and with the King's and Queen's immediate suite and *toute la bâtardise* it was quite full. The King's four sons were there, *signoreggianti tutti,* and the whole thing 'donnait à penser' to those who looked back a little and had seen other days. What a *changement de décoration;* no longer George IV., capricious, luxurious, and misanthropic, liking nothing but the society of listeners and flatterers, with the Conyngham tribe and one or two Tory Ministers and foreign Ambassadors; but a plain, vulgar, hospitable gentleman, opening his doors to all the world, with a numerous family and suite, a Whig Ministry, no foreigners, and no toad-eaters at all. Nothing can be more different, and looking at him one sees how soon this act will be finished, and the same be changed for another probably not less dissimilar. Queen, bastards, Whigs, all will disappear, and God knows what replaces them.

June 7th. Dined with Sefton yesterday, who gave me an account of a dinner at Fowell Buxton's on Saturday to see the brewery, at which Brougham was the 'magnus Apollo.' Sefton is excellent as a commentator on Brougham; he says that he watches him incessantly, never listens to anybody else when he is there, and *rows* him unmercifully afterwards for all the humbug, nonsense, and palaver he hears him talk to people. They were twenty-seven at dinner. Talleyrand was to have gone, but was frightened by being told that he would get nothing but beefsteaks and porter, so he stayed away. They dined in the brewhouse and visited the whole establishment. Lord Grey was there in star, garter, and ribband. There were people ready to show and explain everything, but not a bit—Brougham took the explanation of everything into his own hands—the mode of brewing, the machinery, down to the feeding of the cart horses. After dinner the account books were brought, and the young Buxtons were beckoned up to the top of the table by their father to hear the words of wisdom that flowed from the lips of my Lord Chancellor. He affected to study the ledger, and made various pertinent remarks on the manner of book-keeping. There was a man whom Brougham called 'Cornelius' (Sefton did not know who he was) with whom he seemed very familiar. While Brougham was talking he dropped his voice, on which 'Cornelius' said, 'Earl Grey is listening,' that he might speak louder and so nothing be lost. He was talking of Paley, and said that 'although he did not always understand his own meaning, he always contrived to make it intelligible to others,' on which 'Cornelius' said, 'My good friend, if he made it so clear to others he must have had some comprehension of it himself;' on which Sefton attacked him afterwards, and swore that 'he was a mere child in the hands of "Cornelius,"' that 'he never saw anybody so put down.' These people are all subscribers to the London University, and Sefton swears he overheard Brougham tell them that 'Sir Isaac Newton was nothing compared to some of the present professors,' or something to that effect. I put down all this nonsense because it amused me in the recital, and is excessively characteristic of the man, one of the most remarkable who ever existed. Lady Sefton told me that he went with them to the British Museum, where all the officers of the Museum were in attendance to receive them. He would not let anybody explain anything, but did all the honours himself. At last they came to the collection of minerals, when she thought he must be brought to a standstill. Their conductor began to describe them, when Brougham took the words out of his mouth, and dashed off with as much ease and familiarity as if he had been a Buckland or a Cuvier. Such is the man, a grand mixture of moral, political, and intellectual incongruities.

July 10*th*. They have made a fine business of Cobbett's trial; his insolence and violence were past endurance, but he made an able speech. The Chief Justice was very timid, and favoured and complimented him throughout; very unlike what Ellenborough would have done. The jury were shut up the whole night, and in the morning the Chief Justice, without consulting either party, discharged them, which was probably on the whole the best that could be done. Denman told me that he expected they would have acquitted him without leaving the box, and this principally on account of Brougham's evidence, for Cobbett brought the Chancellor forward and made him prove that *after* these very writings, and while this prosecution was hanging over him,

Brougham wrote to his son 'Dear Sir,' and requesting he would ask his father for some former publications of his, which he thought would be of great use on the present occasion in quieting the labourers. This made a great impression. Gurney overheard one juryman say to another, 'Don't you think we had better stop the case? It is useless to go on.' The other, however, declared for hearing it out, so on the whole it ended as well as it might.

August 9th. On Sunday, overtaken by the most dreadful storm I ever saw—flashes of lightning, crashes of thunder, and the rain descending like a waterspout—I rode to Windsor, to settle with the Queen what sort of crown she would have to be crowned in. I was ushered into the King's presence, who was sitting at a red table in the sitting-room of George IV., looking over the flower garden. A picture of Adolphus Fitzclarence was behind him (a full-length), and one of the parson, Rev. Augustus Fitzclarence, in a Greek dress, opposite. He sent for the Queen, who came with the Landgravine and one of the King's daughters, Lady Augusta Erskine, the widow of Lord Cassilis's son. She looked at the drawings, meant apparently to be civil to me in her ungracious way, and said she would have none of our crowns, that she did not like to wear a hired crown, and asked me if I thought it was right that she should. I said, 'Madam, I can only say that the late King wore one at his coronation.' However she said, 'I do not like it, and I have got jewels enough, so I will have them made up myself.' The King said to me, 'Very well; then *you* will have to pay for the setting.' 'Oh, no,' she said; 'I shall pay for it all myself.'

August 11th. Nothing remarkable in the House of Commons but Lord John Russell's declaration that 'this Bill would not be final if it was not found to work as well as the people desired,' which is sufficiently impudent considering that hitherto they have always pretended that it was to be final, and that it was made so comprehensive only that it might be so; this has been one of their grand arguments, and now we are never to sit down and rest, but go on changing till we get a good fit, and that for a country which will have been made so fidgety that it won't stand still to be measured. Hardinge, whom I found at dinner at the

Athenæum yesterday, told me he was convinced that a revolution in this country was inevitable; and such is the opinion of others who support this Bill, not because they think concession will avert it, but will let it come more gradually and with less violence. I have always been convinced that the country was in no danger of revolution, and still believe that if one does come it will be from the passing of this Bill, which will introduce the principle of change and whet the appetites of those who never will be satisfied with any existing order of things; or if it follows on the rejection of this Bill, which I doubt, it will be owing to the concentration of all the forces that are opposed to our present institutions, and the divisions, jealousies, rivalships, and consequent weakness of all those who ought to defend them. God only knows how it will all end. There has been but one man for many years past able to arrest this torrent, and that was Canning; and him the Tories—idiots that they were, and never discovering that he was their best friend—hunted to death with their besotted and ignorant hostility.

August 20th. A very curious case occurred the other day which shows the inconsistency of the human mind. A man was tried and condemned for ravishing his own daughter; and it appeared in evidence that his mother had died, had been buried, and that he had watched by her grave the whole night, and in the morning had returned home and violated his daughter. Filial piety and parental turpitude meeting together—very strange.

August 30th. Left Stoke yesterday morning; a large party— Talleyrand, De Ros, Fitzroy Somersets, Motteux, John Russell, Alava, Byng. In the evening Talleyrand discoursed, but I did not hear much of him. I was gouty and could not stand, and all the places near him were taken. I have never heard him narrate comfortably, and he is difficult to understand. He talked of Franklin. I asked him if he was remarkable in conversation; he said he was from his great simplicity and the evident strength of his mind. He spoke of the coronation of the Emperor Alexander. Somebody wrote him a letter at the time from Moscow with this expression:

'L'Empereur marchait, précédé des assassins de son grandpère, entouré de ceux de son père, et suivi par les siens.'

He afterwards talked of Madame de Staël and Monti. They met at Madame de Marescalchi's villa near Bologna, and were profuse of compliments and admiration for each other. Each brought a copy of their respective works beautifully bound to present to the other. After a day passed in an interchange of literary flatteries, and the most ardent expressions of delight, they separated, but each forgot to carry away the present of the other, and the books remain in Madame de Marescalchi's library to this day.

September 8th. Dined with the Duke of Wellington yesterday; thirty-one people. After dinner I had much talk with the Duke, who told me a good deal about the late King; talked of his extravagance and love of spending, provided that it was not his own money that he spent; he told an old story he had heard of Mrs. Fitzherbert's being obliged to borrow money for his post-horses to take him to Newmarket, that not a guinea was forthcoming to make stakes for some match, and when on George Leigh's entreaty he allowed some box to be searched that 3,000*l.* was found in it. He always had money. When he died they found 10,000*l.* in his boxes, and money scattered about everywhere, a great deal of gold. There were about 500 pocket-books, of different dates, and in every one money—guineas, one pound notes, one, two, or three in each. There never was anything like the quantity of trinkets and trash that they found. He had never given away or parted with anything. There was a prodigious quantity of hair—women's hair—of all colours and lengths, some locks with the powder and pomatum still sticking to them, heaps of women's gloves, *gages d'amour* which he had got at balls, and with the perspiration still marked on the fingers.

September 17th. The talk of the town has been about the King and a toast he gave at a great dinner at St. James's the other day. He had ninety guests—all his Ministers, all the great people, and all the foreign Ambassadors. After dinner he made a long, rambling speech in French, and ended by giving as 'a sentiment,' as

he called it, 'The land we live in.' This was before the ladies left
the room. After they were gone he made another speech in
French, in the course of which he travelled over every variety of
topic that suggested itself to his excursive mind, and ended with
a very coarse toast and the words 'Honi soit qui mal y pense.'
Sefton, who told it me, said he never felt so ashamed; Lord Grey
was ready to sink into the earth; everybody laughed of course,
and Sefton, who sat next to Talleyrand, said to him, 'Eh bien, que
pensez-vous de cela?' With his unmoved, immovable face he answered only, 'C'est bien remarquable.'

November 14th. For the last two or three days the reports
from Sunderland about the cholera have been of a doubtful
character. The reports exhibit a state of human misery, and necessarily of moral degradation, such as I hardly ever heard of. At
Sunderland they say there are houses with 150 inmates, who are
huddled five and six in a bed. They are in the lowest state of
poverty. The sick in these receptacles are attended by an apothe-
cary's boy, who brings them (or I suppose tosses them) medicines
without distinction or enquiry.

P*ashanger, January 1st, 1832.* Here since Thursday. Went all
over the jail yesterday, which is admirably kept. There are four
treadmills where they work—that is those who are condemned to
hard labour; 130 prisoners, the greatest number there has been
for a long time. So much for legislative amelioration, but some
deny that the effects proceed from the causes. The treadmill has
failed to reform or terrify the prisoners, but the jailer assured us
that private whipping was the most effectual mode of punishment and what they dread the most. The prison allowance varies
with different classes of offenders and with those who labour
and those who do not. The lowest have two pounds of bread a
day and water; others two pounds of bread, soup three times a
week, and milk porridge every morning. The prisoners were remarkably healthy, their cells were warm and dry; the jailer

attributes their good health to the lowness of their diet. What a change in these receptacles within these thirty or forty years! There has been but one execution for a long time—last year a young man was hanged for copulating with a cow.

February 6th. Dined yesterday with Lord Holland; came very late, and found a vacant place between Sir George Robinson and a common-looking man in black. As soon as I had time to look at my neighbour, I began to speculate (as one usually does) as to who he might be, and as he did not for some time open his lips except to eat, I settled that he was some obscure man of letters or of medicine, perhaps a cholera doctor. In a short time the conversation turned upon early and late education, and Lord Holland said he had always remarked that self-educated men were peculiarly conceited and arrogant, and apt to look down upon the generality of mankind, from their being ignorant of how much other people knew; not having been at public schools, they are uninformed of the course of general education. My neighbour observed that he thought the most remarkable example of self-education was that of Alfieri, who had reached the age of thirty without having acquired any accomplishment save that of driving, and who was so ignorant of his own language that he had to learn it like a child, beginning with elementary books. Lord Holland quoted Julius Cæsar and Scaliger as examples of late education, said that the latter had been wounded, and that he had been married and commenced learning Greek the same day, when my neighbour remarked 'that he supposed his learning Greek was not an instantaneous act like his marriage.' This remark, and the manner of it, gave me the notion that he was a dull fellow, for it came out in a way which bordered on the ridiculous, so as to excite something like a sneer. I was a little surprised to hear him continue the thread of conversation (from Scaliger's wound) and talk of Loyola having been wounded at Pampeluna. I wondered how he happened to know anything about Loyola's wound. Having thus settled my opinion, I went on eating my dinner, when Auckland, who was sitting opposite to me, addressed my neighbour, 'Mr. Macaulay, will you drink a glass of wine?' I thought I should have dropped off my chair. It was MACAULAY, the man I had been so long most curious to see and to hear, whose genius, eloquence, astonishing knowledge, and diversified talents have excited my wonder and admiration for such a length of time, and here I had been sitting next to him, hearing him talk, and setting him down for a dull fellow. I felt as if he could have read my thoughts, and the perspiration burst from every pore of my face, and yet it was impossible not to be amused at the idea. It was not till Macaulay stood up that I was aware of all the vulgarity and ungainliness of his appearance; not a ray of intellect beams from his countenance; a lump of more ordinary clay never enclosed a powerful mind and lively imagination. He had a cold and sore throat, the latter of which occasioned a constant contraction of the muscles of the thorax, making him appear as if in momentary danger of a fit. His manner struck me as not pleasing, but it was not assuming, unembarrassed, yet not easy, unpolished, yet not coarse; there was no kind of usurpation of the conversation, no tenacity as to opinion or facts, no assumption of superiority, but the variety and extent of his information were soon apparent, for whatever subject was touched upon he evinced the utmost familiarity with it; quotation, illustration, anecdote, seemed ready in his hands for every topic. Primogeniture in this country, in others, and particularly in ancient Rome, was the principal topic, I think, but Macaulay was not certain what was the law of Rome, except that when a man died intestate his estate was divided between his children. After dinner Talleyrand, and Madame de Dino came in. He was introduced to Talleyrand, who told him that he meant to go to the House of Commons on Tuesday, and that he hoped he would speak, 'qu'il avait entendu tous les grands orateurs, et il désirait à présent entendre Monsieur Macaulay.'

April 1st. At the Duchesse de Dino's ball the night before last I had a very anxious conversation with Melbourne about it all [*the Reform Bill*]. He said that 'he really believed there was no strong feeling in the country for the measure.' We talked of the violence of the Tories, and their notion that they could get rid of the whole thing. I said the notion was absurd *now*, but that I fully agreed with him about the general feeling. 'Why, then,' said he, 'might it not be thrown out?'—a consummation I really believe he would rejoice at, if it could be done. I said because there was a great party which would not let it, which would agitate again, and that the country wished ardently to have it settled; that if it could be disposed of for good and all, it would be a good thing indeed, but that this was now become impossible. I asked him if his colleagues were impressed as he was with this truth, and he said, 'No.' I told him he ought to do everything possible to enforce it, and to make them moderate, and induce them to concede, to which he replied, 'What difficulty can they have in swallowing the rest after they have given up the rotten boroughs? That is, in fact, the essential part of the Bill, and the truth is *I do not see how the Government is to be carried on without them.* Some means may be found; a remedy may possibly present itself, and it may work in practice better than we now know of, but I am not aware of any, and I do not see how any Government can be carried on when these are swept away.' This was, if not his exact words, the exact sense, and a pretty avowal for a man to make at the eleventh hour who has been a party concerned in this Bill during the other ten.

I have refrained for a long time from writing down anything about the cholera, because the subject is intolerably disgusting to me, and I have been bored past endurance by the perpetual questions of every fool about it. It is not, however, devoid of interest. In the first place, what has happened here proves that 'the people' of this enlightened, reading, thinking, reforming nation are not a whit less barbarous than the serfs in Russia, for precisely the same prejudices have been shown here that were found at St. Petersburg and at Berlin. The awful thing is the vast extent of misery and distress which prevails, and the evidence of the rotten foundation on which the whole fabric of this gorgeous society rests, for I call that rotten which exhibits thousands upon thousands of human beings reduced to the lowest stage of moral and physical degradation, with no more of the necessaries

of life than serve to keep body and soul together, whole classes
of artisans without the means of subsistence. However complicated and remote the causes of this state of things, the manifestations present themselves in a frightful presence and reality, and
those whose ingenuity, and experience, and philosophical views
may enable them accurately to point out the causes and the
gradual increase of this distress are totally unable to suggest a
remedy or to foresee an end to it. Can such a state of things permanently go on? can any reform ameliorate it? Is it possible for any
country to be considered in a healthy condition when there is
no such thing as a *general* diffusion of the comforts of life (vary-
ing of course with every variety of circumstance which can affect
the prosperity of individuals or of classes), but when the extremes prevail of the most unbounded luxury and enjoyment and
the most dreadful privation and suffering? To imagine a state of
society in which everybody should be well off, or even tolerably
well off, would be a mere vision, as long as there is a preponder-
ance of vice and folly in the world. There will always be effects
commensurate with their causes, but it has not always been, and
it certainly need not be, that the majority of the population should
be in great difficulty, struggling to keep themselves afloat, and,
what is worse, in uncertainty and in doubt whether they can earn
subsistence for themselves and their families.

London, May 17th. The events of the last few days have
passed with a rapidity which hardly left time to think upon them
—such sudden changes and transitions from rage to triumph on
one side, and from foolish exultation to mortification and despair
on the other. The first impression was that the Duke of Wellington would succeed in forming a Government, with or without
Peel. The first thing he did was to try and prevail upon Peel to
be Prime Minister, but he was inexorable. He then turned to
Baring, who, after much hesitation, agreed to be Chancellor of
the Exchequer. The work went on, but with difficulty, for neither
Peel, Goulburn, nor Croker would take office. They then tried
the Speaker, who was mightily tempted to become Secretary of
State, but still doubting and fearing, and requiring time to make

up his mind. At an interview with the Duke and Lyndhurst at Apsley House he declared his sentiments on the existing state of affairs in a speech of three hours, to the unutterable disgust of Lyndhurst, who returned home, flung himself into a chair, and said that 'he could not endure to have anything to do with such a *damned tiresome old bitch.*' After these three hours of oratory Manners Sutton desired to have till the next morning (Monday) to make up his mind, which he again begged might be extended till the evening. On that evening (Monday) ensued the memorable night in the House of Commons, which everybody agrees was such a scene of violence and excitement as never had been exhibited within those walls. Tavistock told me he had never heard anything at all like it, and to his dying day should not forget it. The House was crammed to suffocation; every violent sentiment and vituperative expression was received with shouts of approbation, yet the violent speakers were listened to with the greatest attention. Tom Duncombe made one of his blustering Radical harangues, full of every sort of impertinence, which was received with immense applause, but which contrasted with an admirable speech, full of dignity, but also of sarcasm and severity, from John Russell—the best he ever made. The conduct of the Duke of Wellington in taking office *to carry the Bill,* which was not denied, but which his friends feebly attempted to justify, was assailed with the most merciless severity, and (what made the greatest impression) was condemned (though in more measured terms) by moderate men and Tories, such as Inglis and Davies Gilbert. Baring, who spoke four times, at last proposed that there should be a compromise, and that the ex-Ministers should resume their seats and carry the Bill. This extraordinary proposition was drawn from him by the state of the House, and the impossibility he at once saw of forming a new Government, and without any previous concert with the Duke, who, however, entirely approved of what he said. After the debate Baring and Sutton went to Apsley House, and related to the Duke what had taken place, the former saying he would face a thousand devils rather than such a House of Commons. From that moment the whole thing was at an end, and the next morning (Tuesday) the Duke repaired to the King, and told him that he could not form an Administration. This communication, for which the debate of the previous night had prepared everybody, was speedily known, and the joy and triumph of the Whigs were complete.

The King desired the Duke and Lyndhurst (for they went together) to advise him what he should do. They advised him to write to Lord Grey (which he did), informing him that the Duke had given up the commission to form a Government, that he had heard of what had fallen from Mr. Baring in the House of Commons the night before on the subject of a compromise, and that he wished Lord Grey to return and resume the Government upon that principle. Lord Grey sent an answer full of the usual expressions of zeal and respect, but saying that he could give no answer until he had consulted his colleagues. He assembled his Cabinet, and at five o'clock the answer was sent.

Yesterday morning Lord Grey saw the King; but up to last night nothing was finally settled, everything turning upon the terms to be exacted, some of the violent of the party desiring they should avail themselves of this opportunity to make Peers, both to show their power and increase their strength; the more moderate, including Lord Grey himself and many of the old Peermakers, were for sparing the King's feelings and using their victory with moderation, all, however, agreeing that the only condition on which they could return was the certainty of carrying the Reform Bill unaltered, either by a creation of Peers or by the secession of its opponents. Up to the present moment the matter stands thus: the King at the mercy of the Whigs, just as averse as ever to make Peers, the violent wishing to press him, the moderate wishing to spare him, all parties railing at each other, the Tories broken and discomfited, and meditating no further resistance to the Reform Bill. The Duke is to make his *exposé* to-night.

Peel, who has kept himself out of the scrape, is strongly suspected of being anything but sorry for the dilemma into which the Duke has got himself, and they think that he secretly encouraged him to persevere, with promises of present support and future co-operation, with a shrewd anticipation of the fate that awaited him. I am by no means indisposed to give credit to this, for I well remember the wrath of Peel when the Duke's Government was broken up in 1830, and the various instances of secret dislike and want of real cordiality which have peeped from under a decent appearance of union and friendship. Nothing can be more certain than that he is in high spirits in the midst of it all, and talks with great complacency of its being very well as it is, and that the salvation of character is everything; and this from him, who fancies he has saved his own, and addressed to those who have forfeited theirs, is amusing.

The joy of the King at what he thought was to be his deliverance from the Whigs was unbounded. He lost no time in putting the Duke of Wellington in possession of everything that had taken place between him and them upon the subject of Reform, and with regard to the creation of Peers, admitting that he had consented, but saying he had been subjected to every species of persecution. His ignorance, weakness, and levity put him in a miserable light, and prove him to be one of the silliest old gentlemen in his dominions; but I believe he is mad, for yesterday he gave a great dinner to the Jockey Club, at which (notwithstanding his cares) he seemed in excellent spirits; and after dinner he made a number of speeches, so ridiculous and nonsensical, beyond all belief but to those who heard them, rambling from one subject to another, repeating the same thing over and over again, and altogether such a mass of confusion, trash, and imbecility as made one laugh and blush at the same time.

August 8th. I dined at Holland House yesterday; a good many people, and the Chancellor came in after dinner, looking like an old clothes man and dirty as the ground. We had a true Holland House dinner, two more people arriving (Melbourne and Tom Duncombe) than there was room for, so that Lady Holland had the pleasure of a couple of general squeezes, and of seeing our arms prettily pinioned. Lord Holland sits at table, but does not dine. He proposed to retire (not from the room), but was not allowed, for that would have given us all space and ease. Lord Holland told some stories of Johnson and Garrick which he had heard from Kemble. Johnson loved to bully Garrick, from a recollection of Garrick's former impertinence. When Garrick was in the zenith of his popularity, and grown rich, and lived with the great, and while Johnson was yet obscure, the Doctor used to drink tea with him, and he would say, 'Davy, I do not envy you your money nor your fine acquaintance, but I envy you your power of drinking such tea as this.' 'Yes,' said Garrick, 'it is very good tea, but it is not my best, nor that which I give to my Lord this and Sir somebody t'other.'

Johnson liked Fox because he defended his pension, and said it was only to blame in not being large enough. 'Fox,' he said, 'is a liberal man; he would always be "aut Cæsar aut nullus;" whenever I have seen him he has been *nullus.*' Lord Holland said Fox made it a rule never to talk in Johnson's presence, because he knew all his conversations were recorded for publication, and he did not choose to figure in them.

Johnson was very bawdy. He said "Talk of pleasure, Sir, there is no pleasure like emission." Garrick on some occasion slept in the same room with him and his wife, and pretended to be asleep to hear Johnson, who mixed up very comically his prayers with his conjugal endearments: "Our Father which art in Heaven— Petty—Tetty."

November 20th. Dined at Holland House the day before yesterday; Lady Holland is unwell, fancies she must dine at five o'clock, and exerts her power over society by making everybody go out there at that hour, though nothing can be more inconvenient than thus shortening the day, and nothing more tiresome than such lengthening of the evening. Rogers and Luttrell were staying there. The *tableau* of the house is this:—Before dinner, Lady Holland affecting illness and almost dissolution, but with a very respectable appetite, and after dinner in high force and vigour; Lord Holland, with his chalkstones and unable to walk, lying on his couch in very good spirits and talking away; Luttrell and Rogers walking about, ever and anon looking despairingly at the clock and making short excursions from the drawing-room; Allen surly and disputatious, poring over the newspapers, and replying in monosyllables (generally negative) to whatever is said to him. The grand topic of interest, far exceeding the Belgian or Portuguese questions, was the illness of Lady Holland's page, who has got a tumour in his thigh. This 'little creature,' as Lady Holland calls a great hulking fellow of about twenty, is called 'Edgar,' his real name being Tom or Jack, which he changed on being elevated to his present dignity, as the Popes do when they are elected to the tiara. More rout is made about him than other people are permitted to make about their children, and the inmates of Holland House are invited and compelled to go and sit with and amuse him. Such is the social despotism of this strange house, which presents an odd mixture of luxury and constraint, of enjoyment physical and intellectual, with an alloy of small *désagréments*. Talleyrand generally comes at ten or eleven o'clock, and stays as long as they will let him. Though everybody who goes there finds something to abuse or to ridicule in the mistress of the house, or its ways, all continue to go; all like it more or less; and whenever, by the death of either, it shall come to an end, a vacuum will be made in society which nothing will supply. It is the house of all Europe; the world will suffer by the loss; and it may with truth be said that it will 'eclipse the gaiety of nations.'

Petworth, December 20th. Came here yesterday. It is a very grand place; house magnificent and full of fine objects, both ancient and modern; the Sir Joshuas and Vandykes particularly interesting, and a great deal of all sorts that is worth seeing. Lord Egremont was eighty-one the day before yesterday, and is still healthy, with faculties and memory apparently unimpaired. He has reigned here for sixty years with great authority and influence. He is shrewd, eccentric, and benevolent, and has always been munificent and charitable in his own way; he patronises the arts and fosters rising genius. Painters and sculptors find employment and welcome in his house; he has built a gallery which is full of pictures and statues, some of which are very fine, and the pictures scattered through the house are interesting and curious. Lord Egremont hates ceremony, and can't bear to be personally meddled with; he likes people to come and go as it suits them, and say nothing about it, never to take leave of him. The party here consists of the Cowpers, his own family, a Lady E. Romney, two nieces, Mrs. Tredcroft a neighbour, Ridsdale a parson, Wynne, Turner, the great landscape painter, and a young artist of the name of Lucas, whom Lord Egremont is bringing into notice, and who will owe his fortune (if he makes it) to him. Lord Egremont is enormously rich, and lives with an abundant though not very refined hospitality. The house wants modern comforts, and the servants are rustic and uncouth; but everything is good, and it all bears an air of solid and aristocratic grandeur. The stud groom told me there are 300 horses of different sorts here. His course, however, is nearly run, and he has the mortification of feeling that, though surrounded with children and grandchildren, he is almost the last of his race, and that his family is about to be extinct. Two old brothers and one childless nephew are all that are left of the Wyndhams, and the latter has been many years married. All his own children are illegitimate, but he has everything in his power, though nobody has any notion of the manner in which he will dispose of his property. It is impossible not to reflect upon the prodigious wealth of the Earls of Northumberland, and of the proud Duke of Somerset who married the last heiress of that house, the betrothed of three husbands. All that Lord Egremont has, all the Duke of Northumberland's property, and the Duke of Rutland's Cambridgeshire estate belonged to them, which together is probably equivalent to between 200,000*l.* and 300,000*l.* a year. Banks told me that the Northumberland property, when settled on Sir H. Smithson, was not above 12,000*l.* a year.[3]

[3] [George O'Brien Wyndham, third Earl of Egremont, to whom Mr. Greville paid this visit, was born on the 18th of December, 1751. He was therefore eighty-two years old at this time; but he lived five years longer, and died in 1837, famous and beloved for his splendid hospitality and for his liberal and judicious patronage of the arts, and likewise of the turf.]

January 22nd, 1833. Dined with Talleyrand the day before yesterday. Nobody there but his *attachés*. After dinner he told me about his first residence in England, and his acquaintance with Fox and Pitt. He always talks in a kind of affectionate tone about the former, and is now meditating a visit to Mrs. Fox at St. Anne's Hill, where he may see her surrounded with the busts, pictures, and recollections of her husband. He delights to dwell on the simplicity, gaiety, childishness, and profoundness of Fox. I asked him if he had ever known Pitt. He said that Pitt came to Rheims to learn French, and he was there at the same time on a visit to the Archbishop, his uncle (whom I remember at Hartwell,[4] a very old prelate with the tic-douloureux), and that

---

[4] [Mr. Greville had paid a visit with his father to the little Court of Louis XVIII. at Hartwell about two years before the Restoration, when he was eighteen years of age. His narrative of this visit has been printed in the fifth volume of the 'Miscellany of the Philobiblon Society,' but it may not be inappropriately inserted here.]

A VISIT TO HARTWELL.

April 14th, 1814.

I have often determined to commit to paper as much as I can remember of my visit to Hartwell; and, as the King is about to ascend the throne of his ancestors, it is not uninteresting to recall to mind the particulars of a visit paid to him while in exile and in poverty.

About two years ago my father and I went to Hartwell by invitation of the King. We dressed at Aylesbury, and proceeded to Hartwell in the afternoon. We had previously taken a walk in the environs of the town, and had met the Duchesse d'Angoulême on horseback, accompanied by a Madame Choisi. At five o'clock we set out to Hartwell. The house is large, but in a dreary, disagreeable situation. The King had completely altered the interior, having subdivided almost all the apartments in order to lodge a greater number of people. There were numerous outhouses, in some of which small shops had been established by the servants, interspersed with gardens, so that the place resembled a little town.

Upon entering the house we were conducted by the Duc de Grammont into the King's private apartment. He received us most graciously and shook hands with both of us. This apartment was exceedingly small, hardly larger than a closet, and I remarked pictures of the late King and Queen, Madame Elizabeth, and the Dauphin, Louis XVII., hanging on the walls. The King had a manner of swinging his body backwards and forwards, which caused the most unpleasant sensations in that small room, and made my father feel something like being sea-sick. The room was just like a cabin, and the mo-

he and Pitt lived together for nearly six weeks, reciprocally
teaching each other French and English. After Chauvelin had
superseded him, and that he and Chauvelin had disagreed, he
went to live near Epsom (at Juniper Hall) with Madame de
Staël; afterwards they came to London, and in the meantime
Pitt had got into the hands of the *émigrés*, who persuaded him

tions of his Majesty exactly resembled the heaving of a ship. After our audience with the King we were taken to the *salon* a large room with a billiard
table at one end. Here the party assembled before dinner, to all of whom
we were presented—the Duchesse d'Angoulême, Monsieur the Duc d'Angoulême, the Duc de Berri, the Prince and Princess de Condé *ci-devant*
Madame de Monaco), and a vast number of ducs, &c.; Madame la Duchesse
de Serron (a little old *dame d'honneur* to Madame d'Angoulême), the Duc
de Lorges, the Duc d'Auray, the Archevêque de Rheims (an infirm old
prelate, tortured with the tic-douloureux), and many others whose names
I cannot remember. At a little after six dinner was announced, when we
went into the next room, the King walking out first. The dinner was extremely
plain, consisting of very few dishes, and no wines except port and sherry.
His Majesty did the honours himself, and was very civil and agreeable. We
were a very short time at table, and the ladies and gentlemen all got up
together. Each of the ladies folded up her napkin, tied it round with a bit
of ribbon, and carried it away. After dinner we returned to the drawing-room
and drank coffee. The whole party remained in conversation about a quarter
of an hour, when the King retired to his closet, upon which all repaired to
their separate apartments. Whenever the King came in or went out of the
room, Madame d'Angoulême made him a low curtsy, which he returned by
bowing and kissing his hand. This little ceremony never failed to take place.
After the party had separated we were taken to the Duc de Grammont's
apartments, where we drank tea. After remaining there about three quarters
of an hour we went to the apartment of Madame d'Angoulême, where a
great part of the company were assembled, and where we stayed about a
quarter of an hour. After this we descended again to the drawing-room,
where several card tables were laid out. The King played at whist with the
Prince and Princess de Condé and my father. His Majesty settled the points
of the game at 'le quart d'un sheling.' The rest of the party played at billiards
or ombre. The King was so civil as to invite us to sleep there, instead of returning to the inn at Aylesbury. When he invited us he said, 'Je crains que
vous serez très-mal logés, mais on donne ce qu'on peut.' Soon after eleven
the King retired, when we separated for the night. We were certainly 'très-mal
logés.' In the morning when I got out of bed, I was alarmed by the appearance of an old woman on the leads before my window, who was hanging
linen to dry. I was forced to retreat hastily to bed, not to shock the old lady's
modesty. At ten the next morning we breakfasted, and at eleven we took
leave of the King (who always went to Mass at that hour) and returned to
London. We saw the whole place before we came away; and they certainly
had shown great ingenuity in contriving to lodge such a number of people
in and about the house—it was exactly like a small rising colony. We were
very much pleased with our expedition; and were invited to return whenever we could make it convenient.

to send Talleyrand away, and accordingly he received orders to quit England in twenty-four hours. He embarked on board a vessel for America, but was detained in the river off Greenwich. Dundas sent to him, and asked him to come and stay with him while the ship was detained, but he said he would not set his foot on English ground again, and remained three weeks on board the ship in the river.

February 14th. Poulett Thomson said to me yesterday that Peel's prodigious superiority over everybody in the House was so evident, his talent for debate and thorough knowledge of Parliamentary tactics, gained by twenty years of experience, so commanding, that he must draw men's minds to him, and that he was evidently playing that game, throwing over the ultra-Tories and ingratiating himself with the House and the country. He, in fact, means to open a house to all comers, and make himself necessary and indispensable. Under that placid exterior he conceals, I believe, a boundless ambition, and hatred and jealousy lurk under his professions of esteem and political attachment. His is one of those contradictory characters, containing in it so much of mixed good and evil, that it is difficult to strike an accurate balance between the two, and the acts of his political life are of a corresponding description, of questionable utility and merit, though always marked by great ability. It is very sure that he has been the instrument of great good, or of enormous evil, and apparently more of the latter. He came into life the child and champion of a political system which has been for a long time crumbling to pieces; and if the perils which are produced by its fall are great, they are mainly attributable to the manner in which it was upheld by Peel, and to his want of sagacity, in a wrong estimate of his means of defence and of the force of the antagonist power with which he had to contend. The leading principles of his political conduct have been constantly erroneous, and his dexterity and ability in supporting them have only made the consequences of his errors more extensively pernicious. If we look back through the long course of Peel's life, and enquire what have been the great political measures with which his name is particularly connected, we shall find, first, the return to cash payments, which almost everybody now agrees was a fatal mistake, though it would not be fair to visit him with extraordinary censure for a measure which was sanctioned by almost all the great financial authorities; secondly, opposition to Reform in Parliament and to religious emancipation of every kind, the maintenance of the exclusive system, and support, untouched and uncorrected, of the Church, both English and Irish. His resistance to alterations on these heads was conducted with great ability, and for a long time with success; but he was endeavouring to uphold a system which was no longer supportable, and having imbibed in his career much of the liberal spirit of the age, he found himself in a state of no small perplexity between his old connections and his more enlarged propensities. Still he was chained down by the former, and consequently being beaten from all his positions, he was continually obliged to give way, but never did so till rather too late for his own credit and much too late for the interest at stake. Notwithstanding, therefore, the reputation he has acquired, the hold he has had of office, and is probably destined to have again, his political life has been a considerable failure, though not such an one as to render it more probable than not that his future life will be a failure too. He has hitherto been encumbered with embarrassing questions and an unmanageable party. Time has disposed of the first, and he is divorced from the last; if his great experience and talents have a fair field to act upon, he may yet, in spite of his selfish and unamiable character, be a distinguished and successful Minister.

London, February 22nd. Goulburn mentioned a curious thing *à propos* of slavery. A slave ran away from his estate in Jamaica many years ago, and got to England. He (the man) called at his house when he was not at home, and Goulburn never could afterwards find out where he was. He remained in England, however, gaining his livelihood by some means, till after some years he returned to Jamaica and to the estate, and desired to be employed as a slave again.

The Reformed Parliament has been sitting for a fortnight or so, and begins to manifest its character and pretensions. The first thing that strikes one is its inferiority in point of composition to preceding Houses of Commons, and the presumption, impertinence, and self-sufficiency of the new members. Formerly new members appeared with some modesty and diffidence, and with some appearance of respect for the assembly into which they were admitted; these fellows behave themselves as if they had taken it by storm, and might riot in all the insolence of victory. There exists no *party* but that of the Government; the Irish act in a body under O'Connell to the number of about forty; the Radicals are scattered up and down without a leader, numerous, restless, turbulent, and bold—Hume, Cobbett, and a multitude such as Roebuck, Faithfull, Buckingham, Major Beauclerck, &c. (most of whom have totally failed in point of speaking)— bent upon doing all the mischief they can and incessantly active; the Tories without a head, frightened, angry, and sulky; Peel without a party, prudent, cautious, and dexterous, playing a deep waiting game of scrutiny and observation. The feelings of these various elements of party, rather than parties, may be thus summed up:—The Radicals are confident and sanguine; the Whigs uneasy; the Tories desponding; moderate men, who belong to no party, but support Government, serious, and not without alarm.

March 4th. Sir Thomas Hardy told my brother he thought the King would certainly go mad; he was so excitable, *loathing* his Ministers, particularly Graham, and dying to go to war. He has some of the cunning of madmen, who fawn upon their keepers when looked at by them, and grin at them and shake their fists when their backs are turned; so he is extravagantly civil when his Ministers are with him, and exhibits every mark of aversion when they are away.

March 13th. Lord Stanley's plan for slave emancipation, [*has*] produced rage and fury among both West Indians and Saints, being too much for the former and not enough for the latter, and both announced their opposition to it. Practical men declared that it is impossible to carry it into effect, and that the details are unmanageable. Even the Government adherents do not pretend that it is a good and safe measure, but the best that could be hit off under the circumstances; these circumstances being the old motive, 'the people will have it.' The night before last Stanley developed his plan in the House of Commons in a speech of three hours, which was very eloquent, but rather disappointing. He handled the preliminary topics of horrors of slavery and colonial obstinacy and misconduct with all the vigour and success that might have been expected, but when he came to his measure he failed to show how it was to be put in operation and to work. The peroration and eulogy on Wilberforce were very brilliant. Howick had previously announced his intention of opposing Stanley, and accordingly he did so in a speech of considerable vehemence which lasted two hours. He was not, however, well received; his father and mother had in vain endeavoured to divert him from his resolution; but though they say his speech was clever, he has damaged himself by it. His plan is immediate emancipation.[5]

May 19*th.* I was marvellously struck (we rode together through St. James's Park) with the profound respect with which the Duke [*of Wellington*] was treated, everybody we met taking off their hats to him, everybody in the park rising as he went by, and every appearance of his inspiring great reverence. I like this symptom, and it is the more remarkable because it is not *popularity,* but a much higher feeling towards him. He has forfeited his popularity more than once; he has taken a line in politics directly counter to the popular bias; but though in moments of excitement he is attacked and vilified (and his broken windows, which I wish he would mend, still preserve a record of the violence of the mob), when the excitement subsides there is always a returning sentiment of admiration and respect for him, kept alive by the recollection of his splendid actions, such as no one else ever inspired.

[5] [The apprenticeship system proposed by Lord Stanley was carried, but failed in execution, and was eventually abandoned.]

June 26th. I have got from Sir Henry Lushington Monk Lewis's journals and his two voyages to the West Indies (one of which I read at Naples), with liberty to publish them, which I mean to do if I can get money enough for him. He says Murray offered him 500*l.* for the manuscripts some years ago. I doubt getting so much now, but they are uncommonly amusing, and it is the right moment for publishing them now that people are full of interest about the West India question.

June 29th. A letter this morning from Sir Henry Lushington about Monk Lewis. He is rather averse to a biographical sketch, because he thinks a true account of his life and character would not do him credit, and adds a sketch of the latter, which is not flattering. Lord Melbourne told me the other day a queer trait of Lewis. He had a long-standing quarrel with Lushington. Having occasion to go to Naples, he wrote beforehand to him, to say that their quarrel had better be *suspended,* and he went and lived with him and his sister (Lady L.) in perfect cordiality during his stay. When he departed he wrote to Lushington to say that now they should resume their quarrel, and put matters in the 'status quo ante pacem,' and accordingly he did resume it, with rather more *acharnement* than before.

July 12th. I have concluded a bargain with Murray for Lewis's journal and sold it him for 400 guineas, the MSS. to be returned to Lushington, and fifteen copies for him, and five for me, gratis.

July 15th. Met Duncannon in the morning. He mentions a man who holds a living of 1,000*l.* a year close to Bessborough, whom he knows. There is no house, no church, and there are no Protestants in the parish. He went there to be inducted, and dined with Duncannon at Bessborough the day after. Duncannon asked him how he had managed the necessary form, and he said he had been obliged to borrow the clerk and three Protestants from a neighbouring parish, and had read the morning and evening service to them within the ruined walls of the old Abbey, and they signed a certificate that he had complied with the forms prescribed by law.

November 13th. On Sunday dined with Rogers, Moore,

Sydney Smith, Macaulay. Sydney less vivacious than usual, and somewhat overpowered and talked down by what Moore called the 'flumen sermonis' of Macaulay. Sydney calls Macauley 'a book in breeches.' All that this latter says, all that he writes, exhibits his great powers and astonishing information, but I don't think he is agreeable. It is more than society requires, and not exactly of the kind; his figure, face, voice, and manner are all bad; he astonishes and instructs, he sometimes entertains, seldom amuses, and still seldomer pleases. He wants variety, elasticity, gracefulness; his is a roaring torrent, and not a meandering stream of talk. I believe we would all of us have been glad to exchange some of his sense for some of Sydney Smith's nonsense. He told me that he had read Sir Charles Grandison fifteen times!

December 18th. Dined with Moore at the Poodle's. He told a good story of Sydney Smith and Leslie the Professor. Leslie had written upon the North Pole; something he had said had been attacked in the 'Edinburgh Review' in a way that displeased him. He called on Jeffrey just as he was getting on horseback, and in a great hurry. Leslie began with a grave complaint on the subject, which Jeffrey interrupted with 'O damn the North Pole.' Leslie went off in high dudgeon, and soon after met Sydney, who, seeing him disturbed, asked what was the matter. He told him what he had been to Jeffrey about, and that he had in a very unpleasant way said, 'Damn the North Pole.' 'It was very bad,' said Sydney; 'but, do you know, I am not surprised at it, for I have heard him speak very disrespectfully of *the Equator.*'

B*urghley, January 28th,* 1834. I heard wonderful things of railroads and steam when I was in Staffordshire, yet by the time anybody reads what I now write (if anybody ever does), how they will smile perhaps at what I gape and stare at, and call wonderful, with such accelerated velocity do we move on. Stephenson, the great engineer, told Lichfield that he had travelled on the Manchester and Liverpool railroad for many miles at the rate of a mile a minute, that his doubt was not how fast his engines could be made to go, but at what pace it would be proper to stop, that he could make them travel with greater speed than any bird can cleave the air, and that he had ascertained that 400 miles an hour was the extreme velocity which the human frame could endure, at which it could move and exist.

May 23rd. On Monday last I went to Petworth, and saw the finest *fête* that could be given. Lord Egremont has been accustomed some time in the winter to feast the poor of the adjoining parishes (women and children, not men) in the riding-house and tennis court, where they were admitted by relays. His illness prevented the dinner taking place; but when he recovered he was bent upon having it, and, as it was put off till the summer, he had it arranged in the open air, and a fine sight it was; fifty-four tables, each fifty feet long, were placed in a vast semicircle on the lawn before the house. Nothing could be more amusing than to look at the preparations. The tables were all spread with cloths, and plates, and dishes; two great tents were erected in the middle to receive the provisions, which were conveyed in carts, like ammunition. Plum puddings and loaves were piled like cannon balls, and innumerable joints of boiled and roast beef were spread out, while hot joints were prepared in the kitchen, and sent forth as soon as the firing of guns announced the hour of the feast. Tickets were given to the inhabitants of a certain district, and the number was about 4,000; but, as many more came, the old Peer could not endure that there should be anybody hungering outside his gates, and he went out himself and ordered the barriers to be taken down and admittance given to all. They think 6,000 were fed. Gentlemen from the neighbourhood carved for them, and waiters were provided from among the peasantry. The food was distributed from the tents and carried off upon hurdles to all parts of the semicircle. A band of music paraded round, playing gay airs. The day was glorious—an unclouded sky and soft southern breeze. Nothing could exceed the pleasure of that fine old fellow; he was in and out of the windows of his room twenty times, enjoying the sight of these poor wretches, all attired in their best, cramming themselves and their brats with as much as they could devour, and snatching a day of relaxation and happiness. After a certain time the women departed, but the park gates were thrown open: all who chose came in, and walked about the shrubbery and up to the windows of the house. At night there was a great display of fireworks, and I should think, at the time they began, not less than 10,000 people were assembled. It was altogether one of the gayest and most beautiful spectacles I ever saw, and there was something affecting in the contemplation of that old man—on the verge of the grave, from which he had only lately been reprieved, with his mind as strong and his heart as warm as ever—rejoicing in the diffusion of happiness and finding keen gratification in relieving the distresses and contributing to the pleasures of the poor. I thought how applicable to him, *mutatis mutandis*, was that panegyric of Burke's on the Indian kings: 'delighting to reign in the dispensation of happiness during the contracted space of human life, strained with all the reachings and graspings of a vivacious mind to extend the dominion of his bounty . . . . and to perpetuate himself from generation to generation as the guardian, the protector, the nourisher of mankind.'

August 19*th*. Creevey says that Brougham is devoured with ambition, and what he wants is to be Prime Minister, but that it is quite impossible he should for ever escape detection and not be regularly *blown up* sooner or later. He now wants to appear on good terms with Lord Grey, and there is a dinner at Edinburgh in contemplation (at which Brougham is to preside) to be given to Lord Grey. His friends want him not to go, but he has a notion that the Scotch have behaved so well to him that he ought not to refuse the invitation. The Chancellor had intended to go junketting on the Rhine with Mrs. P., and this project was only marred by his discovering that he could not leave the country without putting the Great Seal in commission at a cost (to himself) of 1,400*l*. This was a larger price than he was disposed to pay for his trip, so he went off to Brougham instead.

September 4*th*. Stanley told me last night an anecdote of

Melbourne which I can very easily believe. When the King sent for him he told Young 'he thought it a damned bore, and that he was in many minds what he should do—be Minister or no.' Young said, 'Why, damn it, such a position never was occupied by any Greek or Roman, and, if it only lasts two months, it is well worth while to have been Prime Minister of England.' 'By God that's true,' said Melbourne; 'I'll go.'

September 5th. At Holland House yesterday, where I had not been these two years.

As a slight but imperfect sketch of the talk of Holland House I will put down this:—

They talked of Taylor's new poem, 'Philip van Artevelde.' Melbourne had read and admired it. The preface, he said, was affected and foolish, the poem very superior to anything in Milman. There was one fine idea in the 'Fall of Jerusalem'—that of Titus, who felt himself propelled by an irresistible impulse like that of the Greek dramatists, whose fate is the great agent always pervading their dramas. They held Wordsworth cheap, except Spring Rice, who was enthusiastic about him. Holland thought Crabbe the greatest genius of modern poets. Melbourne said he degraded every subject. None of them had known Coleridge; his lectures were very tiresome, but he is a poet of great merit. Then they spoke of Spencer Perceval and Irving preaching in the streets. Irving had called on Melbourne, and eloquently remonstrated that 'they only asked the same licence that was given to puppet-shows and other sights not to be prevented; that the command was express, "Go into the highways," and that they must obey God rather than man.' Melbourne said this was all very true and unanswerable. 'What *did* you answer?' I asked. 'I said, "You must not preach there."' Then of Cambridge and Goulburn, who is a saint and gave lectures in his room, by which he has caught several young men. Lord Holland spoke of George III.'s letters to Lord North; the King liked Lord North, hated the Duke of Richmond. Amongst the few people he liked were Lord Loughborough and Lord Thurlow. Thurlow was always 'endeavouring to undermine the Minister with whom he was acting, and intriguing underhand with his enemies.' Loughborough used to say, 'Do what you think right, and never think of what you are to say to excuse it beforehand'—a good maxim. The Duke of Richmond in 1763 or 1764, after an audience of the King in his closet, told him that 'he had said that to him which if he was a subject he should not scruple to call an untruth.' The King never forgave it, and the Duke had had the imprudence to make a young king his enemy for life. After dinner they discussed women's works: few *chefs-d'œuvres*; Madame de Sévigné the best; the only three of a high class are Madame de Sévigné, Madame de Staël, and (Bobus Smith said) Sappho, but of her not above forty lines are extant: these, however, are unrivalled; Mrs. Somerville is very great in the exact sciences. Lady Holland would not hear of Madame de Staël. They agreed as to Miss Austen that her novels are excellent. Of the early English kings there is no reason to believe that any king before Edward III. understood the English language; the quarrel between Beckett and King Henry II. was attributed (by some writers) to the hostile feeling between Normans and Saxons, and this was the principal motive of the quarrel and the murder of the Archbishop. Klopstock had a *sect* of admirers in Germany; some young students made a pilgrimage from Göttingen to Hamburg, where Klopstock lived in his old age, to ask him the meaning of a passage in one of his works which they could not understand. He looked at it, and then said that he could not then recollect what it was that he meant when he wrote it, but that he knew it was the finest thing he ever wrote, and they could not do better than devote their lives to the discovery of its meaning.

September 7th. No power was ever equal to Chatham's over a public assembly, much greater in the Commons than it was afterwards in the Lords. When Sir Thomas Robinson had been boring the House on some commercial question, and introduced the word 'sugar' so often that there was at last a laugh as often as he did so, Chatham, then Mr. Pitt, who had put him up, grew very angry, and at last his wrath boiled over. When Robinson sat down Pitt rose, and with a tone and manner of the utmost indignation began, 'Mr. Speaker, sir—sugar—I say sugar. Who laughs now?' and nobody did laugh. Once in the House of Lords, on a debate during the American war, he said he hoped the King might be awakened from his slumbers. There was a cry of 'Order! order!' 'Order, my Lords?' burst out Chatham, 'Order? I have not been disorderly, but I *will* be disorderly. I repeat again, I hope that his Majesty may be awakened from his slumbers, but that he may be awakened by such an awful apparition as that which drew King Priam's curtains in the dead of the night and told him of the conflagration of his empire.' Tommy Townshend, a violent, foolish fellow, who was always talking strong language, said in some debate, 'Nothing will satisfy me but to have the noble Lord's head; I will have his head.' Lord North said, 'The honourable gentleman says he will have my head. I bear him no malice in return, for though the honourable gentleman says he will have my head, I can assure him that I would on no account have his.'

September 18*th.*   Henry Taylor brought me a parcel of letters to frank to Southey the other day; they are to supply Southey with materials for Cowper's Life, which he is writing. There is one curious fact revealed in these letters, which accounts for much of Cowper's morbid state of mind and fits of depression, as well as for the circumstance of his running away from his place in the House of Lords. It relates to some defect in his physical conformation; somebody found out his secret, and probably threatened its exposure.

September 23*rd.*   On Saturday at Stoke; came up yesterday with Melbourne. We talked of Canning and the Duke of Wellington, and the breaking up of the Tory Government. I told him that I believed the Duke and the Tories were aware of Canning's communications with Brougham. Brougham wrote to Canning and made him an unqualified offer of support. When the King asked Canning how he was to obtain support enough to carry on the Government, he pulled this letter out of his pocket, gave it to him, and said, 'Sir, your father broke the domination of the Whigs; I hope your Majesty will not endure that of the Tories.'

'No,' said the King; 'I'll be damned if I do;' and he made him Minister. This Canning told Melbourne himself.

November 16*th*. Yesterday morning the town was electrified by the news that Melbourne's Government was at an end. Nobody had the slightest suspicion of such an impending catastrophe; the Ministers themselves reposed in perfect security. I never saw astonishment so great on every side; nobody pretended to have prophesied or expected such an event. Thus it befell:—On Thursday Melbourne went to Brighton to make the arrangements necessary on Lord Spencer's death. He had previously received a letter from the King, which contained nothing indicative of the fate that awaited him. He had his audience on Thursday afternoon, and offered his Majesty the choice of Spring Rice, Lord John Russell, or Abercromby to lead the House of Commons and fill the vacant office. The King made some objections, and said he must take time to consider it. Nothing more passed that night, and the next day, when Melbourne saw the King, his Majesty placed in his hands a letter containing his determination. It was couched in terms personally complimentary to Melbourne, but he said that, having lost the services of Lord Althorp as leader of the House of Commons, he could feel no confidence in the stability of his Government when led by any other member of it; that they were already in a minority in the House of Peers, and he had every reason to believe the removal of Lord Althorp would speedily put them in the same situation in the other House; that under such circumstances he felt other arrangements to be necessary, and that it was his intention to send for the Duke of Wellington. Nothing could be more peremptory and decisive, and not a loophole was left for explanation or arrangements, or endeavour to patch the thing up. The King wrote to the Duke, and, what is rather droll, the letter was despatched by Melbourne's carriage, which returned to town. It is very evident that the King has long determined to seize the first plausible pretext he could find for getting rid of these people, whom he dislikes and fears, and that he thinks (justly or not remains to be proved) the translation of Althorp affords him a good opportunity, and such a one perhaps as may not speedily occur again. It is long since a Government has been so summarily dismissed—regularly kicked out, in the simplest sense of that phrase. Melbourne's colleagues expected his return without a shadow of apprehension or doubt. He got back late, and wrote to none of them. The Chancellor, who had dined at Holland House, called on him and heard the news; the others (except Duncannon, who went to him, and I believe Palmerston) remained in happy ignorance till yesterday morning, when they were saluted at their rising with the astounding intelligence. All the Ministers (except Brougham) read the account of their dismissal in the 'Times' the next morning, and this was the first they heard of it. Melbourne resolved to say nothing that night, but summoned an early Cabinet, when he meant to impart it. Brougham called on him on his way from Holland House. Melbourne told him, but made him promise not to say a word of it to anybody. He promised, and the moment he quitted the house sent to the 'Times' office and told them what had occurred, with the well-known addition that 'the Queen had done it all.'

This morning Lord Lansdowne wrote me word that the Duke had accepted, but it is probable that nothing can be done till Peel returns from Italy. He will accept no post but that of Prime Minister, though the King would prefer to put the Duke there if he would take it.

December 27th. [*Munster*] said that the King is always sending him messages, and the other day "What do you think he did? When I have not seen him for fourteen months he sent to beg I would send down an artist to Windsor to paint his picture for me. And what answer do you think I sent? That I saw no use in having his picture when it was very probable that in less than three years it would be in a pawnbroker's shop."

January 1st, 1835. I heard a ridiculous anecdote of the King the other day. He wrote to the Duke about something—no matter what, but I believe some appointment—and added *à propos de bottes,* 'His Majesty begs to call the attention of the Duke to the *theoretical* state of Persia.' The Duke replied that he was aware of the importance of Persia, but submitted that it was a matter which did not *press* for the moment.

Yesterday I dined with Robarts, and after dinner he gave me an account of the state of his borough (Maidstone), and as it is a tolerably fair sample probably of the real condition of the generality of boroughs, and of the principles and disposition of their constituencies, I will put it down. There are 1,200 voters; the Dissenters are very numerous and of every imaginable sect and persuasion. He has been member seventeen years; the place very corrupt. Formerly (before the Reform Bill), when the constituency was less numerous, the matter was easily and simply conducted; the price of votes was as regularly fixed as the price of bread—so much for a single vote and so much for a plumper, and this he had to pay. After the Reform Bill he resolved to pay no more money, as corruption was to cease. The consequence was that during his canvass none of the people who had formerly voted for him would promise him their votes. They all sulked and hesitated, and, in short, waited to see what would be offered them. I asked him what were the new constituencies. 'If possible worse than the old.' The people are generally alive to public affairs—look into the votes and speeches of members, give their opinions—but are universally corrupt. They have a sour feeling against what are nicknamed abuses, rail against *sinnicures,* as they call them, and descant upon the enormity of such things while they are forced to work all day long and their families have not enough to eat. But the one prevailing object among the whole community is to make money of their votes.

February 17*th.* Yesterday I read Burke's appeal from the new to the old Whigs, which contains astonishing coincidences with the present times. His definition of the people is somewhat tumid and obscure, and involved in a splendid confusion of generalities and abstruse doctrine; but it is a wonderful monument of his genius, and exhibits that extent of knowledge and accuracy of insight into the nature of parties and the workings of political ambition which make him an authority for all times, and show him to be in the political what Shakespeare was in the moral world. But his writings, however as objects of study they may influence the opinions or form the judgment of young men, would have no more power than a piece of musty parchment to arrest the tide of present violence, and superinduce reflection and calmness. A speech of Tom Duncombe's would produce far greater effect than the perusal of a discourse of Burke's. Wisdom never operates directly on masses; it may work upon them through secondary and by indirect means, but it cannot face the noise of actual contest, where passion and not reason is always uppermost.

February 21st. I never was so struck as yesterday by the vulgarity of Peel. In all his ways, his dress, his manner, he looks more like a dapper shopkeeper than a Prime Minister. He eats voraciously, and cuts cream and jellies with his knife. Jersey pointed this out to me. And yet he has genius, and taste, and his thoughts are not vulgar though his manners are to such a degree. I was likewise struck with something worse than vulgarity, the proofs of his insincerity and falseness. Billy Holmes, who is supposed to be in disgrace with this Government came to Peel's last night. To my amazement I saw Sir Robert rush up to him, seize his hand with both his, and nearly wring it off with every mark of affection. Now I know from Jonathan Peel his opinion of Billy Holmes, that he is the greatest rogue unhung and that he betrayed their party to the Whigs last year.

March 22nd. A few nights ago Brougham was speaking in the House of Lords (upon Lord Radnor's motion about university oaths), and was attacking, or rather beginning to attack, the Duke of Wellington in that tone of insolent sarcasm which is so familiar to him, when in the midst of his harangue the Duke from the opposite side lifted up his finger, and said loud enough to be heard, 'Now take care what you say next.' As if panic-struck, Brougham broke off, and ran upon some other tack. The House is so narrow, that Lords can almost whisper to each other across it, and the menacing action and words of the Duke reached Brougham at once.

May 1st. The last day of Parliament was distinguished by a worse attack of O'Connell upon Alvanley for what he had said the day before in the House of Lords. Alvanley has sent him a message through Dawson Damer demanding an apology or satisfaction, and the result I don't yet know.[6]

London, May 17th. Newmarket and gout have between them produced an interval of unusual length in my scribblings. Elections and the affair between Alvanley and O'Connell have been the chief objects of attention; all the newspapers are full of details, which I need not put down here. Alvanley seems to have behaved with great spirit and resolution. There was a meeting at De Ros's house of De Ros, Damer, Lord Worcester, and Duncombe to consider what was to be done on the receipt of Morgan O'Connell's letter, and whether Alvanley should fight him or not. Worcester and Duncombe were against fighting, the other two for it. Alvanley at once said that the boldest course was the best, and he would go out. It was agreed that no time should be lost, so Damer was despatched to Colonel Hodges, and said Alvanley was ready to meet Morgan O'Connell. 'The next morning,' Hodges suggested. 'No, immediately.' The parties joined in Arlington Street and went off in two hackney coaches; Duncombe, Worcester, and De Ros, with Dr. Hume, in a third. Only Hume went on the ground, for Damer had objected to the presence of some Irish friend of O'Connell's, so that Alvanley's friends could only look on from a distance. The only other persons who came near them were an old Irishwoman and a Methodist parson, the latter of whom exhorted the combatants in vain to forego their sinful purpose, and to whom Alvanley replied, 'Pray, sir, go and mind your own affairs, for I have enough to do now to think of mine.' 'Think of your soul,' he said. 'Yes,' said Alvanley, 'but my

---

[6] [O'Connell had called Lord Alvanley a 'bloated buffoon,' and as usual took refuge in his vow never to fight another duel. Upon this his son, Morgan O'Connell, offered to meet Lord Alvanley in lieu of his father, which was accepted and the duel took place.]

body is now in the greatest danger.' The Irishwoman would come and see the fighting, and asked for some money for her attendance. Damer seems to have been a very bad second, and probably lost his head; he ought not to have consented to the third shots upon any account. Alvanley says he execrated him in his heart when he found he had consented to it. Hodges acted like a ruffian, and had anything happened he would have been hanged. It is impossible to know whether the first shot was fired by mistake or not. The impression on the minds of Alvanley's friends is that it was *not,* but it is difficult to believe that any man would endeavour to take such an advantage. However, no shot ought to have been fired after that. The affair made an amazing noise. As O'Connell had threatened to mention it in the House of Commons, Damer went to Peel to put him in possession of all the circumstances, but he said that he was sure O'Connell would not venture to stir the matter there.

June 19th. At Stoke for the Ascot races. Alvanley was there—nobody else remarkable; fine weather and great luxury. Riding to the course on Wednesday, I overtook Adolphus Fitzclarence in the Park, who rode with me, and gave me an account of his father's habits and present state of mind. The former are as follows: —He sleeps in the same room with the Queen, but in a separate bed; at a quarter before eight every morning his *valet de chambre* knocks at the door, and at ten minutes before eight exactly he gets out of bed, puts on a flannel dressing-gown and trousers, and walks into his dressing-room and goes at once to the water closet. Let who will be there, he never takes the slightest notice of them till he emerges from the temple, when, like the *malade imaginaire,* he accosts whoever may be present with a cheerful aspect. He is long at his ablutions, and takes up an hour and a half in dressing. At half-past nine he breakfasts with the Queen, the ladies, and any of his family; he eats a couple of fingers and drinks a dish of coffee. After breakfast he reads the 'Times' and 'Morning Post,' commenting aloud on what he reads in very plain terms, and sometimes they hear 'That's a damned lie,' or some such remark, without knowing to what it applies.

After breakfast he devotes himself with Sir Herbert Taylor to business till two, when he lunches (two cutlets and two glasses of sherry); then he goes out for a drive till dinner time; at dinner he drinks a bottle of sherry—no other wine—and eats moderately; he goes to bed soon after eleven.

July 1st. I went to St. James's to swear in Sir Charles Grey[7] and Charles Fitzroy Privy Councillors, when we had a most curious burst of eloquence from his Majesty. This is the first time I have seen him and his present Ministers together, and certainly they do not strike me as exhibiting any mutual affection. After Sir Charles Grey was sworn the King said to him, 'Stand up,' and up he stood. He then addressed him with great fluency and energy nearly in these words:—'Sir Charles Grey, you are about to proceed upon one of the most important missions which ever left this country, and, from your judgment, ability, and experience, I have no doubt that you will acquit yourself to my entire satisfaction; I desire you, however, to bear in mind that the colony to which you are about to proceed has not, like other British colonies, been peopled from the mother country—that it is not an original possession of the Crown, but that it was obtained *by the sword.* You will take care to assert those undoubted prerogatives which the Crown there possesses, and which I am determined to enforce and maintain, and I charge you by the oath which you have just taken strenuously to assert those prerogatives, *of which persons who ought to have known better have dared even in my presence to deny the existence.'* His speech was something longer than this, but the last words almost precisely the same. The silence was profound.

July 15th. The night before last there was a great concert on the staircase at Stafford House, the most magnificent assembly I ever saw, and such as I think no crowned head in Europe could display, so grand and picturesque. The appearance of the hall was exactly like one of Paul Veronese's pictures, and only wanted some tapestry to be hung over the balustrades. Such prodigious

[7] [Sir Charles Grey had just been appointed Governor of Jamaica.]

space, so cool, so blazing with light; everybody was *comfortable* even, and the concert combined the greatest talents in Europe all together—Grisi, Malibran, Tamburini, Lablache, Rubini, and Ivanhoff. The splendour, the profusion, and the perfect ease of it all were really admirable.

August 9th. On Wednesday last at the levee the King made a scene with Lord Torrington, one of his Lords of the Bedchamber, and a very disgraceful scene. A card was put into Torrington's hands of somebody who was presented, which he read, 'So and so, *Deputy-Governor.*' 'Deputy-Governor?' said the King, 'Deputy-Governor of what?' 'I cannot tell your Majesty,' replied Torrington, 'as it is not upon the card.' 'Hold your tongue, sir,' said the King; 'you had better go home and learn to read;' and shortly after, when some bishop presented an address against (I believe) the Irish Tithe Bill, and the King was going as usual to hand over the papers to the Lord in waiting, he stopped and said to Lord Torrington, who advanced to take them, 'No, Lord Torrington; these are not fit documents to be entrusted to your keeping.' His habitual state of excitement will probably bring on sooner or later the malady of his family.

August 15th. On Wednesday the Lords commenced proceedings on the Corporation Bill—the debate being distinguished by divers sallies of intemperance from Brougham, who thundered, and menaced, and gesticulated in his finest style. When somebody cried, 'Question,' he burst out, 'Do you think to put me down? I have stood against 300 of the House of Commons, and do you think I will give way to *you?*'

August 29th. The House of Lords has become a beargarden since Brougham has been in it; there is no night that is not distinguished by some violent squabble between him and the Tories. Lord Winchelsea directly accused him of cowardice the night before last, to which he replied, 'As to my being *afraid* to say elsewhere what I say here, oh, that is too absurd to require an answer.' It is nevertheless true. Melbourne does very well; his memory served him happily on this night. Brougham had lashed the Lords into a fury by calling them a *mob,* and Melbourne quoted Lord Chesterfield, who said that *all* deliberative assemblies were *mobs*. The other day Lord Howick was inveighing passionately against the Lords for their mutilations of the Corporation Bill, when Melbourne said, with his characteristic *nonchalance*, 'Why, what does it matter? We have gone on tolerably well for 500 years with these corporations, and we may contrive to go on with them for another year or so.'

December 16th. Luttrell was talking of Moore and Rogers—the poetry of the former so licentious, that of the latter so pure; much of its popularity owing to its being so carefully weeded of everything approaching to indelicacy; and the contrast between the *lives* and the *works* of the two men—the former a pattern of conjugal and domestic regularity, the latter of all the men he had ever known the greatest sensualist. He has a passion for little girls and L. said that he cannot walk the streets without being followed by many and he has a police officer in his pay to protect him from impositions and menaces.

December 18th. Melbourne told me that he had been down to Oatlands to consult F. and H. about Dr. Arnold (of Rugby), and to ascertain if he could properly make him a bishop; but they did not encourage him, which I was surprised at, recollecting the religious correspondence which formerly passed between them and him. Arnold, however, shocks the High Churchmen, and is not considered orthodox; and Melbourne said it would make a great uproar to put him on the Bench, and was out of the question. He had been reading his sermons, which he thought very able.

F*ebruary* 1st, 1836. Howick gave me an account yesterday of Spencer Perceval's communications to the Ministers, and other Privy Councillors. He called on Howick, who received him very civilly. Perceval began, 'You will probably be surprised when you learn what has brought me here.' Howick bowed. 'You are aware that God has been pleased in these latter times to make especial communications of His will to certain chosen instruments, in a language not intelligible to those who hear it, nor always to those by whom it is uttered: I am one of those instruments, to whom it has pleased the Almighty to make known His will, and I am come to declare to you, &c. . . .' and then he went off in a rhapsody about the degeneracy of the times, and the people falling off from God. I asked him what Perceval seemed to be driving at, what was his definite object? He said it was not discoverable, but that from the printed paper which he had circulated to all Privy Councillors (for to that body he appears to think that his mission is addressed), in which he specifies all the great acts of legislation for the last five years (beginning with the repeal of the Test and Corporation Acts), as the evidences of a falling off from God, or as the causes of the divine anger, it may perhaps be inferred that he means they should all be repealed. It is a ridiculous and melancholy exposure. His different receptions by different people are amusing and characteristic. Howick listened to him with patient civility. Melbourne argued with and cross-questioned him. He told him 'that he ought to have gone to the Bishops rather than to him,' to which Perceval replied, that one of the brethren (Henry Drummond) was gone to the Archbishop. Stanley turned him out at once. As soon as he began he said, 'There is no use, Mr. Perceval, in going on this way with me. We had, therefore, better put an end to the subject, and I wish you good morning.' He went to Lord Holland, and Lady Holland was with great difficulty persuaded to allow him to go and receive the Apostles. She desired Lord John Russell (who happened to be in the house) to go with him, but John begged to be excused, alleging that he had already had his interview and did not wish for another. So at last she let Lord Holland be wheeled in, but ordered Edgar and Harold, the two pages, to post themselves outside the door, and rush in if they heard Lord Holland scream. Perceval has been with the King, and went to Drayton after Sir Robert Peel, but he complains that he cannot catch the Duke of Wellington.

February 9th. I was talking yesterday with Stephen about Brougham and Macaulay. He said he had known Brougham above thirty years, and well remembers walking with him down to Clapham, to dine with old Zachary Macaulay, and telling him he would find a prodigy of a boy there of whom he must take notice. This was Tom Macaulay. Brougham afterwards put himself forward as the monitor and director of the education of Macaulay, and I remember hearing of a letter he wrote to the father on the subject, which made a great noise at the time; but he was like the man who brought up a young lion, which finished by biting his head off. Brougham and Macaulay disliked each other. Brougham could not forgive his great superiority in many of those accomplishments in which he thought himself unrivalled; and being at no pains to disguise his jealousy and dislike, the other was not behind him in corresponding feelings of aversion. It was unworthy of both, but most of Brougham, who was the aggressor, and who might have considered the world large enough for both of them, and that a sufficiency of fame was attainable by each. Stephen said that, if ever Macaulay's life was written by a competent biographer, it would appear that he had displayed feats of memory which he believed to be unequalled by any human being. He can repeat all Demosthenes by heart, and all Milton, a great part of the Bible, both in English and (the New Testament) in Greek; besides this his memory retains passages innumerable of every description of books, which in discussion he pours forth with incredible facility. He is passionately fond of Greek literature; has not much taste for Latin or French. Old Mill (one of the best Greek scholars of the day) thinks Macaulay has a more extensive and accurate acquaintance with the Greek writers than any man living, and there is no Greek book of any note which he has not read over and over again. In the Bible he takes great delight, and there are few better Biblical scholars. In law he made no proficiency, and mathematics he abominates; but his great forte is history, especially English history. Here his superhuman memory, which appears to have the faculty of digesting and arranging as well as of retaining, has converted his mind into a mighty magazine of knowledge, from which, with the precision and correctness of a kind of intellectual machine, he pours forth stores of learning, information, precept, example, anecdote, and illustration with a familiarity and facility not less astonishing than delightful. He writes as if he had lived in the times and among the people whose actions and characters he records and delineates. A little reading, too, is enough for Macaulay, for by some process impossible to other men he contrives to transfer as it were, by an impression rapid and indelible, the contents of the books he reads to his own mind, where they are deposited, always accessible, and never either forgotten or confused. Far superior to Brougham in general knowledge, in fancy, imagination, and in the art of composition, he is greatly inferior to him in those qualities which raise men to social and political eminence. Brougham, tall, thin, and commanding in figure, with a face which, however ugly, is full of expression, and a voice of great power, variety, and even melody, notwithstanding his occasional prolixity and tediousness, is an orator in every sense of the word. Macaulay, short, fat, and ungraceful, with a round, thick, unmeaning face, and with rather a lisp, though he has made speeches of great merit, and of a very high style of eloquence in point of composition, has no pretensions to be put in competition with Brougham in the House of Commons. Nor is the difference and the inferiority of Macaulay less marked in society. Macaulay, indeed, is a great talker, and pours forth floods of knowledge on all subjects; but the gracefulness, lightness, and variety are wanting in his talk which are so conspicuous in his writings. Brougham, on the other hand, is all life, spirit, and gaiety—'from grave to gay, from lively to severe'; always amusing, always instructive, never tedious.

[*Quantum mutatus!* All this has long ceased to be true of Brougham. Macaulay, without having either the wit or the *charm* which constitutes the highest kind of colloquial excellence or success, is a marvellous, an unrivalled (in his way), and a delightful talker.—1850.]

August 7th. It is surprising to hear how Palmerston is spoken of by those who know him well officially—the Granvilles, for example. Lady Granville, a woman expert in judging, thinks his

capacity first-rate; that it approaches to greatness from his enlarged views, disdain of trivialities, resolution, decision, confidence, and above all his contempt of clamour and abuse. She told
me that Madame de Flahault had a letter written by Talleyrand
soon after his first arrival in England, in which he talked with
great contempt of the Ministers generally, Lord Grey included,
and said there was but one statesman among them, and that was
Palmerston. His ordinary conversation exhibits no such superiority; but when he takes his pen in his hand his intellect seems to
have full play, and probably when engaged exclusively in business.

August 21st. The King at his last levee received Dr. Allen to
do homage for the see of Ely, when he said to him, 'My Lord, I
do not mean to interfere in any way with your vote in Parliament
except on one subject, *the Jews,* and I trust I may depend on your
always voting against them.'

August 30th. At Hillingdon from Saturday to Monday. There
were great festivities at Windsor during the Egham race week,
when the King's daughter Lady Augusta was married at the Castle.[8] It was remarked that on the King's birthday not one of the
Ministers was invited to the Castle, and none except the Household in any way connected with the Government. At the Queen's
birthday a short time before not one individual of that party was
present. Nothing can be more undisguised than the King's aversion to his Ministers, and he seems resolved to intimate that his
compulsory reception of them shall not extend to his society, and
that though he can't help seeing them at St. James's, the gates of
Windsor are shut against them. All his habitual guests are of the
Tory party, and generally those who have distinguished themselves by their violence or are noted for their extreme opinions
—Winchilsea and Wharncliffe, for example, of the former, and the
Duke of Dorset of the latter sort. At the dinner on his birthday

---

[8] [Lady Augusta Fitzclarence, fourth daughter of King William IV. by
Mrs. Jordan, married first, on the 5th of July, 1827, to the Hon. John Kennedy
Erskine, and secondly, on the 26th of August, 1836, to Lord John Frederick
Gordon. She died in 1865.]

the King gave the Princess Victoria's health rather well. Having given the Princess Augusta's he said, 'And now, having given the health of the oldest, I will give that of the youngest member of the Royal Family. I know the interest which the public feel about her, and although *I have not seen so much of her as I could have wished*, I take no less interest in her, and the more I do see of her, both in public and in private, the greater pleasure it will give me.' The whole thing was so civil and gracious that it could hardly be taken ill, but the young Princess sat opposite, and hung her head with not unnatural modesty at being thus talked of in so large a company.

September 21st.   To-day we had a Council, the first since Parliament was prorogued, when his most gracious Majesty behaved most ungraciously to his confidential servants, whom he certainly does not delight to honour. The last article on the list was a petition of Admiral Sartorius praying to be restored to his rank, and when this was read the King, after repeating the usual form of words, added, 'And must be granted. As Captain Napier was restored, so must this gentleman be, for there was this difference between their cases: Admiral Napier knew he was doing wrong, which Admiral Sartorius was not aware of.' Lord Minto said, 'I believe, sir, there was not so much difference between the two cases as your Majesty imagines, for Admiral Sartorius—' Then followed something which I could not catch, but the King did, for he said, with considerable asperity, 'Unless your Lordship is quite sure of that, I must beg leave to say that I differ from you and do not believe it to be so, but since you have expressed your belief that it is so, I desire you will furnish me with proofs of it immediately. The next time I see you you will be prepared with the proofs of what you say, for unless I see them I shall not believe one word of it.' Minto made no reply to this extraordinary sortie, and the rest looked at each other in silence.

This, however, was nothing compared with what took place at Windsor with the Duchess of Kent, of which I heard something a long time ago (August 30th), but never the particulars till last night. It is very remarkable that the thing has not been more talked about. The King invited the Duchess of Kent to go to

Windsor on the 12th of August to celebrate the Queen's birthday
(13th), and to stay there over his own birthday, which was to be
kept (*privately*) on the 21st (the real day, but falling on Sunday) and *publicly* the day following. She sent word that she
wanted to keep her own birthday at Claremont on the 15th (or
whatever the day is), took no notice of the Queen's birthday, but
said she would go to Windsor on the 20th. This put the King in a
fury; he made, however, no reply, and on the 20th he was in town
to prorogue Parliament, having desired that they would not wait
dinner for him at Windsor. After the prorogation he went to Kensington Palace to look about it; when he got there he found that
the Duchess of Kent had appropriated to her own use a suite of
apartments, seventeen in number, for which she had applied last
year, and which he had refused to let her have. This increased
his ill-humour, already excessive. When he arrived at Windsor
and went into the drawing-room (at about ten o'clock at night),
where the whole party was assembled, he went up to the Princess
Victoria, took hold of both her hands, and expressed his pleasure
at seeing her there and his regret at not seeing her oftener. He
then turned to the Duchess and made her a low bow, almost immediately after which he said that 'a most unwarrantable liberty
had been taken with one of his palaces; that he had just come
from Kensington, where he found apartments had been taken
possession of not only without his consent, but contrary to his
commands, and that he neither understood nor would endure
conduct so disrespectful to him.' This was said loudly, publicly,
and in a tone of serious displeasure. It was, however, only the
muttering of the storm which was to break the next day. Adolphus Fitzclarence went into his room on Sunday morning, and
found him in a state of great excitement. It was his birthday, and
though the celebration was what was called private, there were a
hundred people at dinner, either belonging to the Court or from
the neighbourhood. The Duchess of Kent sat on one side of the
King and one of his sisters on the other, the Princess Victoria opposite. Adolphus Fitzclarence sat two or three from the Duchess,
and heard every word of what passed. After dinner, by the
Queen's desire, 'His Majesty's health, and long life to him' was

given, and as soon as it was drunk he made a very long speech, in the course of which he poured forth the following extraordinary and *foudroyante* tirade:—'I trust in God that my life may be spared for nine months longer, after which period, in the event of my death, no regency would take place. I should then have the satisfaction of leaving the royal authority to the personal exercise of that young lady (pointing to the Princess), the heiress presumptive of the Crown, and not in the hands of a person now near me, who is surrounded by evil advisers and who is herself incompetent to act with propriety in the station in which she would be placed. I have no hesitation in saying that I have been insulted—grossly and continually insulted—by that person, but I am determined to endure no longer a course of behaviour so disrespectful to me. Amongst many other things I have particularly to complain of the manner in which that young lady has been kept away from my Court; she has been repeatedly kept from my drawing-rooms, at which she ought always to have been present, but I am fully resolved that this shall not hapen again. I would have her know that I am King, and I am determined to make my authority respected, and for the future I shall insist and command that the Princess do upon all occasions appear at my Court, as it is her duty to do.' He terminated his speech by an allusion to the Princess and her future reign in a tone of paternal interest and affection, which was excellent in its way.

This awful philippic (with a great deal more which I forget) was uttered with a loud voice and excited manner. The Queen looked in deep distress, the Princess burst into tears, and the whole company were aghast. The Duchess of Kent said not a word. Immediately after they rose and retired, and a terrible scene ensued; the Duchess announced her immediate departure and ordered her carriage, but a sort of reconciliation was patched up, and she was prevailed upon to stay till the next day. The following morning, when the King saw Adolphus, he asked him what people said to his speech. He replied that they thought the Duchess of Kent merited his rebuke, but that it ought not to have been given there; that he ought to have sent for her into his closet, and have said all that he felt and thought there, but not at

table before a hundred people. He replied that he did not care
where he said it or before whom, that 'by God he had been insulted by her in a measure that was past all endurance, and he
would not stand it any longer.'

Nothing can be more unaccountable than the Duchess of
Kent's behaviour to the King, nothing more reprehensible; but
his behaviour to her has always been as injudicious and undignified as possible, and this last sortie was monstrous. It was his duty
and his right to send for her, and signify to her both his displeasure at the past and his commands for the future; but such a gross
and public insult offered to her at his own table, sitting by his
side and in the presence of her daughter, admits of no excuse. It
was an unparalleled outrage from a man to a woman, from a host
to his guest, and to the last degree unbecoming the station they
both of them fill. He has never had the firmness and decision of
character a due display of which would have obviated the necessity of such bickerings, and his passion leads him to these indecent exhibitions, which have not the effect of correcting, and
cannot fail to have that of exasperating her, and rendering their
mutual relations more hopelessly disagreeable.

Paris, *January 25th*, 1837. I ended my day (the 25th) by going
to a ball at the Tuileries, one of the great balls, and a magnificent
spectacle indeed. The long line of light gleaming through the
whole length of the palace is striking as it is approached, and the
interior, with the whole suite of apartments brilliantly illuminated, and glittering from one end to the other with diamonds
and feathers and uniforms, and dancing in all the several rooms,
made a splendid display. The supper in the theatre was the finest
thing I ever saw of the kind; all the women sup first, and afterwards the men, the tables being renewed over and over again.
There was an array of servants in gorgeous liveries, and the apartment was lit by thousands of candles (no lamps) and as light as
day. The company amounted to between 3,000 and 4,000, from
all the great people down to national guards, and even private

soldiers. None of the Carlists were there, as they none of them choose to go to Court. The King retired before eleven; it was said that he had received anonymous letters warning him of some intended attempt on his person, and extraordinary precautions were taken to guard against the entrance of any improper people.

January 26th. Having seen all the high society the night before, I resolved to see all the low to-night, and went to Musard's ball—a most curious scene; two large rooms in the rue St. Honoré almost thrown into one, a numerous and excellent orchestra, a prodigious crowd of people, most of them in costume, and all the women masked. There was every description of costume, but that which was the most general was the dress of a French post-boy, in which both males and females seemed to delight. It was well-regulated uproar and orderly confusion. When the music struck up they began dancing all over the rooms; the whole mass was in motion, but though with gestures the most vehement and grotesque, and a licence almost unbounded, the figure of the dance never seemed to be confused, and the dancers were both expert in their capers and perfect in their evolutions. Nothing could be more licentious than the movements of the dancers, and they only seemed to be restrained within limits of common decency by the cocked hats and burnished helmets of the police and gendarmes which towered in the midst of them. After quadrilling and waltzing away, at a signal given they began galloping round the room; then they rushed pellmell, couple after couple, like Bedlamites broke loose, but not the slightest accident occurred. I amused myself with this strange and grotesque sight for an hour or more, and then came home.

March 31st. Among the many old people who have been cut off by this severe weather, one of the most remarkable is Mrs. Fitzherbert, who died at Brighton at above eighty years of age. She was not a clever woman, but of a very noble spirit, disinterested, generous, honest, and affectionate, greatly beloved by her friends and relations, popular in the world, and treated with uniform distinction and respect by the Royal Family. The late King, [*George IV*] who was a despicable creature, grudged her the allowance he was bound to make her, and he was always afraid

lest she should make use of some of the documents in her possession to annoy or injure him. This mean and selfish apprehension
led him to make various efforts to obtain possession of those the
appearance of which he most dreaded, and among others, one
remarkable attempt was made by Sir William Knighton some
years ago. Although a stranger to Mrs. Fitzherbert, he called one
day at her house, when she was ill in bed, insisted upon seeing
her, and forced his way into her bedroom. She contrived (I forget
how) to get rid of him without his getting anything out of her,
but this domiciliary visit determined her to make a final disposition of all the papers she possessed, that in the event of her death
no advantage might be taken of them either against her own
memory or the interests of any other person. She accordingly
selected those papers which she resolved to preserve, and which
are supposed to be the documents and correspondence relating
to her marriage with George IV., and made a packet of them
which was deposited at her banker's, and all other letters and
papers she condemned to the flames. For this purpose she sent
for the Duke of Wellington and Lord Albemarle, told them her
determination, and in their presence had these papers burnt; she
assured them that everything was destroyed, and if after her
death any pretended letters or documents were produced, they
might give the most authoritative contradiction to their authen-
ticity.

June 2nd. The King has been desperately ill, his pulse down
at thirty; they think he will now get over it for this time. His
recovery will not have been accelerated by the Duchess of Kent's
answer to the City of London's address, in which she went into
the history of her life, and talked of her 'friendless state' on arriving in this country, the gist of it being that, having been abandoned or neglected by the Royal Family, she had thrown herself
on the country.

June 11th. At Buckhurst last week for Ascot; went on Monday
and returned on Friday. On Tuesday the Queen came to the
course, but only stayed an hour. They had an immense party at
the Castle notwithstanding the King's illness. I met Adolphus
Fitzclarence at the course, who gave me an account of the King's

state, which was bad enough, though not for the moment alarming; no disease, but excessive weakness without power of rallying. He also gave me an account of the late Kensington quarrel. The King wrote a letter to the Princess offering her 10,000*l.* a year (not out of his privy purse), which he proposed should be at her own disposal and independent of her mother. He sent this letter by Lord Conyngham with orders to deliver it into the Princess's own hands. Conyngham accordingly went to Kensington (where Conroy received him) and asked to be admitted to the Princess. Conroy asked by what authority. He said by his Majesty's orders. Conroy went away, and shortly after Conyngham was ushered into the presence of the Duchess and Princess, when he said that he had waited on her Royal Highness by the King's commands to present to her a letter with which he had been charged by his Majesty. The Duchess put out her hand to take it, when he said he begged her Royal Highness's pardon, but he was expressly commanded by the King to deliver the letter into the Princess's own hands. Her mother then drew back and the Princess took the letter, when Conyngham made his bow and retired. Victoria wrote to the King, thanking him and accepting his offer. He then sent to say that it was his wish to name the person who should receive this money for her, and he proposed to name Stephenson. Then began the dispute. The Duchess of Kent objected to the arrangement, and she put forth her claim, which was that she should have 6,000*l.* of the money and the Princess 4,000*l.* How the matter had ended Adolphus did not know when I saw him. [It never was settled.]

The Duchess of Northumberland had been to Windsor and resigned her office of governess a few days before.

On Wednesday it was announced for the first time that the King was alarmingly ill, on Thursday the account was no better, and in the course of Wednesday and Thursday his immediate dissolution appeared so probable that I concerted with Errol that I should send to the Castle at nine o'clock on Thursday evening for the last report, that I might know whether to go to London directly or not. On Wednesday the physicians wanted to issue a bulletin, but the King would not hear of it. He said as long as he was able to transact public business he would not have the public alarmed on his account; but on Friday, nevertheless, the first bulletin was issued.

June 16th. On Wednesday the King was desperately bad, yesterday he was better, but not so as to afford any hope, though Chambers says his recovery is not impossible. Although the bulletins tell so little, everybody is now aware of his Majesty's state. He dictates these reports himself, and will not allow more to be said; he continues to do business, and his orders are taken as usual, so he is resolved to die with harness on his back. Yesterday Lord Lansdowne sent for me to beg in the first place that everything might be ready, and in the next to say that they were perplexed to know what steps, if any, they ought to take to ascertain whether the Queen is with child, and to beg me to search in our books if any precedent could be found at the accession of James II. But they had forgotten that the case had been provided for in the Regency Bill, and that in the event of the King's death without children, the Queen is to be proclaimed, but the oath of allegiance taken with a saving of the rights of any posthumous child to King William.

In the morning I met Sir Robert Peel in the Park, and talked with him about the beginning of the new reign. He said that it was very desirable that the young Queen should appear as much as possible emancipated from all restraint, and exhibit a capacity for the discharge of her high functions; that the most probable as well as the most expedient course she could adopt, would be to rely entirely upon the advice of Melbourne, and she might with great propriety say that she thought it incumbent on her to follow the example which had been set by her two uncles, her predecessors, William IV. having retained in office the Ministers of his brother, and George IV., although his political predilections were known to lean another way, having also declined to dismiss the Government of his father. Peel said that he concluded King Leopold would be her great adviser. If Leopold is prudent, however, he will not hurry over here at the very first moment, which would look like an impatience to establish his influence, and if he does, the first result will be every sort of jealousy and discord between him and the Duchess of Kent. What renders speculation so easy, and events uncertain, is the absolute ignorance of everybody, without exception, of the character, disposition, and capacity of the Princess. She has been kept in such jealous seclusion by her mother (never having slept out of her bedroom, nor been alone with anybody but herself and the Baroness Lehzen), that not one of her acquaintance, none of the attendants at Kensington, not even the Duchess of Northumberland, her governess, have any idea what she is, or what she promises to be.

June 19th. Yesterday the King was sinking fast; the Sacrament was administered to him by the Archbishop of Canterbury. He said, 'This is the 18th of June; I should like to live to see the sun of Waterloo set.'

June 21st. The King died at twenty minutes after two yesterday morning, and the young Queen met the Council at Kensington Palace at eleven. Never was anything like the first impression she produced, or the chorus of praise and admiration which is raised about her manner and behaviour, and certainly not without justice. It was very extraordinary, and something far beyond what was looked for. Her extreme youth and inexperience, and the ignorance of the world concerning her, naturally excited intense curiosity to see how she would act on this trying occasion, and there was a considerable assemblage at the Palace, notwithstanding the short notice which was given. The first thing to be done was to teach her her lesson, which for this purpose Melbourne had himself to learn. I gave him the Council papers, and explained all that was to be done, and he went and explained all this to her. He asked her if she would enter the room accompanied by the Great Officers of State, but she said she would come in alone. When the Lords were assembled the Lord President informed them of the King's death, and suggested, as they were so numerous, that a few of them should repair to the presence of the Queen and inform her of the event, and that their Lordships were assembled in consequence; and accordingly the two Royal Dukes, the two Archbishops, the Chancellor, and Melbourne went with him. The Queen received them in the adjoining room alone. As soon as they had returned the proclamation was read and the usual order passed, when the doors were thrown open and the Queen entered, accompanied by her two uncles, who advanced to meet her. She bowed to the Lords, took her seat, and then read her speech in a clear, distinct, and audible voice, and without any appearance of fear or embarrassment. She was quite plainly dressed, and in mourning. After she had read her speech and taken and signed the oath for the security of the Church of Scotland, the Privy Councillors were sworn, the two Royal Dukes[9] first, by themselves; and as these two old men, her uncles, knelt before her, swearing allegiance and kissing her hand, I saw her blush up to the eyes, as if she felt the contrast between their civil and their natural relations, and this was the only sign of emotion which she evinced. Her manner to them was very graceful and engaging; she kissed them both, and rose from her chair and moved towards the Duke of Sussex, who was farthest from her and too infirm to reach her. She seemed rather bewildered at the multitude of men who were sworn, and who came one after another to kiss her hand, but she did not speak to anybody, nor did she make the slightest difference in her manner, or show any in her countenance, to any individual of any rank, station, or party. I particularly watched her when Melbourne and the Ministers and the Duke of Wellington and Peel approached her. She went through the whole ceremony, occasionally looking at Melbourne for instruction when she had any doubt what to do, which hardly ever occurred, and with perfect calmness and self-possession, but at the same time with a graceful modesty and propriety particularly interesting and ingratiating. When the business was done she retired as she had entered, and I could see that nobody was in the adjoining room. Lord Lansdowne insisted upon being declared President of the Council (and I was obliged to write a declaration for him to read to that effect), though it was not usual. The speech was admired, except by Brougham, who appeared in a considerable state of excitement. He said to Peel (whom he was standing near, and with whom he is not in the habit of communicating), 'Amelioration,

---

[9] The Dukes of Cumberland and Sussex. The Duke of Cambridge was in Hanover.

that is not English; you might perhaps say *me*lioration, but improvement is the proper word.' 'Oh,' said Peel, 'I see no harm in the word; it is generally used.' 'You object,' said Brougham, 'to the sentiment, I object to the grammar.' 'No,' said Peel, 'I don't object to the sentiment.' 'Well, then, she pledges herself to the policy of *our* Government,' said Brougham. Peel told me this, which passed in the room and near to the Queen. He likewise said how amazed he was at her manner and behaviour, at her apparent deep sense of her situation, her modesty, and at the same time her firmness. She appeared, in fact, to be awed, but not daunted, and afterwards the Duke of Wellington told me the same thing, and added that if she had been his own daughter he could not have desired to see her perform her part better. It was settled that she was to hold a Council at St. James's this day, and be proclaimed there at ten o'clock, and she expressed a wish to see Lord Albemarle, who went to her and told her he was come to take her orders. She said, 'I have no orders to give; you know all this so much better than I do, that I leave it all to you. I am to be at St. James's at ten to-morrow, and must beg you to find me a conveyance proper for the occasion.' Accordingly, he went and fetched her in state with a great escort. The Duchess of Kent was in the carriage with her, but I was surprised to hear so little shouting, and to see so few hats off as she went by. I rode down the Park, and saw her appear at the window when she was proclaimed. The Duchess of Kent was there, but not prominent; the Queen was surrounded by her Ministers, and curtsied repeatedly to the people, who did not, however, hurrah till Lord Lansdowne gave them the signal from the window. At twelve she held a Council, at which she presided with as much ease as if she had been doing nothing else all her life, and though Lord Lansdowne and my colleague had contrived between them to make some confusion with the Council papers, she was not put out by it. She looked very well, and though so small in stature, and without much pretension to beauty, the gracefulness of her manner and the good expression of her countenance give her on the whole a very agreeable appearance, and with her youth inspire an excessive interest in all who approach her, and which I can't help feeling myself. After the Council she received the Archbishops and Bishops, and after them the Judges. They all kissed her hand, but she said nothing to any of them, very different in this from her predecessor, who used to harangue them all, and had a speech ready for everybody.

Conyngham, when he came to her with the intelligence of the King's death, brought a request from the Queen Dowager that she might be permitted to remain at Windsor till after the funeral, and she has written her a letter couched in the kindest terms, begging her to consult nothing but her own health and convenience, and to remain at Windsor just as long as she pleases. In short, she appears to act with every sort of good taste and good feeling, as well as good sense, and as far as it has gone nothing can be more favourable than the impression she has made, and nothing can promise better than her manner and conduct do, though it would be rash to count too confidently upon her judgment and discretion in more weighty matters. No contrast can be greater than that between the personal demeanour of the present and the late sovereigns at their respective accessions. William IV. was a man who, coming to the throne at the mature age of sixty-five, was so excited by the exaltation, that he nearly went mad, and distinguished himself by a thousand extravagances of language and conduct, to the alarm or amusement of all who witnessed his strange freaks; and though he was shortly afterwards sobered down into more becoming habits, he always continued to be something of a blackguard and something more of a buffoon. It is but fair to his memory at the same time to say that he was a good-natured, kind-hearted, and well-meaning man, and he always acted an honourable and straightforward, if not always a sound and discreet, part. The two principal Ministers of his reign, the Duke of Wellington and Lord Grey, have both spoken of him to me with strong expressions of personal regard and esteem. The young Queen, who might well be either dazzled or confounded with the grandeur and novelty of her situation, seems neither the one nor the other, and behaves with a decorum and propriety beyond her years, and with all the sedateness and dignity the want of which was so conspicuous in her uncle.

The Reign
of
Queen Victoria

June 25th, 1837. I remember when George IV died, several years ago, having been struck by the small apparent sensation that his death created. There was, however, at that time a great deal of bustle and considerable excitement, which were caused by the activity of the new Court, and the eccentricities of the King; but in the present instance the Crown has been transferred to the head of the new Queen with a tranquillity which is curious and edifying. The first interest and curiosity to see the young Queen and observe her behaviour having passed off, there appears nothing more to do or to think about; there are no changes, and there is no talk of change. Her Majesty has continued quietly at Kensington, where she transacts business with her Ministers, and everything goes on as if she had been on the throne six years instead of six days. Animated panegyrics were pronounced upon the late King in both Houses of Parliament by those who had served him; and Peel repeated in the House of Commons, in more set phrases, the expressions of his admiration of the conduct of the Queen on her first public appearance, which he uttered to me when I saw him after the Council on Tuesday. Melbourne's funeral oration over William IV was very effective because it was natural and hearty, and as warm as it could be without being exaggerated. He made the most of the virtues the King undoubtedly possessed, and passed lightly over his defects.

King William IV, if he had been born in a private station, would have passed unobserved through life like millions of other men, looked upon as possessing a good-natured and affectionate disposition, but without either elevation of mind or brightness of intellect. During many years of his life the Duke of Clarence was an obscure individual, without consideration, moving in a limited circle, and altogether forgotten by the great world. He resided at Bushey with Mrs. Jordan, and brought up his numerous children with very tender affection: with them, and for them, he seemed entirely to live. The cause of his separation from Mrs. Jordan has not been explained, but it probably arose from his desire to better his condition by a good marriage, and he wanted to marry Miss Wykeham, a half-crazy woman of large fortune, on whom he afterwards conferred a Peerage. George IV., I believe, put a spoke in that wheel, fortunately for the Duke as well as for the country. The death of the Princess Charlotte opened to him a new prospect, and the lack of royal progeny made his marriage as desirable an event to the public as it was convenient to himself. The subsequent death of the Duke of York, which made him heir to the throne, at once exalted him into a personage of political importance, and when the great Tory schism took place, upon the death of Lord Liverpool, Mr. Canning thought the Duke of Clarence's appointment to the office of Lord High Admiral would strengthen his Government, and at the same time relieve him from some of the difficulties which beset him; and he accordingly prevailed upon the King to revive the office in his person. Soon after the Duke of Wellington's elevation he found it necessary to remove the Duke of Clarence, and it is an excellent trait in the character of the latter that, notwithstanding his vexation at the time, which was very great, he harboured no resentment against the Duke of Wellington, and never seems to have hesitated about retaining him as his Minister when he came to the throne. His exaltation (for the moment) completely turned his head, but as his situation got familiar to him he became more composed and rational, if not more dignified in his behaviour. The moral and intellectual qualities of the King, however insignificant in themselves, now became, from their unavoidable influence, an object of great interest and importance, and in the early part of his reign he acquired no small share of popularity. People liked a King whose habits presented such a striking contrast to those of his predecessor. His attention to business, his frank and good-humoured familiarity, and his general hospitality, were advantageously compared with the luxurious and selfish indolence and habits of seclusion in the society of dull and grasping favourites which characterised the former reign.

But although King William was sometimes weak, sometimes obstinate, and miserably deficient in penetration and judgement, he was manly, sincere, honest, and straightforward. The most painful moment of his life, and the greatest humiliation to which a king ever submitted, must have been when he again received the Whig Ministers in 1835; but it is to the credit of Lord Melbourne, as well as of the King, that their subsequent personal intercourse was not disagreeable to either, and greatly to the King's honour that he has never been accused or suspected of any underhand or indirect proceeding for the purpose of emancipating himself from a thraldom so galling. Of political dexterity and artifice he was altogether incapable, and although, if he had been false, able, and artful, he might have caused more perplexity to his Whig Government and have played a better party game, it is perhaps fortunate for the country, and certainly happy for his own reputation, that his virtues thus predominated over his talents. The most remarkable foible of the late King was his passion for speechifying, and I have recorded some of his curious exhibitions in this way. He had considerable facility in expressing himself, but what he said was generally useless or improper. He never received the homage of a Bishop without giving him a lecture; and the custom he introduced of giving toasts and making speeches at all his dinners was more suitable to a tavern than to a palace. He was totally deficient in dignity or refinement, and neither his elevation to the throne nor his association with people of the most distinguished manners could give him any tincture of the one or the other. Though a good-natured and amiable man, he was passionate and hasty, and thus he was led into those bickerings and quarrels with the Duchess of Kent and with his own children, which were a perpetual source of discomfort or disgrace to him, and all of which might have been avoided by a more consistent course of firmness and temper on his part. His sons generally behaved to him with great insolence and ingratitude, except Adolphus. Of the daughters I know nothing.

The various political hopes, fears, and expectations which his death has raised may be very shortly summed up. Nobody can deny that it has given the Whig Government a great advantage over the Tories. Hitherto the Government have been working against the stream, inasmuch as they had the influence of the Crown running dead against them; the tide has now turned in their favour, and to a certain degree they will be able to convert the Tory principle to their own advantage. The object of the Whigs is to remain in office, to put down the Radicals and Radicalism, and go on gradually and safely reforming. This I believe to be the object of Lord Melbourne and Lord John Russell, but at the same time they have colleagues and supporters who have more extensive and less moderate views, and who would like to see the Government more cordially allied to the Radicals than it is, and who are so animated against the Tories that they would do *anything* to prevent their return to power.

July 9th. Yesterday I went to the late King's funeral, who was buried with just the same ceremonial as his predecessor this time seven years. It is a wretched mockery after all, and if I were king, the first thing I would do should be to provide for being committed to the earth with more decency and less pomp. A host of persons of all ranks and stations were congregated, who 'loitered through the lofty halls,' chattering and laughing, and with nothing of woe about them but the garb. I saw two men in an animated conversation, and one laughing heartily at the very foot of the coffin as it was lying in state. The chamber of death in which the body lay, all hung with black and adorned with scutcheons and every sort of funereal finery, was like a scene in a play, and as we passed through it and looked at the scaffolding and rough work behind, it was just like going behind the scenes of a theatre. A soldier's funeral, which I met in the morning—the plain coffin slowly borne along by his comrades, with the cap and helmet and sword of the dead placed upon it—was more impressive, more decent, more affecting than all this pomp with pasteboard crowns, and heralds scampering about, while idleness and indifference were gazing or gossiping round about the royal remains.

Knowsley, July 18th. Tired of doing nothing in London, and of hearing about the Queen, and the elections, I resolved to vary the scene and run down here to see the Birmingham railroad, Liverpool, and Liverpool races. So I started at five o'clock on Sunday evening, got to Birmingham at half-past five on Monday morning, and got upon the railroad at half-past seven. Nothing can be more comfortable than the vehicle in which I was put, a sort of chariot with two places, and there is nothing disagreeable about it but the occasional whiffs of stinking air which it is impossible to exclude altogether. The first sensation is a slight degree of nervousness and a feeling of being run away with, but a sense of security soon supervenes, and the velocity is delightful. Town after town, one park and *château* after another are left behind with the rapid variety of a moving panorama, and the continual bustle and animation of the changes and stoppages make the journey very entertaining. The train was very long, and heads were continually popping out of the several carriages, attracted by well-known voices, and then came the greetings and exclamations of surprise, the 'Where are you going?' and 'How on earth came you here?' Considering the novelty of its establishment, there is very little embarrassment, and it certainly renders all other travelling irksome and tedious by comparison. It was peculiarly gay at this time, because there was so much going on. There were all sorts of people going to Liverpool races, barristers to the assizes, and candidates to their several elections. The day was so wet that I could not see the town of Liverpool.

July 28th. Everything that could be said in praise of the Queen, of her manners, conduct, conversation, and character, having been exhausted, we now hear no more of her. It is an interesting speculation to conjecture how soon she will begin to think and to act for herself upon higher matters, as she has at once done on all minor points connected with her domestic arrangements. It is generally believed that she is perfectly independent of any influence in these things, and while in all political concerns she has put herself implicitly in Melbourne's hands, in all others she is her own mistress. From the beginning she resolved to have nothing to do with Sir John Conroy, but to reward him liberally for his services to her mother. She began by making him a baronet, and she has given him a pension of 3,000*l*. a year; but he has never once been invited to the Palace, or distinguished by the slightest mark of personal favour, so that nothing can be more striking than the contrast between the magnitude of the pecuniary bounty and the complete personal disregard of which he is the object. The Queen has been extremely kind and civil to the Queen Dowager, but she has taken no notice of the King's children, good, bad, or indifferent. Lord Munster asked for an audience to deliver up the keys of the Castle which he had, and was very graciously received by her, but she did not give him back the keys. Adolphus FitzClarence has lost his Lordship of the Bedchamber, but then they only retained Peers, and he keeps the command of the Royal yacht. He has had no intimation whether his pension and his Rangership of Windsor Park are to be continued to him. [In the end, however, they retained everything, and the Queen behaved with equal liberality and kindness towards them all.]

July 30th.   Madame de Lieven told me yesterday that she had an audience of the Queen, who was very civil and gracious, but timid and embarrassed, and talked of nothing but commonplaces. Her Majesty had probably been told that the Princess was an *intrigante*, and was afraid of committing herself. She had afterwards an interview with the Duchess of Kent, who (she told me) it was plain to see is overwhelmed with vexation and disappointment. Her daughter behaves to her with kindness and attention, but has rendered herself quite independent of the Duchess, who painfully feels her own insignificance. The almost contemptuous

way in which Conroy has been dismissed must be a bitter mortification to her. The Duchess said to Madame de Lieven, 'qu'il n'y
avait plus d'avenir pour elle, qu'elle n'était plus rien;' that for
eighteen years this child had been the sole object of her life, of
all her thoughts and hopes, and now she was taken from her, and
there was an end of all for which she had lived heretofore. Madame de Lieven said that she ought to be the happiest of human
beings, to see the elevation of this child, her prodigious success,
and the praise and admiration of which she was universally the
object; that it was a triumph and a glory which ought to be sufficient for her—to which she only shook her head with a melancholy smile, and gave her to understand that all this would not
do, and that the accomplishment of her wishes had only made
her to the last degree unhappy. King William is revenged, he
little anticipated how or by what instrumentality, and if his ghost
is an ill-natured and vindictive shade, it may rejoice in the sight
of this bitter disappointment of his enemy. In the midst of all
her propriety of manner and conduct, the young Queen begins
to exhibit slight signs of a peremptory disposition, and it is impossible not to suspect that, as she gains confidence, and as her
character begins to develope, she will evince a strong will of her
own. In all trifling matters connected with her Court and her
palace, she already enacts the part of Queen and mistress as if it
had long been familiar to her.

August 30th. All that I hear of the young Queen leads to the
conclusion that she will some day play a conspicuous part, and
that she has a great deal of character. It is clear enough that she
had long been silently preparing herself, and had been prepared
by those about her (and very properly) for the situation to which
she was destined. Melbourne, who has a thousand times greater
opportunities of knowing what her disposition and her capacity
are than any other person, thinks highly of her sense, discretion,
and good feeling; but what seem to distinguish her above everything are caution and prudence, the former to a degree which is
almost unnatural in one so young, and unpleasing, because it

suppresses the youthful impulses which are so graceful and attractive.

On the morning of the King's death, the Archbishop of Canterbury and Lord Conyngham arrived at Kensington at five o'clock, and immediately desired to see 'the Queen.' They were ushered into an apartment, and in a few minutes the door opened and she came in wrapped in a dressing-gown and with slippers on her naked feet. Conyngham in a few words told her their errand, and as soon as he uttered the words 'Your Majesty,' she instantly put out her hand to him, intimating that he was to kiss hands before he proceeded. He dropped on one knee, kissed her hand, and then went on to tell her of the late King's death. She presented her hand to the Archbishop, who likewise kissed it, and when he had done so, addressed to her a sort of pastoral charge, which she received graciously and then retired. She lost no time in giving notice to Conroy of her intentions with regard to him; she saw him, and desired him to name the reward he expected for his services to her parents. He asked for the Red Riband, an Irish peerage, and a pension of 3,000*l.* a year. She replied that the two first rested with her Ministers, and she could not engage for them, but that the pension he should have. It is not easy to ascertain the exact cause of her antipathy to him, but it has probably grown with her growth, and results from divers causes. The person in the world she loves best is the Baroness Lehzen, and Lehzen and Conroy were enemies. Her manner to the Duchess is, however, irreproachable, and they appear to be on cordial and affectionate terms. Madame de Lehzen is the only person who is constantly with her. When any of the Ministers come to see her, the Baroness retires at one door as they enter at the other, and the audience over she returns to the Queen. It has been remarked that when applications are made to Her Majesty, she seldom or never gives an immediate answer, but says she will consider of it, and it is supposed that she does this because she consults Melbourne about everything, and waits to have her answer suggested by him. He says, however, that such is her habit even with him, and that when he talks to her upon any subject upon which an opinion is expected from her, she tells him she will think it over, and let him know her sentiments the next day.

The day she went down to visit the Queen Dowager at Windsor, to Melbourne's great surprise she said to him that as the flag on the Round Tower was half-mast high, and they might perhaps think it necessary to elevate it upon her arrival, it would be better to send orders beforehand not to do so. *He* had never thought of the flag, or knew anything about it, but it showed her knowledge of forms and her attention to trifles. Her manner to the Queen was extremely kind and affectionate, and they were both greatly affected at meeting. The Queen Dowager said to her that the only favour she had to ask of her was to provide for the retirement, with their pensions, of the personal attendants of the late King, Whiting and Bachelor, who had likewise been the attendants of George IV.; to which she replied that it should be attended to, but she could not give any promise on the subject.

She is upon terms of the greatest cordiality with Lord Melbourne, and very naturally. Everything is new and delightful to her. She is surrounded with the most exciting and interesting enjoyments; her occupations, her pleasures, her business, her Court, all present an unceasing round of gratifications. With all her prudence and discretion she has great animal spirits, and enters into the magnificent novelties of her position with the zest and curiosity of a child.

No man is more formed to ingratiate himself with her than Melbourne. He treats her with unbounded consideration and respect, he consults her tastes and her wishes, and he puts her at her ease by his frank and natural manners, while he amuses her by the quaint, queer, epigrammatic turn of his mind, and his varied knowledge upon all subjects. It is not therefore surprising that she should be well content with her present Government, and that during the progress of the elections she should have testified great interest in the success of the Whig candidates. Her reliance upon Melbourne's advice extends at present to subjects quite beside his constitutional functions, for the other day somebody asked her permission to dedicate some novel to her, when she said she did not like to grant the permission without knowing the contents of the work, and she desired Melbourne to read the book and let her know if it was fit that she should accept the dedication. Melbourne read the first volume, but found it so dull that he would not read any more, and sent her word that she had better refuse, which she accordingly did. She seems to be liberal, but at the same time prudent with regard to money, for when the Queen Dowager proposed to her to take her band into her service, she declined to incur so great an expense without further consideration, but one of the first things she spoke to Melbourne about was the payment of her father's debts, which she is resolved to discharge.

December 8th. Mr. Disraeli made his first exhibition[1] the other night, beginning with florid assurance, speedily degenerating into ludicrous absurdity, and being at last put down with inextinguishable shouts of laughter.

M*arch 11th*, 1838. I dined yesterday at the Palace, much to my surprise, for I had no expectation of an invitation. There was a very numerous party:—the Hanoverian Minister Baron Münchhausen, Lord and Lady Grey, the Chancellor, the Roseberys, Ossulston, Mahon, &c. We assembled in the round room next the gallery, and just before the dinner was ready the Queen entered with the Duchess of Kent, preceded by the Chamberlain, and followed by her six ladies. She shook hands with the women, and made a sweeping bow to the men, and directly went in to dinner, conducted by Münchhausen, who sat next to her, and Lord Conyngham on the other side. The dinner was like any other great dinner. After the eating was over, the Queen's health was given by Cavendish, who sat at one end of the table, and everybody got up to drink it: a vile, vulgar custom, and, however proper it may be to drink her health elsewhere, it is bad taste to have it given by her own officer at her own table, which, in fact,

---

[1] [*i.e., maiden speech.*]

is the only private table it is ever drunk at. However, this has been customary in the two last reigns. George III. never dined but with his family, never had guests, or a dinner *party*.

The Queen sat for some time at table, talking away very merrily to her neighbours, and the men remained about a quarter of an hour after the ladies. When we went into the drawing-room, and huddled about the door in the sort of half-shy, half-awkward way people do, the Queen advanced to meet us, and spoke to everybody in succession, and if everybody's 'palaver' was as deeply interesting as mine, it would have been worth while to have had Gurney to take it down in short-hand.

I shall now record my dialogue with accurate fidelity:

Q. Have you been riding to-day, Mr. Greville?

G. No, Madam, I have not.

Q. It was a fine day.

G. Yes, Ma'am, a very fine day.

Q. It was rather cold though.

G. (*like Polonius*)—It *was* rather cold, Madam.

Q. Your sister, Lady Francis Egerton, rides, I think, does she not?

G. She does ride sometimes, Madam.

(A pause, when I took the lead, though adhering to the same topic.)

G. Had your Majesty been riding to-day?

Q. (*with animation*)—Oh, yes, a very long ride.

G. Has your Majesty got a nice horse?

Q. Oh, a very nice horse.

Gracious smile and inclination of head on part of Queen, profound bow on mine, she turned again to Lord Grey. Directly after I was (to my satisfaction) deposited at the whist table to make up the Duchess of Kent's party, and all the rest of the company were arranged about a large round table (the Queen on the sofa by it), where they passed about an hour and a half in what was probably the smallest possible talk, interrupted and enlivened, however, by some songs which Lord Ossulston sang. We had plenty of instrumental music during and after dinner. To form an opinion or the slightest notion of her real character and capacity from such a formal affair as this, is manifestly impossible. Nobody expects from her any clever, amusing, or interesting talk, above all no stranger can expect it. She is very civil to everybody, and there is more of frankness, cordiality, and good-humour in her manner than of dignity. She looks and speaks cheerfully: there was nothing to criticise, nothing particularly to admire. The whole thing seemed to be dull, perhaps unavoidably so, but still so dull that it is a marvel how anybody can like such a life. This was an unusually large party, and therefore more than usually dull and formal; but it is much the same sort of thing every day. Melbourne was not there, which I regretted, as I had some curiosity to see Her Majesty and her Minister together.

March 25th. Lady Cowper told me yesterday that the Queen said to Lord Melbourne, 'the first thing which had convinced her he was worthy of her confidence was his conduct in the disputes at Kensington last year about her proposed allowance,' in which, though he knew that the King's life was closing, he had taken his part. She considered this to be a proof of his honesty and determination to do what he thought right. Though she took no part, and never declared herself, it is evident that she, in her heart, sided with the King on that occasion. It is impossible to account for the conduct of the Duchess of Kent and Conroy towards the Princess. Whatever may have been the real amount of coercion or unkindness practiced, it was enough to breed in her mind detestation of him and no doubt a considerable degree of alienation from her mother, nor do they appear to have been the least aware of the strength either of her feelings or her character. It is difficult to attribute to timidity that command over herself and passive obedience which she showed in her whole conduct up to the moment when she learnt that she was Queen; and from that instant, as if inspired with the genius and the spirit of Sixtus V., she at once asserted her dignity and her will. She now evinces in all she does an attachment to the memory of her uncle, and it is not to be doubted that, in the disputes which took place

between him and her mother, her secret sympathies were with
the King; and in that celebrated scene at Windsor, when the
King made so fierce an attack upon the Duchess's advisers, and
expressed his earnest hope that he might live to see the majority
of his niece, Victoria must have inwardly rejoiced at the expression of sentiments so accordant with her own. Her attentions and
cordiality to Queen Adelaide, her bounty and civility to the King's
children, and the disgrace of Conroy, amply prove what her sentiments have all along been.

May 11th. Last night I was at the ball at the Palace—a poor
affair in comparison with the Tuileries. Gallery ill-lit; rest of
the rooms tolerable. The Queen's manner and bearing perfect.
She danced, first with Prince George, then young Esterhazy, then
Lord FitzAlan. Before supper, and after dancing, she sat on a sofa
somewhat elevated in the drawing-room, looking at the waltzing;
she did not waltz herself. Her mother sat on one side of her, and
the Princess Augusta on the other; then the Duchesses of Gloucester and Cambridge and the Princess of Cambridge; her household, with their wands, standing all round; her manners exceedingly graceful, and, blended with dignity and cordiality, a
simplicity and good humour, when she talks to people, which are
mighty captivating. When supper was announced she moved
from her seat, all her officers going before her—she, first, alone,
and the Royal Family following; her exceeding youth strikingly
contrasted with their mature ages, but she did it well. I was struck
last night for the first time with the great change in the Duke of
Wellington's looks; others have noted it before. He is no longer
so straight and upright, and old age is taking possession of his
features in a way that is distressing to see. He has lived long
enough for his own renown, but he cannot live long enough for
the good of his country, let what will happen and when it may.
It is a fine sight to regard the noble manner in which he is playing
the last act of his glorious life.

My brother writes me word from Paris that Leopold is deadly
sick of his Belgian crown, and impatient to abdicate, thinking
that it is a better thing to be an English Prince, uncle to the

Queen, with 50,000*l.* a year, than to be monarch of a troublesome vulgar little kingdom which all its neighbours regard with an evil or a covetous eye. Louis Philippe is in a mighty fright about it, and he is right, for Leopold's abdication would be almost sure to disturb the peace of Europe.

May 23rd.   Talleyrand is dead. He died after a short illness some day last week. It would require a nice discrimination of character and intimate knowledge of the man to delineate his, a great deal more of both than I possess, therefore I shall not attempt it. During the period of his embassy in England I lived a good deal with him, his house being always open to me, and I dined there *en famille* whenever I pleased. Nothing could be more hospitable, nothing more urbane and kind than he was; and it was fine to see, after his stormy youth and middle age, after a life spent in the very tempest and whirlwind of political agitation, how tranquilly and honourably his declining years ebbed away. Still retaining his faculties unimpaired, and his memory stored with the recollections of his extraordinary and eventful career, and an inexhaustible mine of anecdotes, his delight was to narrate, which he used to do with an abundance, a vivacity, and a *finesse* peculiar to himself, and to the highest degree interesting and attractive. No name was once held in greater detestation in England than that of Talleyrand. He was looked upon universally as a sink of moral and political profligacy. Born at the end of Louis XV.'s reign, and bred up in the social pleasures and corruptions of that polite but vicious aristocracy, he was distinguished in his early youth for his successful gallantries, for the influence he obtained over women, and the dexterity with which he converted it to his advancement. A debauched abbé and bishop, one of the champions and then one of the victims of the Revolution, afterwards (having scrambled through the perilous period of Terrorism) discarding his clerical character, he became the Minister of the Consulate and the Empire, and was looked upon all over Europe as a man of consummate ability, but totally destitute of principle in public or in private life. Disgraced by Napoleon, he reappeared after his fall, and was greatly concerned in the restoration of the Bourbons. For a short time only employed, but always treated by them with consideration and respect, the Revolution of July again brought Talleyrand prominently on the stage, and, to the surprise of all men, he accepted the embassy to London. The years he passed here were probably the most peaceful of his life, and they served to create for him a reputation altogether new, and such as to cancel all former recollections. His age was venerable, his society was delightful, and there was an exhibition of conservative wisdom, 'of moderate and healing counsels,' in all his thoughts, words, and actions very becoming to his age and station, vastly influential from his sagacity and experience, and which presented him to the eyes of men as a statesman like Burleigh or Clarendon for prudence, temperance, and discretion. Here therefore he acquired golden opinions, and was regarded by all ranks and all parties with respect, and by many with sincere regard. When he was attacked in the House of Lords the Duke of Wellington rose in his defence, and rebuked the acrimony of his own friends. Talleyrand was deeply affected at this behaviour of the Duke. I regret much not having availed myself of the opportunities I might have had to listen to and record the talk of Talleyrand, but the fact is, he was so inarticulate, and I so deaf, that the labour would have been greater than I could go through for the object. The account which my brother has sent me of the circumstances which preceded his death, and of his reconciliation with the Church, are very curious. He had always desired to die at Valençay, in order to avoid the scandal which he apprehended there might be in Paris from the severity of the Archbishop, but it was contrived to get everything quietly and decently settled, and he died in peace with the Church, and with all the absolutions and benedictions that she could have bestowed upon the most faithful of her sons.

June 21st. Much talked of is the speech which Lord Anglesey made at the Waterloo dinner when he gave the Duke's health. He said that 'it was superfluous to talk of his military achievements, but that he must express his admiration of his conduct in civil matters, especially in the House of Lords during the present session, when he had shown how superior he was to all party considerations and purposes, and when he had given his support to a Government in which it was well known he placed no confidence, because he thought that the national honour and interest required that they should be supported.' Of course, a speech reported at second or third hand is not very correctly given, but this was the gist of it, extremely well done by all accounts, not perhaps palatable to all who heard him, but which gave great pleasure to the Duke himself. Anglesey said that the Duke, when he sat down, squeezed his hand hard and long, and said to him, 'I cannot tell you what pleasure you have given me.' The Queen sent the Duke a gracious message, desiring he would bring the whole of his party to her ball, which gratified him very much, and he wrote a very grateful and respectful answer. The French were exceedingly annoyed at the ball being given on that particular night (the 18th), and begged to be excused from attending, not angrily however. It was unfortunate that this day was chosen for the ball, but it was accidental, and not intended as a celebration.

June 29th. The Coronation (which, thank God, is over) went off very well. The appearance of the Abbey was beautiful, particularly the benches of the Peeresses, who were blazing with diamonds. The entry of Soult was striking. He was saluted with a murmur of curiosity and applause as he passed through the nave, and nearly the same as he advanced along the choir. His appearance is that of a veteran warrior, and he walked alone, with his numerous suite following at a respectful distance, preceded by heralds and ushers, who received him with marked attention, more certainly than any of the other Ambassadors. The Queen looked very diminutive, and the effect of the procession itself was spoilt by being too crowded; there was not interval enough between the Queen and the Lords and others going before her. The Bishop of London (Blomfield) preached a very good sermon. The different actors in the ceremonial were very imperfect in their parts, and had neglected to rehearse them. Lord John Thynne, who officiated for the Dean of Westminster, told me that nobody knew what was to be done except the Archbishop and himself (who had rehearsed), Lord Willoughby (who is experienced in these matters), and the Duke of Wellington, and consequently there was a continual difficulty and embarrassment, and the Queen never knew what she was to do next. They made her leave her chair and enter into St. Edward's Chapel before the prayers were concluded, much to the discomfiture of the Archbishop. She said to John Thynne, 'Pray tell me what I am to do, for they don't know;' and at the end, when the orb was put into her hand, she said to him, 'What am I to do with it?' 'Your Majesty is to carry it, if you please, in your hand.' 'Am I?' she said; 'it is very heavy.' The ruby ring was made for her little finger instead of the fourth, on which the rubric prescribes that it should be put. When the Archbishop was to put it on, she extended the former, but he said it must be on the latter. She said it was too small, and she could not get it on. He said it was right to put it there, and, as he insisted, she yielded, but had first to take off her other rings, and then this was forced on, but it hurt her very much, and as soon as the ceremony was over she was obliged to bathe her finger in iced water in order to get it off. The noise and confusion were very great when the medals were thrown about by Lord Surrey, everybody scrambling with all their might and main to get them, and none more vigorously than the Maids of Honour. There was a great demonstration of applause when the Duke of Wellington did homage. Lord Rolle, who is between eighty and ninety, fell down as he was getting up the steps of the throne. Her first impulse was to rise, and when afterwards he came again to do homage she said, 'May I not get up and meet him?' and then rose from the throne and advanced down one or two of the steps to prevent his coming up, an act of graciousness and kindness which made a great sensation. It is, in fact, the remarkable union of *naïveté*, kindness, nature, good nature, with propriety and dignity, which makes her so admirable and so endearing to those about her, as she certainly is. I have been repeatedly told that they are all warmly attached to her, but that all feel the impossibility of for a moment losing sight of the respect which they owe her. She never ceases to be a Queen, but is always the most charming, cheerful, obliging, unaffected Queen in the world. The procession was very handsome, and the Extraordinary Ambassadors produced some gorgeous equipages. This sort of procession is incomparably better than the old ceremonial which so much fuss was made about, for the banquet would only have benefited the privileged few and the rich, and for one person who would have witnessed the procession on the platform five hundred enjoyed a sight of this. In fact, the thing best worth seeing was the town itself, and the countless multitudes through which the procession passed. The Chancellor of the Exchequer told me that he had been informed 200,000*l.* had been paid for seats alone, and the number of people who have flocked into London has been estimated at five hundred thousand. It is said that a million have had a sight of the show in one way or another. These numbers are possibly exaggerated, but they really were prodigious. From Buckingham Palace to Westminster Abbey, by the way they took, which must be two or three miles in length, there was a dense mass of people; the seats and benches were all full, every window was occupied, the roofs of the houses were covered with spectators, for the most part well dressed, and, from the great space through which they were distributed, there was no extraordinary pressure, and consequently no room for violence or ill-humour.

July 24th. High Church has been recently reading lectures to Her Majesty the Queen in the shape of two sermons preached at the Chapel Royal by Mr. Perceval and Mr. Hook. Hook's sermon appears to have been the stronger of the two. He told the Queen that the Church would endure, let what would happen to the throne. On her return to Buckingham House, Normanby, who had been at the chapel, said to her, 'Did not your Majesty find it very hot?' She said, 'Yes, and the sermon was very hot too.'

August 8th. James Stephen yesterday was talking to me about Macaulay. He came to him soon after his return from India, and told him that when there he used to get up at five every morning (as everybody else did), and till nine or ten he read Greek and

Latin, and went through the whole range of classical literature
of every sort and kind; that one day in the Government library
he had met with the works of Chrysostom, fourteen Greek folios,
and that he had taken home first one volume and then another,
till he had read the whole through, that is, he had not read every
word, because he had found that it contained a great deal of
stuff not worth reading, but he had carefully looked at every
page, and had actually read the greater part. His object now is
to devote himself to literature, and his present project, to write
a History of England for the last 150 years, in which Stephen
says he would give scope to his fine imagination in the delinea-
tion of character, and bring his vast stores of knowledge to the
composition of the narrative, and would, without doubt, produce
a work of astonishing power and interest. Macaulay says if he
had the power of recalling everything he has ever written and
published and of destroying it all, he would do so, for he thinks
that his time has been thrown away upon *opuscula* unworthy of
his talents. I asked Stephen by what mental process Macaulay
had contrived to accumulate such boundless stores of information,
and how it was all so sorted and arranged in his head that it
was always producible at will. He said that he had first of all the
power of abstraction, of giving his undivided attention to the
book and the subject on which he was occupied; then, as other
men read by syllables or by words, he had the faculty, acquired
by use, of reading by whole sentences, of swallowing, as it were,
whole paragraphs at once, and thus he infinitely abbreviated
the mere mechanical part of study; that as an educated man
would read any number of pages much more quickly than an
uneducated man, so much more quickly would Macaulay read
than any ordinary man.

September 7th. Nothing to record of any sort or kind: London
a desert; I went to-day to Windsor for a Council, was invited by
the Queen (through Melbourne) to stay and dine, but made an
excuse on the score of business, and luckily had a plausible one
to make. It is too much of a good thing to cool one's heels for
some four and a half hours in order to be bored for three more

in the evening, and then end with a nocturnal jaunt to town. To sit at the Royal table and play at shilling whist with the Duchess of Kent are great honors, but le jeu ne vaut pas la chandelle.

September 12th. George Villiers, who came from Windsor on Monday, told me he had been exceedingly struck with Lord Melbourne's manner to the Queen, and hers to him: his, so parental and anxious, but always so respectful and deferential; hers, indicative of such entire confidence, such pleasure in his society. She is continually talking to him; let who will be there, he always sits next her at dinner, and evidently by arrangement, because he always takes in the lady-in-waiting, which necessarily places him next her, the etiquette being that the lady-in-waiting sits next but one to the Queen. It is not unnatural, and to him it is peculiarly interesting. I have no doubt he is passionately fond of her as he might be of his daughter if he had one, and the more because he is a man with a capacity for loving without having anything in the world to love. It is become his province to educate, instruct, and form the most interesting mind and character in the world. No occupation was ever more engrossing or involved greater responsibility. I have no doubt that Melbourne is both equal to and worthy of the task, and that it is fortunate she has fallen into his hands, and that he discharges this great duty wisely, honourably, and conscientiously. There are, however, or rather may be hereafter, inconveniences in the establishment of such an intimacy, and in a connexion of so close and affectionate a nature between the young Queen and her Minister; for whenever the Government, which hangs by a thread, shall be broken up, the parting will be painful, and their subsequent relations will not be without embarrassment to themselves, nor fail to be the cause of jealousy in others. It is a great proof of the discretion and purity of his conduct and behaviour, that he is admired, respected, and liked by all the Court.

Yesterday I went to Battersea and dined with Robert Eden, the Rector,[2] and he took me before dinner to see his lions, and

[2] Afterwards Bishop of Bath and Wells.

introduced me to scenes very different from those which I am used to see. We went to different manufactories, a saw-mill, a pottery, to the lunatic asylum, to the workhouse, and we visited several poor people at their cottages, when he enquired into the circumstances of the sick or the indigent; but what struck me most forcibly was the school (upon Bell's system) and the extraordinary acquirements of the boys. Eden examined them, and invited me to do so, in arithmetic, geography, English history, and the Bible, and their readiness and correctness were really surprising. I doubt whether many of the children of the rich, who are educated at a vast expense at private or public schools, could pass such an examination as these young paupers who are instructed at the cost of about one guinea a year. The greatest punishment that can be inflicted on one of these boys is to banish him from school, such delight do they take in acquiring knowledge. He gave me a curious account of the state of his parish: there is no middle class of tradesmen in good circumstances; they are divided between the extremes of wealth and of poverty, masters and operatives; but amongst the latter there is a considerable amount of knowledge, though their minds are ill-regulated and their principles perverted. When first he came there the place abounded in disciples of Carlile, pure atheists, and when Carlile was in prison he was supported by their contributions; but though totally without religion they were not immoral, and among these men were some of the best husbands and fathers in the place, so much so that when Carlile told them that men might indulge in polygamy and take two wives, they were scandalised and disgusted, and began immediately to abandon him.

September 15*th*. Yesterday again at Windsor for a Council. I had made up my mind not to stay if invited, and meant to hasten away; but before I could do so Melbourne came after me and said, 'You will stay here? the Queen desired me to ask you.' I said I had no evening dress, had come by the railroad, and walked from Slough; could not assume that I should be asked, and did not know what to do. He said, 'She meant it as a civility, and thought you would like it.' There was a sort of reproach con-

veyed in the tone, and that induced me to say, 'So I should if
I had only known of it, but as it is I can send for my things if
you like.' He ended by desiring I would do what I liked best
myself, promised that he would take care the Queen was not
offended, and that nobody else would know anything of the matter. I accordingly resolved to go, and went away with Lord
Albemarle. My mind misgave me, and I had a great mind to
stay, especially as Lord Albemarle told me they did not mean to
turn me out after dinner, but that sleeping there was a matter
of course. Then I was sorry I had not stayed, which I might just
as well have done, for I had nothing else to do. At these Councils
we meet in common morning dress, which we used not to do.

November 18*th, Wolbeding.*   Came here to-day and brought
Lord Fitzroy Somerset[3] with me, who told me a great deal about
the Duke and their old campaigns. He never saw a man so cool
and indifferent to danger, at the same time without any personal
rashness or bravado, never putting himself in unnecessary danger, never avoiding any that was necessary. He was close to the
Duke, his left arm touching the Duke's right, when he was shot
in the arm at Waterloo, and so was Lord Anglesey when he received his wound in the leg. When Lord Anglesey was shot he
turned to the Duke and said, 'By G— I have lost my leg.' The
Duke replied, 'Have you? by G—.' The only time the Duke ever
was hit was at Orthez, by a spent ball, which struck him on the
side and knocked him down. He and Alava were standing together having both dismounted, and they were laughing at a
Portuguese soldier who had just passed by saying he was 'offendido' when the Duke was struck down, but he immediately
rose and laughed all the more at being 'offendido' himself. During
the battles of the Pyrenees Cole proposed to the Duke and his
staff to go and eat a very good dinner he had ordered for himself
at his house in the village he occupied, as he could not leave his
division. They went and dined, and then the Duke went into
the next room and threw himself upon a bed without a mattress,

[3] [Afterwards Lord Raglan. He lost his arm at Waterloo, and commanded
the British army in the Crimea, where he died in 1855.]

on the boards of which he presently went to sleep with his des-
patch-box for a pillow. Fitzroy and the aides-de-camp slept in
chairs or on the floor scattered about. Presently arrived, in great
haste and alarm, two officers of artillery, Captain Cairne and
another, who begged to see the Duke, the former saying that he
had just brought up some guns from the rear, and that he had
suddenly found himself close to the enemy and did not know
what to do. They went and woke the Duke, who desired him to
be brought in. The officer entered and told his story, when the
Duke said, very composedly, 'Well, Sir, you are certainly in a
very bad position, and you must get out of it in the best way you
can,' turned round, and was asleep again in a moment.

December 15*th*.   Went on Wednesday to a Council at Windsor, and after the Council was invited to stay that night; rode
with the Queen, and after riding Melbourne came to me and said
Her Majesty wished me to stay the next day also. This was very
gracious and very considerate, because it was done for the express purpose of showing that she was not displeased at my not
staying when asked on a former occasion, and as she can have
no object whatever in being civil to me, it was a proof of her
good-nature and thoughtfulness about other people's little vani-
ties, even those of the most insignificant. Accordingly I remained
till Friday morning, when I went with the rest of her suite to
see the hounds throw off, which she herself saw for the first time.
The Court is certainly not gay, but it is perhaps impossible that
any Court should be gay where there is no social equality; where
some ceremony, and a continual air of deference and respect
must be observed, there can be no ease, and without ease there
can be no real pleasure. The Queen is natural, good-humoured,
and cheerful, but still she is Queen, and by her must the social
habits and the tone of conversation be regulated, and for this she
is too young and inexperienced. She sits at a large round table,
her guests around it, and Melbourne always in a chair beside her,
where two mortal hours are consumed in such conversation as
can be found, which appears to be, and really is, very up-hill
work. This, however, is the only bad part of the whole; the rest

of the day is passed without the slightest constraint, trouble, or annoyance to anybody; each person is at liberty to employ himself or herself as best pleases them, though very little is done in common, and in this respect Windsor is totally unlike any other place. There is none of the sociability which makes the agreeableness of an English country house; there is no room in which the guests assemble, sit, lounge, and talk as they please and when they please; there is a billiard table, but in such a remote corner of the Castle that it might as well be in the town of Windsor; and there is a library well stocked with books, but hardly accessible, imperfectly warmed, and only tenanted by the librarian: it is a mere library, too, unfurnished, and offering none of the comforts and luxuries of a habitable room. There are two breakfast rooms, one for the ladies and the guests, and the other for the equerries, but when the meal is over everybody disperses, and nothing but another meal reunites the company, so that, in fact, there is no society whatever, little trouble, little etiquette, but very little resource or amusement.

The life which the Queen leads is this: she gets up soon after eight o'clock, breakfasts in her own room, and is employed the whole morning in transacting business; she reads all the despatches, and has every matter of interest and importance in every department laid before her. At eleven or twelve Melbourne comes to her and stays an hour, more or less, according to the business he may have to transact. At two she rides with a large suite (and she likes to have it numerous); Melbourne always rides on her left hand, and the equerry in waiting generally on her right; she rides for two hours along the road, and the greater part of the time at a full gallop; after riding she amuses herself for the rest of the afternoon with music and singing, playing, romping with children, if there are any in the Castle (and she is so fond of them that she generally contrives to have some there), or in any other way she fancies. The hour of dinner is nominally half-past seven o'clock, soon after which time the guests assemble, but she seldom appears till near eight. The lord in waiting comes into the drawing-room and instructs each gentleman which lady he is to take in to dinner. When the guests are all assembled the Queen comes in, preceded by the gentlemen of her household, and followed by the Duchess of Kent and all her ladies; she speaks to each lady, bows to the men, and goes immediately into the dining-room. She generally takes the arm of the man of the highest rank, but on this occasion she went with Mr. Stephenson, the American Minister (though he has no rank), which was very wisely done. Melbourne invariably sits on her left, no matter who may be there; she remains at table the usual time, but does not suffer the men to sit long after her, and we were summoned to coffee in less than a quarter of an hour. In the drawing-room she never sits down till the men make their appearance. Coffee is served to them in the adjoining room, and then they go into the drawing-room, when she goes round and says a few words to each, of the most trivial nature, all however very civil and cordial in manner and expression. When this little ceremony is over the Duchess of Kent's whist table is arranged, and then the round table is marshalled, Melbourne invariably sitting on the left hand of the Queen and remaining there without moving till the evening is at an end. At about half-past eleven she goes to bed, or whenever the Duchess has played her usual number of rubbers, and the band have performed all the pieces on their list for the night. This is the whole history of her day: she orders and regulates every detail herself, she knows where everybody is lodged in the Castle, settles about the riding or driving, and enters into every particular with minute attention. But while she personally gives her orders to her various attendants, and does everything that is civil to all the inmates of the Castle, she really has nothing to do with anybody but Melbourne, and with him she passes (if not in *tête-à-tête* yet in intimate communication) more hours than any two people, in any relation of life, perhaps ever do pass together besides. He is at her side for at least six hours every day—an hour in the morning, two on horseback, one at dinner, and two in the evening. This monopoly is certainly not judicious; it is not altogether consistent with social usage, and it leads to an infraction of those rules of etiquette which it is better to observe with regularity at Court. But it is more peculiarly inexpedient with reference to her own future enjoyment, for if Melbourne should be compelled to resign, her privation will be the more bitter on account of the exclusiveness of her intimacy with him. Accordingly, her terror when any danger menaces the Government, her nervous apprehension at any appearance of change, affect her health, and upon one occasion during the last session she actually fretted herself into an illness at the notion of their going out. It must be owned that her feelings are not unnatural, any more than those which Melbourne entertains towards her. His manner to her is perfect, always respectful, and never presuming upon the extraordinary distinction he enjoys; hers to him is simple and natural, indicative of the confidence she reposes in him, and of her lively taste for his society, but not marked by any unbecoming familiarity. Interesting as his position is, and flattered, gratified, and touched as he must be by the confiding devotion with which she places herself in his hands, it is still marvellous that he should be able to overcome the force of habit so completely as to endure the life he leads. Month after month he remains at the Castle, submitting to this daily routine: of all men he appeared to be the last to be broken in to the trammels of a Court, and never was such a revolution seen in anybody's occupations and habits. Instead of indolently sprawling in all the attitudes of luxurious ease, he is always sitting bolt upright; his free and easy language interlarded with 'damns' is carefully guarded and regulated with the strictest propriety, and he has exchanged the good talk of Holland House for the trivial, laboured, and wearisome inanities of the Royal circle.

December 24th. Dined yesterday at the Hollands': Normanby, Melbourne, and Luttrell; pretty good talk. Lord Holland gave me an account of Fox's death, with all the details of the operations (he was thrice tapped), and his behaviour; and till then I was not entirely aware that Fox was no believer in religion. Mrs. Fox was very anxious to have prayers read, to which he consented, but paid little attention to the ceremony, remaining quiescent merely, not liking, as Lord Holland said, to refuse any wish of hers, nor to pretend any sentiments he did not entertain.

February 17*th*, 1839. I dined at Lady Blessington's yesterday, to meet Durham and Brougham; but, after all, the latter did not come, and the excuse he made was, that it was better not; and as he was taking, or going to take (we shall see), a moderate course about Canada, it would impair his efficacy if the press were to trumpet forth, and comment on, his meeting with Durham. There was that sort of strange *omnium gatherum* party which is to be met with nowhere else, and which for that reason alone is curious. We had Prince Louis Napoleon and his A.D.C.[4] He is a short, thickish, vulgar-looking man, without the slightest resemblance to his Imperial uncle, or any intelligence in his countenance. Then we had the ex-Governor of Canada, Captain Marriott, the Count Alfred de Vigny (author of 'Cinq Mars' &c.), Sir Edward Lytton Bulwer, and a proper sprinkling of ordinary persons to mix up with these celebrities. In the evening, Forster, sub-editor of the 'Examiner;' Chorley, editor of the 'Athenæum;' Macready, and Charles Buller. Lady Blessington's existence is a curiosity, and her house and society have at least the merit of being singular, though the latter is not so agreeable as from its composition it ought to be. There is no end to the men of consequence and distinction in the world who go there occasionally —Brougham, Lyndhurst, Abinger, Canterbury, Durham, and many others; all the *minor* poets, *literati*, and journalists, without exception, together with some of the highest pretensions. Moore is a sort of friend of hers; she *has been* very intimate with Byron, and *is* with Walter Savage Landor. Her house is furnished with a luxury and splendour not to be surpassed; her dinners are frequent and good; and D'Orsay does the honours with a frankness and cordiality which are very successful; but all this does not

---

[4] [The first mention of His Imperial Majesty Napoleon III., who was an *habitué* of Gore House, and well known to all who frequented it.]

make society, in the real meaning of the term. There is a vast deal of coming and going, and eating and drinking, and a corresponding amount of noise, but little or no conversation, discussion, easy quiet interchange of ideas and opinions, no regular social foundation of men of intellectual or literary calibre ensuring a perennial flow of conversation, and which, if it existed, would derive strength and assistance from the light superstructure of occasional visitors, with the much or the little they might individually contribute. The reason of this is that the woman herself, who must give the tone to her own society, and influence its character, is ignorant, vulgar, and commonplace.[5] Nothing can be more dull and uninteresting than her conversation, which is never enriched by a particle of knowledge, or enlivened by a ray of genius or imagination. The fact of her existence as an authoress is an enigma, poor as her pretensions are; for while it is very difficult to write good books, it is not easy to compose even bad ones, and volumes have come forth under her name for which hundreds of pounds have been paid, because (Heaven only can tell how) thousands are found who will read them. Her 'Works' have been published in America, in one huge folio, where it seems they meet with peculiar success; and this trash goes down, because it is written by a Countess, in a country where rank is eschewed, and equality is the universal passion. It would be not uninteresting to trace this current of success to its source. First and foremost, her magnificent house and luxurious dinners; then the alliance offensive and defensive which she has contrived (principally through the means of said house and dinners) to establish with a host of authors, booksellers, and publishers, and above all with journalists. Her name is eternally before the public;

---

[5] [Lady Blessington had a good deal more talent and reading than Mr. Greville gives her credit for. She was well read in the best English authors, and even in translations of the classics; but the talent to which she owed her success in society was her incomparable tact and skill in drawing out the best qualities of her guests. What Mr. Greville terms her vulgarity might be more charitably described as her Irish cordiality and *bonhomie*. I have no doubt that her 'Conversations with Lord Byron' were entirely written by herself. It is true that, writing, as she did, to make money, many of her other books were exceedingly worthless.]

she produces those gorgeous inanities, called 'Books of Beauty,' and other trashy things of the same description, to get up which all the fashion and beauty, the taste and talent, of London are laid under contribution. And so, by all this puffing and stuffing, and untiring industry, and practising on the vanity of some, and the good-nature of others, the end is attained; and she takes her place confidently and complacently as one of the literary celebrities of her day.

March 2nd. The whole town has been engrossed for some days with a scandalous story at Court, and although of course great exaggerations and falsehoods are grafted upon the real case, and it is not easy to ascertain what and how much is true, enough is known and indubitable, to show that it is a very discreditable transaction. It appears that Lady Flora Hastings, the Duchess of Kent's lady, has been accused of being with child. It was at first whispered about, and at last swelled into a report, and finally into a charge. With whom it originated is not clear; but the Queen appears to have been apprised of the rumour, and so far to have entered into it as to sanction an intimation to the lady that she must not appear at Court till she could clear herself of the imputation. Medical examination was either demanded by her or submitted to, and the result was satisfactory to the virtue of the accused damsel. Then naturally exploded the just indignation of insulted honour. Her brother, Lord Hastings, came up to town, saw Melbourne, who is said to have endeavoured to smother the affair, and to have tried to persuade Lord Hastings to do so; but he was not at all so inclined, and if he had been, it was too late, as all the world had begun to talk of it, and he demanded and obtained an audience of the Queen. I abstain from noticing the various reports of what this or that person did or said, for the truth of which I could not vouch; but it is certain that the Court is plunged in shame and mortification at the exposure, that the palace is full of bickerings and heart-burnings, while the whole proceeding is looked upon by society at large as to the last degree disgusting and disgraceful. It is really an exemplification of the saying, that 'les Rois et les Valets' are made of the refuse clay of creation, for though such things sometimes happen in the servants' hall, and housekeepers charge still-room and kitchen-maids with frailty, they are unprecedented and un-heard of in good society, and among people in high or even in respectable stations. It is inconceivable how Melbourne can have permitted this disgraceful and mischievous scandal, which can-not fail to lower the character of the Court in the eyes of the world. There may be objections to Melbourne's extraordinary domiciliation in the palace; but the compensation ought to be found in his good sense and experience preventing the possibility of such transactions and *tracasseries* as these.

March 8th. I went last night to the first representation of Bulwer's play 'Richelieu:' a fine play, admirably got up, and very well acted by Macready, except the last scene, the conception of which was altogether bad. He turned Richelieu into an exag-gerated Sixtus V., who completely lost sight of his dignity, and swaggered about the stage, taunting his foes, and hugging his friends with an exultation quite unbecoming and out of char-acter. With this exception it was a fine performance; the success was unbounded, and the audience transported. After Macready had been called on, they found out Bulwer, who was in a small private box next the one I was in with Lady Blessington and D'Orsay, and were vociferous for his appearance to receive their applause. After a long delay, he bowed two or three times, and instantly retreated. Directly after he came into our box, looking very serious and rather agitated; while Lady Blessington burst into floods of tears at his success, which was certainly very bril-liant.

March 12th. The affair of Lady Flora Hastings at the Palace excites greater interest than any matter of a public and political character. It is still unsettled, for Lord Hastings wants to make a fresh stir about it, probably thinking that if there is to be pub-licity the more of it the better. The Duke of Wellington wrote a capital letter to the Duchess of Kent, advising conciliation and quiet.

April 21st. [*John Russell*] afterwards told me a great deal about the Hastings affair, which has been rendered much worse and more mischievous by the publication of the correspondence between Lady Hastings and Melbourne (by the former). The letters are very bad productions on both sides; the Lady's ill written, intemperate and rhapsodical, the Minister's rude and unbecoming. The whole affair has done incredible harm, and has played the devil with the Queen's popularity and cast dreadful odium and discredit on the Court, especially in the country where a thousand exaggerated reports are rife. It is next to impossible to repair the mischief because so much mystery is still thrown over the transaction and its origin. The public takes it up (as it took Queen Caroline) on the principle of favoring an injured person, and one who appears to have obtained no reparation for the injuries inflicted on her. Since Lord Harewood came to town he has taken it up on account of his daughter Lady Portman, and he went to the Duke of Wellington, to whose wisdom and integrity all have recourse in seasons of difficulty. The truth is it is to take the Duke *par son foible,* for he likes being consulted and being mixed up in *messes;* but upon this occasion besides the excitement of the tracasserie he is actuated by higher and graver considerations, and he sees and deplores all the evils which result from this miserable affair and its disgraceful publicity. Lord Portman went to him and entreated him to interpose to set matters straight, and he at once said that he would do anything; he would see Melbourne, or the Queen, or the Duchess of Kent, and do anything in his power to suppress the scandal. He told Lord Harewood that he was cognisant of everything that had occurred, and that both his daughter and Lady Tavistock had done exactly what they ought—their duty neither more nor less—and that his opinion might be told to everybody. Lord Portman went to Melbourne yesterday and entreated him to see the Duke. 'Why, damn it,' said Melbourne, 'I can't see him now, I am shaving and then I am going to a Cabinet.' However Lord Portman insisted, and while Melbourne finished 'questa barba maledetta' he went and fetched the Duke. It appears that in the first instance the affair would have blown over, and that

Lady Flora was well disposed to be satisfied, and even thanked
Lady Portman cordially for her conduct, if it had not been for
Conroy, who was the grand mover of all the subsequent hubbub.
He it was who incited the Duchess and Lady Flora to jeter feu et
flamme; and the young Lady is said to have acted with great
duplicity, for while she was affecting amicable feelings at the
Palace and to have made it up with everybody, she was writing
to her Uncle those statements which he afterwards published,
and preparing for the explosion which eventually took place.
Besides being a miserable subject, full of disgrace and evil, it
is very unsatisfactory to discuss, because the whole truth is still
concealed and no judgment can be fairly pronounced upon the
conduct of any of the parties concerned. Melbourne appears to
blame for not having quashed it in the first instance; then it is
said if all were known Melbourne would not appear so blamable.
But the public will not brook delay and it will rush to an opinion.
If it have not all the facts it forms it on those it has, and if therefore all the truth can't be told those who know it and conceal it
(no matter what their motives) must abide by the consequences.

May 10*th.* I left town on Monday, having in the morning
seen Le Marchant, who knows better than anybody the numbers and details of divisions; and he told me that they should
have a majority of twenty: little, therefore, was I prepared to
hear on Tuesday morning that they had been left with only a
majority of five. It was not till they were in the House of Commons that they were aware of the defections, and of the probability of a close division, if not of a defeat. About ten of the Radicals voted against them, and ten or a dozen stayed away; six
of the Tories voted with Government, but the balance was quite
enough to reduce the old majority to an equality. On Tuesday
the Cabinet met, and resolved to resign. The Queen had not been
prepared for this catastrophe and was completely upset by it.
Her agitation and grief were very great. In her interview with
Lord John Russell she was all the time dissolved in tears; and
she dined in her own room, and never appeared on the Tuesday
evening. Melbourne advised her to send for the Duke, and on

Wednesday morning she sent for him. By this time she had re-
gained her calmness and self-possession. She told him that she
was very sorry for what had occurred, and for having to part
with her Ministers, particularly Lord Melbourne, for whom she
felt the warmest regard, and who had acted an almost parental
part towards her. The Duke was excessively pleased with her
behaviour and with her frankness. He told her that his age and
his deafness incapacitated him from serving her as efficiently as
he could desire, and that the leader of the House of Commons
ought to be her Prime Minister, and he advised her to send for
Peel. She said, 'Will you desire him to come to me?' He told her
that he would do anything; but, he thought, under the circumstances, it would be better that she should write to him herself.
She said she would, but begged him to go and announce to Peel
that he might expect her letter. This the Duke did, and when
Peel received it, he went to the Palace (in full dress according
to etiquette), and received her commands to form a Government. She received him (though she dislikes him) extremely
well, and he was perfectly satisfied.

While, however, there was yesterday this uncertainty and agitation in the Whig camp, and the Tories were waiting in perfect
security for the tranquil arrangement of the new Government, a
storm suddenly arose, which threatens to scatter to the winds
the new combinations, and the ultimate effects of which it is
impossible for anybody to foresee. The Queen insisted upon
keeping the ladies of her household, and Peel objected, but without shaking her determination. He begged her to see the Duke
of Wellington, and she agreed to see the Duke and him together.
He had, however, before this gone to the Palace with Lord Ashley, whom he had taken with him, fancying that because he had
been in the habit of seeing a great deal of the Queen, he might
have some influence with her—a notion altogether preposterous,
and exhibiting the deficiency of Peel in worldly dexterity and
tact, and in knowledge of character. Ashley made no impression
on the Queen. When the Duke and Peel saw her, and endeavoured to persuade her to yield this point, they found her firm

and immoveable, and not only resolved not to give way, but prepared with answers to all they said, and arguments in support of her determination. They told her that she must consider her *Ladies* in the same light as *Lords:* she said, 'No, I have Lords besides, and these I give up to you.' And when they still pressed her, she said, 'Now suppose the case had been reversed, that you had been in office when I had come to the Throne, and that Lord Melbourne would not have required this sacrifice of me.' Finding that she would not give way, Peel informed her that under these circumstances he must consult his friends; and a meeting took place at his house yesterday afternoon.

In the meantime the old Ministers were apprised of the difficulty that had occurred, and Lord John Russell, who knew that there was a meeting at Peel's to consider what was to be done, entreated Melbourne, if the thing was broken off upon this difficulty, not to give any advice, but to call the Cabinet and have a general consultation. At nine in the evening he was summoned to a Cabinet at Melbourne's house, and from this he inferred that negotiations with Peel had closed. The ministers were collected from all quarters: (Hobhouse from dinner at Wilton's, Morpeth from the opera), and Melbourne laid before them a letter from the Queen,[6] written in a bitter spirit, and in a strain such as Elizabeth might have used. She said, 'Do not fear that I was not calm and composed. They wanted to deprive me of my Ladies, and I suppose they would deprive me next of my dresses and my housemaids; they wished to treat me like a girl, but I will show them that I am Queen of England!' They consulted, and a suggestion was thrown out that Lady Normanby (and some other I think) should resign. This was overruled, as was a proposition of John Russell's, that the Queen should require from Peel a precise statement of the extent of his demands. The end was, that a letter was composed for her, in which she simply declined to place the Ladies of her household at Peel's discretion. This was sent yesterday morning; when Peel wrote an answer resigning

[6] [Melbourne, it appears, from his own statement in the House of Lords, was sent for at six o'clock on Thursday.]

his commission into Her Majesty's hands; but recapitulating everything that had passed. When the difficulty first arose, Peel
asked her to see the Duke; she acquiesced; he fetched him, and
the Duke was with her alone. The Duke it was who argued *the
principle* with her—Peel had touched upon its application.

In the meantime Lord Melbourne and Lord John Russell went
to the Queen, who told them her whole story. I met the latter
coming from her; he said, 'I have just been for an hour with the
Queen; she told me her story, and ended by saying, 'I have stood
by you, you must now stand by me.' They thought her case a
good one, and resolved to stand by her. Such was the state of
things and such the case as reported to me by several members
of the Whig party yesterday morning, and my impression was
that Peel had been unreasonable in his demands and impolitic
in breaking off the negotiation on such grounds. Nevertheless
I had some misgivings, because I thought the Duke of Wellington unlikely to concur in any proceeding harsh towards the
Queen, or ill-considered in a political sense; but the assertion
was at the same time so positive, that Peel had required the dismissal of *all* the ladies, and the Tories defended instead of deny-
ing this, that I did not doubt the fact to have been so; and
moreover I was told that Peel's behaviour had created a strong
sentiment of dislike towards him in the Queen, and from her
representations and the language of her letter it was clear the
impression on her mind was that no consideration was intended
to be shown to her feelings and wishes, but, on the contrary, that
they meant to abuse their power to the utmost. At the ball last
night I put the question directly to Lord Normanby and Ben
Stanley, and they both declared that the Queen's understanding
was that the demand for power to dismiss the Ladies was unqualified by any intimation of an intention not to exercise that
power to the utmost extent; that she believed they were *all* to
be taken from her, and under this impression she had sent her
ultimatum by which the whole thing was terminated. But I had
afterwards a conversation with Lord Wharncliffe, who gave me
an account of all that had passed, placed the matter in a very

different light, and proved beyond a doubt that there was no lack of deference and consideration on the part of Peel, but, on the contrary, the clearest indication of an intention and desire to consult her wishes and feelings in every respect, and that, instead of a sweeping demand for the dismissal of *all* her Ladies, he had approached that subject with delicacy and caution, and merely suggested the expediency of some partial changes, for reasons (especially when taken with other things) by no means insufficient. So little disposition was there on the part of Peel to regard her with distrust or to fetter her social habits, that when she said, 'You must not expect me to give up the society of Lord Melbourne,' he replied that 'Nothing could be further from his thoughts than to interfere with Her Majesty's society in any way, or to object to her receiving Lord Melbourne as she pleased, and that he should always feel perfectly secure in the honour of Lord Melbourne, that he would not avail himself improperly of his intercourse with her.' When she said that she should like to have Lord Liverpool about her, he immediately acquiesced, and proposed that he should be Lord Steward, and he suggested certain other persons, whom he said he proposed because he believed they were personally agreeable to her; but when he began to talk of 'some modification of the Ladies of her household,' she stopped him at once, and declared she would not part with any of them. Thenceforward this became the whole matter in dispute; but there had been some circumstances even in the first interview which Peel and the Duke regarded as ominous and indicative of her having been primed as to the part she should play. The principal of these was an intimation of her desire that there should be *no dissolution of Parliament.* This surprised Peel very much, but he only replied that it was impossible for him to come to any determination on that point, as he might be beaten on one of the first divisions, in which case it would be inevitable. It was indeed the fact of his taking the Government with a *minority* in the House of Commons which was his principal argument for desiring the power of dismissing the Ladies, or rather of changing the household, that he might not, he said, give to the world the spectacle of a Court entirely hostile to him, consisting of ladies whose husbands were his strongest political opponents, thereby creating an impression that the confidence of the Crown was bestowed on his enemies rather than on himself. In the Duke's first interview with the Queen, he had entreated her to place her whole confidence in Peel, and had then said that, though some changes might be necessary in her household, she would find him in all the arrangements anxious to meet her wishes and consult her feelings. Notwithstanding her assurance to Melbourne that she was calm, she was greatly excited, though still preserving a becoming dignity in her outward behaviour.

June 14th. After the death of George II someone asked if the Princess Emily, whose virtue was not thought immaculate, was to have Guards. George Selwyn said, "One every now and then."

June 24th. The continuation of the violent and libellous articles in the *Morning Post* about Lady Flora Hastings, and the unappeased wrath of Hastings, again stirred the question of explanations and apologies; and now Brougham mixed himself up in it as the Adviser of Hastings with whom he has struck up a mighty friendship, and he has been wonderfully zealous and active in the business. Lady Hastings, it seems, has never got over the letter which Melbourne wrote to her, and her son is indignant both at that letter and at the unredressed wrong to his sister. However Brougham thought he would be satisfied if Melbourne would make some apology to Lady Hastings, and to effect this he began to work. After conferring with Duncannon about it he went to the Duke, and the Duke agreed with him that Melbourne might and ought to do this, and he undertook to speak to him about it. Accordingly Melbourne went to Apsley House by appointment where they talked it over, but Melbourne convinced the Duke that it would be better not to write an apology or explanation to Lady Hastings, though what his arguments were I do not know. So the matter stands, and in the meantime they are in a great fright lest Lady Flora should die; because she is very ill, and if she should die the public will certainly hold an inquest on her body and bring in a verdict of wilful murder against Buckingham Palace. As if one scandal of this sort was not enough there has been another, not so serious but unbecoming and disreputable, concerning the Duchess of Montrose and Lady Sarah Ingestre, who were said to have hissed the Queen from Erroll's stand at Ascot as Her Majesty drove up the course. This story was rife in London, and the Duchess, when she found it so, insisted upon vindicating herself; and besides appealing to Lady Litchfield who was in the stand, went to Buckingham House and sent for Uxbridge to complain, and through him to ask for an audience of the Queen. The Queen declined seeing her, and the Duke of Montrose applied (through Melbourne) for one for himself; but this affair has ended by a gracious reception of the Ladies at the drawing-room, and an assurance from Melbourne that the Queen never had believed a word of the story, and he hoped therefore that the Duke of Montrose would not press for an audience. The fact however, in spite of the indignant denial of the Ladies, is true. These two foolish vulgar women (for such they are) at a moment of great excitement (for it was shortly after the grand scompiglio), did by some not decorous or feminine noises testify their dislike or contempt, not probably of the Queen particularly but of the general contents of the procession, and this was so openly even ostentatiously done that it could not escape the notice of the other women in the stand, more than one of whom—and one (Duchess of Beaufort) a Tory—told me. It is a miserable matter, but it does harm. The Queen is to blame to listen to such tales, and to allow anybody to tell her them, whether true or false. It would be more dignified to treat such tittle-tattle with contempt, and discourage its being told to her at all.

July 7th.   Came to town yesterday from Basingstoke by railroad, found that Lady Flora Hastings was dead, and a great majority in the House of Lords against the Education, the Bishop of London having made an extraordinary fine speech. Lady Flora said to have died of dropsy in the womb, which also accounts for her appearance of pregnancy. She suffered dreadfully in mind and body, the latter from the exertions she was compelled to

make in going about, and the former from being such an object
of attention and curiosity, and still more because every sort of
excitement was kept up in and around her by the faction who
made an instrument of her.

July 19th. There have been angry debates in the Lords about
the Birmingham riots, chiefly remarkable for the excitement, so
unlike his usual manner, exhibited by the Duke of Wellington,
who assailed the Government with a fierceness which betrayed
him into much exaggeration and some injustice. Lord Tavistock,
who, although a partisan, is a fair one, and who has a great esteem and respect for the Duke, told me that he had seen and
heard him with great pain, and that his whole tone was alarmingly indicative of a decay of mental power. This is not the first
time that such a suspicion has been excited: George Villiers told
me, soon after he came over, how much struck he had been with
the change he observed in him, and from whatever cause, he is
become in speaking much more indistinct and embarrassed, continually repeating and not always intelligible, but his speeches,
when reported, present much the same appearance, and the sense
and soundness (when the reporters have lopped off the redun-
dancies and trimmed them according to their fashion) seem to
be unimpaired. It is, however, a serious and melancholy thing
to contemplate the possibly approaching decay of that great
mind, and I find he always contemplates it himself, his mother's
mind having failed some years before her death. It will be sad
if, after exploits as brilliant as Marlborough's, and a career far
more important, useful, and honourable, he should be destined
for an end like Marlborough's, and it is devoutly to be hoped
that his eyes may be closed in death before 'streams of dotage'
shall begin to flow from them. The Tories, with whom nothing
goes down but violence, were delighted with his angry vein,
and see proofs of vigour in what his opponents consider as evidence of decay; his bodily health is wonderfully good, which is
perhaps rather alarming than reassuring as to the safety of his
mind.

August 15th. For a long time past Tavistock has been worried to death by the attacks on his wife in the *Morning Post* about her share in the affair of Lady Flora Hastings, and has over and over again attempted to get some sort of explanation made in her behalf in Parliament or elsewhere; but for one reason or another nothing was ever said or done. At length the matter seemed to have dropt, when about a week ago it broke out afresh, by the publication of Lady Flora's original letter to Mr. Hamilton Fitzgerald, accompanied by the usual tirade of the *Morning Post*. This might have been passed over, as a hundred such publications had been, but the following day the matter was taken up by the *Morning Chronicle;* and in an apologetical article in reply to the *Morning Post* it thought fit to admit that Ladies Tavistock and Portman had been the persons who had first told the Queen of Lady Flora's supposed pregnancy, and then went on to express all the sorrow and contrition they had felt for the mistake they had made. This defence, which was tantamount to a confession of guilt with extenuating circumstances, naturally excited fresh and stronger annoyance and resentment in Tavistock's mind, which were stimulated by a letter from Brougham to whom he wrote (as well as to me) on the subject. Brougham, who hates the Queen cordially and would gladly increase the prejudice against her, urged upon Tavistock the duty of defending the character of his wife without any regard to the consequences as they might affect the Queen, and went on to say that unless she dismissed Baroness Lehzen she would be exposed to increased odium. This letter, together with his own reflections and my advice that he should without delay do something, determined him to write a letter containing an explanation of Lady Tavistock's share in the transaction, and stating how she had communicated with Melbourne but not with Her Majesty. This letter he sent to me desiring it might be inserted in the *Morning Chronicle* of the day; but as soon as I had read it I saw that it would not do, not being calculated to set Lady Tavistock's conduct in a fair point of view, but on the contrary to leave it exposed to more obloquy than before, and the introduction of Melbourne's name would have embarrassed without at all satisfactorily explaining the matter, and have opened a new and extensive field of discussion.

I resolved therefore not to publish this letter; but as I had full power to alter it I doubted whether I should send an altered version of it *immediately* as his, or whether I should refer again to him and take on myself the responsibility of the delay. Not chusing however to act entirely on my own judgement I resolved to consult the Duke of Wellington, who had all along been in communication with Tavistock on this subject, and who was thoroughly acquainted with all its details. Accordingly I went to Apsley House, told the Duke what had passed and the article that had appeared in the *Chronicle* (which he had never seen), and then read Tavistock's proposed letter to him. He at once said that this letter ought not to be published; that no names should be mentioned; above all that care should be taken to say nothing which might implicate the Queen or excite any fresh prejudice against *her—that* being the most essential evil to guard against; and that in whatever Tavistock might think it necessary to say, he should confine himself to generalities and avoid all details. In all this I concurred, and I showed him the amendment I had sketched to Tavistock's letter, of which (after suggesting some alterations) he approved. But not chusing to publish a letter as *Tavistock's* so different from that which he had written, I returned all the papers to him at Buxton, and determined to take on myself the responsibility of the delay. But this morning I have heard from him that in full confidence of the publication of his letter this morning he had written to Melbourne to announce it, and to give his reasons for not having previously notified to him his intention.

I was with the Duke of Wellington for above two hours, in the course of which he entered into all the details of this affair and of the part he had been called upon to act in it; and told me besides many particulars of his interviews with the Queen at the time of the Ministerial changes, together with various other things, all more or less interesting, and rendered particularly so by his quaint natural and lively style of narration, together with the certainty that every syllable was strictly true. In the Hastings affair he has been consulted or appealed to by all parties, and in communication with the Duchess of Kent, Conroy, the Queen, the Ministers and Lord Hastings. The Duchess of Kent first sent for him, told him her story and showed him all the papers—for the details of Lady Flora's ailments and the opinion of the Doctor were all committed to paper. His advice was to hush the matter up, on every account to prevent the story going out of the four walls of the Palace—'it is now between these four walls; if they were to tumble down it would be for ever buried in the ruins— so let it be.' He thinks it would have been hushed up and that all the mischief would have been avoided, if after the explanations and reconciliations more pains had been taken to conciliate the Duchess of Kent; but that the omission in this respect and the importunities of Conroy, and his influence over the Duchess and Lady Flora kept bad feelings alive, and led to the original letter to Mr. Hamilton Fitzgerald, which the Duke says was the primary cause of the subsequent exposure. Against the removal of the Doctor the Duke always protested, because he could not be dismissed as a *punishment* without a previous inquiry, and this inquiry would have been attended with the most painful results to all parties. There were no doubt circumstances which, if not sufficient to justify the suspicions that were raised, at least were to render them very natural; but they never were intended to assume the shape of a serious charge, and in the first instance were rather matter of joke and loose talk. Not only did Lady Flora's shape exhibit all the appearances of pregnancy, both as to its size and its gradual increase, but there was the constitutional change usually attending that state; and they knew that she and Conroy had travelled up from Scotland together in a post chaise, which, coupled with his familiar habits in the Duchess's apartments and certain jokes which had been previously current about her, created very easily the unfortunate impression that had prevailed. The first intimation to Lady Flora was from the Doctor, who told her the Ladies of the Palace said she was secretly married, or at all events if she was not that she ought to be. The Duke thought that the thing might have been suppressed then as well as at the subsequent period of Melbourne's correspondence with Lady Hastings, if there had been judicious management and greater efforts at conciliation. The Duchess of

Kent consulted the Duke on every occasion and in every step of
the affair; and he appears uniformly to have given the soundest
and honestest advice, and to have kept his eyes steadfastly fixed
on the two great objects of saving the character of the Queen,
and putting her and her mother upon decently amicable terms.
This latter seems to have been all along next to impossible, for
the Queen has neither a particle of affection nor of respect for
her Mother, and is either so thoughtless or so careless of consequences that she desires no better than that the Duchess should
quit the Palace, and take up her abode elsewhere. Against this
separation the Duke strenuously worked, and he continually enforced the expediency of harmony, mutual forbearance and conciliation. One of the people with whom the Duke had most
communication was the Speaker (Abercrombie), who was much
mixed up in it, and consulted by the Duchess; and he was so
struck with the sentiments expressed by the Duke in conversation
with him, that he entreated him to write the substance of what
he had said to the Duchess. He did so, and his letter, together
with another to the same effect and for the same end, was communicated (by the Duke's desire) to the Queen, and by the
Queen to the Cabinet. The Queen then wrote a very kind letter
to the Duchess, in which she said that if she had made any sacrifice out of regard to her, she thanked her most warmly for what
she had done. This letter, the Duke told the Duchess, ought to
satisfy her, but she said it was not in the Queen's own hand-
writing, though the Duke says it certainly was. (I remember
hearing of this letter and that the idea it was not written by herself was much commented on.) In the course of his conversation
with the Duchess, and when urging her to resume her place in
the Court circle (from which she had absented herself) and to
adopt a good-humoured and conciliatory tone generally, she said,
'But what am I to do if Lord Melbourne comes up to me?'—'Do?
Why, receive him with civility and cordiality. He is your daughter's Prime Minister, and as such you are bound to treat him in
this manner; and besides, why should you not? What reason can
you have for doing otherwise?'—'O, I don't approve of the way
in which he comes here.'—'Nonsense—all stuff and nonsense—

don't tell me of his coming here. He is quite right to come as he does, and if I found any fault, it would be that he is not here enough. Now I'll tell you what I should have done if I had been Minister when the Queen came to the throne—I would have instantly taken up my abode at Kensington Palace, and when she removed to Buckingham Palace, I would have had an apartment there; and if I could not have had one I would have taken a lodging as near the Palace as I could find one, in order that I might have been every day and every hour in the day at hand to assist and advise her upon every possible occasion and in every matter in which she might require my advice. Lord Melbourne has done nothing but his duty, and I tell you that if I had been in his place I should not only have done the same, but have done more than he has done.'—'Well,' said she, 'I must say you are a just man—but what must I do if she asks me to shake hands with Letzen?'—'Do? Why, take her in your arms and kiss her.' Here the Duchess burst out laughing, in which the Duke joined, when he said, 'I don't mean you are to take *Letzen* in your arms and kiss *her*, but the Queen. She is your daughter, and this is the way you must treat her, and be civil to Lord Melbourne, and Letzen and all the persons in attendance upon her.'

It was the Duke, and he alone, who got Conroy to resign and leave the country; and this he did by cajoling and flattering Conroy himself, and representing to him that his conduct in retiring would not only be gratifying to the Duchess's family but be honorable to himself, and appreciated by the public; and by honied words like these he prevailed on him at last to go. The primary motive of his retirement was, however, the unanimous opposition which he met with from the Coburg family; all the Duchess's brothers,[7] her son,[8] her daughter and son-in-law,[9] all joined with

[7] The three brothers were: Ernest, Duke of Saxe-Coburg (1784–1844), eldest brother of the Duchess of Kent and father of Prince Albert; Prince Ferdinand of Saxe-Coburg (1785–1851); and Leopold I, King of the Belgians.
[8] Charles Frederick, Prince of Leiningen (1804–56); only son of the Duchess of Kent by her first husband, the Prince of Leiningen; married Maria, Countess of Klebelsberg, 1829.
[9] Princess Feodora, only daughter of the Duchess of Kent by the Prince of Leiningen; married Ernest, Prince of Hohenlohe (1794–1860), in 1828.

the Queen and against Conroy, and on one occasion the Duke was obliged to interfere in his and her defence. They had a common sitting-room at the Palace in the Dss.'s apartments, and they complained that Conroy used insolently to come and sit there, and they asked the Duke whether it was not fit that he should be formally warned off. But the Duke said that this could not be; the Duchess was a great Princess, independent, and having an undoubted right to select her own servants and attendants, with whom nobody could with decency interfere; and to prohibit her officer from entering her apartments would be an outrage to her. But the Duchess told the Duke that the whole family had insisted upon her never taking any step but by his advice, and consulting him on all occasions, which she had engaged to do. They wanted her to appoint a successor to Conroy, but the Duke advised her not, and to make some arrangement with her other gentlemen so that she should always (take) one of them when necessary; but not to put anybody in Conroy's place till she took up her abode elsewhere and formed an establishment. On which she desired to have this opinion in writing, and he accordingly gave it her—so necessary did she think it to have proofs to show to her family of having been governed by the Duke's advice. The cause of the Queen's alienation from the Duchess and hatred of Conroy, the Duke said was unquestionably owing to her having witnessed some familiarities between them. What she had seen she repeated to the Baroness Spaeth, and Spaeth not only did not hold her tongue, but (he thinks) remonstrated with the Duchess herself on the subject. The consequence was that they got rid of Spaeth, and they would have got rid of Letzen too if they had been able; but Letzen, who knew very well what was going on, was prudent enough not to commit herself, and she was besides powerfully protected by George IV and William IV so that they did not dare to attempt to expel her.

The ample discussion we had upon these matters led naturally to the question of the Queen's character and capacity, and I asked him what he thought of it. He said as far as he had seen that she expressed herself well, but he did not appear to be impressed with a very positive and high opinion of her abilities. In the communications which took place about the changes she had been very civil and gracious to him, but rather irritable particularly the second day. I said she detested Peel. He said that he must say he had never seen Peel so gentle and conciliatory in his manner as he was to her, and that there was nothing at which she ought to have taken umbrage. At his first interview he implored her to put her whole confidence in Peel, and above all to make no conditions; that he could not come in upon conditions. 'But what am I to do if he proposes appointments that are disagreeable to me?'—'Fight upon the details as much as you please, but make no conditions as to principles, and depend upon it, there will be every disposition to consult your wishes and feelings in every respect. It is especially necessary and desirable in your peculiar situation that this should be done, and you will find such to be his anxious desire and intention.' She said 'You must promise me to be Secretary of State for Foreign affairs.' But he represented to her that it was impossible he could make any such promise; and that it would never do to put the formation of a Government into Peel's hands, and then to inform him that she and the Duke of Wellington had settled between them that he (the Duke) should have a particular office. She owned this was true and did not insist.

In the grand discussion (on Thursday), it was after expressing his desire that the appointments in the household should be personally agreeable to herself, and after her own suggestion of Lord Liverpool, that Peel proceeded to say it was his wish that the changes which might be necessary in the female part of the household should be governed by the same principle—meaning (the Duke said) that she should herself express her own wishes as to who should retire, and the persons by whom they should be replaced. But she stopt him at once by saying 'She did not mean *any* of her Ladies to be changed.' When the Duke arrived at the Palace, after the rupture was begun, he said on entering 'Well, I am very sorry to find there is a difficulty.'—To which she instantly replied with a naïveté so very girlish, 'Oh, *he* began it and not

me.' The Duke argued the point with her, and tried to persuade
her that nothing had been proposed to her but what the circumstances of the case rendered necessary, and employed all the
arguments which have been repeatedly urged on the subject, to
which she replied: 'But I thought you said that my situation demanded peculiar consideration, and that my feelings and wishes
were entitled to especial regard.' He said: 'So I did say, Madam,
and to-day I say so ten times more, and I told your Majesty that
you might depend upon it, every regard and attention would be
(as it ought to be) shown to your Majesty's wishes, but I warned
you against any contest upon principles, and told you that however you might make any objections you pleased upon details, it
was impossible for you without the creation of insuperable difficulties to make any upon principles.' When we talked about the
ladies, she said with some marks of irritation: 'It is offensive to
me to suppose that I talk to any of my ladies upon public affairs.'
He said: 'I know you do not. I am quite certain you do not, but
the public does not know this, and it is on account of the impression necessarily to be produced on the public mind, and not on
account of any doubt of your Majesty's refraining from talking
politics with your ladies, that the proposal is made to you.'

London, November 8th. Nothing has excited so much interest
as the hoax of Brougham's pretended death,[10] which was generally believed for twenty-four hours, and the report elicited a
host of criticisms and panegyrics on his life and character, for
the most part flattering, except that in the 'Times,' which was
very able but very severe, and not less severe than true. As soon
as it was discovered that he was not dead, the liveliest indignation was testified at the joke that had been played off, and the

---

[10] [A letter from Brougham purporting to be from Mr. Shafto was received by Mr. Alfred Montgomery, which contained the particulars of Lord
Brougham's death by a carriage accident. Mr. Montgomery brought the letter
to Lady Blessington's at Gore House, where I happened to be, and I confess
we were all taken in by the hoax. Montgomery went off in a post-chaise to
break the news to Lord Wellesley at Fernhill; and meeting Lord Alfred
Paget in Windsor Park, he sent the news to the Castle. The trick was kept
up for twenty-four hours, but the next day I received a note from Brougham
himself, full of his usual spirits and vitality.—H. R.]

utmost anxiety to discover its origin. General suspicion immediately fixed itself on Brougham himself, who, finding the bad impression produced, hastened to remove it by a vehement but indirect denial of having had any share in, or knowledge of, the hoax. But so little reliance is placed upon his word, that everybody laughs at his denials, and hardly anybody has a shadow of a doubt that he was himself at the bottom of it. He has taken the trouble to write to all sorts of people, old friends and new, to exonerate himself from the charge; but never was trouble more thrown away. D'Orsay says that he carefully compared the (supposed) letter of Shafto with one of Brougham's to him, and that they were evidently written by the same hand. The paper, with all its marks, was the same, together with various other minute resemblances, leaving no doubt of the fact.

November 13th. At Holland House for three days last week. Lord Holland told many stories of Lord Chatham, some of which I had heard before, and some not. His stories are always excellent, and excellently told, and those who have heard them before can very well bear to hear them again. [*One*] of his sayings was in the House of Lords, when, on I forget what question, he was unsupported: 'My Lords, I stand like our First Parents—alone, naked, but not ashamed.' This was fine. Lord Holland said there was nothing like real oratory in Parliament before the American war.

He had received several letters from Brougham in a most strange, incoherent style, avowedly for the purpose of thanking Lady Holland for the interest he heard she had shown about him when his death was reported, and at the same time to explain that he had no hand in the report, which he did with the utmost solemnity of asseveration[11].

November 13th. I had much talk with Lady Cowper about the Court. She lamented the obstinate character of the Queen, from which she thought that hereafter great evils might be apprehended. She said she did not think anything would induce the

---

[11] [It was well known, eventually, that the hoax was entirely his own, and the letter dictated by himself.]

Queen to give way upon the point on which the former difference arose. It is very revolting to hear of a girl of 19 albeit Queen, pronouncing an opinion upon the conduct of the Duke of Wellington and deciding what it was his duty to do, and that in a matter personal to herself. It is the worst trait of her character I have met with, because it is arrogant, vain and ungrateful. As to the matter itself I hope some way will be found of preventing any future collision upon it, but if not, she will have to learn the disagreeable lesson that her opinion does not make right, nor her volition law.

November 23rd. At Wolbeding for three days. Then news came of the Duke's illness, which, though it turned out to be exaggerated, will, I fear, prove to have given him a shake. The Council being summoned to declare the Queen's marriage to-day, I have come up to town for it, and am just returned from the declaration, which took place in the lower apartments of the palace. About eighty Privy Councillors present, all who were within call having attended. Peel, Lyndhurst, and the Duke. The Duke arrived last night for the purpose; he looked very old, very feeble, and decrepit. I thought a great change was observable in him, but he was cheerful as usual, and evidently tried to make the best of it. The Queen had sent in the morning to enquire after him, and the answer was, 'He had had a restless night.' All the Privy Councillors seated themselves, when the folding-doors were thrown open, and the Queen came in, attired in a plain morning-gown, but wearing a bracelet containing Prince Albert's picture. She read the declaration in a clear, sonorous, sweet-toned voice, but her hands trembled so excessively that I wonder she was able to read the paper which she held. Lord Lansdowne made a little speech, asking her permission to have the declaration made public. She bowed assent, placed the paper in his hands, and then retired.

November 26th. The Queen wrote to all her family and announced her marriage to them. When she saw the Duchess of Gloucester in town, and told her she was to make her declaration the next day, the Duchess asked her if it was not a nervous thing to do. She said, 'Yes; but I did a much more nervous thing a little while ago.' 'What was that?' 'I proposed to Prince Albert.'

The Duke of Cambridge hunted Brougham round the room, saying, 'Oh, by God, you wrote the letter; by God, you did it yourself.'

December 14th. I was at Oatlands a fortnight ago, where I met Croker—not overbearing, and rather agreeable. He said he dined and passed the evening *tête-à-tête* with the Duke of Wellington (then Sir Arthur Wellesley) before his departure for Portugal to take the command of the army. He was then Irish Secretary, and had committed to Croker's management the bills he had to carry through Parliament. After dinner he was very thoughtful, and did not speak. Croker said, 'Sir Arthur, you don't talk; what is it you are thinking about?' He said, 'Of the French. I have never seen them; they have beaten all Europe. I think I shall beat them, but I can't help thinking about them.'

J *anuary 26th,* 1840. Everybody (except those who have an interest in defending it) thinks the allowance proposed for Prince Albert very exorbitant: 50,000*l.* a year given for pocket money is quite monstrous, and it would have been prudent to propose a more moderate grant for the sake of his popularity. Prince George of Denmark had 50,000*l.* a year (as it is said), but the Queen gave it him, and he had a household four times more numerous than is intended for Prince Albert.

January 29th. On Monday night Government were beaten by 104 on the question of reducing the Prince's allowance from 50,-000*l.* to 30,000*l.* a year. They knew they should be beaten, but nevertheless John Russell would go doggedly on and encounter this mortifying defeat, instead of giving way with the best grace he could. He lost his temper, and flung dirt at Peel, like a sulky boy flinging rotten eggs; in short, exposed himself sadly.

February 13th. The wedding on Monday went off tolerably

well.[12] The week before was fine, and Albert drove about the town with a mob shouting at his heels. Tuesday, Wednesday, and to-day, all beautiful days; but Monday, as if by a malignant influence, was a dreadful day—torrents of rain, and violent gusts of wind. Nevertheless a countless multitude thronged the park, and was scattered over the town. I never beheld such a congregation as there was, in spite of the weather. The Queen proceeded in state from Buckingham House to St. James's without any cheering, but then it was raining enough to damp warmer loyalty than that of a London mob. The procession in the Palace was pretty enough by all accounts, and she went through the ceremony with much grace and propriety, not without emotion, though sufficiently subdued, and her manner to her family was very pretty and becoming. She [the Queen] had been as wilful, obstinate, and wrong-headed as usual about her invitations, and some of her foolish and mischievous Courtiers were boasting that out of above 300 people in the Chapel there would only be five Tories; of these five, two were the joint Great Chamberlains Willoughby and Cholmondeley, whom they could hardly omit, and one Ashley, the husband of Melbourne's niece, the other two were Lord Liverpool her own old friend, and the Duke, but there was a hesitation about inviting them. The Duke and Duchess of Northumberland were not there, and she did worse than not invite them, for though the day of the ceremony had been fixed a month before, and it was well known that they were at Alnwick, the invitation was sent to them so late that they could not have got it in time to come, and the truth is that it was intended not to invite them at all. Nothing could be more improper and foolish than to make this a mere Whig party, and if she was to make a selection she might with great propriety have invited all those, such as the Dukes of Rutland and Exeter, who had formerly received and entertained her at their houses, but she would not, and stuffed in a parcel of Whigs, taken apparently at haphazard, in preference to any of these. Upon leaving the Palace for Windsor

---

[12] [Queen Victoria was married to Prince Albert of Saxe-Coburg-Gotha on the 10th February, 1840.]

she and her young husband were pretty well received; but they went off in a very poor and shabby style. Instead of the new chariot in which most married people are accustomed to dash along, they were in one of the old travelling coaches, the postilions in undress liveries, and with a small escort, three other coaches with post-horses following. The crowds on the road were so great that they did not reach the Castle till eight o'clock. Her honeymoon seems to be a very curious affair, more strange than delicate, and even her best friends are shocked and hurt at her not conforming more than she is doing to English customs and at not continuing for a short space in that retirement, which modesty and native delicacy generally prescribe, and which few Englishwomen would be content to avoid, but she does not think any such restraint necessary. Married on Monday, she collected an immense party on Wednesday, and she sent off in a hurry for Clarence Paget, to go down and assist at a ball or rather dance, which she chose to have at the Castle last night. This is a proceeding quite unparalleled, and Lady Palmerston said to me last night that she was much vexed that she had nobody about her who could venture to tell her that this was not becoming and would appear indelicate; but she has nobody who dares tell her, or she will not endure to hear such truth. Normanby said to me the same thing. It is a pity Melbourne, when she desired him to go there on Wednesday, did not tell her she had better not have him, nor anybody except perhaps her own family. He probably did not think about it. It was much remarked too that she and Prince Albert were up very early on Tuesday morning, walking about, which is very contrary to her former habits. Strange that a bridal night should be so short, and I told Lady Palmerston that this was not the way to provide us with a Prince of Wales.

February 15*th*. It is a sad sight to see the Duke of Wellington almost insulted by the Court, just as his Sun is about to set. It turns out to be quite true that it was with great difficulty the Queen was induced to invite him to her wedding, and at last only when it was hinted to her that if he was not there, there would very likely be some unpleasant manifestation of public opinion.

He is well aware of this, and he told Lord Lyndhurst (who told me) that she said 'I won't have that Old rebel'—not however that I believe she did say this. This is one of the inventions I have no doubt of the busy mischief-makers and angry Tories, who make bad as much worse as they can.

It is a curious fact but perfectly true that a few days before her marriage she felt considerable misgivings about the step she was going to take. She was very nervous and feverish, so much so that they fancied she was going to have the measles. In this state she got alarmed for the result of her matrimonial venture, and she said:—'After all it is a very hazardous experiment, and how unhappy I shall be if it does not answer. I have always had my own way, and particularly for the last two years, and suppose he should endeavor to thwart me and oppose me in what I like, what a dreadful thing it would be.' I daresay the words are incorrectly reported, but the fact and the substance are correct and true; and this, though they say she is so in love with him. It is her dread of being thwarted and her love of power, stronger than love, which stirred up these doubts and this emotion. The best thing for her will be that he should have some firmness and resolution, and should show it for her guidance and restraint.

February 16th.   The Duke of Wellington (although his life was in such danger on Thursday night, that the chances were he died) has thrown off his attack in a marvellous manner, and is now rapidly approaching to convalescence, all dangerous symptoms subsiding.

February 19th.   Went yesterday morning to Apsley House. Duke going on well, but his people indignant that while all the Royal Family have been sending continually to enquire after him, and all London has been at his door, the Queen alone has never taken the slightest notice of him. This afflicted me and I resolved to speak to Melbourne. Accordingly I wrote him a note begging for God's sake he would get the Queen to send and enquire, and representing the injury it was to *herself* not to do so. I took it to the Palace where I knew he would be (for the Addresses) and sent it up to him. I then went to my office, where

I had not been five minutes before he sent for me. He began by saying he thought she *had* sent; but he had seen a paragraph in the *Morning Post* (which I had not), stating that she had not, on which he had asked her and she had owned it was true. But it appeared he had not then himself suggested it, nor would have done but for the note. He asked if it would not then be late. I said certainly it would, but it was better late than not at all, as it enabled one to say, when she was accused of not sending, that she had sent. He sat down, wrote her a note, and sent it off directly. I said 'I suppose she will send now'—'O yes, she will send now' he replied. He then talked about her; said she was very resentful, but that people pressed her too much, did not give her time. They complained of *him* for being dilatory and not urging things, but there was everything in not being urgent and giving time. I did not quite make out to what his allusions were especially directed, but I said 'time would not wait, nor people either; it was just not what it was reasonable to expect.' I then told him that it really was lamentable that she did the things she does, and that I had no scruple in saying so to him, as I knew he did his utmost to keep her straight. 'By God' (he said) 'I am moving noon and night at it'—to which I answered that 'it was not to be endured that he should exert himself in vain; that she must know he had only her good at heart, and that his experience and knowledge of the world entitled him to attention; and that there was no use in his occupying the station he did, if he could not persuade her against the suggestions of her own fancies or the weak people about her.' He said 'she was very resentful'—I said 'depend upon it, she will get into a great scrape. The people of England will not endure that she should treat the Duke of Wellington with disrespect; and it is not the mere act of sending or not that will make an impression of the badness of her heart and disposition. Everybody knows her Father was the greatest rascal that ever went unhung, and they will say that it is the bad blood coming out in her.' He said 'she had none of her Father's faults'; to which I said 'certainly not, but the evil disposition which showed itself in him in one way might show itself in her in another.'

February 26th.   Called on the Duke of Bedford yesterday morning, and had a long talk about the Court, when he told me several little things (in great confidence) about Prince Albert's position, how little to be envied, and possibly hereafter to be pitied. Taken from his family, who adored him, and from his country and habits, and put down in the midst of a grandeur which is so very heavy and dull, and which unless something is done to improve the social gaiety of the Court must end by fatiguing and disgusting him. The Duchess of Bedford's impression is that the Queen is excessively in love with him, but he not a bit with her. All the courtiers point with admiration to their walking together arm in arm in the garden, and say how charming it is to see such signs of mutual passion, but the Duchess does not think it is mutual, and he gives her the impression of not being happy. The Duchess of Saxe-Coburg told her (or some of them) that there never were such heartbreaking scenes as his leave-taking of his family, eternal as it must be.

One day the Duchess was in the Queen's room with the Baroness, when the Queen said she knew that she was very wilful, when the Baroness (Lehzen) said, 'To know your faults is the first step toward correcting them.' This was honest, and it was well received, but her consciousness does not seem to produce amendment, and it was only the other day that Bedford says he is sure there was a battle between her and Melbourne. He overheard Melbourne say to her with great earnestness, 'No. For God's sake, don't do that.' Though he does not know what it was about; and he is sure there was one about the men's sitting after dinner, for he overheard her say to him rather angrily, 'It is a horrid custom.' But when the ladies left the room (he dined there) directions were given that the men should remain *five minutes* longer. Adolphus Fitzclarence told me that at the Queen Dowager's party, when the Queen was going away, her shawl was not forthcoming and the Duchess of Bedford, her lady in waiting, could not find it. While she was looking, Lady Clinton did find it and went up with it, offering to put it on, but the Queen would not let her, and said it was for the Duchess of Bedford to do it, and when a moment later the latter returned, she said, 'Duchess of Bedford, I have been waiting some time for my shawl.'

March 29th. We had M. Guizot at dinner.[13] They all say he is agreeable, but I have not been in the way of his talk. He is enchanted and elated with his position, and it is amusing to see his apprehension lest anybody should, either by design or inadvertence, rob him of his precedence; and the alacrity with which he seizes on the arm of the lady of the house on going out to dinner, so demonstrative of the uneasy grandeur of a man who has not yet learnt to be familiar with his own position. With reference to diplomatic rank, I only heard last night, for the first time, that the Duke of Sutherland had, some time ago, addressed a formal remonstrance to Palmerston, against Foreign Ministers (not Ambassadors) having place given them at the Palace (which means going first out to dinner over himself *et suos pares*), a most extraordinary thing for a sensible man to have done, especially in such high favour as his wife and her whole family are. He got for answer, that Her Majesty exercised her own pleasure in this respect in her own palace. The rule always has been that Ambassadors (who represent the persons of their Sovereigns) have precedence of everybody; Ministers (who are only agents) have not; but the Queen, it appears, has given the *pas* to Ministers Plenipotentiaries, as well as to Ambassadors, and ordered them to go out at her dinners before her own subjects of the highest rank.[14]

May 7th. Lord Ashburton told me an anecdote of General Maitland (Sir Thomas), which happened at some place in the West Indies or South America. He had taken some town, and the soldiers were restrained from committing violence on the inhabitants, when a shot was fired from a window, and one of his men killed. They entered the house, went to the room from the win-

[13] [M. Guizot had just been appointed French Ambassador in London under the Government of M. Thiers.]

[14] [It was afterwards settled by Her Majesty that Foreign Ministers should take precedence *after* Dukes and before Marquesses.]

dow of which the shot had been fired, and found a number of
men playing at billiards. They insisted on the culprit being given
up, when a man was pointed out as the one who had fired the
shot. They all agreed as to the culprit, and he was carried off. Sir
Thomas considering that a severe example was necessary, ordered the man to be tied to the mouth of a cannon, and shot
away. He was present, but turned his head away when the signal
was given for blowing this wretch's body to atoms. The explosion
took place, when to his amazement the man appeared alive, but
with his hair literally standing 'like quills upon the fretful por-
cupine,' with terror. In the agony of the moment he had contrived
to squeeze himself through the ropes, which were loosely tied,
and get on one side of the cannon's mouth, so that the ball missed
him. He approached Maitland and said, 'You see, General, that
it was the will of Heaven my life should be spared; and I sol-
emnly assure you that I am innocent.' Maitland would not allow
him to be executed after this miraculous escape, and it turned
out, upon further enquiry, that he *was* innocent, and it was some
other man who had fired the shot.

June 12th. On Wednesday afternoon, as the Queen and Prince
Albert were driving in a low carriage up Constitution Hill, about
four or five in the afternoon, they were shot at by a lad of eighteen
years old, who fired two pistols at them successively, neither shots
taking effect. He was in the Green Park without the rails, and as
he was only a few yards from the carriage, and, moreover, very
cool and collected, it is marvellous he should have missed his aim.
In a few moments the young man was seized, without any attempt on his part to escape or to deny the deed, and was carried
off to prison. The Queen, who appeared perfectly cool, and not
the least alarmed, instantly drove to the Duchess of Kent's, to
anticipate any report that might reach her mother, and, having
done so, she continued her drive and went to the Park. By this
time the attempt upon her life had become generally known, and
she was received with the utmost enthusiasm by the immense
crowd that was congregated in carriages, on horseback, and on
foot. All the equestrians formed themselves into an escort, and

attended her back to the Palace, cheering vehemently, while she acknowledged, with great appearance of feeling, these loyal manifestations. She behaved on this occasion with perfect courage and self-possession, and exceeding propriety; and the assembled multitude, being a high-class mob, evinced a lively and spontaneous feeling for her—a depth of interest which, however natural under such circumstances, must be very gratifying to her, and was satisfactory to witness.

September 22nd. There has been a Court *tracasserie* and the Queen has been very angry with the Duke of Cambridge for what he said of her at the Mansion House the day Prince Albert received the freedom of the City. The day had long been fixed for his dining at the Mansion House, when in consequence of a bad account of Princess Augusta, Prince Albert wrote (on the day previous) and said he could not attend. The Lord Mayor posted down to Windsor and represented that after all the trouble and expense that had been incurred, it would be a grievous disappointment if he did not go, so (the account of the Princess being better) he agreed to attend. The Duke of Cambridge, who had been invited to meet him, wrote to him to say that if he liked it, he would meet him in the morning (wherever it was he was to go) and that as he was not accustomed to these ceremonies he might be of some use to him. The Prince never answered his letter, but when they met, he said to the Duke that he had a favour to ask him which was that he would not stay and dine there, as he did not himself mean to do so. The Duke said he would do no such thing and asked why he did not.—On account of the Princess Augusta, he said, and he had promised the Queen to return. The Duke said the Princess Augusta was better than she had been for some time. He, Prince Albert, might do as he pleased, but that he, the Duke, could not now make an excuse to the Lord Mayor. When Prince Albert was gone, the Lord Mayor came to the Duke and said he really did not know what to do, but people were so indignant at his departure that if his health was proposed he was afraid they would turn down their glasses. On this the Duke said he would do the best he could to get him out of the scrape, and for this purpose he made the speech in which, in not very refined terms, and in somewhat too familiar phrase, he talked of his having married "a fine young girl," and that they were "very fond of each other's company." It took very well, and answered the purpose, but Her Majesty was very indignant at being called "a fine young girl," thought it very impertinent, and signified her displeasure in a letter to the Duchess of Gloucester which she desired her to show to the Duke. She is mighty tenacious of her dignity, and as she fancies everything is to bend her will, she was probably very angry that the Duke did not comply with Albert's request and go away when he did.

Downham, October 23rd. From Livermere to Riddlesworth last Monday, and home to-day. This morning I learnt (by reading it in the *Globe*) the sudden death of Lord Holland, after a few hours' illness, whom I left not a fortnight ago in his usual health, and likely to live many years. There did not, probably, exist an individual whose loss will be more sincerely lamented and severely felt than his. Never was popularity so great and so general, and his death will produce a social revolution, utterly extinguishing not only the most brilliant, but the only great house of reception and constant society in England. His marvellous social qualities, imperturbable temper, unflagging vivacity and spirit, his inexhaustible fund of anecdote, extensive information, sprightly wit, with universal toleration and urbanity, inspired all who approached him with the keenest taste for his company, and those who lived with him in intimacy with the warmest regard for his person. This event may be said with perfect truth to 'eclipse the gaiety of nations,' for besides being an irreparable loss to the world at large, it turns adrift, as it were, the innumerable *habitués* who, according to their different degrees of intimacy, or the accidents of their social habits, made Holland House their regular and constant resort. It is impossible to overrate the privation, the blank, which it will make to the old friends and associates, political and personal, to whom Holland House has always been open like a home, and there cannot be a sadder sight than to see the curtain suddenly fall upon a scene so brilliant and apparently prosperous, and the light which for nearly half a century has adorned and cheered the world, thus suddenly and for ever extinguished. Although I did not rank among the old and intimate friends of Holland House, I came among the first of the second class of those who were always welcome, passed much of my time there, and have been continually treated with the greatest cordiality and kindness, and I partake largely and sincerely of the regret that must be so deep and universal.

December 19*th*. I dined with Erroll yesterday who told me some gossiping details of the Queen's accouchement.[15] Her health and strength through the operation seem to have been marvellous. She desired that as few persons as possible should be present, and actually in the room there were only Locock (no other doctor) the Prince and Mrs. Lilly, the nurse. In the next room (with the door so open so that Erroll said he could see the Queen plainly the whole time and hear what she said) were the Cabinet ministers, the Archbishop of Canterbury, and Bishop of London. When the child was born, Locock said: 'Oh, Madam, it is a Princess.' She said, 'Never mind, the next will be a Prince.' The baby was then brought stark naked into the room where the Councillors were and laid on a table (already prepared) for their inspection and having thus verified the birth, they went away. The Queen's delivery was so little expected that the wet nurse was at her own home on the Isle of Wight, and Whiting the Page (and formerly private valet de chambre of George IV) went off for her, brought her over in an open boat from Cowes to Southampton and had her at the Palace by two in the morning.

January 9*th*, 1841. The other day at Windsor, when Clarendon was sitting talking with Melbourne, the latter in his lounging way, as if thinking aloud, said, 'In all my experience, I never remember such a state of things as the present; I never remember, in the

---

15 [*Of the future Empress Frederick and mother of Kaiser Wilhelm.*]

course of my political life, anything at all like it; it can't last—it's
impossible this Government can go on; Palmerston in communication with the Tories—Palmerston and Ashley—' and then he
stopped. Clarendon said, 'What! you think Palmerston and the
Tories will come together?' To which Melbourne nodded assent.
'And which,' Clarendon persevered, 'will come to the other: will
Palmerston go to Ashley, or will Ashley come to Palmerston?' To
which Melbourne chuckled and grunted, laughed and rubbed his
hands, and only said, 'Oh, I don't know.' These are the sentiments
of the Prime Minister about his own Government—a strange state
of things: while Palmerston is in confidential communication with
the Tories, or some of them, for the purpose of obtaining their
support to his policy, half of his own colleagues, though committed, being adverse to it, and regarded by him as his worst
adversaries. He and John Russell, the two Secretaries of State—
the latter leader of the House of Commons—pass some days together in the house of the former, without exchanging one word
upon the subject of foreign policy, and Lord John is reduced to
the necessity of gathering in conversation from Neumann and
Esterhazy what Palmerston's views and opinions are. These two
diplomats expressed the greatest indignation at Ponsonby's proceedings, and Palmerston himself has renewed to Bourqueney
the assurances of his resolution to adhere to the engagements he
had already made to France with regard to Egypt. Melbourne,
however, acknowledged that he was entirely in the dark as to
Palmerston's real views and opinions, as he believed was every
one of his colleagues. He has no intimacy, no interchange of
thought and complete openness with anybody, and all they know
is (and that only as soon as he thinks fit to impart it) his notions
with regard to each particular question as its exigencies become
pressing. His position, however, is now a very remarkable one.
Belonging to a Government almost every member of which dislikes or distrusts him, he has acquired, by recent events, a great
reputation, and is looked upon generally as a bold, able, and successful statesman. In the event of a dislocation of parties, he is

free to adopt any course, and to join with any party.[16] Almost all the domestic questions which have hitherto excited interest have been settled, compromised, or thrown aside, and a sudden interest has been awakened, and attention generally drawn to our foreign policy and international relations. All that has recently occurred—our treaties and our warlike operations—are not looked upon as the work of the Government, but as that of Palmerston alone—Palmerston, in some degree, as contradistinguished from the Government. All this confers upon him a vast importance, and enables him, neither unreasonably nor improbably, to aspire to head and direct any Government that may hereafter be formed by a dissolution and fresh combination of parties.

January 13th. The other day died the Duchess of Cannizzaro, a woman of rather amusing notoriety, whom the world laughed with and laughed at, while she was alive, and will regret a little because she contributed in some degree to their entertainment. She was a Miss Johnstone, and got from her brother a large fortune; she was very short and fat, with rather a handsome face, totally uneducated, but full of humour, vivacity, and natural drollery, at the same time passionate and capricious. Her all-absorbing interest and taste was music, to which all her faculties and time were devoted. She was eternally surrounded with musical artists, was their great patroness, and at her house the world was regaled with the best music that art could supply. Soon after her brother's death, she married the Count St. Antonio (who was afterwards made Duke of Cannizzaro), a good-looking, intelli-

16 [I believe at this time, Lord Palmerston, irritated by the opposition and distrust of his own colleagues, and encouraged by the applause of the Tories, who were delighted at the rupture of the alliance with France, and eager to bully that country, did contemplate a junction with the Tory party. But to this there was an insurmountable obstacle, the deep distrust and dislike of Sir Robert Peel, who thought Palmerston a dangerous and mischievous Foreign Minister, and the hostility of Lord Aberdeen. In fact, when these statesmen came into office a few months later, they applied themselves mainly to obliterate the traces of Palmerston's quarrels. Nothing would have induced Sir Robert Peel to take Palmerston into his Cabinet. It was otherwise, some years later, when Lord Stanley had succeeded to the leadership of the Conservative Party, and at that time the negotiations between him and Lord Palmerston were renewed, though without any result.—H. R.]

gent, but penniless Sicilian of high birth, who was pretty successful in all ways in society here. He became disgusted with her, however, and went off to Italy, on a separate allowance which she made him. After a few years he returned to England, and they lived together again; he not only became more disgusted than before, but he had in the meantime formed a *liaison* at Milan with a very distinguished woman there, once a magnificent beauty, but now as old and as large as his own wife, and to her he was very anxious to return. This was Madame Visconti (mother of the notorious Princess Belgioso), who, though no longer young, had fine remains of good looks, and was eminently pleasing and attractive. Accordingly, St. Antonio took occasion to elope (by himself) from some party of pleasure at which he was present with his spouse, and when she found that he had gone off without notice or warning, she first fell into violent fits of grief, which were rather ludicrous than affecting, and then set off in pursuit of her faithless lord. She got to Dover, where the sight of the rolling billows terrified her so much, that she resolved to return, and weep away her vexation in London. Not long afterwards, however, she plucked up courage, and taking advantage of a smooth sea she ventured over the Straits, and set off for Milan, if not to recover her fugitive better half, at all events to terrify her rival and disturb their joys. The advent of the Cannizzaro woman was to the Visconti like the irruption of the Huns of old. She fled to a villa near Milan, which she proceeded to garrison and fortify, but finding that the other was not provided with any implements for a siege, and did not stir from Milan, she ventured to return to the city, and for some time these ancient heroines drove about the town glaring defiance and hate at each other, which was the whole amount of the hostilities that took place between them. Finding her husband was irrecoverable, she at length got tired of the hopeless pursuit, and resolved to return home, and console herself with her music and whatever other gratifications she could command. Not long after, she fell in love with a fiddler at a second-rate theatre in Milan, and carried him off to England, which he found, if not the most agreeable, the most profitable business he could engage in. The affair was singular and curious, as showing what society may be induced to put up with. There was not the slightest attempt to conceal this connexion; on the contrary it was most ostentatiously exhibited to the world, but the world agreed to treat it as a joke, and do nothing but laugh at it. The only difference 'the Duchesse' ever found was, that her Sunday parties were less well attended; but this was because the world (which often grows religious, but never grows moral) had begun to take it into its head that it would keep holy the Sabbath *night*. The worst part of the story was, that this profligate blackguard bullied and plundered her without mercy or shame, and she had managed very nearly to ruin herself before her death. What she had left, she bequeathed to her husband, notwithstanding his infidelities and his absence.

January 21st. I dined with Lady Holland yesterday. Everything there is exactly the same as it used to be, excepting only the person of Lord Holland, who seems to be pretty well forgotten. The same talk went merrily round, the laugh rang loudly and frequently, and, but for the black and the mob-cap of the lady, one might have fancied he had never lived or had died half a century ago. Such are, however, affections and friendships, and such is the world. Macaulay dined there, and I never was more struck than upon this occasion by the inexhaustible variety and extent of his information. It is impossible to mention any book in any language with which he is not familiar. If he could tread less heavily on the ground, if he could touch the subjects he handles with a lighter hand, if he knew when to stop as well as he knows what to say, his talk would be as attractive as it is wonderful. What Henry Taylor said of him is epigrammatic and true, 'that his memory has swamped his mind.' We had yesterday a party well composed for talk, for there were listeners of intelligence and a good specimen of the sort of society of this house—Macaulay, Melbourne, Morpeth, Duncannon, Baron Rolfe, Allen and Lady Holland, and John Russell came in the evening. I wish that a shorthand writer could have been there to take down all the conversation, or that I could have carried it away in my head; because it was curious in itself, and curiously illustrative of the characters of the performers. Before dinner some mention was made of the portraits of the Speakers in the Speaker's House, and I asked how far they went back. Macaulay said he was not sure, but certainly as far as Sir Thomas More. 'Sir Thomas More,' said Lady Holland, 'I did not know he had been Speaker.' 'Oh, yes,' said Macaulay, 'don't you remember when Cardinal Wolsey came down to the House of Commons and More was in the chair?' and then he told the whole of that well-known transaction, and all More had said. At dinner the name of Sir Thomas Munro came uppermost. Lady Holland did not know why Sir Thomas Munro was so distinguished; when Macaulay explained all that he had ever said, done, written, or thought, and vindicated his claim to the title of a great man, till Lady Holland got bored with Sir Thomas, told Macaulay she had had enough of him, and would have no more. This would have dashed and silenced an ordinary talker, but to Macaulay it was no more than replacing a book on its shelf, and he was as ready as ever to open on any other topic. When we went upstairs we got upon the Fathers of the Church. Allen asked Macaulay if he had read much of the Fathers. He said, not a great deal. He had read Chrysostom when he was in India; that is, he had turned over the leaves and for a few months had read him for two or three hours every morning before breakfast; and he had read some of Athanasius. 'I remember a sermon,' he said, 'of Chrysostom's in praise of the Bishop of Antioch;' and then he proceeded to give us the substance of this sermon till Lady Holland got tired of the Fathers, again put her extinguisher on Chrysostom as she had done on Munro, and with a sort of derision, and as if to have the pleasure of puzzling Macaulay, she turned to him and said, 'Pray, Macaulay, what was the origin of a *doll?* when were dolls first mentioned in history?' Macaulay was, however, just as much up to the dolls as he was to the Fathers, and instantly replied that the Roman children had their dolls, which they offered up to Venus when they grew older; and quoted Persius for

'Veneri donatæ a virgine puppæ,'

and I have not the least doubt, if he had been allowed to proceed, he would have told us who was the Chenevix of ancient Rome, and the name of the first baby that ever handled a doll.

May 8th. Mr. Barnes died yesterday morning, suddenly, after having suffered an operation. His death is an incalculable loss to the 'Times,' of which he was the principal editor and director; and his talents, good sense, and numerous connexions gave him a preponderating influence in the affairs of the paper. The vast power exercised by the 'Times' renders this a most important event, and it will be curious to see in what hands the regulating and directing power will hereafter be placed. Latterly it must be owned that its apparent caprices and inconsistency have deprived it of all right and title, and much of its power, to influence the opinions of others, but this has been the consequence of the extraordinary variety of its connexions and the conflicting opinions which have been alternately, and sometimes almost, if not quite, simultaneously, admitted to discharge themselves in its columns. Barnes was a man of considerable acquirements, a good scholar, and well versed in English, especially old dramatic literature.[17]

June 6th. The division took place on Friday night, and there was a majority of one against the Government. For the last day or two it was a complete toss-up which side won, and it evidently depended on the few uncertain men who might or might not choose to vote. As it was, it all turned on an accident. John Russell wrote to Sir Gilbert Heathcote (who never votes), and begged him to come up on Thursday, and to vote. Sir Gilbert did come, but, as there was no division that night, he went home again,

---

[17] [Mr. Barnes was succeeded in the Editorship of the 'Times' by Mr. John Delane, then a young man of about four and twenty. The friendly relations which had for some time subsisted between Mr. Greville and Mr. Barnes were strengthened and consolidated under the administration of his successor. Mr. Delane was well aware that he could nowhere meet with a more sagacious adviser or a more valuable ally. He owed to Mr. Greville his first introduction to political society, of which he made so excellent a use, and where he gradually acquired the esteem of men of all parties and a position which no editor of a newspaper had before enjoyed. The influence of the 'Times' newspaper during the ensuing ten or fifteen years can hardly be exaggerated.

and his vote was lost. They left no stone unturned to procure a majority, and brought down a lord who is in a state of drivelling idiotcy, and quite incapable of comprehending what he was about. This poor wretch was brought in a chair; they got him into the House, and then wheeled him past the tellers. Charles Howard, Melbourne's private secretary, told me he thought it a monstrous and indecent proceeding.

June 20th. At Chiswick yesterday morning a party for the Queen and Prince Albert, who wished to see the place. It rained half the time and it was very formal. She cannot, or will not, encourage conversation; nothing of the kind is ever attempted; and as Melbourne was not there (being ill) she had nobody to talk to.

June 23rd. Prince Albert would not go to the Duke's Waterloo dinner. The Duke invited him when they met at Oxford, and the Prince said he would send an answer. He sent an excuse, which was a mistake, for the invitation was a great compliment, and this is a sort of national commemoration at which he might have felt a pride at being present. But the enthusiasm which is universally felt for the Duke, and the deep veneration with which he is regarded everywhere else, have no existence in the Palace, and the Queen (for there can be no doubt it was her doing) chose that he should send some trumpery excuse rather than accept as he ought to have done with alacrity the invitation.

July 11th. I find London rather empty and tolerably calm. The elections are sufficiently over to exhibit a pretty certain result, and the termination of the great Yorkshire contest by the signal victory of the Tories—a defeat, the magnitude of which there is no possibility of palliating, or finding any excuse for—seems to have had the effect of closing the contest. The Whigs give the whole thing up as irretrievably lost; and though some of them with whom I have conversed still maintain that they did right to dissolve, they do not affect to deny that the result has disappointed all their hopes and calculations, and been disastrous beyond their worst fears. They now give Peel a majority of sixty or seventy.

August 4th. The next thing from which the Whigs hope to

derive benefit is the hostile disposition of the Queen towards the Tory Government, and this they do their utmost to foster and keep up as far as writings and speeches go; but I do not believe that Melbourne does any such thing, and he alone has access to the Queen's ear and to her secret thoughts. With him alone she communicates without reserve, and to none of his colleagues, not even to John Russell, does he impart *all* that passes between them. The best thing she can possibly do is to continue in her confidential habits with him as far as possible, for I am persuaded he will give her sound and honest advice; he will mitigate instead of exasperating her angry feelings, and instruct her in the duties and obligations of her position, and try at least to persuade her that her dignity, her happiness and her interest are all concerned in her properly discharging them. He has faults enough of various kinds, but he is a man of honour and of sense, and he is deeply attached to the Queen. He will prefer her honour and repose to any interests of party, and it is my firm conviction that he will labour to inspire her with just notions and sound principles, and as far as in him lies will smooth the difficulties which would be apt to clog her intercourse with his successors.

September 4th. In the evening I dined at Stafford House and met Melbourne. After dinner he took me aside and said, 'Have you any means of speaking to *these chaps?*' I said, 'Yes, I can say anything to them.' 'Well,' he said, 'I think there are one or two things Peel ought to be told, and I wish you would tell him. Don't let him suffer any appointment he is going to make to be talked about, and don't let her hear it through anybody but himself; and whenever he does anything, or has anything to propose, let him explain to her clearly his reasons. The Queen is not conceited; she is aware there are many things she cannot understand, and she likes to have them explained to her elementarily, not at length and in detail, but shortly and clearly; neither does she like long audiences, and I never stayed with her a long time. This morning I called on Peel and told him word for word what Melbourne had said to me. He said, 'It was very kind of Lord Melbourne, and I am much obliged to him; but do you mean that this refers to anything that has already occurred?' I said, 'Not at all, but to the future.' Melbourne, knowing the Queen's mind better than Sir Robert possibly could, wished to tell him these things in order that matters might go on more smoothly.

September 29th. Mellish told me another anecdote of Palmerston, that eleven thousand pounds (I put it in letters, because in figures some error might have been suspected) had been spent in *one year*, at the Foreign Office, in chaises and four conveying messengers to overtake the mail with his private letters, which never were ready in time. Nothing ever equalled the detestation in which he is regarded at that Office.

November 24th. The Duke of Wellington is remarkably well. I saw him yesterday for the first time since the Council at Windsor, and he said he never was better. But he is altered in character strangely. He has now a morbid aversion to seeing people, which nearly amounts to madness. Nobody can get access to him, not even his nearest relations. When anybody applies for an interview, he flies into a passion, and the answers which he dictates to letters asking for audiences, or asking for anything, are so brutally uncivil and harsh that my brother Algy constantly modifies or alters them. The Duke fancies he is so engaged that he cannot spare time to see anybody. This peculiarity is the more remarkable, because formerly his weakness was a love of being consulted by everybody, and mixed up with everything. Nobody was ever in a difficulty without applying to him; innumerable were the quarrels, *tracasseries*, scandals, intrigues, and scrapes which he had to arrange and compose.

December 15th. I have been employed in reading the Duchess of Marlborough's correspondence with her two granddaughters, successively Duchesses of Bedford, and most amusing it is. I have urged the Duke to publish it, and, if Lord John, who is going to publish a volume or more of Bedford papers, does not choose to take the Duchess of Marlborough's letters in hand, to let me arrange them for the press, which he has promised to do. I hardly ever read any letters more expressive of character, and more natural than these, and they abound in shrewd observation and knowledge of human nature, besides a very good sprinkling of anecdotes, some very entertaining. I took Lord Spencer down with me to the librarian's room to look at them, when he told me two anecdotes of John Spencer, her grandson, to whom, after quarrelling with him violently, as she did with everybody else, she left all the property at her disposal. The first was about the cause of their quarrel. She gave a great dinner on her birthday to all her family, and she said that 'there she was, like a great tree, herself the root, and all her branches flourishing round her;' when John Spencer said to his neighbour that 'the branches would flourish more when the root was under ground.' This produced great hilarity, which attracted the notice of old Sarah, who insisted on knowing the cause, when John Spencer himself told her his own *bon mot,* at which—and no wonder—she took great offence. She afterwards forgave him, and desired him to marry. He expressed his readiness to marry anybody she pleased, and at last she sent him a list, alphabetically arranged, of suitable matches. He said he might as well take the first on the list, which happened to be letter C, a Carteret, daughter of Lord Granville's, and her he accordingly married.

December 23rd. Three days passed very agreeably [*at Bowood*]. Charles Austin came yesterday, Dundas and John Russell to-day. Last night Mrs. Butler read the first three acts of the 'Hunchback,' which she was to have finished to-night, but she ran restive, pretended that some of the party did not like it, and no persuasion could induce her to go on. Another night, Moore sang some of his own Melodies, and Macaulay has been always talking. Never certainly was anything heard like him. I had at one time a notion of trying to remember and record some of the conversation that has been going on, and some of the anecdotes that have been told, but I find it is in vain to attempt it. The drollest thing is to see the effect upon Rogers, who is nearly extinguished, and can neither make himself heard, nor find an interval to get in a word. He is exceedingly provoked, though he can't help admiring, and he will revive to-morrow when Macaulay goes. We walked together for a long time the day before yester-

day, when he talked of the History he is writing. I asked him if
he was still collecting materials, or had begun to write. He said
he was writing while collecting, going on upon the fund of his
already acquired knowledge, and he added, that it was very mortifying to find how much there was of which he was wholly ignorant. I said if he felt that, with his superhuman memory and
wonderful scope of knowledge, what must ordinary men feel? He
said that it was a mistake to impute to him either such a memory
or so much knowledge; that Whewell and Brougham had more
universal knowledge than he had, but that what he did possess
was the ready, perhaps too ready, use of all he knew. I said what
surprised me most was, his having had time to read certain books
over and over again; *e.g.* he said he had read Don Quixote in
Spanish, five or six times; and I am afraid to say how often he
told me he had read 'Clarissa.' He said that he read no modern
books, none of the novels or travels that come out day after day.
He had read 'Tom Jones' repeatedly, but 'Cecil a Peer,' not at all;
and as to 'Clarissa,' he had read it so often that, if the work were
lost, he could give a very tolerable idea of it, could narrate the
story completely, and many of the most remarkable passages and
expressions. However, it would be vain, nor is it worth while, to
attempt to recollect and record all his various talk. Wonderful as
it is, it is certainly oppressive after a time, and his departure is
rather a relief than otherwise. Dundas, who is very agreeable, and
very well informed, said to-day that he was a bore; but *that* he is
not, because what comes from him is always good, and it comes
naturally, and without any assumption of superiority. His memory
treasures up all sorts of trash and nonsense, as well as the most
serious and most important matter; but there is never any confusion.

December 26th. Macaulay went away the day before Christ-
mas Day, and it was wonderful how quiet the house seemed after
he was gone, and it was not less agreeable. Rogers was all alive
again, Austin and Dundas talked much more than they would
have done, and Lord Lansdowne too, and on the whole we were
as well without him. It does not do for more than two or three

days; but I never passed a week with so much good talk, almost all literary and miscellaneous, very little political, no scandal and gossip. And this is the sort of society which I might have kept instead of that which I have.

January 24th, 1842.   Met Sutton Sharpe the other night, who told me some amusing stories of Lord Ellenborough and his treatment of counsel. A man was opening his speech, and said, 'My Lord, my unfortunate client,' and then repeated the words again. 'Go on, sir,' said Lord Ellenborough, 'the Court is with you so far.' Another man said, 'And now, if your Lordship pleases, I will proceed so and so.' 'Sir, we sit here not to court, but to endure arguments.'

February 5th.   Francis Baring, who is come over from Paris to see Lord Ashburton before he goes, tells me that if Palmerston had continued for a year or two more at the Foreign Office, nothing, he is persuaded, could have prevented a war between us and France, for that he intrigued against France in every part of the world, and with a tenacity of purpose that was like insanity; he was constantly engaged in thwarting, counteracting, and insulting her, so that the exasperation against him and against this country was so great and universal that a collision would have been inevitable.

March 13th.   On Friday night in the midst of the most intense and general interest and curiosity, heightened by the closeness and fidelity with which the Government measures had been kept secret, Peel brought forward his financial plans in a speech of three hours and forty minutes, acknowledged by everybody to have been a masterpiece of financial statement. The success was complete; he took the House by storm; and his opponents, though of course differing and objecting on particular points, did him ample justice. A few people expected an income tax, but the majority did not. Hitherto the Opposition have been talking very big about opposing all taxes, but they have quite altered their tone. It is really remarkable to see the attitude Peel has taken in this Parliament, his complete mastery over both his friends and his foes. His own party, *nolentes aut volentes,* have surrendered at discretion, and he has got them as well disciplined and as obedient as the crew of a man-of-war. This just measure, so lofty in conception, right in direction, and able in execution, places him at once on a pinnacle of power, and establishes his Government on such a foundation as accident alone can shake. Political predictions are always rash, but certainly there is every probability of Peel's being Minister for as many years as his health and vigour may endure. Only a few weeks ago I heard from my Whig friends of nothing but his weakness and embarrassments, and of all the difficulties his own supporters would cause him, what a poor figure he cut, &c.; but now they have not a word to say, and one of them who had been loudest in that strain brought to the Travellers', where I was dining, an account of Peel's speech, and said, 'One felt, all the time he was speaking, "Thank God, Peel is Minister!"' There can be no doubt that he is now a very great man, and it depends on himself to establish a lasting reputation. Wharncliffe told me that the principle of their measure, the imposition of an income-tax, was settled six weeks after they came into office, which makes the wonder greater that nothing of it got out.

March 19th. This day Lord Hertford[18] is buried at Ragley, a man whose death excited much greater interest than anything he ever did in his life, because the world was curious to learn the amount of his wealth, and how he had disposed of it. A pompous funeral left Dorchester House three days ago, followed by innumerable carriages of private individuals, pretending to show a respect which not one of them felt for the deceased; on the contrary, no man ever lived more despised or died less regretted. His life and his death were equally disgusting and revolting to every good and moral feeling. As Lord Yarmouth he was known as a sharp, cunning, luxurious, avaricious man of the world, with some

---

[18][*From whom Thackeray is supposed to have drawn Lord Steyne in* VANITY FAIR.]

talent, the favourite of George IV. (the worst of kings) when Lady Hertford, his mother, was that Prince's mistress. He was celebrated for his success at play, by which he supplied himself with the large sums of money required for his pleasures, and which his father had no inclination to give him, and the son had none to ask of him. He won largely, not by any cheating or unfairness, but by coolness, calculation, always backing the best players, and getting the odds on his side. He was a *bon vivant*, and when young and gay his parties were agreeable, and he contributed his share to their hilarity. But after he became Lord Hertford and the possessor of an enormous property he was puffed up with vulgar pride, very unlike the real scion of a noble race; he loved nothing but dull pomp and ceremony, and could only endure people who paid him court and homage. After a great deal of coarse and vulgar gallantry, generally purchased at a high rate, he formed a connexion with Lady Strachan, which thenceforward determined all the habits of his life. She was a very infamous and shameless woman, and his love after some years was changed to hatred; and she, after getting very large sums out of him, married a Sicilian. But her children, three daughters, he in a manner adopted; though eventually all his partiality centred upon one, Charlotte by name, who married Count Zichy-Ferraris, a Hungarian nobleman. She continued to live with Hertford on and off, here and abroad, until his habits became in his last years so ostentatiously crapulous that her residence in his house, in England at least, ceased to be compatible with common decency. She was, however, here till within a week or ten days of his death, and her departure appears curiously enough to have led to the circumstances which immediately occasioned it. There has been, as far as I know, no example of undisguised debauchery exhibited to the world like that of Lord Hertford, and his age and infirmities rendered it at once the more remarkable and the more shocking. Between sixty and seventy years old, broken with various infirmities, and almost unintelligible from a paralysis of the tongue, he has been in the habit of travelling about with a company of prostitutes, who formed his principal society, and by whom he was surrounded up to the moment of his death, generally picking them up from the dregs of that class, and changing them according to his fancy and caprice. Here he was to be seen driving about the town, and lifted by two footmen from his carriage into the brothel, and he never seems to have thought it necessary to throw the slightest veil over the habits he pursued. For some months or weeks past he lived at Dorchester House, and the Zichys with him; but every day at a certain hour his women, who were quartered elsewhere, arrived, passed the greater part of the day, and one or other of them all the night in his room. He found the presence of the Countess Zichy troublesome and embarrassing to his pleasures, and he made her comprehend that her absence would not be disagreeable to him, and accordingly she went away. He had then been ill in bed for many days, but as soon as she was gone, as if to celebrate his liberation by a jubilee, he got up and posted with his seraglio down to Richmond. No room was ready, no fire lit, nevertheless he chose to dine there amidst damp and cold, drank a quantity of champagne, came back chilled and exhausted, took to his bed, grew gradually worse, and in ten days he died. And what a life, terminating in what a death! without a serious thought or a kindly feeling, lavishing sums incalculable on the worthless objects of his pleasures or caprices, never doing a generous or a charitable action, caring and cared for by no human being, the very objects of his bounty only regarding him for what they could get out of him; faculties, far beyond mediocrity, wasted and degraded, immersed in pride without dignity, in avarice and sensuality; all his relations estranged from him, and surrounded to the last by a venal harem, who pandered to the disgusting exigencies. He left vast sums to the Strachan family, a considerable legacy to Croker, to whom he had been formerly under obligations, largely provided for his servants, and, with the exception of a few bequests to his executors and one or two other people, and a very large property to an old mistress (formerly Lady Strachan's maid), he left everything to his son

Lord Yarmouth, with whom he had always been on very moderate terms.

June 5th. Last week the Queen was shot at, very much in the same manner and on the same spot as two years ago. She was aware that the attempt had been meditated the day before, and that the perpetrator was at large, still she would go out, and without any additional precautions. This was very brave, but imprudent. It would have been better to stay at home, or go to Claremont, and let the police look for the man, or to have taken some precautionary measures. It is certainly very extraordinary, for there is no semblance of insanity in the assassin, and no apparent motive or reason for the crime. This young Queen, who is an object of interest, and has made no enemies, has twice had attempts made on her life within two years. George III., a very popular king, was exposed to similar attempts, but in his case the perpetrators were really insane; while George IV., a man neither beloved nor respected, and at different times very odious and unpopular, was never attacked by anyone.

Last night I went to Hullah's choral meeting, at Exeter Hall, where the Queen Dowager appeared. It was fine to see, and fine and curious to hear; but the finest thing was when the Duke of Wellington came in, almost at the end. The piece they were singing stopped at once; the whole audience rose, and a burst of acclamation and waving of handkerchiefs saluted the great old man, who is now the idol of the people. It was grand and affecting, and seemed to move everybody but himself.

September 1st. Peel began the Session with his great financial measures, which were received, on their first appearance, with considerable applause by the Opposition, and with a sulky acquiescence on the part of the Tories. The former, however, soon began to change their note and to pick holes, but probably this rather was of service to him than otherwise, for the semblance of an Opposition—and it was no more—kept together the masses of the Government party, and the tone of superiority and even supremacy which he assumed from the beginning has imposed upon both friend and foe, and enabled him to get through a very laborious and troublesome session without any serious difficulty. John Russell not only showed no disposition to lead his party in regular attacks on the Government, but he very soon became impatient to go and seek rural recreation, and some time before the close of the session he abandoned them to their fate. Before his departure, however, a sort of guerilla warfare had begun, which afterwards became more desultory, but more brisk and incessant. Charles Buller, Tom Duncombe, Hawes, and Vernon Smith took different departments, and, Palmerston taking the post of leader, they all kept up an incessant fire upon the Treasury Bench. The Whigs were exceedingly provoked with Lord John for quitting his post, and equally delighted with Palmerston for retaining his with such constancy and for taking so active a part. Nothing, however, occurred very remarkable in the way of debate till the last night of the session, when Palmerston made a grand attack upon the Government, *à la* Lyndhurst, in a speech of great ability, as his opponents themselves allow. Peel, however, replied to him in a still abler speech, and, with this brilliant single combat, which took place in a very empty House, the session ended.

Parliament was no sooner up, than the riots broke out, sufficiently alarming but for the railroads, which enabled the Government to pour troops into the disturbed districts, and extinguish the conflagration at once. The immediate danger is over, but those who are best informed look with great anxiety and apprehension to the future, and only consider what has recently happened as the beginning of a series of disorders. It is remarkable that whilst England and Scotland have been thus disturbed, Ireland has been in the profoundest tranquillity, and when everybody, themselves included, feared that Ireland would be hardly governable under Tory rule, they have not had the slightest difficulty in that quarter. O'Connell has been much quieter since Peel came into office than he was before, and is evidently doing all he can to keep the country quiet. The Queen, too, is to all appearance on just as good terms with the present Government as she was with the last. There is no such intimacy with anybody as there was with Melbourne, but she is very civil to all her Ministers, invites them constantly to her house, and, what is curious, hardly ever takes any notice of those members of the late Government and Household whom she appeared not to be able to live without; even Melbourne is very rarely a guest either at Windsor or Buckingham House.

September 24th. Adolphus Fitz-Clarence told me nothing could be more agreeable and amiable than [*the Queen*] was, and the Prince too, on board the yacht, conversing all the time with perfect ease and good humour, and on all subjects, taking great interest and very curious about everything in the ship, dining on deck in the midst of the sailors, making them dance, talking to the boatswain, and, in short, doing everything that was popular and ingratiating. Her chief fault, in little things and in great, seems to be impatience; in sea phrase, she always wants to *go ahead;* she can't bear contradiction nor to be thwarted. She was put out because she could not get quicker to the end of her voyage, and land so soon as she wished. She insisted on landing as soon as it was possible, and would not wait till the authorities were ready and the people assembled to receive her. An hour or two of delay would have satisfied everybody, and though it might be unreasonable to expect this, as Peel said it was, it would have been wise to have conceded it. Adolphus says there was very alarming excitement in the town for a little while, and much discontent among the crowds who had come from distant parts, and who had paid large sums for seats and windows to see her go by.

October 5th. The Baroness Lehzen has left Windsor Castle, and is gone abroad for her health (as she says), to stay five or six months, but it is supposed never to return. This lady, who is much beloved by the women and much esteemed and liked by all who frequent the Court, who is very intelligent, and has been a faithful and devoted servant to the Queen from her birth, has for some time been supposed to be obnoxious to the Prince, and as he is now all-powerful her retirement was not unexpected. I do not know the reason of it, nor how it has been brought about;

Melbourne told me long ago that the Prince would acquire unbounded influence.

October 23rd. To the Grove on Thursday; came back yesterday
to dine with Mr. Grenville; passed the whole morning of Saturday at the British Museum, where I had not been for many years,
but where I propose to go henceforward very often. The number
of readers is now on an average three hundred a day; in the
time of Gray, as may be seen by his letters, it was not half a
dozen. I had never dined with Mr. Grenville before, though he
has more than once asked me, and I was glad to go there. He is
a man whom I have always looked at with respect and pleasure.
It is a goodly sight, to see him thus placidly and slowly going
down the hill of life, with all his faculties of mind and body, not
unimpaired, but still fresh and strong. One would rejoice to procure a new lease for such a man. He may well look round him,
as he sits in his unrivalled library and surrounded by his friends,
serene and full of enjoyment, and say, like Mazarin, 'Et il faut
quitter tout cela!' but no reflexions or anticipations seem to over-
cast the mild sunshine of his existence. I certainly never saw so
graceful and enviable an old age; and though he is eighty-six,
and I am forty-eight, I would willingly change lives with him. I
would much rather be approaching the end of life as he is approaching it, than live any number of years that I may yet chance
to have in store as I am likely to live them. Mr. Grenville is rather
deaf, and he complains of loss of memory, but he hears well
enough for social purposes, and he is full of recollections of former times and remarkable people. He told a story of Porson,[19]
which I will put in his own words:—'When I was a young man,
which is now about seventy years ago, I used to live with
Cracherode and other literary men of that day, who were good
enough to allow me to come among them, and listen to their
conversation, which I used to take great delight in doing, and I
remember one day going into the room, and finding Cracherode
and another person disputing about language, and whether a certain English word had ever been used by any good authority. In

[19] [*After Bentley, the greatest classical scholar of the 18th century.*]

the middle of the dispute, one of them said, "But why do we go on talking here, when that little fellow in the corner can tell us in a moment which of us is in the right?" The little fellow was Porson, who was on his knees poring over a book. They called him up, told him what they were disputing about, and asked if he knew of the word having been used, and by whom. He at once replied, "I only know of one instance, and that is in Fisher's funeral sermon on the death of Margaret of Richmond, the mother of Henry VII., and you will find it about the third or fourth page on the right-hand side;" and there accordingly they did find it.'

November 2nd. Lord Wharncliffe and Kay Shuttleworth, who are both come from the north, have given me an account of the state of the country and of the people which is perfectly appalling. There is an immense and continually increasing population, deep distress and privation, no adequate demand for labour, no demand for anything, no confidence, but a universal alarm, disquietude, and discontent. Nobody can sell anything. Somebody said, speaking of some part of Yorkshire, 'This is certainly the happiest country in the world, for *nobody wants anything.*' Kay says that nobody can conceive the state of demoralisation of the people, of the masses, and that the only thing which restrains them from acts of violence against property is a sort of instinctive consciousness that, bad as things are, their own existence depends upon the security of property *in the long run.* It is in these parts that the worst symptoms are apparent, but there are indications of the same kind more or less all over the country, and certainly I have never seen, in the course of my life, so serious a state of things as that which now stares us in the face; and this, after thirty years of uninterrupted peace, and the most ample scope afforded for the development of all our resources, when we have been altering, amending, and improving, wherever we could find anything to work upon, and being, according to our own ideas, not only the most free and powerful, but the most moral and the wisest people in the world. One remarkable feature in the present condition of affairs is that nobody can account for it, and nobody pretends to be able to point out any remedy; for those who clamour for the repeal of the Corn Laws, at least those who know anything of the matter, do not really believe that repeal would supply a cure for our distempers. It is certainly a very dismal matter for reflexion, and well worthy the consideration of the profoundest political philosophers, that the possession of such a Constitution, all our wealth, industry, ingenuity, peace, and that superiority in wisdom and virtue which we so confidently claim, are not sufficient to prevent the existence of a huge mountain of human misery, of one stratum in society in the most deplorable state, both moral and physical, to which mankind can be reduced, and that all our advantages do not secure us against the occurrence of evils and mischiefs so great as to threaten a mighty social and political convulsion.

November 18th. Called on Mr. Grenville yesterday morning. He told me he was eighty-eight, and had never been ill in all his life; had colds, but never been ill enough to keep his bed a whole day since he was born. His memory, he said, failed as to dates and names. He told me a curious anecdote of Wolfe. In Pitt's (Lord Chatham's) administration, when Wolfe was going out to take the command of the army in America, at that time a post of the greatest importance, Mr. Pitt had him to dinner with no other person present but Lord Temple (Mr. Grenville's uncle). After dinner Wolfe got greatly excited, drew his sword, flourished it about, and boasted of the great things he would do with it in a wonderfully braggart style. Lord Temple and Mr. Pitt were horror-struck, and when the General was gone, they lifted up their hands and eyes, and said what an awful thing it was to think that they were about to trust interests so vital to the discretion of a man who could talk and bluster in such a way. Mr. Grenville said he had never liked to repeat this anecdote, and had never done so till very lately, for he had been reluctant to say anything which might, by possibility, throw a slur on the reputation of Wolfe. But I told him it was too curious to be suppressed; curious as a peculiar trait of character, and that the heights of Abraham had secured the fame of Wolfe beyond the possibility of being injured by anything that could now be said.

April 5th, 1843. In the course of conversation with Arbuthnot the other day on various matters, he told me something about Lord Spencer's taking office in '30, which I thought rather curious. Lord Spencer told it him himself. When Lord Grey was sent for by King William to form an administration, he went to Althorp and asked him what place he would have. Althorp said he would not have any. Lord Grey said, 'If you won't take office with me, I will not undertake to form the Government, but will give it up.' 'If that's the case,' said the other, 'I must; but if I do take office, I will be Chancellor of the Exchequer and lead the House of Commons.' 'Lead the House of Commons?' said Lord Grey; 'but you know you can't speak!' 'I know that,' he said, 'but I know I can be of more use to you in that capacity than in any other, and I will either be that or nothing.' He became the very best leader of the House of Commons that any party ever had. Peel said that he never failed on every question to say a few words entirely to the point, and no argument open to reply escaped him. The whole House liked him, his own party followed him with devoted attachment. This was a curious piece of confidence and self-reliance in a very modest man. There is an anecdote of him, exemplifying the reliance placed in his word and on his character, which has often been told, and may probably be recorded elsewhere. I forget the particulars of the story, but the gist of it is this. During the discussion of some Bill, a particular clause was objected to, and by his own friends. Althorp said that he knew when the Bill was framed, very cogent reasons were produced in favour of this clause, but to say the truth he could not at the moment recollect what they were. He invited them to waive these objections in deference to these excellent but unknown reasons, and they did so at his request. It would be long enough before Canning or Peel would have obtained such a mark of confidence from their supporters.

Good Friday, April 14th. Came back from Brighton on Sunday evening. The same night John Allen died, after a week's illness, much regretted by all the friends of Holland House. He was seventy-two years old, and had lived for forty years at Holland House, more exclusively devoted to literary pursuits and abdicating his independent existence more entirely than any man ever did. It is rather remarkable that no great work ever was produced by him; but perhaps his social habits, and still more the personal exigencies of Lady Holland, are sufficient to account for this. He was originally recommended to Lord Holland as a physician, being at that time a distinguished member of that remarkable literary circle at Edinburgh which contained Brougham, Horner, Jeffrey, and Sydney Smith, who revered Dugald Stewart as their master, and who originated the 'Edinburgh Review.' Allen does not seem to have been considered for any length of time as belonging to Holland House in a medical capacity. He soon was established there permanently as a friend, and looked upon (as he was) as an immense literary acquisition. From that time he became an essential and remarkable ingredient of the great Holland House establishment, the like of which we shall never see again. Allen became one of the family, was in all their confidence, and indispensable to both Lord and Lady Holland. Lord Holland treated him with uniform consideration, affection, and amenity; she worried, bullied, flattered, and cajoled him by turns. He was a mixture of pride, humility, and independence; he was disinterested, warm-hearted, and choleric, very liberal in his political, still more in his religious opinions, in fact, a universal sceptic. He used for a long time in derision to be called 'Lady Holland's Atheist,' and in point of fact I do not know whether he believed in the existence of a First Cause, or whether, like Dupuis, he regarded the world as *l'univers Dieu*. Though not, I think, feeling quite certain on the point, he was inclined to believe that the history of Jesus Christ was altogether fabulous or mythical, and that no such man had ever existed. He told me he could not get over the total silence of Josephus as to the existence and history of Christ. It was not, however, the custom at Holland House to discuss religious subjects, except rarely and incidentally. Everybody knew that the House was sceptical, none of them ever thought of going to church, and they went on as if there was no such thing as religion. But there was no danger of the most devout person being shocked or offended by any unseemly controversy, by any mockery, or insult offered to their feelings and convictions. Amongst the innumerable friends and habitual guests of the House were many clergymen, very sincere and orthodox, and many persons of both sexes entertaining avowedly the strongest religious opinions, amongst them Miss Fox, Lord Holland's sister, and his daughter, Lady Lilford. Allen's learning and still more his general information were prodigious, and as he lived amongst books, the stock was continually increasing. He was the oracle of Holland House on all literary subjects, and in every discussion some reference was sure to be made to Allen for information, upon which he never was at fault. He was not accustomed to take much part in general conversation, but was always ready to converse with anybody who sought him, and when warmed up would often argue away with great vigour and animation, and sometimes with no little excitement. After Lord Holland's death, which he felt with an intensity of grief that showed the warmth of his affections, he devoted himself entirely to Lady Holland, and never left her for a moment. His loss is, therefore, to her quite irreparable. He was for twenty-two years Master of Dulwich College, but he never was allowed to live there, or to absent himself from Holland House, except for the few hours in each week when his attendance at Dulwich was indispensable.

June 14th. The Duke of Bedford told me the other day that Prince Albert talked to his brother, Lord Wriothesley (with whom as one of their chaplains he is, it seems, in the habit of conversing) about the future education of the Prince of Wales, and he said that "the great object must be to make him as unlike as possible to any of his great uncles." This was an imprudent and ungracious speech, and not at all justifiable. There is not perhaps one of them whom it is desirable he should closely re-

semble, but there are some who possessed qualities in which it
will be well that he should be like them. His own grandfather
was by far the worst of the family, and it will be fortunate if no
portion of that blood is eventually found flowing in his veins and
tainting his disposition.

Frankfort, June 24th. Frankfort is not very gay or amusing.
There is very little society; the rich people here live very quietly,
and only display their wealth in occasional banquets, which are
splendid, but long and tiresome. The old mother of the Rothschilds, the grandmother of the present generation, is here, living
in the Jews' quarter in the old home of the family, which she
will not be persuaded to quit. It is miserable-looking on the outside, but is said to be very different within. The old woman, who
is ninety-four years old, drives about and goes constantly to the
opera or play.

Mannheim, June 29th. I went to Frankfort yesterday; went
to see the Jews' street, the most curious part of the town. It is
very narrow, the houses all of great antiquity, and not one new
or modern in the whole street. This street exhibits a perfect specimen of a town of the fifteenth or sixteenth century. The houses
are very lofty, a good deal ornamented, but they look dark and
dirty, and as if their interior had undergone as little alteration as
the exterior. Strange figures were loitering about the street, standing in the doorways or looking out of the windows. There was a
man who might have presented himself on the stage in the character of Shylock, with the gaberdine and the beard; and old
crones of the most miserable and squalid, but strange aspect. We
had the good luck to see the old mother of the Rothschilds, and a
curious contrast she presented. The house she inhabits appears
not a bit better than any of the others; it is the same dark and
decayed mansion. In this narrow gloomy street, and before this
wretched tenement, a smart *calèche* was standing, fitted up with
blue silk, and a footman in blue livery was at the door. Presently
the door opened, and the old woman was seen descending a dark,
narrow staircase, supported by her grand-daughter, the Baroness
Charles Rothschild, whose carriage was also in waiting at the end

of the street. Two footmen and some maids were in attendance to
help the old lady into the carriage, and a number of the inhabitants collected opposite to see her get in. A more curious and
striking contrast I never saw than the dress of the ladies, both
the old and the young one, and their equipages and liveries, with
the dilapidated locality in which the old woman persists in remaining. The family allow her 4,000*l.* a year, and they say she
never in her life has been out of Frankfort, and never inhabited
any other house than this, in which she is resolved to die. The
street was formerly closed at both ends, and the Jews were confined to that quarter. The French took away the gates and they
have never been replaced. The Jews now live in any part of the
town they please. The Rothschilds, of whom there are several
residing at Frankfort, are said to do a great deal of good both to
Christians and Jews.

August 6th. Since I have had time to look about me and hear
what people say, I am of opinion that no serious injury has been
done to the stability of the Government, whatever blows may
have been inflicted on its credit; no other party, no other individuals, have gained, whatever they may have lost, on the score
of popularity and character. The Court is entirely on their side.
The Queen never cared for any individual of her old Government
but Melbourne, and she knows that his political life is closed; she
feels that her own personal comfort is much greater with Peel's
Government and large majority, than it ever was, or is likely to be
again, with the Whigs. She remembers what a state of continual
agitation she was kept in, when they never knew from day to day
whether they should not be beaten and turned out, and she infinitely prefers her present state of security and repose, especially
as the present Ministers do all they can to please her, and her
husband is their strenuous and avowed friend. I see nothing to
alter my opinion that the principle on which Peel resolved to act,
and has acted, was the wisest and best he could adopt—that of
steering between extreme parties, of guiding, regulating, and restraining forward movements, the advance of which was, he
knew, inevitable, and which he did not deem undesirable. He

might have foreseen that this was a difficult part to play well. It was pretty sure to make him unpopular with his friends, as it has done, and it was equally sure not to conciliate his enemies, who, on the contrary, rejoiced to see him weakened by dissensions with his allies, and hastened to place him between two fires, and by embarrassing his march as much as they could to cast universal discredit upon him. The way to meet these difficulties was, in the first place, to be perfectly single-minded; to be open, bold, and resolute; and with his friends frank and conciliatory. Unhappily, Peel's character is not such as enabled him to display these qualities. He acts rather like the cautious leader of a party, than like a great and powerful Minister determined to do what he thinks right, casting himself upon public opinion, and trusting to its bearing them out in the long run. Then he is so cold, so reserved, and his ways are so little winning and attractive, that he cannot attach people to him personally, and induce them to bear with the Ministers for the sake of the man. Although I think his general views are sound, his way of working out his measures is not happy, and therefore the clamour against him is very general, and he finds very few defenders, admirers, and friends.

Nevertheless the Opposition pretenders to power are mistaken if they think he is at all near his downfall, or themselves likely to succeed him. The Tories and landlords do not want to turn him out; none of the great interests which support him and look to him for protection have begun to turn their thoughts and wishes to any other quarter; and if the 'volvenda dies' brings about a better state of things, if trade revives, and Irish agitation stagnates, it will be found that the clamour against Peel's Government had no great foundation of facts to rest upon.

Since I have been away nothing very interesting has occurred. The King of Hanover has been the great lion of London, all the Tories feasting and entertaining him with extraordinary demonstrations of civility and regard; but not so the Court, for the Queen has taken hardly any notice of him. He seems to have behaved very well, taking great pleasure in the attentions he has received, but giving no cause for complaint by any indecorous or imprudent language; in fact, he seems not to have meddled with politics in any way whatever. They tell a story of him, that one day at Buckingham Palace he proposed to Prince Albert to go out and walk with him. The Prince excused himself, saying he could not walk in the streets, as they should be exposed to inconvenience from the crowd of people. The King replied, 'Oh, never mind that. I was still more unpopular than you are now, and used to walk about with perfect impunity.'

August 8th. Yesterday morning I found the Duke of Wellington in my brother's room and in high good-humour. I began talking to him about the discovery lately made at Woodstock of the Duke of Marlborough's correspondence, which Sir George Murray had told me of; and this led him to talk of the Duke of Marlborough, of his character and military genius, and so on to other things. He said that he considered the principal characteristic of the Duke of Marlborough to have been his strong sound sense and great practical sagacity. That it was a mistake to say he was illiterate. People fancied so because of the way in which his words were misspelt, but in his time they spelt them as they were pronounced. He thought the errors he had committed were owing to his wife. As to his character, we must not judge of it according to the maxims by which men in our time were governed; besides that, they were less strict in his day; the condition of affairs itself produced a laxity; and though it was true he communicated with the Pretender and acted a double part, that was no more than many men in France did during Napoleon's reign, and he told a curious anecdote of Talleyrand. He said that at the Congress held at Erfurt, not long before Napoleon's marriage, he and the Emperor Alexander met for the purpose of discussing what should be done with Austria, Napoleon being anxious to plunder and degrade her to a great extent. He brought Talleyrand with him to this meeting, and Talleyrand completely threw him over. Every evening there was a meeting at the house of the Princess of Thurn and Taxis, between Alexander, Talleyrand, and Vincent, the Austrian Minister, at which they concerted what should be said to Napoleon the next day, and how they should parry his propositions. The Duke said that both Vincent and the Emperor Alexander had given him an account of all this transaction. He added, that though it was a sort of treachery on the part of Talleyrand towards Napoleon, he had no doubt he was really of opinion that it was very fit he should be thwarted, and that it was inexpedient to destroy the Austrian empire. He said many men, and respectable ones, in employment under Napoleon had been in constant communication with the Duke of Orleans.

The Duke then talked of the military genius of Marlborough, and said that though he was a very great man, the art of war was so far advanced since his time that it was impossible to compare him with more modern generals; and unquestionably Napoleon was the greatest military genius that ever existed; that he had advantages which no other man ever possessed in the unlimited means at his command and his absolute power and irresponsibility, and that he never scrupled at any expenditure of human life; but nevertheless his employment of his means and resources was wonderful. I told him that I remembered to have heard him say that he considered Napoleon's campaign of '14 to have been one of the greatest, if not the greatest, of his exploits, and that he was then ruined by his own impatience. He said it was quite true, and then repeated (what he had once before told me) that nothing could exceed the ability of Napoleon's operations, and if he had continued to act for a little longer in the same way, he would have forced the Allies to retreat, which they were in fact preparing to do. [The Duke] also mentioned, that though he had taken about 3,000 pieces of cannon of different sorts, he had never in his life lost a single gun.

August 26th. The day before yesterday the Queen prorogued Parliament. She was received much as usual—that is, with indifference; the Speech was reckoned good, well written, and Ireland, the principal topic, properly alluded to. I reserve for another day to speak about the session and its events. On Wednesday I went with Adolphus FitzClarence on board the new yacht 'Victoria and Albert,' and steamed as far as Gravesend. It is luxuriously fitted up, but everything is sacrificed to the com-

fort of the Court, the whole ship's company being crammed into
wretched dog-holes, officers included. I breakfasted with one of
the lieutenants, and he showed me their berths. They are packed
two officers in one berth, about seven feet by five at most, and, as
he said, they have not room to move, or dress themselves. The
whole of the arrangements were submitted to the Queen and
Prince, so that they were apprised of all this; what I heard on this
matter exemplifies the selfishness and absence of all consideration for others engendered by unbroken habits of indulgence
and eternal adulation. There is a large room, a sort of waiting-
room, allotted to the pages, who are in fact footmen, and
round this on both sides their berths, one to each. It was pointed
out that the room for the officers was insufficient, and suggested
that one half of these berths should be allotted to them and the
other half to the pages; the other pages they proposed to put on
board the attendant steamers. This proposal, which was only to
put the officers and the royal footmen on the same level as to
accommodation, was rejected, because it might possibly be inconvenient not to have *all* the servants together. They preferred
condemning the officers (all picked men and distinguished) to
be thus disgracefully treated rather than run the risk of sustain-
ing even a momentary inconvenience. The Admiralty are much
to blame for suffering the officers to be used with such indignity,
but flattery seems to be the order of the day.

September 19*th.* On Sunday I went to Richmond to call on
Miss Berry,[20] and found her in great indignation at Croker's recent
article in the 'Quarterly' upon the series just published of Lord
Orford's [*i.e., Horace Walpole's*] letters to Mann, angry on his account and on her own. Croker says, what has been often reported,

[20] [Miss Berry and her sister Agnes, who both died at a very advanced age
in 1852, were the last surviving friends of Horace Walpole, who called them
his 'Strawberries,' and had established a great intimacy between their youth
and his own age. Miss Berry's house in Curzon Street was one of the last
salons that existed in London, and the most agreeable. It was frequented by
all the rank, beauty, and talent of those times. Whenever the lamp over the
hall door was lit, any *habitué* of the house was welcome. Of the two sisters,
Mary Berry was born in March 1763, and died in November 1852; Agnes
Berry was born in May 1764, and died in January 1852.]

that Lord Orford offered to marry Mary Berry, and on her refusal, to marry Agnes. She says it is altogether false. He never
thought of marrying Agnes, and what passed with regard to herself was this: The Duchess of Gloster was very jealous of his
intimacy with the Berrys, though she treated them with civility.
At last her natural impetuosity broke out, and she said to him,
'Do you mean to marry Miss Berry or do you not?' To which he
replied, 'That is as Miss Berry herself pleases;' and that, as I understood her, is all that passed about it. She said nothing could
be more beautiful and touching than his affection for her, devoid
as it was of any particle of sensual feeling, and she should ever
feel proud of having inspired such a man with such a sentiment.

October 16th. I have been laid up with the gout more or less
during the last three weeks, and when that is upon me I am always disinclined to write. Just before I was attacked I went to
breakfast with George Lewis to meet Ranke, the author of 'The
Popes of the Sixteenth and Seventeenth Century.' He had got
Macaulay, who had reviewed his book, to meet him, Sir Alexander Duff Gordon and his wife (daughter of Mrs. Austin, his
translator), and Sir Edmund Head. I went prepared to listen to
some first-rate literary talk between such luminaries as Ranke
and Macaulay, but there never was a greater failure. The professor, a vivacious little man, not distinguished in appearance,
could talk no English, and his French, though spoken fluently,
was quite unintelligible. On the other hand, Macaulay could not
speak German, and he spoke French without any facility and
with a very vile accent. It was comical to see the abundance of
his matter struggling with his embarrassment in giving utterance
to it, to hear the torrent of knowledge trying to force its way
through the impediment of a limited acquaintance with the
French language and the want of habit of conversing in it. But
the struggle was of short duration. He began in French, but very
soon could bear the restraint no longer, and broke into English,
pouring forth his stores to the utterly unconscious and uncompre-
hending professor. This babel of a breakfast, at which it was impossible for seven people to converse in any common language,

soon came to an end, and Ranke was evidently glad to go off to the State Paper Office, where he was working every day. After he was gone, Macaulay held forth.

December 13*th*.   Duncannon in the evening told me the story of George II.'s robbery in Kensington Gardens, which I had heard before, but remembered imperfectly. He was walking with William IV., he said, in Kensington Gardens one day, and when they got to a certain spot the King said to him, 'It was here, my Lord, that my great-grandfather, King George II., was robbed. He was in the habit of walking every morning alone round the garden, and one day a man jumped over the wall, approached the King, but with great respect, and told him he was in distress, and was compelled to ask him for his money, his watch, and the buckles in his shoes. The King gave him what he had about him, and the man knelt down to take off his buckles, all the time with profound respect. When he had got everything, the King told him that there was a seal on the watch-chain of little or no value, but which he wished to have back, and requested he would take it off the chain and restore it. The man said, 'Your Majesty must be aware that we have already been here some time, and that it is not safe for me to stay longer, but if you will give me your word not to say anything of what has passed for twenty-four hours, I will place the seal at the same hour to-morrow morning on that stone,' pointing to a particular place. The King promised, went the next morning at the appointed hour, the man appeared, brought the seal, and then jumped over the wall and went off. 'His Majesty,' added King William, 'never afterwards walked alone in Kensington Gardens.'

All the people who have been at the Royal progress say there never was anything so grand as Chatsworth; and the Duke, albeit he would have willingly dispensed with this visit, treated the Queen right royally. He met her at the station and brought her in his own coach and six, with a coach and four following, and eight outriders. The finest sight was the illumination of the garden and the fountains; and after seeing the whole place covered with innumerable lamps and all the material of the illuminations, the guests were astonished and delighted when they got up the following morning not to find a vestige of them left, and the whole garden as trim and neat as if nothing had occurred. This was accomplished by Paxton, who got 200 men, set them to work, and worked with them the whole night till they had cleared away everything belonging to the exhibition of the preceding night.

February 22nd, 1844. The other day Bobus Smith gave us at dinner at Lady Holland's a good pun of Jekyll's (I so regret never having met him). He was asked to dine at Lansdowne House, but was engaged to the Chief Justice. It happened that the ceiling of the dining-room at Lansdowne House fell in, which when Jekyll heard, he said he had been invited to 'ruat cœlum,' but was engaged to 'fiat Justitia.'

March 16th. Writing of Mr. Grenville, I must mention an anecdote he told me the other day, illustrating the facility with which Pitt gave peerages to anybody who had a fancy for the honour. Mr. Grenville one day asked his cousin, Lord Glastonbury, what had induced him to get made a peer, for he could not think he had ever cared much for a title. He said, 'God, Devil!' (for such it seems was his queer habit of expressing himself) 'I'll tell you. I never thought of a peerage; but one day I took up the newspaper, and I read in it that Tommy Townshend was made a peer. Confound the fellow, said I, what right had he to be made a peer I should like to know. Why, I am as rich again as he is, and have a much better right. So I resolved to write to Pitt and tell him so. I wrote, and was made a peer the following week.'

June 10th. For the last week this town has been kept in a fever by the brief and unexpected visit of the Emperor of Russia. Brunnow told me he was at Petersburg, and had given up all idea of coming here, and the very next day the telegraph announced that he was at the Hague, and would arrive in London in twenty-four hours. Nobody knows now what was the cause of

this sudden and rapid expedition, for he travelled without stopping, and with extraordinary rapidity, from Petersburg, with the
exception of twenty-four hours at Berlin, and forty-eight hours
at the Hague. He alighted at the Palace, embraced the Queen,
and after his interview went to establish himself at Brunnow's.
He immediately visited all the Royal Family, and the Duke of
Wellington. The Duke attired himself in the costume of a Russian
Field-Marshal to receive the Emperor. On Monday he went to
Windsor, Tuesday to Ascot, Wednesday they gave him a Review, which went off very badly, owing to mistakes and bad
arrangement, but with which he expressed himself very well satisfied. The sight was pretty, glorious weather, 3,000 or 4,000
Guards, Horse, Foot, and Artillery in the Park, the Queen *en
calèche* with a brilliant suite. It was striking when the Duke went
and put himself at the head of his regiment, marched past, and
saluted the Queen and Emperor. The air resounded with acclamations as the old warrior passed, and the Emperor rode up to
him and shook him by the hand. He did the same by the Prince
and Duke of Cambridge as they respectively marched by at the
head of their regiments, but neither of them was so cheered as
the Duke. There was a blunder about the artillery. The Queen
cannot endure firing, and the Duke had ordered that the guns
should not be fired till she left the ground. By some mistake contrary orders were given, and they advanced and fired not far
from Her Majesty. The Duke was furious, and would not be
pacified, though Emperor, Queen, and Prince did their best to
appease him; he blew up, and swore lustily, and ordered the
luckless artillery into the rear. It was a mighty small concern for
the Emperor, who reviews 100,000 men, and sees 15,000 mount
guard every day; but he expressed his satisfaction, and when the
Queen said her troops were few in number, he told her that she
must consider his troops at her disposal exactly the same as her
own.

On Thursday they went to Ascot again, where they were received very well by a dense multitude; on Friday to London,
where they gave him a party at the Palace, omitting to ask half

the remarkable people, especially of the Opposition. On Saturday a breakfast at Chiswick, a beautiful *fête*, and perfectly
successful. Everything that was distinguished in London was collected to see and be seen by the Emperor. All the statesmen,
fine ladies, poets, artists, beauties, were collected in the midst of
a display of luxury and magnificence, set off by the most delicious
weather. The Emperor lunched in a room fitted up with his arms
and ensigns, and afterwards held a sort of circle on the grass,
where people were presented to him, and he went round talking
to one after another. His appearance on the whole disappointed
me. He is not so tall as I had heard he was—about 6 feet 2, I
should guess; and he has no remains of the beauty for which he
was once so celebrated, and which at his age, forty-eight, need
not have so entirely faded away; but the cares of such an Empire
may well have ravaged that head on which they sit not lightly.
He is become bald and bulky, but nevertheless is still a very fine
and grand-looking personage. He accepts his age and its consequences, and does not try to avert them by any artificial appli-
ances, and looks all the better for so doing. Though he has a very
imposing air, I have seen much nobler men; he does not bear the
highest aristocratic stamp; his general appearance is inferior to
that of Lord Anglesey or Lord Granville (both twenty-five years
older), and to others. He gives me more the idea of a Thracian
peasant raised to Empire, than of the descendant of a line of
kings; still his head, and especially his profile, is very fine, and his
manners are admirable, affable without familiarity, cordial yet
dignified, and particularly full of deference and gallantry to
women. As he moved round the circle all smiling and urbane, I
felt a sensation of awe mixed with that of curiosity at reflecting
that I saw before me a potentate so mighty and despotic, on
whose will and pleasure or caprice depended the fortune, the
happiness, and the lives of millions of creatures; and when the
condition of these subject millions and the frequent exercise of
such unbounded power flitted over my mind, I felt a pleasant
consciousness that I was beyond the sphere of its influence, free
as the birds in the air, at least from him, and I enjoyed that in-

voluntary comparison of my freedom with the slavery of his sub-jects, which is in itself happiness, or something like it.

The Emperor seems to have a keen eye for beauty, and most of the good-looking women were presented to him. He was very civil to M. de St. Aulaire (and so he had been to Van de Weyer the night before), and very civil to Lord Harrowby, Lord Gran-ville, Lord Lansdowne, to Clarendon, whom he had known in Russia, and to Palmerston. Lord John Russell was not presented to him, which was very wrong and ill-managed. Of all men he ought to have made acquaintance with the remarkable leader of the Whig party; but the Queen had not asked him to her party the night before, so that he never approached the Emperor at all. His Majesty thanked Lord Melbourne for having come to the breakfast, and afforded him the opportunity of making his ac-quaintance. He went away early, and the departure was pretty; the Royal equipages, the escort of Lancers with their pennons glancing in the sun, the steps and balcony clustered over with women to speed the parting guest; and as he bade the Duke of Devonshire a kind farewell, and mounted his carriage, while the Russian Hymn struck up, and he took his departure for ever from the gay scene and brilliant assemblage, proceeding on the march of his high and hard destiny, while we all turned to our humble, obscure, peaceful, and uneventful occupations, it was an exhibition to stir the imagination and excite busy thoughts.

At the opera, which was crowded from top to bottom, he was very well received and would have been better, if the Queen had had the tact and the grace to bring him forward to receive the burst of acclamations with which the audience was ready to hail him; but she did not, and he could not present himself of his own accord. They say he is excessively disgusted with the dullness of the Court, and well he may be. The Queen has no conversation, and no attempt was made to amuse him. Lady Clanricarde, to whom he paid a visit, told me that she was struck with his saying not one word expressive of admiration or satisfaction about any-body or anything at Court—not a syllable in praise either of the Queen or Prince.

February 25th, 1845. Yesterday we heard of the death of Sydney Smith, which took place on Sunday. His case had for some time been hopeless, and it was merely a question how long he could be kept alive by the remedies applied to stop the water on his chest. It is the extinction of a great luminary, such as we shall hardly see the like of again, and who has reigned without a rival in wit and humour for a great length of time. It is almost impossible to overrate his wit, humour, and drollery, or their effect in society. Innumerable comical sayings and jokes of his are or have been current, but their repetition gives but an imperfect idea of the flavour and zest of the original. His appearance, voice, and manner added immensely to the effect, and the bursting and uproarious merriment with which he poured forth his good things, never failed to communicate itself to his audience, who were always in fits of laughter. If there was a fault in it, it was that it was too amusing. People so entirely expected to be made to die of laughing, and he was so aware of this, that there never seemed to be any question of conversation when he was of the party, or at least no more than just to afford Sydney pegs to hang his jokes on. This is the misfortune of all great professed wits, and I have very little doubt that Sydney often felt oppressed with the weight of his comical obligations, and came on the stage like a great actor, forced to exert himself, but not always in the vein to play his part. It is well known that he was subject at home to frequent fits of depression, but I believe in his own house in the country he could often be a very agreeable companion, on a lower and less ambitious level, for his talk never could be otherwise than seasoned with his rich vein of humour and wit, as the current, though it did not always flow with the same force, was never dry. He was full of varied information, and a liberal, kind-hearted, charitable man. The favourite objects of his jokes were the men of his own cloth, especially the bishops, among whom he once probably aspired to sit. I do not suppose he had any dogmatic and doctrinal opinions in respect to religion, and that in his heart of hearts he despised and derided all that the world wrangles and squabbles about; but he had the true religion of benevolence and charity.

London, August 28th. Beauvale told me another thing which I did not know before. When the proposal to give the prince fifty thousand a year was cut down by the Tories to thirty thousand, [*the Queen*] was not angry but pleased. She did not wish him to be made so rich, and said the Coburgs were already sufficiently exalted and it was well that they should have this little check. Her sentiments are very different now, when nothing is great enough for her husband, and she even insists on a throne like her own being erected for him under the royal canopy.

September 7th. A complete absence of events, till a few days ago, when after a very short illness Lord Spencer died at his house near Doncaster. My own acquaintance with him was not intimate, but I had a great respect and esteem for him, and no man ever died with a fairer character, or more generally regretted. In his county he was exceedingly beloved and respected. The career of Lord Spencer presents few materials to the biographer, for he had neither the brilliant nor even plausible exterior which interests and captivates vulgar imaginations, but he had sterling qualities of mind and character which made him one of the most useful and valuable, as he was one of the best and most amiable men of his day. He was the very model and type of an English gentleman, filling with propriety the station in which fortune had placed him, and making the best use of the abilities which Nature had bestowed upon him. Modest without diffidence, confident without vanity, ardently desiring the good of his country, without the slightest personal ambition, he took that part in public affairs which his station and his opinions prompted, and he marched through the mazes of politics with that straightforward bravery, which was the result of sincerity, singleness of purpose, the absence of all selfishness, and a true, genuine, but unpretending patriotism. His tastes, habits, and turn of mind were peculiarly and essentially English; he was a high-minded,

unaffected, sensible, well-educated English gentleman, addicted
to all those rural pursuits and amusements which are considered
national, a practical farmer and fond of field sports, but enjoying
all things in moderation. In his political principles he was consistent, liberal, and enlightened, but he was too much of a philosopher, and had too deeply studied the book of life to entertain
any wild notions of human perfectibility. He observed, therefore, a just proportion, and a perfect moderation in his political
views and objects, firmly believing in the capacity of the Constitution to combine the utmost extent of civil and religious liberty with the predominance of law, and a safe and vigorous
administration of public affairs. His whole life, therefore, was
devoted to abrogating exclusive and oppressive laws, extending
political franchises, giving freedom to commerce, and by the
progress of a policy at once sound and safe, to promote the welfare and happiness of the mass of the people, and the power and
prosperity of the country.

Lord Spencer came into office as Chancellor of the Exchequer
and leader of the House of Commons with Lord Grey's Government in 1830; on the death of his father in 1834, his elevation
to the House of Lords obliged him to relinquish that office, upon
which, as is well known, King William dismissed the Whig Government, on the pretext that it was so weakened as to be unworthy of public confidence and incapable of carrying on the
business of the State. This was indeed only a pretext for getting
rid of an obnoxious Ministry; but the King's venturing upon so
bold a step upon such grounds affords a convincing proof of the
high consideration which Lord Spencer enjoyed in the House of
Commons and in the country. Nor, indeed, was it possible to exag-
gerate that consideration. The greatest homage that ever was
rendered to character and public virtue was exhibited in his
popularity and authority during the four eventful years when
he led the Whig Government and party in the House of Commons. Without one showy accomplishment, without wit to amuse
or eloquence to persuade, with a voice unmelodious and a manner ungraceful, and barely able to speak plain sense in still plainer

language, he exercised in the House of Commons an influence and even a dominion greater than any leader either after or before him. Neither Pitt the father, nor Pitt the son, in the plenitude of their magnificent dictatorships, nor Canning in the days of his most brilliant displays of oratory and wit, nor Castlereagh, returning in all the glory of an ovation from the overthrow of Napoleon, could govern with the same sway the most unruly and fastidious assembly which the world ever saw.

November 16th. All the world went last night to the St. James's Theatre to see the second representation of 'Every Man in his Humour,' by Dickens and the 'Punch' people. The house was crammed full. I was in a bad place, heard very ill, and was so bored that at the end of the third act I went away. Dickens acted Bobadil very well indeed, and Douglas Jerrold (the author of the Caudle Lectures in 'Punch') Master Stephen well also; the rest were very moderate and the play intolerably heavy. A play 200 years old, a comedy of character only, without plot or story, or interest of any sort or kind, can hardly go down. The audience were cold as ice, because, it was said, they were too fine; but I believe because they were not at all amused.[21]

Worsley, November 22nd. I came here, for the first time, on Monday last, to see the fine new house Francis Egerton has built.

I have passed these few days in seeing this place and some of the manufacturing wonders at Manchester. On Tuesday I went over the house and place; and then to Francis' yard, a sort of small dockyard and manufactory; then on the canal in the Trust boat—a luxurious barge fitted up with every convenience and comfort, with a fireplace, and where one may write, read, and live just as in the house; a kitchen behind. The boat is drawn by two horses with postilions in livery, and they trot along at a

[21] [I went to see this performance with Lord Melbourne, Mrs. Norton, and my cousin Lady Duff Gordon, who gave me a place in their box. Lord Melbourne said before the curtain rose that it was a dull play, 'with no μῦθος in it,' that was his expression. Between the acts he exclaimed in a stentorian voice, heard across the pit, 'I knew this play would be dull, but that it would be so damnably dull as this I did not suppose!'—H. R.]

merry pace, all the craft (except, by compact, 'the Swift boats,' as they are called) giving way to the Trust boat. On Wednesday I went through the subterraneous canal, about a mile and a half long, into the coalpit, saw the working in the mine, and came up by the shaft; a black and dirty expedition, scarcely worth the trouble, but which I am glad to have made. The colliers seem a very coarse set, but they are not hard worked, and, in fact, do no more than they choose. There are many miles of this under-ground canal. On Thursday I went to Manchester, and saw one of the great cotton and one of the great silk manufactories; very curious even to me, who am ignorant of mechanics, and could only stare and wonder, without being able to understand the niceties of the beautiful and complicated machinery by which all the operations of these trades are performed. The heat of the rooms in the former of them was intense, but the man who showed them to us told us it was caused by the prodigious fric-tion, and the room might be much cooler, but the people liked the heat. Yesterday I went to the infant school, admirably man-aged; then to the recreation ground of the colliers and working hands—a recent establishment. It is a large piece of ground, planted and levelled round about what is called the paying-house, where the men are paid their wages once a fortnight. The object is to encourage sports and occupations in the open air, and induce them not to go to the alehouse. There are cricket, quoits, and football, and ginger-beer and coffee are sold to the people, but no beer or spirits. This has only a partial success. Afterwards to Patricroft, to see Messrs. Nasmyth's great establishment for making locomotive engines, every part of which I went over. I asked at all the places about the wages and habits of the work-people. In Birley's cotton factory 1,200 are employed, the ma-jority girls, who earn from ten to fourteen shillings a week. At Nasmyth's the men make from twenty to thirty-two shillings a week. They love to change about, and seldom stay very long at one place; some will go away in a week, and some after a day. In the hot factory rooms the women look very wan, very dirty, and one should guess very miserable. They work eleven hours generally, but though it might be thought that domestic service must be preferable, there is the greatest difficulty in procuring women-servants here. All the girls go to the factory in spite of the confinement, labour, close atmosphere, dirt, and moral danger which await them. The parents make them go, because they earn money which they bring home, and they like the independence and the hours every evening, and the days from Saturday to Monday, of which they can dispose.

Worsley, November 24th. The day I came here Lady Holland died, that is, she died at two o'clock in the preceding night. She evinced during her illness a very philosophical calmness and resolution, and perfect good humour, aware that she was dying, and not afraid of death. The religious people don't know what to make of it. She never seems to have given the least sign of any religious feeling or belief. Though she was a woman for whom nobody felt any affection, and whose death therefore will have excited no grief, she will be regretted by a great many people, some from kindly, more from selfish motives, and all who had been accustomed to live at Holland House and continued to be her *habitués* will lament over the fall of the curtain on that long drama, and the final extinction of the flickering remnant of a social light which illuminated and adorned England and even Europe for half a century. The world never has seen and never will again see anything like Holland House, and though it was by no means the same thing as it was during Lord Holland's life, Lady Holland contrived to assemble round her to the last a great society, comprising almost everybody that was conspicuous, remarkable, and agreeable. The closing of her house, therefore, will be a serious and an irreparable loss, especially to those old friends who are too old to look out for new places of resort and to form new social habits. She was a very strange woman, whose character it would not be easy to describe, and who can only be perfectly understood from a knowledge and consideration of her habits and peculiarities. She was certainly clever, and she had acquired a great deal of information both from books and men, having passed her whole life amidst people remarkable for their abilities and knowledge. She cared very little for her children, but she sometimes pretended to care for them, and she also pretended to entertain strong feelings of friendship for many individuals; and this was not all insincerity, for, in fact, she did entertain them as strongly as her nature permitted. She was often capricious, tyrannical, and troublesome, liking to provoke, and disappoint, and thwart her acquaintances, and she was often obliging, good-natured, and considerate to the same people. To those who were ill and suffering, to whom she could show any personal kindness and attention, among her intimate friends, she never failed to do so. She was always intensely selfish, dreading solitude above everything, and eternally working to enlarge the circle of her society, and to retain all who ever came within it. She could not live alone for a single minute; she never was alone, and even in her moments of greatest grief it was not in solitude but in society that she sought her consolation. Her love and habit of domination were both unbounded, and they made her do strange and often unwarrantable things. None ever lived who assumed such privileges as Lady Holland, and the docility with which the world submitted to her vagaries was wonderful. Never was anybody more invariably kind to her servants or more solicitous for their comfort. In this probably selfish considerations principally moved her; it was essential to her comfort to be diligently and zealously served, and she secured by her conduct to them their devoted attachment. It used often to be said in joke that they were very much better off than her guests.

January 13*th*, 1846.　There has been a curious scene with Melbourne at Windsor, which was told me by Jocelyn, who was present. It was at dinner, when Melbourne was sitting next to the Queen. Some allusion was made to passing events and to the expected measure, when Melbourne suddenly broke out, 'Ma'am, it is a damned dishonest act.' The Queen laughed, and tried to quiet him, but he repeated, 'I say again it is a very dishonest act,' and then he continued a tirade against abolition of Corn Laws, the people not knowing how to look, and the Queen only laughing. The Court is very strong in favour of Free Trade, and not less in favour of Peel.

Newmarket, Sunday [*no date.*] Arbuthnot told the Duke of Bedford an anecdote, which I have great difficulty in believing. It is this: that when he was at the Treasury one day, old Sir Robert Peel called on him and said, 'I am come to you about a matter of great importance to myself, but which I think is also of importance to your Government. If you do not speedily confer high office on my son he will go over to the Whigs, and be for ever lost to the party.' He told Lord Liverpool this, who immediately made young Peel Irish Secretary. If it is true, never did any father do a greater injury to a son, for if Peel had joined a more congenial party he might have followed the bent of his political inclination, and would have escaped all the false positions in which he has been placed; instead of the insincere career that he has pursued, which must have been replete with internal mortification, disgust, and shame, he might have given out his real sentiments and acted upon them. He would neither have fettered nor perverted his understanding, and he would have been an abler, a better, and a happier man, besides incomparably more useful to the country. As it is, his whole life has been spent in doing enormous mischief, and in attempts to repair that mischief. It will be a curious biography whenever it comes to be written, but not a creditable one.

May 21st. Last week the debate in the House of Commons came to a close at last, wound up by a speech of Disraeli's, very clever, in which he hacked and mangled Peel with the most unsparing severity, and positively tortured his victim. It was a miserable and degrading spectacle. The whole mass of the Protectionists cheered him with vociferous delight, making the roof ring again; and when Peel spoke, they screamed and hooted at him in the most brutal manner. When he vindicated himself, and talked of honour and conscience, they assailed him with shouts of derision and gestures of contempt. Such treatment in a House of Commons where for years he had been an object of deference and respect, nearly overcame him. The Speaker told me that for a minute and more he was obliged to stop, and for the first time in his life, probably, he lost his self-possession; and the Speaker thought he would have been obliged to sit down, and expected him to burst into tears. They hunt him like a fox, and they are eager to run him down and kill him in the open, and they are full of exultation at thinking they have nearly accomplished this object. It is high time such a state of things should finish. To see the Prime Minister and leader in the House of Commons thus beaten and degraded, treated with contumely by three-fourths of the party he has been used to lead, is a sorry sight, and very prejudicial to the public weal. He is no longer able to conduct the business of the country in Parliament.

March 8th, 1847. George Anson told me yesterday that the Queen's affairs are in such good order and so well managed, that she will be able to provide for the whole expense of Osborne out of her income without difficulty, and that by the time it is furnished it will have cost 200,000*l*. He said, also, that the Prince of Wales when he came of age would not have less than 70,000*l*. a year from the Duchy of Cornwall. They have already saved 100,000*l*. The Queen takes for his maintenance whatever she pleases, and the rest, after paying charges, is invested in the funds or in land, and accumulates for him.

April 2nd. Yesterday Le Marchant told me an anecdote illustrative of the power of the press. He called late one night many years ago on Barnes at his house, and while there another visitor arrived whom he did not see, but who was shown into another room. Barnes went to him and after a quarter of an hour returned, when Le Marchant said, 'Shall I tell you who your visitor is?' Barnes said yes, if he knew. 'Well, then, I know his step and his voice; it is Lord Durham.' Barnes owned it was, when

Le Marchant said, 'What does he come for?' Barnes said he came on behalf of King Leopold, who had been much annoyed by some article in the 'Times,' to entreat they would put one in of a contrary and healing description. As Le Marchant said, here was the proudest man in England come to solicit the editor of a newspaper for a crowned head!

Moxon told me on Wednesday that some years ago Disraeli had asked him to take him into partnership, but he refused, not thinking he was sufficiently prudent to be trusted. He added he did not know how Dizzy would like to be reminded of that now.

June 2nd. The death of O'Connell, I have said, made little or no sensation here. He had quarrelled with half of his followers, he had ceased to be the head of a great party animated by any great principle, or encouraged to pursue any attainable object; the Repeal cause was become despicable and hopeless without ceasing to be noisy and mischievous. O'Connell knew not what to say or what to do; he had become bankrupt in reputation and in power, and was no longer able to do much good or much harm. History will speak of him as one of the most remarkable men who ever existed; he will fill a great space in its pages; his position was unique; there never was before, and there never will be again, anything at all resembling it. To rise from the humblest situation to the height of empire like Napoleon is no uncommon destiny; there have been innumerable successful adventurers and usurpers; but there never was a man who, without altering his social position in the slightest degree, without obtaining any office or station whatever, raised himself to a height of political power which gave him an enormous capacity for good or evil, and made him the most important and most conspicuous man of his time and country. It would not be a very easy matter to do him perfect justice. A careful examination of his career and an accurate knowledge of his character would be necessary for the purpose. It is impossible to question the greatness of his abilities or the sincerity of his patriotism. His dependence on his country's bounty, in the rent that was levied for so many years, was alike honourable to the contributors and the recipient; it was an income nobly given and nobly earned. Up to the conquest of Catholic Emancipation his was certainly a great and glorious career. What he might have done and what he ought to have done after that, it is not easy to say, but undoubtedly he did far more mischief than good, and exhibited anything but a wise, generous, and patriotic spirit. In Peel's administration he did nothing but mischief, and it is difficult to comprehend with what object and what hope he threw Ireland into confusion, and got up that Repeal agitation, the folly and impracticability of which nobody must have known so well as himself.

July 13th. The Cambridge installation went off with prodigious *éclat,* and the Queen was enchanted at the enthusiastic reception she met with; but the Duke of Wellington was if possible received with even more enthusism. It is incredible what popularity environs him in his latter days; he is followed like a show wherever he goes, and the feeling of the people *for him* seems to be the liveliest of all popular sentiments; yet he does nothing to excite it, and hardly appears to notice it. He is in wonderful vigour of body, but strangely altered in mind, which is in a fitful uncertain state, and there is no knowing in what mood he may be found; everybody is afraid of him, nobody dares to say anything to him; he is sometimes very amiable and good-humoured, sometimes very irritable and morose. About this affair of the Statue, Croker and Trench contrived to work him up to a state of frenzy; he was as near as possible resigning upon it. When Lord John wrote to him the other day in consequence of what passed in the House of Commons, he wrote a long rigmarole of an answer, which Lord John did not read yesterday, but gave the substance of it. All this is very unlike him. Then he is astonishing the world by a strange intimacy he has struck up with Miss [*Burdett Coutts*], with whom he passes his life, and all sorts of reports have been rife of his intention to marry her. Such are the lamentable appearances of decay in his vigorous mind, which are the more to be regretted because he is in most enviable circumstances, without any political responsibility, yet associated with public affairs, and surrounded with every sort of respect and consideration on every side—at Court, in Parliament, in society, and in the country.

October 23rd. The most remarkable circumstance is the intense interest and curiosity which are felt about Peel's opinions and intentions. Everybody asks with anxiety what he says, what he thinks, what he will do. His vanity may well be gratified by the immense importance which is attached to his opinions and to the course he may take and recommend; his power seems to be as great out of office as it ever was in office; nothing was ever so strange or anomalous as his position. Half the commercial world attributes the distress and danger to his Bill; he is liked by nobody. The Conservatives detest him with unquenched hatred, and abuse him with unmitigated virulence. The Whigs regard him with a mixture of fear, suspicion, and dislike, but treat him with great deference and respect. There is a party which is called by others and by itself, but not (publicly at least) acknowledged by him as his party; it is far from numerous, and too weak for substantive power. He has never opened his lips on the great questions of the day, and is an oracle shrouded in mystery. It would seem as if a man thus abandoned by the majority of his former political friends and adherents, without personal attachments and following, an object of hatred to one party and of suspicion to the other, the country at large or a great proportion of it attributing to his financial measures the distress by which all are afflicted or endangered, could by no possibility occupy any great and important position in the country: nevertheless he does. All eyes are turned upon him as if by a sort of fascination. If the country could be polled to decide who should be Minister, he would be elected by an immense majority. There is a prevalent opinion that he *must* return to power; nobody knows when or how, but the notion is that the present men are weak, that the public necessities and perils are great, and if a crisis of difficulty and danger should arrive, that Peel is the only man capable of extricating the country from it. The consequence of all this is that his *prestige* and his influence are enormous.

December 22nd. I went yesterday to St. George's Hospital to see the chloroform tried. A boy two years and a half old was cut for a stone. He was put to sleep in a minute; the stone was so large and the bladder so contracted, the operator could not get hold of it, and the operation lasted above twenty minutes, with repeated probings by different instruments; the chloroform was applied from time to time, and the child never exhibited the slightest sign of consciousness, and it was exactly the same as operating on a dead body. A curious example was shown of what is called the *étiquette* of the profession. The operator (whose name I forget) could not extract the stone, so at last he handed the instrument to Keate, who is the finest operator possible, and he got hold of the stone. When he announced that he had done so, the first man begged to have the forceps back that he might draw it out, and it was transferred to him; but in taking it he let go the stone, and the whole thing had to be done over again. It was accomplished, but not of course without increasing the local inflammation, and endangering the life of the child. I asked Keate why, when he had got hold of the stone, he did not draw it out. He said the other man's 'dignity' would have been hurt if he had not been allowed to complete what he had begun! I have no words to express my admiration for this invention, which is the greatest blessing ever bestowed on mankind, and the inventor of it the greatest of benefactors, whose memory ought to be venerated by countless millions for ages yet to come. All the great discoveries of science sink into insignificance when compared with this. It is a great privilege to have lived in the times which saw the production of steam, of electricity, and now of ether—that is, of the development and application of them to human purposes, to the multiplication of enjoyments and the mitigation of pain. But wonderful as are the powers and the feats of the steam-engine and the electric telegraph, the chloroform far transcends them all in its beneficent and consolatory operations.

January 22nd, 1848. Lady Beauvale told me some anecdotes of the royal children. The Princess Royal is very clever, strong in body and in mind; the Prince of Wales weaker, more timid, and

the Queen says he is a stupid boy; but the hereditary and un-
failing antipathy of our sovereigns to their heirs apparent seems
thus early to be taking root. He seems too to have an incipient
propensity to that sort of romancing which distinguished his uncle, George IV. The child told Lady Beauvale that during their
cruise he was very nearly thrown overboard and was proceeding
to tell her how, when the Queen overheard him, sent him off with
a flea in his ear, and told her it was totally untrue.

January 26th. Came back from Brocket on Monday. Melbourne not much inclined to talk; he dines at a quarter-past
seven, and he went to bed, or at least to his room, at half-past
eight. He is as anti-Palmerstonian as his brother, agreed with me
that Palmerston had all along greatly exaggerated the importance
of the Spanish marriage. Much talk with Beauvale, particularly
about Palmerston; he told me an anecdote of him which shows
the man and how difficult he is to manage. During the Spanish
discussions Beauvale was at Windsor, and one day when the
Prince was in his room the draft of a despatch from Palmerston
arrived to Lord John Russell, which he wanted to show to the
Prince, and afterwards to submit to the Queen for her sanction.
Finding the Prince was in Beauvale's room, he came there and
read out the despatch. There was a paragraph in it saying the
succession of the Duchesse de Montpensier's children would be
inadmissible by the constitutional law of Spain (or words to this
effect). Lord John said he thought this ought to be expunged;
that we might say what we pleased as to the effect of treaties,
but it did not become *us* to lay down the constitutional law of
Spain; the Prince and Beauvale both concurred, and Lord John
said he would strike out this passage, and submit it so amended
to the Queen. He did so, and Her Majesty took the same view. It
was returned so altered to Palmerston; but when the despatch
was published, it was found that Palmerston had re-inserted the
paragraph, and so it stood. What more may have passed I know
not, but it is clear that they all *stood* it, as they always will.

Lady Beauvale gave me an account of the scene at dinner at
Windsor when Melbourne broke out against Peel (about the Corn

Laws). She was sitting next Melbourne, who was between her and the Queen; he said pretty much what I have somewhere else stated, and he would go on though it was evidently disagreeable to the Queen, and embarrassing to everybody else. At last the Queen said to him, 'Lord Melbourne, I must beg you not to say anything more on this subject now; I shall be very glad to discuss it with you at any other time,' and then he held his tongue. It is however an amiable trait in her, that while she is austere to almost everybody else, she has never varied in her attachment to him, and to him everything has always been permitted; he might say and do what he liked. Now she constantly writes to him, never forgets his birthday.

February 13*th.* On Friday I was with Graham for a long time, who talked a good deal of colonial matters, and said the change in our commercial policy brought about the necessity of a great one in our colonial policy, that we ought to limit instead of extending our colonial empire, that Canada must soon be independent. He condemned the Caffre war, and extension of the Cape Colony, that we ought only to have a *Gibraltar* there, a house of call; condemned New Zealand and Labuan and Hong Kong; considered the West India interest as gone, and dilated at great length (and very well) on these points.

London, February 28*th.* The French Revolution has driven for the time every other subject out of thought, and so astounding has the event been, so awful and surprising from its inconceivable rapidity and the immensity of the operation, that every mind has been kept in a restless whirl and tumult incompatible with calm reflexion; while from the quick succession of events crowding on each other, all dashed with lies, false reports, exaggerations, and errors, it has been almost impossible to sit down and give a clear, connected, and true account of what has happened. By degrees the facts develope themselves and the fictions are cast aside; but the time is not yet arrived for completing this historical process. There are people alive who remember the whole of the first Revolution, and we of middle age are all familiar with the second; but this, the third, transcends them both.

The first Revolution was a long and gradual act, extending over years. The second was not unexpected; the causes were working openly and ominously; and at last the great stroke so rashly attempted, was only the concluding scene of a drama which long had been before the world. In 1789 everybody saw that a revolution was inevitable; in 1830 everybody thought that it was probable; but in 1848, up to the very moment at which the explosion took place, no human being dreamt of a revolution and of the dethronement of the King. The power of the Government appeared to be immense and unimpaired. The King was still considered one of the wisest and boldest of men, with a thorough knowledge of the country and the people he ruled; and though his prudence and that of his Ministers had been greatly impugned by their mode of dealing with the question of Parliamentary reform, the worst that anybody anticipated was the fall of Guizot's Cabinet, and that reform of some sort would be found necessary. But no one imagined that the King, defended by an army of 100,000 men and the fortifications of Paris (which it was always said he had cunningly devised to give himself full power over the capital), was exposed to any personal risk and danger. There was a strong reforming and, it might be, a strong republican or revolutionary spirit abroad, but the principal leaders of Opposition were understood to have no designs against the monarchy, and it was believed by those who had good opportunities of knowing that the *bourgeoisie* of Paris were comparatively indifferent to political questions, averse to revolutionary movements, and the determined advocates of order and tranquillity. For some time before the day appointed for the Reform banquet, much anxiety prevailed for the peace of the capital; but when it was announced that the Government did not mean to interfere, all apprehension subsided; and when the proclamation of Odilon Barrot and the chiefs of the Banquet appeared, it was regarded as a false and imprudent step, which by putting the Ministers in the right would only seem to strengthen their authority and avert their downfall, which otherwise had been probable. Duchâtel made a very good speech in the Chamber of Deputies, and proved that this last act was so clearly illegal and mischievous that the Ministers were bound to take the course they did; and as the banqueters showed a disposition to obey the Government, nobody doubted that the whole affair would end quietly.

When therefore this great and sudden insurrection took place, sweeping everything before it with the irresistible speed and violence of a hurricane, everybody here stood aghast; but for the first two days no one anticipated the final catastrophe. At Paris, from the King downwards, all seem to have lost their presence of mind and judgement. Everything was involved in perplexity and confusion; the roar of insurrectionary Paris affrighted the ears and bewildered the senses of the inmates of the Tuileries. At the moment I am writing we are still ignorant of the minute details of all that passed, of what the King said and did, and how others played their several parts. We know that Guizot resigned, that Molé was appointed—a capital fault, for Molé was another Guizot, and the selection only proved how unconscious the King was of the precipice on the brink of which he was standing. Some precious hours were lost in Molé's abortive attempt. Then came Thiers and Odilon Barrot, Ministers of a few hours, who, seduced by the deceptive applause of the rabble, fancied they could command and restrain the people of Paris, and who persuaded the King to withdraw the troops, telling him they would answer for the people. This fatal advice cost him the Crown. The tide swept on; a host of people, and among them Emile Girardin, rushed to the Tuileries, told the King his life was menaced, and advised him to abdicate; he refused. The people about him, and his own son amongst them (Duc de Montpensier), pressed him, and he signed the act of abdication. Still the crowd pressed on, and the palace was unprotected. He resolved, or was persuaded, to fly; and with the Queen and such of his family as were with him he quitted the palace with such precipitation that they had no time to take anything, and they had scarcely any money amongst them. They proceeded to Dreux, where they separated, and as yet no one knows where the King is, or where those of his family are who are not yet arrived in England.

The Duchesse d'Orléans, after the terrible scene in the Chamber of Deputies, was taken to some house in or near Paris, where she now lies concealed. All these events passed with the velocity of an express train; hardly an interval was placed between circumstances and conditions of the most opposite description. No monarchy or monarch ever fell with such superhuman rapidity. There is something awful and full of fear and pity in the contemplation of such a tremendous vicissitude: of a great King and a numerous and prosperous family, not many hours before reposing in the security of an apparently impregnable power, suddenly toppled down from this magnificent eminence and laid prostrate in the dust, covered with ignominy and reproach, and pursued by terror and grief. All at once the whole edifice of grandeur and happiness fell to the ground. The flight was undignified. It would be hard to accuse Louis Philippe of want of courage, of which he has given on various occasions many signal proofs; but he certainly displayed no resolution on this occasion. It is very doubtful whether his person would have been injured; the people have evinced no thirst for blood. It was then, indeed, too late for resistance, for the means had been withdrawn; but it may fairly be asked if it would not have been the wiser course to affront the danger of popular rage, and to have tried what might have been done by firmness, by reason, and by concession at the same time. All this is speculation. It may be that his life and that of his Queen would have been sacrificed; but on a more terrible occasion, when the same palace was invaded by a more formidable mob, a King still more unpopular and a detested Queen were left uninjured; and it is far more probable that the abdication of Louis Philippe would have satisfied and disarmed the wrath and fury of the people.

There is a strong impression that if they had unsparingly used the military means at their disposal while it was still time, the monarchy would have been saved and the tumult suppressed. The recollection of the 13th Vendémiaire and the Place St. Roch, when the troops of the Convention defeated the Sections of Paris, produces this notion. But when the time was given to the *émeute* to grow and expand, and when the National Guards took part in it, all was over; for the troops of the line, who would have repressed the mob, would not fight against the National Guards. Between blunders, bad advice, and delay, the insurrection sprang at once into gigantic proportions, and the world has seen with amazement a King who was considered so astute and courageous, with sons full of spirit and intelligence, sink without striking a blow for their kingdom. Louis Philippe has been seventeen years on the throne; in many respects a very amiable man, and, though crafty and unscrupulous as a politician, and neither beloved nor respected, he has never done anything to make himself an object of the excessive hatred and bitter feelings which have been exhibited against him and his family. The mob, though, on the whole, moderate and good-humoured, have been violent against his person, and they plundered the Palais Royal, invaded the Tuileries, and burnt Neuilly to show their abhorrence of him.

London, March 5th. The fugitives have all arrived here day by day with the exception of the Duchesse d'Orléans and her children, who are supposed to be in Germany. The King and Queen came yesterday from Newhaven, where they landed; Madame de Lieven and Guizot the day before, the one from Paris, the other through Belgium; they were in the same train (leaving Paris at seven o'clock on Thursday night), but neither knew the other was there. The King, as soon as he reached England, wrote a letter to the Queen, in which he gave her to understand that he considered all as over with him, and he said that it was the *Comte de Neuilly* who thanked her for all her past and present kindness to himself and his family. It was a very good letter (Lord Lansdowne tells me), and the Queen was much moved by it. Her personal resentment had long ceased; Aberdeen told me last night that she had told him so not long ago, and that though the political question was another thing, her personal feelings towards the French Royal Family were what they had ever been.

Yesterday I saw Madame de Lieven, and heard her narrative,

both personal and historical. With the sufferers, as with the spectators, the predominant feeling is one of intense astonishment amounting to a sort of incredulity; every one repeats that nothing that history has recorded, or fiction invented, ever approached this wonderful reality. The beginning, the middle, and the end of the contest have been equally wonderful: the conduct of the old Government and the conduct of the new; the events of months or years crammed into a few days or hours; the whole change so vast and complete, made as at the stroke of an enchanter's wand. France, on Monday, February 22nd, a powerful, peaceful, and apparently impregnable Monarchy; on Wednesday, 24th of the same month, the whole of her Royalty scattered over the face of the earth, and France become a Republic no less powerful and peaceful.

Madame de Lieven's story runs thus. On Sunday—that is, this day fortnight—she had a reception as usual. No alarm prevailed, but she was a little struck by Delessert telling her that there was a good deal of agitation amongst some of the lower orders of workmen, and those who were known to the Government as Communists; still he did not appear to attach much importance to it. On Monday evening Guizot told her that it was possible there might be some rioting and disturbance in the streets the following day, and he advised her to go out of her house for a few hours in the morning, which she did, ordering her dinner and meaning to return. That same day the commotions began, but still the Ministers were unterrified; and though the affair began to be serious, they never doubted that they should be able to suppress the tumult and restore order. Everything went on, as is well known, up to Wednesday morning, when Guizot saw the King, told him all would go right, and went to the Chamber. While there Duchâtel called him out, and told him the King wanted him directly at the Tuileries. He was surprised, asked for what, and proposed they should go together, which they did. When they got there they found the King much disturbed; he said the Commandant of a Legion of the National Guard had been to him and told him they must have reform, and he was afraid the rest of the National Guard would follow the example. 'Well,' said Guizot, 'if they do, we shall have no difficulty in putting down such a demonstration.' 'Oh, but,' said the King, 'that will produce bloodshed, and may lead to lamentable events;' and then, after beating about the bush a good deal, and with many expressions of personal attachment to Guizot, he said, 'Perhaps a change of Ministers might settle everything, and relieve him from his embarrassment.' Guizot at once said that the mere suggestion of such a thing made it 'une affaire résolue,' and if His Majesty thought that by taking any other Ministers he could improve the state of his affairs, he, of course, ought to do so. The King then talked of his regrets, and that he would rather abdicate than part with him. Guizot said abdication was not to be thought of. The King then talked of sending for Molé, and Guizot assured him of his readiness to support Molé, or any other man who would maintain Conservative principles. He then returned to the Chamber, and announced that the Ministers were out. The Conservatives were struck with astonishment and alarm; crowded round Guizot, and asked him if he had resigned. He said 'No; that he had been dismissed.' Molé was sent for, and said he would try and form a Government. The King said he had only one exclusion to insist on: that Bugeaud should not command the troops. Molé said it was the very first appointment he should propose to His Majesty. The King wanted to keep the command in the hands of his sons. Molé went away to try his hand. Meanwhile the agitation of Paris increased. At night, hearing nothing of Molé, the King sent Pasquier to him; he found him alone. 'Well, is your Government formed?' 'No, not yet; but I expect to see Passy to-morrow morning.' He was told this would not do, and while he had been thus wasting time, the movement was swelling and advancing. So Molé went to the Palace at ten at night, and threw the thing up. Then the King sent for Thiers and Odilon Barrot. Thiers made it a condition that the troops should not act for twelve hours, and said he would meanwhile answer for the people. The King consented, and he and Odilon Barrot went out into the streets on horseback to harangue the mob, announce their Minis-

try, and send them home satisfied; they were received with menaces and shots, and sent about their business. They went back to
the Tuileries and said all was over, and they could do nothing.
Early in the morning the state of affairs having become more
and more formidable, a host of people came to the Tuileries, and
all urged the King to abdicate. He asked Thiers what he advised.
Thiers had lost his head, and said he was not his Minister, and
could give no advice; all the rest (none more urgently than the
Duc de Montpensier) pressed the King to abdicate. The King
was reluctant, and Piscatory alone entreated him not to do so.
'Il ne faut jamais abdiquer, Sire,' he said to him; 'voilà le moment
de monter à cheval et de vous montrer.' The Queen behaved
like a heroine. She who was so mild and religious, and who never
took any part in public affairs, alone showed firmness and resolution; she thanked Piscatory for his advice to the King, and said,
'Mon ami, il ne faut pas abdiquer; plutôt mourez en Roi.' But the
more disgraceful counsel prevailed. He abdicated, and hurried
off, as we know. Piscatory was with him to the last, and the
Queen, on parting from him, told him to tell Guizot that she owed
to him all she had enjoyed of happiness for the last six years.
Thus fell the Orleans dynasty, *pitoyablement, honteusement,*
without respect or sympathy. 'Where,' I asked, 'were the sons,
and what did they do?' Madame de Lieven only shook her head.
She herself had taken refuge at St. Aulaire's, then at Apponyi's,
then at an Austrian attaché's; then Pierre d'Aremberg took her
under his care, and hid her at Mr. Roberts', the English painter,
who brought her to England as Mrs. Roberts, with gold and
jewels secreted in her dress. Guizot was concealed one day at
Piscatory's, the other at the Duc de Broglie's.

In all this great drama Lamartine stands forth pre-eminently
as the principal character; how long it may last God only knows,
but such a fortnight of greatness the world has hardly ever seen;
for fame and glory with posterity it were well for him to die now.
His position is something superhuman *at this moment;* the eyes of
the universe are upon him, and he is not only the theme of general admiration and praise, but on him almost alone the hopes

of the world are placed. He is the principal author of this Revolution; they say that his book has been a prime cause of it;[22] and that which he has had the glory of directing, moderating, restraining. His labour has been stupendous, his eloquence wonderful. When the new Government was surrounded by thousands of armed rabble, bellowing and raging for they knew not what, Lamartine contrived to appease their rage, to soften, control, and eventually master them; so great a trial of eloquence was hardly ever heard of. Then from the beginning he has exhibited undaunted courage and consummate skill, proclaiming order, peace, humanity, respect for persons and property. This improvised Cabinet, strangely composed, has evinced most curious vigour, activity, and wisdom; they have forced everybody to respect them; but Lamartine towers above them all, and is the presiding genius of the new creation. He has acted like a man of honour and of feeling too. He offered the King an escort; he wrote to Madame Guizot and told her her son was safe in England, and caused the report of this to be spread abroad that he might not be sought for; and, moreover, he sent to Guizot to say if he was not in safety where he was he might come to his house. When he first proposed the abolition of the punishment of death he was overruled; but the next day he proposed it again, and declared if his colleagues would not consent he would throw up his office, quit the concern, and they might make him if they pleased the first victim of the law they would not abolish. All this is very great in the man who the Duc de Broglie told me was so bad, 'un mauvais livre par un mauvais homme,' and consequently all France is praying for the continuation of the life and power of Lamartine; and the exiles whom he has been principally instrumental in driving from their country are all loud in praise and admiration of his humanity and his capacity.

Aberdeen saw Guizot yesterday; he is in good health and spirits, and wants for nothing. He told Aberdeen that for the last two years he thought there was a considerable alteration in the

---

[22] 'The Girondins,' and still more Dumas' play of the 'Chevaliers de la Maison Rouge.'

King's mind; that he was *occasionally* as vigorous as ever, but on the whole that he was changed for the worse. This makes Guizot's conduct during these two years only the more inexcusable. He thinks (as everybody else does) that this fine fabric which has risen like an exhalation will not last long, and he said, 'You English bet about everything; if I was compelled to bet, I should for choice take the Duchesse d'Orléans and her sons as the most probable eventuality where everything is so uncertain.'

March 6th. I called on Guizot yesterday. Guizot told me that the Government had long been aware of the secret societies, but never could ascertain who were their chiefs; that their intention had been to delay their republican attempt till the death of the King, but that they had changed this plan on the Tuesday night, and resolved to seize the present occasion. I told him we had always supposed the *bourgeoisie* of Paris, composing the bulk of the National Guard, to be disposed to order, and that they would have maintained it. He said the great majority of them were so, but that the well-disposed had not come forth, while the factious minority had. Moreover, 'you English cannot conceive what our lowest class is: your own is a mere mob without courage or organisation, and not given to politics; ours on the contrary, the lowest class, is eager about politics and with a perfect military organisation, and therefore most formidable.' Guizot said all this could not last; that France had no desire for a Republic; everybody had adhered from fear or prudence. He expected, however, that there would be a great battle in the streets of Paris within a few days between the Republicans and the Communists, in which the former would prevail, because the National Guard would support the former.[23]

He gave us an account of his own personal adventures, which were very simple. He left the Ministry of the Interior with Madame Duchâtel, Duc de Broglie, and two other people; and he was first taken to a house where he was told he would be safe, and conducted by the *portière au cinquième*. She entered the room after him and said, 'You are M. Guizot.' He said, 'I am.'

[23] His prediction was exactly accomplished, only a good deal later.

'Fear nothing,' she said; 'you are safe here. You have always defended honest people, and I will take care nobody comes near
you.' In the evening he went to the Duc de Broglie's; he was one
day at Piscatory's; and on Wednesday night he left Paris as
somebody's servant. He said he was never in danger, as the Government would have been sorry to apprehend him.

March 10th. Yesterday I saw Southern and Mrs. Austin, both
just arrived from Paris. They both agree that all France abhors
this Revolution, but notwithstanding the bitter and universal regret that it has occasioned, and will still more hereafter, that
nobody thinks of endeavouring to restore the monarchy in any
way or under any head. The King was not so unpopular as Guizot,
and they confirm all previous impressions, that not only he might
have been saved, but that nothing but a series of fatal and inconceivable blunders and the most deplorable weakness could
have upset him. The causes of this prodigious effect were ludi-
crously small. Southern declares there were not above 4,000
armed men of the populace actually employed; but the troops
were everywhere paralysed, boys carried off the cannon from the
midst of them without resistance.

March 12th. Yesterday Lady Granville and Lady Georgiana
Fullerton went to Claremont to see the Royal Family. The Queen
was gone to town, but they were received by the King, who
talked to them for an hour and gave them a narrative of his adventures, which they related to me last night. It was very curious,
that is, curious as an exhibition of his character. He described his
flight, and all his subsequent adventures, his travels, his disguises,
his privations, the dangers he incurred, the kindness and assistance he met with, all very minutely. They said it was very interesting, and even very amusing; admirably well told. He was
occasionally pathetic and occasionally droll; his story was told
with a mixture of the serious and the comic—sometimes laughing and at others almost crying—that was very strange. It struck
them that he was very undignified, even vulgar, and above all
that he seemed to be animated with no feeling towards his country, but to view the whole history through the medium of *self*.

He said of the French, 'Ils ont choisi leur sort; je dois supporter le mien.' He gave a very different account of what passed from that of Guizot. He said he was in personal danger when he was on horseback reviewing the National Guard on Thursday morning; that they pressed round him, shouting for reform. He cried out, 'Mais vous l'avez, la réforme; laissez-moi passer donc;' and that he was obliged to spur his horse through the mob, and got back to the Tuileries with difficulty. He said he had *posé la question* of resistance to Guizot, who had refused to entertain it, said that he could not give orders to fire on the National Guards. Their two statements are quite irreconcileable, and thus occur historical perplexities and the errors and untruths which crowd all history. It appears that the Royal Family have no money, the King having invested his whole fortune in France, and beggary is actually staring them in the face.

March 14th. The Government had a capital division last night, and Lord John made a very good and stout speech. In France everything is going down hill at railroad pace. This fine Revolution, which may be termed the madness of a few for the ruin of many, is already making the French people weep tears of blood. Hitherto there has been little or no violence, and fine professions of justice and philanthropy; up to this time, not a month from the beginning, the account may be thus balanced: they have got rid of a King and a Royal Family and the cost thereof; they have got a reform so radical and complete, that it can go no further; they have repealed some laws and some taxes which were obnoxious to different persons or different classes, but none of which were grievous or sensibly injurious to the nation at large. In short, it is difficult to point out any considerable advantage either of a positive or a negative character which they have obtained, or have got the prospect of obtaining. However, it remains to be seen whether they can work out any advantage from their new institutions.

Meanwhile, the other side of the account presents some formidable items for a political balance sheet. They have got a Government composed of men who have not the slightest idea how to govern, albeit they are men of energy, activity, and some capacity. The country is full of fear and distrust. Ruin and bankruptcy are stalking through the streets of the capital. The old revolutionary principles and expedients are more and more drawn forth and displayed by the present rulers; they are assuming despotic power, and using it without scruple; they confer it on their agents; they proclaim social and political maxims fraught with ruin and desolation, and incompatible with the existence of any Government. The different Ministers vie with one another in the extravagance of their several manifestoes. Louis Blanc holds a parliament of operatives, whom he feeds with soft sawder and and delusive expectations, giving them for political truths all the most dangerous absurdities of his book. Garnier Pagès, in his frank *exposé* of the finances of the country, approaches to the very verge of national bankruptcy, and is evidently prepared for the next step. Carnot instructs the people to elect for their representatives not men of property and education, but any men who have republican ideas; and Ledru Rollin desires his agents to act in the same spirit, and with all the authority (which means despotism) that a revolutionary government always assumes it to be its right to exercise. In short, all is terror, distress, and misery, both material and moral; everybody fleeing away from the turbulent capital, and hiding what money he can collect; funds falling, everything depreciated in value, the shops unfrequented, no buyers, tranquillity still doubtfully preserved by factitious means, but the duration of which no one counts upon. All the letters that arrive here, whether they come from Legitimists, or Liberals, or Orleanists, or indifferents to all parties, tell the same tale of disgust, distress, and dread.

March 20th. There has been all sorts of botheration about Louis Philippe and his affairs, particularly about his remaining at Claremont. Soon after he came, a notification was made to him *by Palmerston* that he was not to remain there permanently.[24] He complained of this to all the people he saw (talking

[24] [Lord Palmerston made an unsuccessful attempt to remove Louis Philippe from Claremont, although it was not even an English royal palace at that time, but belonged to the King's own son-in-law, Leopold, King of the Belgians.]

very loosely and foolishly), and it got wind and made a noise. Soon after, the Duke of Wellington went to see him, and told him that Claremont was the fit place for him, and the other day a letter arrived from Leopold telling him he might stay there as long as he liked; he is therefore to stay. Everything in France gets more serious and alarming every day. The clubs of Paris are omnipotent, the National Guards are *écrasés*, the Provisional Government makes a show of independence, and Lamartine makes fine speeches; but they are at the mercy of the Parisian mob, whose organisation is wonderful.

March 25th. Nothing is more extraordinary than to look back at my last date and see what has happened in the course of *five days*. A tenth part of any one of the events would have lasted us for as many months; but now we are perplexed, overwhelmed, and carried away with excitement, and the most stupendous events are become like matters of every-day occurrence. Within these last four or five days there has been a desperate battle in the streets of Berlin between the soldiers and the mob; the flight of the Prince of Prussia; the King's convocation of his States; concessions to and reconciliation with his people; and his invitation to all Germany to form a Federal State; and his notification of what is tantamount to removing the Imperial Crown from the head of the wretched *crétin* at Vienna, and placing it on his own.

Next, a revolution in Austria; an *émeute* at Vienna; downfall and flight of Metternich, and announcement of a constitutional *régime; émeutes* at Milan; expulsion of Austrians, and Milanese independence; Hungary up and doing, and the whole empire in a state of dissolution. Throughout Germany all the people stirring; all the sovereigns yielding to the popular demands; the King of Hanover submitting to the terms demanded of him; the King of Bavaria abdicating. To attempt to describe historically and narratively these events as they occur would be impossible if I were to attempt it; and it is unnecessary, because they are chronicled in a thousand publications.

March 31st. The Queen and the Prince have taken to seize

everything in the way of patronage they can lay their hands on.
The Chamberlain formerly used to have it all, even to the appointment of domestic servants. First they took Hampton Court
and the distribution of the apartments there. Spencer found matters there, and acquiesced; but on the vacancy made by Gosset's
death they wanted to seize his place also. Spencer resisted, or
half asserted his right. He wrote to the Prince and said he proposed to appoint Charles Russell; and he told me he should resign if they refused their assent. On the course at Northampton
a messenger arrived with the reply, which was an assent, but
not a very willing one, and giving him to understand that they
considered the appointment as their own.

April 2nd. There is nothing to record but odds and ends: no
new revolution, no fresh deposition. Madame de Lieven told
me yesterday what she had heard from Flahault of the outbreak
at Vienna and the downfall of Metternich. When the people rose
and demanded liberal measures, they were informed that the
Council would be convened and deliberate, and an answer should
be given them in two hours. The Council assembled, consisting
of the Ministers and the Archdukes. The question was stated,
when Metternich rose and harangued them for an hour and a
half without their appearing nearly to approach a close. On this
the Archduke John pulled out his watch and said, 'Prince, in half
an hour we must give an answer to the people, and we have not
yet begun to consider what we shall say to them.' On this Kolowrath said, 'Sir, I have sat in Council with Prince Metternich for
twenty-five years, and it has always been his habit to speak thus
without coming to the point.' 'But,' said the Archduke, 'we must
come to the point, and that without delay. Are you aware, Prince,'
turning to Metternich, 'that the first of the people's demands is
that you should resign?' Metternich said that he had promised the
Emperor Francis on his deathbed never to desert his son, the
present Emperor, nor would he. They intimated that his remaining would be difficult. Oh, he said, if the Imperial Family wished
him to resign, he should feel that he was released from his engagement, and he was ready to yield to their wishes. They said

they did wish it, and he instantly acquiesced. Then the Emperor himself interposed and said, 'But, after all, I am the Emperor, and it is for me to decide; and I yield everything. Tell the people I consent to all their demands.' And thus *the Crétin* settled it all; and the great Minister, who was in his own person considered as *the Empire*, and had governed despotically for forty years, slunk away, and to this hour nobody knows where he is concealed.

June 3rd. I saw Lord Grey, who talked to me about the state of the Government, and what had passed between Lord John and him touching Palmerston. He said that he only came into office with a distinct understanding that Lord John should exercise a control over the Foreign Office and secure the Cabinet against any imprudence of Palmerston's.

The Government are now getting seriously uneasy about the Chartist manifestations in various parts of the country, especially in London, and at the repeated assemblings and marchings of great bodies of men. Le Marchant told me that two or three months ago, when he was at the Home Office, he received accounts he thought very alarming of the wide-spreading disaffection of the people, and particularly of the enormous increase of cheap publications of the most mischievous and inflammatory character, which were disseminated among the masses and eagerly read; and lately, accounts have been received from well-informed persons, whose occupations lead them to mix with the people, clergymen—particularly Roman Catholic—and medical men, who report that they find a great change for the worse amongst them, an increasing spirit of discontent and disaffection, and that many who on the 10th of April went out as special constables declare they would not do so again if another manifestation required it. The speeches which are made at the different meetings are remarkable for the coarse language and savage spirit they display. It is quite new to hear any Englishmen coolly recommend assassination, and the other day a police superintendent was wounded in the leg by some sharp instrument. These are new and very bad symptoms, and it is impossible not to feel alarm when we consider the vast amount of the population as compared with any repressive power we possess. The extent and reality of the distress they suffer, the impossibility of expecting such masses of people to be eternally patient and forbearing, to restrain all their natural impulses, and endure tamely severe privations when they are encouraged and stimulated to do otherwise,—all these considerations may well beget a serious presentiment of danger. But though many do feel this and brood much over it, there appears to be a fatal security amongst the majority, whose sluggish minds cannot be awakened to the possibility of a great convulsion here, notwithstanding the continental conflagration that stares them in the face. What we principally want is a strong Government which shall obtain public confidence and respect, and which may have a chance of conciliating, satisfying, and keeping in check public opinion. This the divisions and subdivisions of parties, and the enduring enmities and vindictive feelings of the Conservatives, effectually prevent. The only strong Government that could be formed would be a Liberal one under Peel, and the Protectionists would rather encounter the chances of revolution than see the man whom they detest so bitterly at the head of affairs again. They are so blind to their own interest, or so insane in their resentment, that they would prefer to run the risk of all that Radicals or Chartists could do than owe their safety to Peel, whom they affect to think the enemy of their best interests, and a man not to be trusted; and this they go on harping upon, although half of them now admit that it is the greatest blessing to them to have been saved by his measures from the dangerous predicament in which they would now otherwise be.

June 10th. The Government have at last taken strong measures against the Chartists; but in spite of the arrest of some of their leaders, another demonstration is expected on Monday, for which great preparations are to be made. The townspeople, who are thus perpetually alarmed, are growing very angry, and the military are so savage that Lord Londonderry told the Duke of Wellington he was sure, if a collision took place, the officers of his regiment would not be able to restrain their men. Many people think that a severe chastisement of these mobs will alone put a stop to their proceedings. But if these multitudes of discontented men can be daunted into submission, fearful considerations remain behind. We have an enormous overgrown population, a vast proportion of which are in undeniable misery and distress, and are soured and exasperated by their sufferings. To expect such beings to be reasonable, and still more to be logical, is to expect a moral impossibility. While the minds of the masses are in a combustible state, and they are ready to listen to anybody who appears to sympathise with them, and who pretends to be able to put them in the way of mending their condition, there are not wanting agents who strive with all their might, and not without success, to inflame and mislead them. The suffering people are prompt to believe that that cannot be a sound and just condition of society in which they are abandoned to starvation and destitution, while other classes are revelling in luxury and enjoyment. They have confused notions that this is all wrong, and that under some different political dispensation their interests would be better cared for, and according to their necessities they would be comforted and relieved. They are neither able to comprehend nor disposed to listen to the long processes of argument by which it might be demonstrated to them that all the prevailing misery and distress are attributable to causes over which Government has no control, and which no legislation can counteract: the unhappy state of the world, the confusion which prevails everywhere, the interruption of regular industry, the disturbance of the ordinary course of social life. We seem to have got into another stage of existence, our world is almost suddenly altered, we deal with new questions, men seem to be animated with fresh objects; what are called politics, international questions and the strife of parties, sink into insignificance; society is stirred up from its lowest depths, and we are obliged to turn our eyes and thoughts and faculties to the vast spectacle that is laid bare before us—and an appalling and awful spectacle it is.

June 26th. The details which reach us of the extraordinary contest which has just taken place at Paris are equally horrible and curious. Hitherto we have been struck by the absence of that ferocity which distinguished the first Revolution, and the little taste there seemed for shedding blood; but the ferocity of the people broke out upon this occasion in the most terrible examples. The people not only murdered, but tortured, their prisoners. Since the victory the prisoners have been executed by hundreds, and with hardly any form of trial; indeed, no trial was possible or necessary, they were rebels taken *en flagrant délit*, at once rebels and prisoners of war. One man, when he was going to be shot, said he did not care, for he had had his revenge already, and he pulled out of his pocket twenty tongues that had been cut out. All agree that the organisation, the military skill displayed, and the vast resources the insurgents possessed in the material of war, were as extraordinary as unaccountable. The preparations must have been long before made, for the houses of their principal fortifications were perforated for the purpose of communication and escape, the staircase removed, and there were telegraphic signals arranged by lights on the tops of the buildings. There certainly was a commander-in-chief who presided over the whole, but nobody knows who he was; and the Government have never yet been able to ascertain who the leaders were. Although distress and famine were the prime causes of this great struggle, it is remarkable that there was no plundering or robbery; on the contrary, they were strictly forbidden and apparently never attempted. It is the only example, so far as I know, that history records of a pitched battle in the streets of a great capital between the regular army and the armed civil power on one side, and the populace of the town militarily armed and organised also on the other, nobody knowing how the latter were organised or by whom directed. Prodigies of valour seem to have been performed on both sides, and the incidents were to the last degree romantic. There was one boy, not above fifteen or sixteen, a frightful little urchin, who scaled three barricades one after another and carried off the colours from each; Cavaignac embraced him and gave him the Legion of Honour from his own person, and he was carried in triumph and crowned with laurels to a great banquet of his comrades.

July 31st. I dined at Holland House yesterday, and sat next to old Sir Robert Adair, eighty-five years old, but with mind very fresh. He lived in great intimacy with all the 'great of old, who still rule our spirits from their own,' and I believe possesses a great store of anecdotes of bygone days. He gave me an account of young Burke's preventing the reconciliation between his father and Fox, which, however, is too well known to require repetition; but he told me how the Duke of Portland came to be put at the head of the Whig party on the death of Lord Rockingham in 1782, which I had not heard before. There was a meeting of the party to choose their chief; the Duke of Richmond put forth his pretensions, but he was so great a Radical (having views of Parliamentary Reform not only far beyond those of any man of that day, but beyond the Reform we have actually got), that they were afraid of him; and Charles Fox got up and said that he thought he, as leader of the House of Commons, had claims at least as good as the Duke of Richmond's, but that they ought both of them to waive their own claims, and in his judgement the man they ought to place at their head was the Duke of Portland. This compromise was agreed to, but the Duke of Richmond was so disgusted that he joined Lord Shelburne. My grandfather was a very honourable, high-minded, but ordinary man; his abilities were very second-rate, and he had no power of speaking; and his election to the post of leader of the great Whig party only shows how aristocratic that party was, and what weight and influence the aristocracy possessed in those days; they would never have endured to be led by a Peel or a Canning. Adair told me that old Lord George Cavendish expressed the greatest indignation at their party being led by Burke in the House of Commons, and it was this prevalent feeling, together with the extraordinary modesty of Burke, who had no vanity for himself, though a great deal for his son, which accounts for the fact, so extraordinary according to our ideas and practice, that though Burke led the Whig party in the House of Commons for four or

five years, when that party came into power he was not offered
a place in the Cabinet, but put in a subordinate office, which he
condescended to accept, seeing men so immeasurably inferior
to himself occupying the highest posts.

August 8th. At Latimers from Saturday till Monday. Called
on Wriothesley Russell at Chenies, and Lady Wriothesley told
me that there is not far off a Chartist establishment; a society of
Chartists located and living on land bought by Chartist subscrip-
tions; a sort of communist society. It has existed some years, but
is now falling into decay. Feargus O'Connor spoke to Charles
Russell about it, and said he wished his brother would take
some notice of them, *for they liked to be noticed by people of
rank;* and, he added, 'Collectively they are with me, but individually they are with you.' In these words a great lesson and significant fact are contained well worth attention.

November 29th. Lord Melbourne died on Friday night at
Brocket, without suffering pain, but having had a succession of
epileptic fits the whole day, most painful and distressing to his
family collected about him.

His friends are deeply annoyed and angry at a biographical
article on Melbourne which appeared in the 'Times' the morning
after his death; and it certainly was coarse, vulgar, and to a
great degree unjust. It was a mere daub and caricature, and very
discreditable to the paper.

But it is a difficult thing to write a good article upon Melbourne, one which shall delineate his character with impartiality
and discrimination, and describe fairly and truly his political career. I have known a great deal of him in the course of my life,
but I never lived in real intimacy with him; and as he at no time
seemed to have much inclination for my company, though we
were always very good friends, I saw but little of him; but every
now and then we had something to say to each other, and at rare
intervals we met on intimate and confidential terms. He was certainly a very singular man, resembling in character and manner,
as he did remarkably in feature, his father, the late Lord Egre-

mont.[25] He was exceedingly handsome, when first I knew him, which was in 1815 or thereabouts. It was at this period that the irregularities of his wife had partly estranged him from her, though they were not yet separated, and he was occasionally amused by her into condonation of her amours, and into a sort of half-laughing, half-resentful reconciliation. They lived in this queer way. He, good-natured, eccentric, and not nice; she, profligate, romantic, and comical. Both were kept together, as they had been brought together, by the influence and management of their common relations and connexions; but it was during this period that he devoted himself with ardour to study, and that he acquired the vast fund of miscellaneous knowledge with which his conversation was always replete, and which, mixed up with his characteristic peculiarities, gave an extraordinary zest and pungency to his society. His taste for reading and information, which was confirmed into a habit by the circumstances of these years, continued to the end of his life, unbroken, though unavoidably interrupted by his political avocations. He lived surrounded by books, and nothing prevented him, even when Prime Minister, and with all the calls on his time to which he was compelled to attend, from reading every new publication of interest or merit, as well as frequently revelling amongst the favourite authors of his early studies. His memory was extremely retentive, and amply stored with choice passages of every imaginable variety, so that he could converse learnedly upon almost all subjects, and was never at a loss for copious illustrations, amusing anecdotes, and happy quotations. This richness of talk was rendered more piquant by the quaintness and oddity of his manner, and an ease and naturalness proceeding in no small degree from habits of self-indulgence and freedom, a license for which was conceded

[25] [This sounds strange, but it was believed by those who were acquainted with the *chronique scandaleuse* of a former generation, in the last century, that William Lamb and Lady Cowper (afterwards Lady Palmerston) were not the children of their putative father, the Lord Melbourne of that day, but of Lord Egremont, who never married, but had numerous illegitimate offspring. William, Lord Melbourne, whose death is here recorded, was the husband of Lady Caroline, celebrated for her passion for Lord Byron and her subsequent quarrel with him.]

to him by common consent, even by the Queen herself, who, partly from regard for him, and partly from being amused at his ways, permitted him to say and do whatever he pleased in her presence. He was often paradoxical, and often coarse, terse, epigrammatic, acute, droll, with fits of silence and abstraction, from which he would suddenly break out with a vehemence and vigour which amused those who were accustomed to him, and filled with indescribable astonishment those who were not. His mother-in-law, Lady Bessborough, told me that high office was tendered to him many years before he began to play any political part, but at that time he preferred a life of lettered and social idleness, and he would not accept it. He never was really well fitted for political life, for he had a great deal too much candour, and was too fastidious to be a good party man. It may be said of him, at least in his earlier days, that he was

'For a patriot too cool, for a drudge disobedient,
    And too fond of the right to pursue the expedient.'

And still less was he fit to be the leader of a party and the head of a Government, for he had neither the strong convictions, nor the eager ambition, nor the firmness and resolution which such a post requires. From education and turn of mind, and from the society in which he was bred and always lived, he was a Whig; but he was a very moderate one, abhorring all extremes, a thorough Conservative at heart, and consequently he was only half identified in opinion and sympathy with the party to which he belonged when in office; he often dreaded and distrusted his colleagues, and was secretly the enemy of the measures which his own Government originated, and of which he was obliged to take the credit or bear the obloquy. No position could be more false than the position in which Melbourne was often placed, and no man ever was more perplexed and tormented than he was by it, for he was remarkably sensitive; and most of the latter years of his administration were passed in a state of dissatisfaction with himself and with all about him. He hated the Reform Bill, which he was obliged to advocate. He saw, indeed, that Reform had become irresistible, and therefore he reconciled it to his conscience to support the Bill; but he had not sufficient energy of character or strength of will to make a stand against the lengths which he disapproved, and he contented himself with those indirect attempts to modify it which I have narrated in their proper place. It was probably his personal popularity, and the reluctance of Lord Lansdowne to take so laborious a post, which led to his being made Prime Minister on the resignation of Lord Grey, for there never was a man more incapable of exercising the vigilance and supremacy which that office demands. After the great breach of 1835, and the abortive attempt of William IV. to throw over the Whig Government, his relations with his Ministers became very uncomfortable; but Melbourne was a good-natured man, and a gentleman, and perhaps no one else would have gone on with the King so harmoniously as he managed it.

But it was upon the accession of the Queen that his post suddenly grew into one of immense importance and interest, for he found himself placed in the most curious and delicate position which any statesman ever occupied. Victoria was transferred at once from the nursery to the throne—ignorant, inexperienced, and without one human being about her on whom she could rely for counsel and aid. She found in her Prime Minister and constitutional adviser a man of mature age, who instantly captivated her feelings and her fancy by his deferential solicitude, and by a shrewd, sagacious, and entertaining conversation, which were equally new and delightful to her. She at once cast herself with implicit confidence upon Melbourne, and, from the first day of her reign, their relations assumed a peculiar character, and were marked by an intimacy which he never abused; on the contrary, he only availed himself of his great influence to impress upon her mind sound maxims of constitutional government, and truths of every description that it behoved her to learn. It is impossible to imagine anything more interesting than the situation which had thus devolved upon him, or one more calculated to excite all the latent sensibility of his nature. His loyal devotion soon warmed into a parental affection, which she repaid by unbounded manifestations of confidence and regard. He set himself wisely, and with perfect disinterestedness, to form her mind and character, and to cure the defects and eradicate the prejudices from which the mistakes and faults of her education had not left her entirely free. In all that Melbourne said or did, he appears to have been guided by a regard to justice and truth. He never scrupled to tell her what none other would have dared to say; and in the midst of that atmosphere of flattery and deceit which kings and queens are almost always destined to breathe, and by which their minds are so often perverted, he never scrupled to declare boldly and frankly his real opinions, strange as they sometimes sounded, and unpalateable as they often were, and to wage war with her prejudices and false impressions with regard to people or things whenever he saw that she was led astray by them. He acted in all things an affectionate, conscientious, and patriotic part, endeavouring to make her happy as a woman, and popular as a queen.

It is notorious that he committed two great errors in judgement, both of which were attended with disastrous consequences, and I believe that in both cases his discretion was misled by his feelings, and that it was his care for her ease and happiness which betrayed him into these fatal mistakes. The first was the Flora Hastings affair, the scandal of which he might certainly have prevented; the other was the Bedchamber quarrel, when her reluctance to part with him, and his tenderness for her, overruled his better judgement, and made him adopt a course he must have known to be both impossible and wrong. In these affairs (especially the first), Melbourne must have suffered torments, for his tender solicitude for the Queen, and the deep sense of his own responsibility, were sure to weigh heavily upon him. His influence and authority at Court were not diminished, nor his position there altered by her marriage; but the Prince, though always living on very friendly terms with him, was secretly rejoiced when the political power of this great favourite was brought to a close; for, so long as Melbourne was there, he undoubtedly played but an obscure and secondary part. When the inevitable change of Government at last took place, the parting between the Queen and her Minister was very sorrowful to both of them, and it was then that he gave his last and generous proof of his anxiety for her happiness in sending me with his advice to Peel.

It would be rendering imperfect justice to Melbourne's character to look upon him rather as a courtier than as a statesman, and to fancy that he made his political principles subordinate to his personal predilections. He was deeply attached to the Queen, but he had all the patriotism of an English gentleman, and was jealous of the honour and proud of the greatness of his country. He held office with a profound sense of its responsibilities; there never was a Minister more conscientious in the distribution of patronage, more especially of his ecclesiastical patronage. He was perfectly disinterested, without nepotism, and without vanity; he sought no emoluments for his connexions, and steadily declined all honours for himself. The Queen often pressed him to accept the Garter, but he never would consent, and it was remarked that the Prime Minister of England was conspicuous at Court for being alone undecorated amidst the stars and ribands which glittered around him.

At the time Melbourne left office he was only an occasional guest at Court, but the Queen continued to correspond with him constantly, and gave him frequent proofs that her regard for him was undiminished. He took very little part in politics after 1841, and it was not long before his health began to give way. He had been so completely absorbed by the Court, that for many years he had been almost lost to society; but as soon as he was out of office, he resumed his old habits, and was continually to be found at Holland House, at Lady Palmerston's, and with a few other intimate friends. There he loved to lounge and sprawl at his ease, pouring out a rough but original stream of talk, shrewd, playful, and instructive. His distinctive qualities were strong sound sense, and an innate taste for what was great and good, either in action or sentiment. His mind kindled, his eye brightened, and his tongue grew eloquent when noble examples or sublime conceptions presented themselves before him. But while he pursued truth, as a philosopher, his love of paradox made him often appear a strange mass of contradiction and inconsistency. A sensualist and a Sybarite, without much refinement or delicacy, a keen observer of the follies and vices of mankind, taking the world as he found it, and content to extract as much pleasure and diversion as he could from it, he at one time would edify and astonish his hearers with the most exalted sentiments, and at another would terrify and shock them by indications of the lowest morality and worldly feelings, and by thoughts and opinions fraught with the most cold-hearted mocking and sarcasm. His mind seems all his life long, and on almost every subject, to have been vigorous and stirring, but unsettled and unsatisfied. It certainly was so on the two great questions of religion and politics, and he had no profound convictions, no certain assurance about either. He studied divinity eagerly and constantly, and was no contemptible theologian; but he never succeeded in arriving at any fixed belief, or in anchoring himself on any system of religious faith. It was the same thing in politics. All the Liberal and Constitutional theories which he had ever entertained had been long ago more than realised, and he was filled with alarm at the prospect of their further extension. All his notions were aristocratic, and he had not a particle of sympathy for what was called progressive reform. He was a vehement supporter of the Corn Laws, abused Peel with all the rancour of a Protectionist, and died in the conviction that his measures will prove the ruin of the landed interest.

During his administration his great object seemed to be to keep a rickety concern together, less from political ambition than from his personal feelings for the Queen. He abhorred disputes and quarrels of every description, and he was constantly temporising and patching them up when they occurred in his Cabinet (as they often did) by all sorts of expedients, seldom asserting either the dignity or the authority of his position as head of the Government. Such weak and unworthy misrule brought his Cabinet, his party, and himself into contempt, and it was unquestionably in great measure owing to his want of judgement and firmness that they became so unpopular, and at last fell with so little credit and dignity as they did in 1841. He was capricious about money, and generous and stingy by fits and starts. Easy and indolent, he suffered himself to be plundered by his servants, and took little trouble in looking after his affairs. He was fond of his family, and much beloved by them, but, both with regard to them and his friends, he was full of a jealousy and touchiness, which made him keenly alive to any appearance of indifference, and equally sensible of any attentions that were shown him. This grew into a morbid feeling after his health had given way, and tinged his latter days with melancholy, for he fancied himself neglected and uncared for. On the promotion of Lord John Russell's Government, he was mortified at not being invited to take a share in it. It was evident that he was conscious of, and bitterly felt, the decay of his own powers, and the insignificance to which he was reduced. He would, if he could, have disguised this from himself and others, but it preyed on his mind, and made him very unhappy, and often apparently morose. Sometimes his feelings would find vent in these lines from the 'Samson Agonistes,' which he would repeat with a sad memory of the past, and sense of the present:

> *So much I feel my genial spirits droop,*
> *My hopes all flat, nature within me seems*
> *In all her functions weary of herself,*
> *My race of glory run, and race of shame,*
> *And I shall shortly be with them that rest.*

Taking him altogether, he was a very remarkable man in his abilities and his acquirements, in his character and in his career, with virtues and vices, faults and merits, curiously intermingled, and producing as eccentric results as society has often beheld.

February 9th, 1849. Ireland is like a strong man with an enormous cancer in one limb of his body. The distress is confined to particular districts, but there it is frightful and apparently irremediable. It is like a region desolated by pestilence and war. The people really are dying of hunger, and the means of aiding them do not exist. Here is a country, part and parcel of England, a few hours removed from the richest and most civilised community in the world, in a state so savage, barbarous, and destitute, that we must go back to the Middle Ages or to the most inhospitable regions of the globe to look for a parallel. Nobody knows what to do; everybody hints at some scheme or plan to which his next neighbour objects. Most people are inclined to consider the case as hopeless, to rest on that conviction, and let the evil work itself out, like a consuming fire, which dies away when there is nothing left for it to destroy. All call on the Government for a plan and a remedy, but the Government have no plan and no remedy; there is nothing but disagreement among them; and while they are discussing and disputing, the masses are dying. God only knows what is to be the end of all this, and how and when Ireland is to recover from such a deplorable calamity.

London, September 15th. On Monday, the 3rd, on returning from Hillingdon, I found a summons from John Russell to be at Balmoral on Wednesday 5th at half-past two, for a Council, to order a Prayer for relief against the cholera. No time was to be lost, so I started by the five o'clock train, dined at Birmingham, went on by the mail train to Crewe, where I slept; breakfasted the next morning at Crewe Hall, which I had never seen, and went on by the express to Perth, which I reached at half-past twelve. I started on Wednesday morning at half-past six, and arrived at Balmoral exactly at half-past two. It is a beautiful road from Perth to Balmoral, particularly from Blairgowrie to the Spital of Glenshee, and thence to Braemar. Much as I dislike Courts and all that appertains to them, I am glad to have made this expedition, and to have seen the Queen and Prince in their Highland retreat, where they certainly appear to great advantage. The place is very pretty, the house very small. They live there without any state whatever; they live not merely like private gentlefolks, but like very small gentlefolks,[26] small house, small rooms, small establishment. There are no soldiers, and the

---

[26] [The present castle of Balmoral was not then built. The residence was at this time simply that of a Scotch laird.]

whole guard of the Sovereign and the whole Royal Family is a single policeman, who walks about the grounds to keep off impertinent intruders or improper characters. Their attendants consisted of Lady Douro and Miss Dawson, Lady and Maid of Honour; George Anson and Gordon; Birch, the Prince of Wales's tutor; and Miss Hildyard, the governess of the children. They live with the greatest simplicity and ease. The Prince shoots every morning, returns to luncheon, and then they walk and drive. The Queen is running in and out of the house all day long, and often goes about alone, walks into the cottages, and sits down and chats with the old women. I never before was in society with the Prince, or had any conversation with him. On Thursday morning John Russell and I were sitting together after breakfast, when he came in and sat down with us, and we conversed for about three-quarters of an hour. I was greatly struck with him. I saw at once (what I had always heard) that he is very intelligent and highly cultivated, and moreover that he has a thoughtful mind, and thinks of subjects worth thinking about. He seemed very much at his ease, very gay, pleasant, and without the least stiffness or air of dignity. After luncheon we went to the Highland gathering at Braemar—the Queen, the Prince, four children and two ladies in one pony carriage; John Russell, Mr. Birch, Miss Hildyard, and I in another; Anson and Gordon on the box; one groom, no more. The gathering was at the old Castle of Braemar, and a pretty sight enough. We returned as we came, and then everybody strolled about till dinner. We were only nine people, and it was all very easy and really agreeable, the Queen in very good humour and talkative; the Prince still more so, and talking very well; no form, and everybody seemed at their ease. In the evening we withdrew to the only room there is besides the dining-room, which serves for billiards, library (hardly any books in it), and drawing-room. The Queen and Prince and her ladies and Gordon soon went back to the dining-room, where they had a Highland dancing-master, who gave them lessons in reels. We (John Russell and I) were not admitted to this exercise, so we played at billiards. In process of time they came back, when there

was a little talk, and soon after they went to bed. So much for
my visit to Balmoral. I was asked to stay there the first night, but
was compelled to remain there the second, as the Braemar gathering took all the horses, and it was impossible to get away. The
Prince was very civil about my staying when this was explained
to him.

J*anuary 23rd*, 1850. If I had not been too lazy to write about
anybody or anything, I should not have suffered the death of
Lord Alvanley to pass without some notice. The world, however,
has no time to think of people who are out of its sight, and a long
illness which had confined him entirely, and limited his society
to a few old friends, caused him to be forgotten, and his departure
out of life to be almost unobserved. There was a time when it
would have been very different, during those many years when
his constant spirits and good humour, together with his marvellous wit and drollery, made him the delight and ornament of
society. He was originally in the army, came early into the world,
and at once plunged into every sort of dissipation and extravagance. He was the most distinguished of that set of *roués* and
spendthrifts who were at the height of the fashion for some years
—consisting of Brummel, Sir H. Mildmay, Lord Sidney Osborne,
Foley, John Payne, Scrope Davies, and several others, and when
all of them were ruined and dispersed (most of them never to
recover), Alvanley still survived, invulnerable in his person, from
being a Peer, and with the means of existence in consequence of
the provident arrangement of his uncle, who left him a considerable property in the hand of trustees, and thus preserved from
the grasp of his creditors. He was naturally of a kind and affectionate disposition, good-natured, obliging, and inclined to be
generous; but he was to the last degree reckless and profligate
about money; he cared not what debts he incurred, and he made
nothing of violating every sort of pecuniary engagement or obligation. He left the friends who assisted him in the lurch without

remorse, and such was the *bonhomie* of his character, and the irresistible attraction of his society, that they invariably forgave him, and after exhausting their indignation in complaints and reproaches, they became more intimate with him than before. Many a person has been astonished, after hearing the tale of Alvanley's abominable dishonesty and deceit, to see the plaintiff and the culprit the dearest of friends in the world. When I recollect his constant treacheries, and the never-failing placability of his dupes, I always think of the story of Manon l'Escaut, of whom he appears to me to have been a male prototype. It would be very difficult to convey any idea of the sort of agreeableness which was so captivating in him. He did not often say very witty things; it was not uproarious mirth, and jokes exciting fits of laughter like Sydney Smith; he was unlike any of the great luminaries of his own or of bygone times; but he was delightful. He was so gay, so natural, so irresistibly comical, he diffused such cheerfulness around him, he was never ill-natured; if he quizzed anybody and bantered them, he made them neither angry nor unhappy; he had an even and constant flow of spirits, and till his health became impaired you were *sure* of him in society. He was vain, but it was a harmless and amusing vanity, which those who knew him well understood and laughed at. He had rioted in all the dissipations of play and wine and women, and for many years (a *liaison* which began when neither were very young, and was the *réchauffé* of an earlier affair, before she was married) he was the notorious and avowed lover of Lady [*Fitzroy Somerset*]. What Burke says with a sort of mock modesty of himself, was true of Alvanley—he had 'read the book of life for a long time, and other books a little!' For the first years of his life he was too entirely plunged in dissipation and debauchery to repair in any way the deficiencies of a neglected education; later, he read a good deal in a desultory way, and acquired a good store of miscellaneous information. At one period he addicted himself to politics, but he never made any figure in the House of Lords, having no parliamentary experience, no oratorical genius, and no foundation of knowledge. But it was during this period that he signalised his courage in his duel with young O'Connell. Before that event, for no particular reason but that he was only known as a voluptuary, no very high idea was entertained of his personal bravery; but on this occasion it shone forth with great lustre, for no man ever exhibited more resolution or indifference to danger. For the last four years of his life he was afflicted with painful diseases, and his sufferings were incessant and intense. He bore them all with a fortitude and a cheerfulness which never failed him, and which excited universal sympathy and admiration.

February 22nd. Last night I met Clarendon at dinner at Bath House. He gave me an account of what had passed between the Queen and Prince and himself. He dined at the Palace on Tuesday. I told him they were sure to talk to him on foreign affairs, but he said he should avoid it. However, he could not avoid it. The moment he came into the drawing-room after dinner the Queen exploded, and went with the utmost vehemence and bitterness into the whole of Palmerston's conduct, all the effects produced all over the world, and all her own feelings and sentiments about it. He could only listen and profess his own almost entire ignorance of the details. After she had done Prince Albert began, but not finding time and opportunity to say all he wished, he asked him to call on him the next day. He went and had a conversation of two hours and a half, in the course of which he went into every detail, and poured forth without stint or reserve all the pent-up indignation, resentment, and bitterness with which the Queen and himself have been boiling for a long time past. He commented on Palmerston's policy and conduct much in the same terms in which the 'Times' does, and as I and others do. But what he enlarged upon with the strongest feeling was the humiliating position in which the Queen was placed in the eyes of the whole world. The remonstrances and complaints, the sentiments and resentments of other Sovereigns —of the King of Naples, and of the Emperor of Russia, for instance—directly affected her dignity as the Sovereign and Representative of this Nation; and the consciousness that these Sovereigns and all the world knew that she utterly disapproved of all that was done in her name, but that she was powerless to prevent it, was inconceivably mortifying and degrading. Prince Albert said he knew well enough the Constitutional position of the Sovereign of this country, and that it was the policy and measures which the nation desired and approved which the Government must carry out; but that the nation disapproved of Palmerston's proceedings, and so did his own colleagues, Lord Lansdowne particularly; yet by their weak connivance he was allowed to set at defiance the Sovereign, the Government, and public opinion, while the Queen could get neither redress nor support from John Russell, and was forced to submit to such degradation. He then mentioned various instances in which the Queen's remonstrances and suggestions had been disregarded. Minutes submitted to her in one form and changed by Palmerston into other forms; the refusal of Austria to send any Ambassador here, because he could not transact business with her Secretary of State. Clarendon asked him if he had ever endeavoured to influence Palmerston himself, and remonstrated with him on those matters which had justly excited the strong feelings of the Queen and himself. He said that he had done so repeatedly, and for a long time; that he always found him easy, good-humoured, very pleasant to talk to, but that it was utterly impossible to turn him from his purposes, or to place the least reliance on anything he said or engaged to do, and that at length the conviction which had been forced upon him of the uselessness of speaking to him had caused him entirely to leave it off, and for above a year past neither the Queen nor he had ever said one word to him; that it was in vain they had appealed to John Russell. He supposed it was the etiquette for Cabinet Ministers never to admit there was anything censurable in the conduct of each other, for though he was certain many things were done of which John Russell could not approve, and for which he was unable to make any defence, he never would admit that what had been done had been wrong; that the consequence of this had been to impair considerably the relations of confidence and openness which ought to exist between the Queen and her Prime Minister, and to place her in an unsatisfactory position *vis-à-vis* of him. After dilating at great length on this topic, he said something from which Clarendon inferred that his object was to make *him* a channel of communication with John Russell, and thus to make their sentiments known to him more clearly and unreservedly than they could do themselves, and he means to tell Lord John all that passed. He said the Prince talked very sensibly and very calmly, very strong, but without excitement of manner. I shall be curious to hear what Lord John says to it all; but though it can hardly fail somewhat to disturb his mind, I don't believe it will make the least alteration in his conduct, or change an iota of the 'unconquerable will and study of revenge' of Palmerston, or prevent his doing just what he pleases in spite of all the world.

March 8th.   I met Brunnow a few days ago coming from Palmerston, where he had been (though he did not say so) to present the Emperor's indignant note. He was laughing as he always does when he speaks of Palmerston; said of this affair, 'que c'était une bêtise; qu'il ne pouvait pas faire comprendre à Palmerston l'humiliation de l'affaire.' So far from acknowledging this, or evincing the least sign of regret or shame, when Hume asked him a question in the House the other night, he replied with the utmost effrontery, and with rather more than his usual insolence and audacity. As on every occasion, the House laughed and nobody said a word. All that relates to him, his character, conduct, and career, will hereafter form one of the most curious passages in history and the most astounding and unaccountable.

May 17th.   This has been a day of agitation. On Wednesday night all London was excited by the announcement at Devonshire House (where there was a great rout) that Drouyn de Lhuys had been recalled and was gone to Paris, and that neither Brunnow nor Cetto had been present at Palmerston's birthday dinner. Everybody was talking yesterday in the two Houses of these things and of the cause of them, which of course had to do with Greece. Questions were put to Lord Lansdowne and to Palmerston, when both of them said that the French Government had desired the presence of Drouyn de Lhuys at Paris in order to explain matters, and they both said what was tantamount to a denial of his having been recalled. At the very moment that they were making these statements in Parliament, the French Minister for Foreign Affairs was reading in the tribune of the National Assembly the formal letter of recall which had been sent to their Ambassador, which he was instructed to communicate, and which he read to Palmerston on the preceding day, and he was at the same time explaining that the Ambassador had been recalled on account of the manner in which the English Government had behaved to that of France, which rendered it incompatible with the dignity of the Republic to leave any longer an Ambassador in London. After a series of blunders and a long course of impolitic and unjustifiable acts, Palmerston has contrived to involve us in a *quasi* quarrel with France, and to break up in the most wanton manner, and for the most ridiculous object, the good understanding which existed between the two countries.

This is the greatest scrape into which Palmerston has ever got, and it will be curious enough too how he gets out of it. Our Government stands charged by that of France with breach of faith and violation of compact.

May 19th. Lord John said that the first thing to be done was to settle this matter as they best might; that they must support Palmerston's assertions, to which they were bound to give credit; but that when this business was concluded, in about a month perhaps, he would bring matters to a crisis, that is, announce to Palmerston that he could not go on in the Foreign Office. Lord John is at present very angry, and therefore very stout, but I never can feel sure of him. He is to see the Queen on Tuesday, who will of course be boiling over with indignation, and if she finds Lord John at last disposed to take her views of the matter, the affair may possibly be settled between them.

May 25th. The morning before yesterday the Duke of Bedford came here again. He had seen Lord John since, and heard what passed with the Queen. She was full of this affair, and again urged all her objections to Palmerston. This time she found Lord

John better disposed than heretofore, and he is certainly revolving in his mind how the thing can be done. He does not by any means contemplate going out himself, or breaking up the Government. What he looks to is this, that the Queen should take the initiative, and urge Palmerston's removal from the Foreign Office. She is quite ready to do this as soon as she is assured of her wishes being attended to. For various reasons it would not do to put Clarendon in his place. Clarendon would not like it, and it would make Palmerston furious; therefore this is out of the question. The only possible arrangement is that Lord John should himself take the Foreign Office, provisionally, and he is quite prepared to take it.

June 21st. John Russell made his statement last night, giving the reasons why he did not resign, quoting two precedents, one above a century ago, and one in 1833, for not resigning in consequence of an adverse vote of the House of Lords. I concur in the constitutional doctrine he laid down on that score, but the rest of what he said was very imprudent and ill-judged. He has now committed himself more than ever to Palmerston, and has thrown down a defiance to all Europe, announcing that they will make no difference whatever in their administration of foreign affairs.

On Saturday afternoon the news came of the difference being settled, by our conceding to the French all they demanded. Nobody seems to care, or it would be a mortifying and a ridiculous conclusion.

June 29th. I have been for two days in the country, while the great debate was going on. Palmerston came out the second night with prodigious force and success. He delivered an oration four hours and three-quarters long, which has excited unusual admiration, boundless enthusiasm amongst his friends, and drawn forth the most flattering compliments from every quarter. It is impossible to deny its great ability; parts of it are strikingly eloquent and inimitably adroit. It was a wonderful effort to speak for nearly five hours without ever flagging, and his voice nearly as strong at last as at first. The ability of it is the more remarkable, because on an attentive and calm perusal of it, the insufficiency of it as an answer and a defence against the various charges which have been brought against him is manifest; but it is admirably arranged and got up, entirely free from the flippancy and impertinence in which he usually indulges, full of moderation and good taste, and adorned with a profusion of magnificent and successful clap-traps. The success of the speech has been complete, and his position is now unassailable. John Russell may save himself the trouble of considering, when this is all over, how he may effect some change involving the withdrawal of the Foreign Office from Palmerston's hands, for they are now all tied and bound to him in respect to the future as completely as to the present and the past. These discussions and attacks, which were to have shaken him in his seat, have only made *him* more powerful than he was before.

London, July 1st. The day before yesterday Sir Robert Peel had a fall from his horse and hurt himself seriously. Last night he was in imminent danger. His accident has excited the greatest interest, and his doors are beset with enquirers of all parties without distinction. He was in high spirits that day, for he was pleased with the division which saved the Government, and with his own speech, which for his purpose was very dexterous and successful.

July 6th. The death of Sir Robert Peel, which took place on Tuesday night, has absorbed every other subject of interest. The suddenness of such an accident took the world by surprise, and in consequence of the mystery in which great people's illnesses are always shrouded, the majority of the public were not aware of his danger till they heard of his death. The sympathy, the feeling, and the regret which have been displayed on every side and in all quarters, are to the last degree striking. Every imaginable honour has been lavished on his memory. The Sovereign, both Houses of Parliament, the press and the people, from the highest to the lowest, have all joined in acts of homage to his character, and in magnifying the loss which the nation has sustained. When we remember that Peel was an object of bitter hatred to one great party, that he was never liked by the other party, and that he had no popular and ingratiating qualities, and very few intimate friends, it is surprising to see the warm and universal feeling which his death has elicited. It is a prodigious testimony to the greatness of his capacity, to the profound conviction of his public usefulness and importance, and of the purity of the motives by which his public conduct has been guided. I need not record details with which every newspaper teems. Those who were opposed to him do not venture or are not inclined to try and stem the current of grief and praise which is bursting forth in all directions, and most assuredly no man who in life was so hated and reviled was ever so lamented and honoured at his death. The Duke of Wellington pronounced in the House of Lords a few nights ago a panegyric on his love of truth, and declared that during his long connexion with him he had never known him to deviate from the strictest veracity. This praise would be undeserved if he had ever been guilty of any underhand, clandestine, and insincere conduct in political matters, and it leads me to suspect that resentment and disappointment may have caused an unfair and unwarrantable interpretation to be put upon his motives and his behaviour on some important occasions. My acquaintance with Peel was slight and superficial. I never associated with him, and never was in his house except on two or three occasions at rare intervals. He scarcely lived at all in society; he was reserved but cordial in his manner, had few intimate friends, and it may be doubted whether there was any one person, except his wife, to whom he was in the habit of disclosing his thoughts, feelings, and intentions with entire frankness and freedom. In his private relations he was not merely irreproachable, but good, kind, and amiable. The remarkable decorum of his life, the domestic harmony and happiness he enjoyed, and the simplicity of his habits and demeanour, contributed largely without doubt to the estimation in which he was held. He was easy of access, courteous and patient, and those who approached him generally left him astonished at the extensive and accurate knowledge, as well as the sound practical sense and judgement, which he displayed on all subjects. It was by the continual exhibition of these qualities that he gained such a mastery over the public mind, and such prodigious influence in the House of Commons. Nothing but a careful and accurate survey of his career, an intimate knowledge of the secret transactions of his political life, and a minute analysis of his character, can enable any one to form a correct judgement concerning him. He might easily be made the subject of a studied panegyric, or as easily of a studied invective; but either the one or the other would of necessity be exaggerated and untrue. The sacrifices which he made upon two memorable occasions forbid us to believe that he was ever influenced by any considerations but such as were honest and conscientious. Notwithstanding his great sagacity, it may, however, be doubted whether his judgement was not often faulty, and whether he was not led to erroneous conclusions as to the obligations imposed upon him, and the course which it was his duty to pursue. It is very difficult to account satisfactorily for his conduct on the Catholic question. We must indeed make great allowance for the position in which he was placed by his birth, education, and connexions. His father was a Tory, imbued with all the old Tory prejudices, one of those followers of Mr. Pitt who could not comprehend and never embraced his liberal sentiments, and who clung to the bigoted and narrow-minded opinions of Addington and George III. It is no wonder then that Peel was originally an anti-Catholic. The death of Perceval left the Protestant party without a head, and not long after his entrance into public life, and while the convictions of his youth were still unshaken, he became their elected chief. For about fourteen years he continued to fight their battle in opposition to a host of able men, and in spite of a course of events which might have satisfied a far less sagacious man that this contest must end in defeat. Nevertheless, the man who eventually proved himself to be one of the wisest and most liberal of statesmen maintained for years a struggle against religious liberty, a struggle by which he was involved in inconsistencies injurious to his own character, and which brought the kingdom to the brink of a civil war. It is now impossible to fathom the depths of Peel's mind, and to ascertain whether during that long period he had any doubts and misgivings as to the cause in which he was embarked, or whether he really and sincerely believed that Catholic Emancipation could be resisted and prevented. It is strange that he did not perceive the contest to be hopeless, and that such a contest was more perilous than any concession could possibly be. But he declared that up to the period of Lord Liverpool's death his opinions were unchanged, and that he thought the prolongation of this contest was not unreasonable. I do not see how he can be acquitted of insincerity save at the expense of his sagacity and foresight. His mind was not enthralled by the old-fashioned and obsolete maxims which were so deeply rooted in the minds of Eldon and Perceval; his spirit was more congenial to that of Pitt; and if he had let his excellent understanding act with perfect freedom, and his opinions take their natural course, it is impossible to doubt that he would have concurred and co-operated with the able men of different parties who were advocates of Emancipation, instead of continuing to encourage and lead on those masses of bigotry and prejudice whose resistance produced so much direct and indirect mischief. The truth is that having become pledged and committed in the cause, it was a matter of infinite difficulty for him to back out of it, to recant his opinions, and change his course; although any one who watched the signs of the times (and no man watched or studied them more carefully than Peel), might have seen that Catholic Emancipation was steadily but surely progressing towards its consummation. To change the whole mind of Peel, something more was required than the accustomed signs of agitation, and the accumulated power of eloquent speeches and able writings. At length the crash came by which the moral revolution was effected. The Clare election did what reason, and eloquence, and authority had failed to do. The Duke of Wellington and Peel simultaneously determined to strike their colours, to abandon a cause which they had sustained at great risks and by enormous sacrifices, and to carry out the measure which their whole lives had been spent in opposing, and which they had denounced as incompatible with the safety of the country. Whatever [*Peel's*] errors may have been, he made a noble atonement for them, and having once changed his mind, he flung himself into his new career with a gallantry and devotion deserving of the highest praise. He encountered without flinching the storm which he knew would burst upon him, and bravely exposed his character and reputation to suspicions, resentments, and reproaches, which might for aught he knew be fatal to his future prospects. Upon this occasion indeed, he shared the obloquy with the Duke of Wellington, upon whom as Prime Minister the responsibility principally rested. But the indignation and resentment of the Tories fell, though unjustly, much more upon Peel than upon the Duke.

Their ill-humour and resentment led to the destruction of the Duke's Government, and the change of Ministry brought about the Reform Bill and the overthrow of the Tory party. It is difficult to discern any proofs of sound judgement and foresight in Peel's conduct in regard to Parliamentary Reform. If he had manifested a disposition to concede some moderate and reasonable reforms as fit occasions presented themselves, it is by no means improbable that the country might have been satisfied; but his opposition to the transfer of the East Retford franchise to Birmingham, together with the Duke's celebrated declaration that the representative system could not be improved, and that as long as he was in office he would oppose any measure of Parliamentary Reform, convinced the Reformers that they were resolved to make no concessions, however slight, and not to suffer any change to be made in the existing representative system. Peel evidently made an incorrect estimate of the state of the public mind upon the question of Parliamentary Reform. He could not indeed foresee the French Revolution or its contagious effects here; but unless the country had been already combustible, it would not have been so inflamed as it was; and if he had been aware of its temper and disposition, he never would have opposed the general sentiment so pertinaciously as he did. I think, therefore, that his course in respect to Reform exhibits a deficiency in sagacity and foresight, and must be accounted one of the blemishes of his political career. He fought the Reform battle with extraordinary energy, and the skill and perseverance with which he afterwards rallied the broken forces and restored the fallen spirits of his party were admirable. In 1835 the rash and abortive attempt of William IV. to get rid of the Whigs made Peel the Minister of a hundred days. This was the most brilliant period of his life, and it was during that magnificent campaign that he established the vast reputation which, while clouds of suspicion and distrust, of enmity and dislike, were all the while gathering about him, made him for nearly twenty years by far the most conspicuous, important, and powerful of English statesmen. He not only reorganised his party, but he revived its political influence, and laid the foundation for regaining its former power. His policy was as successful as it was wise. He flung himself cheerfully and confidently into the new order of things, associated himself with the sentiments and the wants of the nation, and day by day saw his reputation increasing both in Parliament and throughout the country. The Tories abandoned themselves to his guidance with a mixture of passive reliance and admiration and of lurking resentment for the past with distrust and suspicion for the future. They rejoiced in the chief who made them once more powerful, and led them on to victory; but they felt that there were no real sympathies between themselves and him. While he was boldly advancing with the spirit of the age, they were lagging behind, gloomily regarding his manifestation of Liberal principles, in which they did not participate, and lingering on those traditions of the past which they saw that he had entirely forsaken.

At length, ten years after the Reform Bill, the Whig Government was overthrown, and Peel became Minister. At this time the great bulk of his supporters coveted power principally for the sake of Protection. They believed that it was the duty, the inclination, and the intention of Peel to maintain the Corn Laws, and they had a right to think so. He had been the vigorous and ingenious advocate of the protective system, not, however, without some qualifications and reservations, which, though they were enough to excite the jealousy and mistrust of the most suspi-

cious, were still insufficient to neutralise the effect of his general
professions. It is almost impossible to discover what the process
was by which he was gradually led to embrace the whole doctrine of Free Trade. We cannot distinguish what effect was made
upon his mind by the reasoning, and what by the organisation
and agitation, of the Anti-Corn Law League. It would be interesting, if it were possible, to sum up periodically the exact state
of Peel's opinions upon commercial and fiscal questions, and to
know how he combined them with other political as well as party
considerations, which he was obliged constantly to keep in view.
No man but himself could explain and vindicate the whole
course of his conduct. It may safely be assumed that when he
began to reorganise the Conservative party, he did not contemplate a repeal of the Corn Laws, and that it was by a severely
inductive process of study and meditation that he was gradually
led to the conception and elaboration of the commercial system
which the last years of his life were spent in carrying out. The
modification, and possibly the ultimate repeal, of the Corn Laws
must have formed a part of that system, but what he hoped and
intended probably was to bring round the minds of his party by
degrees to the doctrines of Free Trade, and to conquer their
repugnance to a great alteration of the Corn Laws, both by showing the imprudence of endeavouring to maintain them, and by
the gradual development of those countervailing advantages
with which Free Trade was fraught. That, I believe, was his
secret desire, hope, and expectation; and if the Irish famine had
not deranged his plans and precipitated his measures, if more
time had been afforded him, it is not impossible that his projects
might have been realised. He has been bitterly accused of de-
ceiving and betraying his party, of 'close designs, and crooked
counsels,' and there is no term of reproach and invective which
rage and fear, mortification and resentment, have not heaped
upon him. He has been unjustly reviled; but, on the other hand,
it must be acknowledged that, wise as his views, and pure as his
motives may have been, his manner of dealing with his party in
reference to the changes he contemplated, could not fail to ex-

cite their indignation. If they were convinced that the Corn Laws were essential, not merely to the prosperity, but to the existence, of the landed interest, he had been mainly instrumental in confirming this conviction. It was indeed a matter of extraordinary difficulty and nicety to determine at what precise period he should begin to disclose to his supporters the extent of the plans which he meditated. His reserve may have been prudent, possibly indispensable; but although they were not unsuspicious of his intentions, and distrusted and disliked him accordingly, they were wholly unprepared for the great revolution which he suddenly proclaimed; and at such a moment of terror and dismay it was not unnatural that despair and rage should supersede every other sentiment, and that they should loudly complain of having been deceived, betrayed, and abandoned.

The misfortune of Peel all along was, that there was no real community of sentiment between him and his party, except in respect to certain great principles, which had ceased to be in jeopardy, and which therefore required no united efforts to defend them. There was no longer any danger of organic reforms; the House of Lords and the Church were not threatened; the great purposes for which Peel had rallied the Conservative interest had been accomplished; almost from the first moment of his advent to power in 1841 he and his party stood in a false position towards each other. He was the liberal chief of a party in which the old anti-liberal spirit was still rife; they regarded with jealousy and fear the middle classes, those formidable masses, occupying the vast space between aristocracy and democracy, with whom Peel was evidently anxious to ingratiate himself, and whose support he considered his best reliance. His treatment of both the Catholics and Dissenters was reluctantly submitted to by his followers, and above all his fiscal and commercial meaures kept them in a state of constant uncertainty and alarm. There was an unexpressed but complete difference in their understanding and his of the obligations by which the Government and the party were mutually connected. They considered Peel to be not only the Minister, but the creature, of the Conservative party, bound above all things to support and protect their especial interests according to their own views and opinions. He considered himself the Minister of the Nation, whose mission it was to combine the interest of all classes in one homogeneous system, by which the prosperity and happiness of the whole commonwealth would be promoted. They thought of nothing but the present sacrifices which this system would entail on the proprietors of land, while he thought only of the great benefits which it would ultimately confer upon the people at large. Whether in 1847 he was prepared for the unappeasable wrath and the general insurrection of the Protectionists, I know not; but even if he viewed it as a possible alternative, involving the loss of political power and a second dissolution of the Conservative party, I believe he would have nevertheless encountered the danger and accepted the sacrifice. If his party were disgusted with him, he was no less disgusted with them, and it is easy to conceive that he must have been sickened by their ignorance and presumption, their obstinacy and ingratitude. He turned to the nation for that justice which his old associates denied him, and from the day of his resignation till the day of his death he seemed to live only for the purpose of watching over the progress of his own measures, in undiminished confidence that time and the hour would prove their wisdom, and vindicate his character to the world. Though he was little beholden to the Whigs in his last struggle in office, he gave John Russell's Government a constant, and at the same time unostentatious support. His abstinence from political conflicts, his rare appearance in debate, and the remarkable moderation of his speeches made some fancy that the vigour of his faculties was impaired; but if this was at all the case, it was only by negative symptoms that it appeared, and was by no means suspected by the community. Nevertheless, though his death was so sudden and premature, and he was cut off in the vigour of life, he could not have died at a moment and in circumstances more opportune for his own fame; for time and political events might perhaps have diminished, but could not have increased, his great reputation.

It is impossible to foresee the political effects of Peel's death. [*It*] is a great loss to the Queen, who felt a security in knowing that he was at hand in any case of danger or difficulty, and that she could always rely upon his devotion to her person and upon the good counsel he would give her. But his relations with the Court at different periods are amongst the most curious passages of his political history. In 1838, when the Bedchamber quarrel prevented his forming a Government, there was probably no man in her dominions whom the Queen so cordially detested as Sir Robert Peel. Two years afterwards he became her Prime Minister, and in a very short time he found means to remove all her former prejudice against him, and to establish himself high in her favour. His influence continued to increase during the whole period of his administration, and when he resigned in 1846 the Queen evinced a personal regard for him scarcely inferior to that which she had manifested to Lord Melbourne, while her political reliance on him was infinitely greater. To have produced such a total change of sentiment is no small proof of the tact and adroitness of Peel; but it was an immense object to him to ingratiate himself with his Royal Mistress; he spared no pains for that end, and his success was complete.

He appears to have suffered dreadful pain during the three days which elapsed between his accident and his death. He was sensible, but scarcely ever spoke. Sir Benjamin Brodie says that he never saw any human frame so susceptible of pain, for his moral and physical organisation was one of exquisite sensibility. He was certainly a good, and in some respects a great man; but when future historians shall describe his career and sum up his character, they will pass a more sober and qualified judgement than that of his admiring and sorrowing contemporaries. It is impossible to forget that there never was a statesman who so often embraced erroneous opinions himself, and contributed so much to mislead the opinions of others.

Brighton, August 27th. Yesterday morning Louis Philippe expired at Claremont quite unexpectedly, for though he had been ill for a long time, it was supposed he might still live many

months. Not long ago his life was the most important in the
world, and his death would have produced a profound sensation
and general consternation. Now hardly more importance at-
taches to the event than there would to the death of one of the
old bathing-women opposite my window.

London, November 8th, 1851. At Newmarket I seldom hear or
think of politics, but this time an incident occurred in which I
took a part, and which was very near leading to serious consequences. About three weeks ago Kossuth arrived in England,
and was received at Southampton and Winchester with prodigious demonstrations and a great uproar on the part of Mayors
and Corporations, the rabble and a sprinkling of Radicals, of
whom the most conspicuous were Cobden and Dudley Stuart.
While Kossuth was still at Southampton, but about to proceed to
London, on Monday, October 24th, I received a letter from my
brother Henry, informing me that he had just received information that Palmerston was going to receive Kossuth, and he entreated me, if I had any influence with the Government, to try
and prevent such an outrage, and that he believed if it was done
Buol would be recalled. I could not doubt that the information
from such a quarter was correct, and it was confirmed by a notice
in one of the *pro*-Kossuth papers, that Lord Palmerston was going
to receive Mr. Kossuth 'privately and unofficially.' Thinking that
it would be an outrage, and one in all probability attended with
serious consequences, I resolved to write to John Russell at once.
I sent him a copy of my brother's letter, only putting the names
in blank, said that the authority on which this was notified to me
compelled me to attend to it, and added, 'I send you this without
comment; you will deal with it as you think fit, "liberavi animam
meam."' The result of this communication was that Lord John
Russell addressed a remonstrance to Lord Palmerston. Lord
Palmerston replied with his usual audacity that 'he would not be
dictated to and should receive whomsoever he pleased in his

own house, but that his office was at the disposal of the Government.' On receiving this answer Lord John instantly summoned a Cabinet and laid it before them. Ministers were of opinion (all but one) that Lord Palmerston should not receive Kossuth, and he accordingly submitted to the decision of his colleagues.

November 16th. I was at Windsor for a Council on Friday. There I saw Palmerston and Lord John mighty merry and cordial, talking and laughing together. Those breezes leave nothing behind, particularly with Palmerston, who never loses his temper, and treats everything with gaiety and levity.

November 22nd. At Brocket on Tuesday and Wednesday last. I found Beauvale knew all about the Palmerston and Kossuth affair, and was of course mightily pleased at his brother-in-law's defeat, and at the interview not having taken place. But on Wednesday afternoon we were both of us astounded at reading in the paper the account of the deputation to Palmerston, the addresses and his answers.[27] We both agreed that he had only *reculé pour mieux sauter,* and that what he had now done was a great deal worse and more offensive than if he had received Kossuth. The breach of faith and the defiance towards John Russell and his colleagues are flagrant, and the whole affair astonishing even in him who has done such things that nothing ought to astonish me. I am waiting with the greatest curiosity to see what John Russell will do, and how he will take it, and how it will be taken by the Queen and the foreign Courts and Ministers. To receive an address in which the Emperors of Russia and Austria are called despots, tyrants, and odious assassins, and to express great gratification at it, is an unparalleled outrage, and when to this is added a speech breathing Radical sentiments and interference, it is difficult to believe that the whole thing can pass off without notice.

December 3rd. At twelve o'clock yesterday morning the won-

[27] [On November 18, a deputation from Finsbury and Islington waited upon Lord Palmerston to congratulate him on the liberation of Kossuth. Lord Palmerston took the opportunity of expressing his strong sympathy and that of the British nation with the Hungarian cause.]

derful Electric Telegraph brought us word that two hours before the President had accomplished his *Coup d'État* at Paris with success.

Panshanger, December 14th. Naturally the French Revolution has absorbed all interest. The success of Louis Napoleon's *Coup d'État* has been complete, and his audacity and unscrupulousness marvellous. The French are indeed a strange people, so restless, fierce, and excitable that they are ready to upset governments with the smallest possible show of reason or necessity—with cause as in 1830, or without cause as in 1848—and they acquiesce without a struggle, and tamely endure the impudent and vulgar democratic rule of the blackguards and mountebanks of the Provisional Government at the latter period, and now the unlimited and severe military despotism of Louis Napoleon.

London, December 22nd. On Friday last Mr. Luttrell died, at the age of eighty-one, having been long ill and confined to his bed with great suffering. When I first came into the world, nearly forty years ago, he was one of the most brilliant members of society, celebrated for his wit and repartee, and for many years we lived in great intimacy and in the same society. He was the natural son of old Lord Carhampton, but was always on bad terms with his father. He had been a member of the Irish Parliament, and obtained a place, afterwards commuted for a pension, on which he lived. He never took any part in public life, was always in narrow circumstances, and had the air, and I think the feeling, of a disappointed man. He was, in fact, conscious of powers which ought to have raised him to a higher place than that which he occupied in the world. Why he never did advance, whether it was from pride and shyness, or from disinclination, or the unkind neglect of those who might have helped him on, I know not. As it was, he never had any but a social position, but that was one of great eminence and success. He was looked upon as one of the most accomplished, agreeable, and entertaining men of his day; he lived in the very best society, was one of the cherished and favoured *habitués* of Holland House, and the intimate friend and associate of Sydney Smith, Rogers, Lord Dudley, and all the men most distinguished in politics, literature, or social eminence. Rogers and Luttrell especially were always bracketed together, intimate friends, seldom apart, and always hating, abusing, and ridiculing each other. Luttrell's *bons mots* and repartees were excellent, but he was less caustic, more good-natured, but in some respects less striking in conversation, than his companion, who had more knowledge, more imagination, and, though in a different way, as much wit. His literary performances were few and far between, consisting of little more than occasional verses, and 'Crockford House,' an amusing but rather flimsy satire. His contribution to the pleasures of society was in talk, and he was too idle and too much of a Sybarite to devote himself to any grave and laborious pursuit. There are, however, so many more good writers than good talkers, and the two qualities are so rarely found united in the same person, that we owe a debt of gratitude to Luttrell for having cultivated his conversational rather than his literary powers, and for having adorned and delighted society for so many years with his remarkable vivacity and wit. It used to be said that he was less amusing, though in the same style, as his father; but of this I cannot judge, as I do not remember Lord Carhampton. Luttrell had excellent qualities, was an honourable, high-minded gentleman, true and sincere, grateful for kindness and attentions without being punctilious or exacting, full of good feelings and warm affections, a man of excellent sense, a philosopher in all things, and especially in religion. For several years past he had disappeared from the world, and lived in great retirement, suffering under much bad health and bodily pain, but cheerful and in possession of his faculties nearly to the last. His death has removed one of the last survivors of a brilliant generation.

December 23rd. Palmerston is out!—actually, really, and irretrievably out. I nearly dropped off my chair yesterday afternoon, when at five o'clock, a few moments after the Cabinet had broken up, Granville rushed into my room and said, 'It is none of the things we talked over; Pam is out, the offer of the Foreign Office goes to Clarendon to-night, and if he refuses, which of course he will not, it is to be offered to me!!' It now appears that the cause of Palmerston's dismissal, for dismissed he is, is his having committed the Government to a full and unqualified approval of Louis Napoleon's *Coup d'État*, which he did in conversation with Walewski, but so formally and officially, that Walewski wrote word to his own Government that ours approved entirely of all that Louis Napoleon had done. Upon this piece of indiscretion, to which it is probable that Palmerston attached no importance, being so used to act off his own bat, and never dreaming of any danger from it, Lord John determined to act. I do not know the details of the correspondence, only that he signified to Palmerston his displeasure at his having thus committed the Government to an approbation they did not feel, and it ended in his turning Palmerston out, for this was in fact what he did. But though this was the pretext, the *causa causans* was without any doubt the Islington speech and deputations, and his whole conduct in that affair. The Queen had deeply resented it, and had had a discussion with Lord John about it, for he rather defended Palmerston, and accepted his excuses and denials. It is evident that he did this, because he did not dare to quarrel with him on grounds which would have enabled him to cast himself on the Radicals, to appeal to all the Kossuthian sympathies of the country, and to represent himself as the victim of our disgraceful subserviency to Austria. But having thus passed over what would have been a sufficient cause of quarrel, he at once seized upon one much less sufficient, but which was not liable to the same difficulties and objections. In fully approving Louis Napoleon's *coup d'état*, Palmerston has taken a part against the feelings of the Radicals, and if the cause of the quarrel is made public, their approval will *ad hoc* be rather with John Russell than with him.

February 5th, 1852.   I might have saved myself the trouble of writing down a scattered and imperfect notice of the Palmerstonian dismissal, since John Russell told the whole story on Tues-

day night. The public interest and curiosity to hear the 'explanations' were intense. Up to almost the last moment the confidence
and the *jactance* of the Palmerston clique were boundless. At
length the moment arrived. In all my experience I never recollect
such a triumph as John Russell achieved, and such complete discomfiture as Palmerston's. Lord John made a very able speech,
and disclosed as much as was necessary, and no more. Beyond
all doubt his great *coup* was the Queen's Minute in 1850, which
was absolutely crushing. Some grave persons think the introduction of her name was going too far, but it was irresistible. The
effect was prodigious. Palmerston was weak and inefficient, and
it is pretty certain that he was taken by surprise, and was unprepared for all that John Russell brought forward. Not a man of
weight or influence said a word for him, nobody but Milnes and
Dudley Stuart. The Queen's letter was decisive, for it was evident
that his conduct must have been intolerable to elicit such charges
and rebukes; and it cannot fail to strike everybody that no man
of common spirit, and who felt a consciousness of innocence,
would have brooked anything so insulting. Such a man would
have indignantly resigned, and have demanded what John Russell meant by making himself the organ of such accusations; but
he submitted to them.

August 9th.   The death of D'Orsay, which took place the other
day at Paris, is a matter not of political, but of some social interest.
Nature had given him powers which might have raised him to
very honourable distinction, and have procured him every sort
of success, if they had been well and wisely employed, instead
of the very reverse. He was extremely good-looking, very quick,
lively, good-natured, and agreeable, with considerable talent,
taste for, and knowledge of art, and very tolerably well-informed.
Few *amateurs* have excelled him as a painter and a sculptor,
though his merit was not so great as it appeared, because he
constantly got helped, and his works retouched by eminent artists, whose society he cultivated, and many of whom were his
intimate friends. His early life and connexion with the Blessington
family was enveloped in a sort of half mystery, for it was never

exactly known how his ill-omened marriage was brought about; but the general notion was, that Lord Blessington and Lady Blessington were equally in love with him, and it is certain that his influence over the Earl was unbounded.[28] Whatever his relations may have been with the rest of the family, he at all events devoted his whole life to *her,* and employed all his faculties in making Gore House, where they resided together for many years, an attractive and agreeable abode. His extravagance at one period had plunged him into inextricable difficulties, from which neither his wife's fortune, a large portion of which was sacrificed, nor the pecuniary aid of friends on whom he levied frequent contributions, were sufficient to relieve him, and for some years he made himself a prisoner at Gore House, and never stirred beyond its four walls, except on a Sunday, to avoid being incarcerated in a more irksome confinement. Nothing, however, damped his gaiety, and he procured the enjoyment of constant society, and devoted himself assiduously to the cultivation of his talent for painting and sculpture, for which he erected a studio in the garden. He was extremely hospitable, and managed to collect a society which was very miscellaneous, but included many eminent and remarkable men of all descriptions, professions, and countries, so that it was always curious and often entertaining. Foreigners of all nations were to be met with there, especially exiles and notabilities of any kind. He was the friend of Louis Napoleon and the friend of Louis Blanc, both of whom at different times I met at Gore House. He had a peculiar talent for drawing people out, and society might have been remarkably agreeable there if the lady of the house had contributed more to make it so. Of course no women ever went there, except a few who were in some way connected with D'Orsay and Lady Bles-

[28] [It was Lord Blessington who induced Alfred D'Orsay, then a very young man, to throw up his commission in the Guards of the King of France (for which the French never forgave him), and to become a member of the Blessington family. This was done with a formal promise to the Count's family that he should be provided for, and a marriage was accordingly brought about between him and the only daughter and heiress of Lord Blessington by his first marriage, which turned out very ill.]

sington; and exotic personages, such as Madame Guiccioli, who
lived with them whenever she came to England. There never was
a foreigner who so completely took root in England as D'Orsay,
except perhaps the Russian Matuscewitz. He spoke and wrote
English perfectly, and he thoroughly understood the country. He
was always ridiculing the crude and absurd notions which his
own countrymen formed of England; they came here, and after
passing a few weeks in scampering about seeing sights, they fancied they thoroughly understood the genius and the institutions
of the country, and talked with a pretension and vain complacency which D'Orsay used to treat with excessive contempt, and
lash with unsparing ridicule. He had in fact become thoroughly
English in tastes, habits and pursuits; his antecedent life, his connexion with Lady Blessington, and the vague but prevalent notion of his profligate and immoral character, made it impossible
for him to obtain admission into the best society, but he managed
to gather about him a miscellaneous but numerous assemblage
of personages not fastidious, or troubled by any scruples of a
refined morality, which made Gore House a considerable social
notability in its way. Lyndhurst and Brougham were constant
guests; the Bulwers, Landseer, Macready, all authors, artists, and
men eminent in any liberal profession, mixed with strangers of
every country and colour; and D'Orsay's fashionable associates
made the house a very gay and often agreeable resort. Whatever his faults may have been, and his necessities made him unscrupulous and indelicate about money matters, he was very
obliging, good-natured, and *serviable;* partly from vanity and
ostentation, but also in great measure from humane motives he
was always putting himself forward to promote works of charity
and beneficence, and he exerted all the influence he possessed,
which was not inconsiderable, to assist distressed genius and merit
in every class. He was very anti-Orleanist during the reign of
Louis Philippe, and though his connexions were Legitimist, his
personal sympathies were enlisted on the side of Louis Napoleon,
with whom he had considerable intimacy here, and whose future
greatness he always anticipated and predicted. When the de-

rangement of Lady Blessington's affairs broke up the establishment at Gore House, and compelled her to migrate to Paris, D'Orsay naturally expected that the elevation of Louis Napoleon would lead to some good appointment for himself, and he no doubt was deeply mortified at not obtaining any, and became a *frondeur* in consequence. It was, however, understood that the President wished to give him a mission, and he certainly was very near being made Minister at Hanover, but that the French Ministers would not consent to it. He was unpopular in France and ill-looked upon, in consequence of having quitted the army when ordered on active service, in what was considered a discreditable manner, and consequently his social position at Paris was not near so good as that which he enjoyed in England, though it was of the same description, as he lived chiefly with authors, artists, and actors, or rather actresses; but a short time ago, when the President was become omnipotent and could dispense his patronage and his favours as he pleased, he created a place for D'Orsay connected with the Department of the Fine Arts, which exactly suited his taste, and would have made the rest of his life easy, if he had continued to live, and his patron continued to reign.

London, September 18th. It was at Doncaster on Wednesday morning last that I heard of the Duke of Wellington's death, which at first nobody believed, but they speedily telegraphed to London, and the answer proved that the report was correct. Doncaster was probably the only place in the kingdom where the sensation caused by this event was not absorbing and profound; but there, on the morning of the St. Leger,[29] most people were too much occupied with their own concerns to bestow much thought or lamentation on this great national loss. Everywhere else the excitement and regret have been unexampled, and the press has been admirable, especially the 'Times,' the biographical notice and article in which paper were both composed many months ago, and shown to me. Indeed the notices of the Duke and the characters drawn of him have been so able and elaborate

[29] [*One of England's great annual racing events.*]

in all the newspapers, that they leave little or nothing to be said. Still, there were minute traits of character and peculiarities about the Duke which it was impossible for mere public writers and men personally unacquainted with him to seize, but the knowledge and appreciation of which are necessary in order to form a just and complete conception of the man. In spite of some foibles and faults, he was, beyond all doubt, a very great man—the only great man of the present time—and comparable, in point of greatness, to the most eminent of those who have lived before him. His greatness was the result of a few striking qualities—a perfect simplicity of character without a particle of vanity or conceit, but with a thorough and strenuous self-reliance, a severe truthfulness, never misled by fancy or exaggeration, and an ever-abiding sense of duty and obligation which made him the humblest of citizens and most obedient of subjects. The Crown never possessed a more faithful, devoted, and disinterested subject. Without personal attachment to any of the monarchs whom he served, and fully understanding and appreciating their individual merits and demerits, he alike reverenced their great office in the persons of each of them, and would at any time have sacrificed his ease, his fortune, or his life, to serve the Sovereign and the State. Passing almost his whole life in command and authority, and regarded with universal deference and submission, his head was never turned by the exalted position he occupied, and there was no duty, however humble, he would not have been ready to undertake at the bidding of his lawful superiors, whose behests he would never have hesitated to obey. Notwithstanding his age and his diminished strength, he would most assuredly have gone anywhere and have accepted any post in which his personal assistance might have been essential to the safety or advantage of the realm. He had more pride in obeying than in commanding, and he never for a moment considered that his great position and elevation above all other subjects released him from the same obligation which the humblest of them acknowledged. He was utterly devoid of personal and selfish ambition, and there never was a man whose greatness was so *thrust* upon him. It was in this

dispassionate unselfishness, and sense of duty and moral obligation, that he was so superior to Napoleon Bonaparte, who, with
more genius and fertility of invention, was the slave of his own
passions, unacquainted with moral restraint, indifferent to the
well-being and happiness of his fellow-creatures. The Duke was a
good-natured, but not an amiable man; he had no tenderness in
his disposition, and never evinced much affection for any of his
relations. His nature was hard, and he does not appear to have
had any real affection for anybody, man or woman, during the
latter years of his life, since the death of Mrs. Arbuthnot, to whom
he probably was attached, and in whom he certainly confided.
Domestic enjoyment he never possessed, and, as his wife was intolerable to him, though he always kept on decent terms with
her, at least, ostensibly, he sought the pleasure of women's society in a variety of capricious *liaisons*, from which his age took
off all scandal: these he took up or laid aside and changed as
fancy and inclination prompted him. His intimate friends and
adherents used to smile at these senile *engouements*, but sometimes had to regret the ridicule to which they would have exposed him if a general reverence and regard had not made him
a privileged person, and permitted him to do what no other man
could have done with impunity. In his younger days he was extremely addicted to gallantry, and had great success with women,
of whom one in Spain gained great influence over him, and his
passion for whom very nearly involved him in serious difficulties.
His other ladies did little more than amuse his idle hours and
subserve his social habits, and with most of them his *liaisons* were
certainly very innocent. He had been very fond of Grassini, and
the successful lover of some women of fashion, whose weaknesses
have never been known, though perhaps suspected. These habits
of female intimacy and gossip led him to take a great interest in
a thousand petty affairs, in which he delighted to be mixed up
and consulted. He was always ready to enter into any personal
matters, intrigues, or quarrels, political or social difficulties, and
to give his advice, which generally (though not invariably) was
very sound and good; but latterly he became morose and inac-

cessible, and cursed and swore at the people who sought to approach him, even on the most serious and necessary occasions.

Although the Duke's mind was still very vigorous, and he wrote very good papers on the various subjects which were submitted for his judgement and opinion, his prejudices had become so much stronger and more unassailable, that he gave great annoyance and a good deal of difficulty to the Ministers who had to transact business with him. He was opposed to almost every sort of change and reform in the military administration, and it was a task of no small difficulty to steer between the exigencies of public opinion and his objections and resistance. As it was always deemed an object to keep him in good humour, and many considerations forbade anything like a dissension with him, or an appeal against him to the public, the late Ministers often acted, or refrained from acting, in deference to his opinions and against their own, and took on themselves all the responsibility of maintaining his views and measures, even when they thought he was wrong. His habits were latterly very solitary, and after the death of Arbuthnot he had no intimacy with any one, nor any friend to whom he could talk freely and confidentially. As long as Arbuthnot lived he confided everything to him, and those who wished to communicate with the Duke almost always did so through him.

Notwithstanding the friendly and eulogistic terms in which he spoke of Sir Robert Peel just after his death, it is very certain that the Duke disliked him, and during the latter part of their Administration he seldom had any communication with Peel except such as passed through Arbuthnot. The Duke deeply resented, and I believe never heartily forgave, Peel's refusal to have anything to do with the Administration he so unwisely undertook to form on Lord Grey's sudden resignation in 1832, in the middle of the Reform contest; but this did not prevent his advising King William to make Peel Prime Minister, and taking office under him in 1835, and again in 1841. They acted together very harmoniously during Peel's Administration, but the Duke (though he sided with Sir Robert when the schism took place) in his heart bitterly lamented and disapproved his course about the Repeal of the Corn Laws, not so much from aversion to Free Trade as because it produced a fresh and final break-up of the Conservative party, which he considered the greatest evil which could befall the country. But whatever may have been his real sentiments with regard to various public men, he never allowed any partialities or antipathies to appear in his manner or behaviour towards them, and he was always courteous, friendly, and accessible to all, especially those in office, who had recourse to him for his advice and opinion. He had all his life been long accustomed to be consulted, and he certainly liked it till the last, and was pleased with the marks of deference and attention which were continually paid to him.

His position was eminently singular and exceptional, something between the Royal Family and other subjects. He was treated with greater respect than any individual not of Royal birth, and the whole Royal Family admitted him to a peculiar and exclusive familiarity and intimacy in their intercourse with him, which, while he took it in the easiest manner, and as if naturally due to him, he never abused or presumed upon. No man was more respectful or deferential towards the Sovereign and other Royal personages, but at the same time he always gave them his opinions and counsels with perfect frankness and sincerity, and never condescended to modify them to suit their prejudices or wishes. Upon every occasion of difficulty, public or private, he was always appealed to, and he was always ready to come forward and give his assistance and advice in his characteristic, plain, and straightforward manner. If he had written his own memoirs, he might have given to the world the most curious history of his own times that ever was composed, but he was the last man to deal in autobiography. One of his peculiarities was never to tell anybody where he was going, and when my brother or his own sons wished to be acquainted with his intentions, they were obliged to apply to the housekeeper, to whom he was in the habit of making them known, and nobody ever dared to ask him any questions on the subject. He was profuse but careless and indiscriminating in his charities, and consequently he was continually imposed upon, especially by people who pretended to have served under him, or to be the descendants or connexions of those who had, and it was very difficult to restrain his disposition to send money to every applicant who approached him under that pretence. Partly from a lofty feeling of independence and disinterestedness, and partly from indifference, he was a very bad patron to his relations and adherents, and never would make any applications for their benefit. The consequence was that he was not an object of affection, even to those who looked up to him with profound veneration and respect. He held popularity in great contempt, and never seemed touched or pleased at the manifestations of popular admiration and attachment of which he was the object.

October 22nd. Since the Duke's death I have had nothing to write about. The distribution of his offices and honors has not given satisfaction. The Prince has shown little judgment in making himself the heir of his military appointments; and there is something ridiculous as well as odious in his doing so.

November 16th. I went yesterday to the lying in state of the Duke of Wellington; it was fine and well done, but too gaudy and theatrical, though this is unavoidable. Afterwards to St. Paul's to see it lit up. The effect was very good, but it was like a great rout; all London was there strolling and staring about in the midst of a thousand workmen going on with their business all the same, and all the fine ladies scrambling over vast masses of timber, or ducking to avoid the great beams that were constantly sweeping along. These public funerals are very disgusting *meâ sententiâ.*

November 21st. An incident occurred the other night in the House of Commons, which exposed Disraeli to much ridicule and severe criticism. He pronounced a pompous funeral oration on the Duke of Wellington, and the next day the 'Globe' showed that half of it was taken word for word from a panegyric of Thiers on Marshal Gouvion de St. Cyr. Disraeli has been unmercifully pelted ever since, and well deserves it for such a piece of folly and bad taste. His excuse is, that he was struck by the passage, wrote it down, and, when he referred to it recently, forgot what it was, and thought it was his own composition.

On Saturday night, about twelve o'clock, Miss Mary Berry died after a few weeks' illness, without suffering, and in possession of her faculties, the machine worn out, for she was in her 90th year. As she was born nearly a century ago, and was the contemporary of my grandfathers and grandmothers, she was already a very old woman when I first became acquainted with her, and it was not till a later period, about twenty years ago, that I began to live in an intimacy with her which continued uninterrupted to the last. My knowledge of her early life is necessarily only traditional. She must have been exceedingly goodlooking, for I can remember her with a fine commanding figure and a very handsome face, full of expression and intelligence. It is well known that she was the object of Horace Walpole's octogenarian attachment, and it has been generally believed that he was anxious to marry her for the sake of bestowing upon her a title and a jointure, which advantages her disinterested and independent spirit would not allow her to accept. She continued nevertheless to make the charm and consolation of his latter days, and at his death she became his literary executrix, in which capacity she edited Madame du Deffand's letters. She always preserved a great veneration for the memory of Lord Orford, and has often talked to me about him. I gathered from what she said that she never was herself quite sure whether he wished to marry her, but inclined to believe that she might have been his wife had she chosen it. She seems to have been very early initiated into the best and most refined society, was a constant inmate of Devonshire House and an intimate friend of the Duchess, a friendship which descended to her children, all of whom treated Miss Berry to the last with unceasing marks of attention, respect, and affection. She had been very carefully educated, and was full of literary tastes and general information, but her greatest merit was her amiable and benevolent disposition, which secured to her a very large circle of friends. For a great many years the Misses Berry were amongst the social celebrities of London, and their house was the continual resort of the most distinguished people of both sexes in politics, literature, and fashion.

December 23rd. The other day twenty ruffians of the Carlton Club gave a dinner there. After dinner, when they got drunk, they went upstairs, and finding Gladstone alone in the drawing-room, some of them proposed to throw him out of the window. This they did not quite dare to do, but contented themselves with giving some insulting message or order to the waiter, and then went away.

J*anuary 30th*, 1853. Yesterday morning Frederic Lamb, Lord Beauvale and Melbourne, with whom both titles cease, died at Brocket after a short but severe attack of influenza, fever and gout. He was in his seventy-first year. Lady Palmerston[30] thus becomes a rich heiress. He was not so remarkable a man in character as his brother William, less peculiar and eccentric, more like other people, with much less of literary acquirement, less caustic humour and pungent wit, but he had a vigorous under-standing, great quickness, a good deal of general information, he was likewise well versed in business and public affairs, and a very sensible and intelligent converser and correspondent. He took a deep and lively interest in politics to the last moment of his life, was insatiably curious about all that was going on, and was much confided in and consulted by many people of very dif-ferent parties and opinions. He never was in Parliament, but engaged all his life in a diplomatic career, for which he was very well fitted, having been extremely handsome in his youth, and always very clever, agreeable, and adroit. He consequently ran it with great success, and was in high estimation at Vienna, where his brother-in-law, Palmerston, sent him as Ambassador. He was always much addicted to gallantry, and had endless liaisons with women, most of whom continued to be his friends long after they

[30] [*His sister.*]

had ceased to be his mistresses, much to the credit of all parties. After having led a very free and dissolute life, he had the good fortune at sixty years old, and with a broken and enfeebled constitution, to settle (as it is called), by marrying a charming girl of twenty, the daughter of the Prussian Minister at Vienna, Count Maltzahn. This Adine, who was content to unite her May to his December, was to him a perfect angel, devoting her youthful energies to sustain and cheer his valetudinarian existence with a cheerful unselfishness, which he repaid by a grateful and tender affection, having an air at once marital and paternal. She never cared to go anywhere, gave up all commerce with the world and all its amusements and pleasures, contenting herself with such society as it suited him to gather about them, his old friends and some new ones, to whom she did the honours with infinite grace and cordiality, and who all regarded her with great admiration and respect. In such social intercourse, in political gossip, and in her untiring attentions, his last years glided away, not without enjoyment. His most intimate friends abroad were the Metternichs and Madame de Lieven, and his notions of foreign policy were extremely congenial to theirs. Brougham, Ellice, and myself were the men he was most intimate with. He was very fond of his sister, but never much liked Palmerston.

February 8th. Yesterday I went to see the unhappy Lady Beauvale, and, apart from the sorrow of witnessing so much bodily and mental suffering, it is really a singular and extraordinary case. Here is a woman thirty-two years old, and therefore in the prime of life, who has lost a husband of seventy-one deprived of the use of his limbs, and whom she had nursed for ten years, the period of their union, with the probable or possible fatal termination of his frequent attacks of gout constantly before her eyes, and she is not merely plunged in great grief at the loss she has sustained, but in a blank and hopeless despair, which in its moral and physical effects seriously menaces her own existence. She is calm, reasonable and docile, talks of him and his illness without any excitement, and is ready to do everything that her friends advise; but she is earnestly desirous to die, considers

her sole business on earth as finished, and talks as if the prolongation of her own life could only be an unmitigated evil and intolerable burden, and that no ray of hope was left for her of any
possibility of happiness or even peace and ease for the future.
She is in fact brokenhearted, and that for a man old enough to
be her grandfather and a martyr to disease and infirmity; but to
her he was everything; she had consecrated her life to the pres-
ervation of his, and she kept his vital flame alive with the un-
wearied watching of a Vestal priestess. She had made him an
object and an idol round which all the feelings and even passion
of an affectionate heart had entwined themselves, till at last she
had merged her very existence in his, and only lived in, with,
and for him. She saw and felt that he enjoyed life, and she made
it her object to promote and prolong this enjoyment. 'Why,' she
says, 'could I not save him now, as I saved him heretofore?' and
not having been able to do so, she regards her own life as utterly
useless and unnecessary, and only hopes to be relieved of it.

February 9th.   Yesterday Clarendon told me a curious thing
about the Emperor Napoleon and his marriage, which came in a
roundabout way, but which no doubt is true. Madame de Montijo's[31] most intimate friend is the Marchioness of Santa Cruz,
and to her she wrote an account of what had passed about her
daughter's marriage and the Emperor's proposal to her. When he
offered her marriage, she expressed her sense of the greatness of
the position to which he proposed to raise her. He replied, 'It
is only fair that I should set before you the whole truth, and let
you know that if the position is very high, it is also perhaps very
dangerous and insecure.' He then represented to her in detail
all the dangers with which he was environed, his unpopularity
with the higher classes, the *malveillance* of the Great Powers,
the possibility of his being any day assassinated at her side, his
popularity indeed with the masses, but the fleeting character of
their favour, but above all the existence of a good deal of disaffection and hostility in the army, the most serious thing of all. If this

---

[31] [*The mother of Eugénie.*]

latter danger, he said, were to become more formidable, he knew very well how to avert it by a war; and though his earnest desire was to maintain peace, if no other means of self-preservation should remain, he should not shrink from that, which would at once rally the whole army to one common feeling. All this he told her with entire frankness, and without concealing the perils of his position, or his sense of them, and it is one of the most creditable traits I have ever heard of him. It was, of course, calculated to engage and attach any woman of high spirit and generosity, and it seems to have had that effect upon her.

March 24th. Lady Lyttelton, whom I met at Althorp, told me a great deal about the Queen and her children. She said the Queen was very fond of them, but severe in her manner, and a strict disciplinarian in her family. She described the Prince of Wales to be extremely shy and timid, with very good principles, and particularly an exact observer of truth. I wrote this because it will hereafter be curious to see how the boy grows up, and what sort of performance follows this promise, though I shall not live to see it.

April 21st. The great event of Gladstone's Budget came off on Monday night. He had kept his secret so well, that nobody had the least idea what it was to be, only it oozed out that the Income Tax was not to be differentiated. He spoke for five hours, and by universal consent it was one of the grandest displays and most able financial statement that ever was heard in the House of Commons; a great scheme, boldly, skilfully, and honestly devised, disdaining popular clamour and pressure from without, and the execution of it absolute perfection. Even those who do not admire the Budget, or who are injured by it, admit the merit of the performance. It has raised Gladstone to a great political elevation, and, what is of far greater consequence than the measure itself, has given the country assurance of a *man* equal to great political necessities, and fit to lead parties and direct governments.

April 22nd. I met Gladstone last night, and had the pleasure of congratulating him and his wife, which I did with great sin-

cerity, for his success is a public benefit. They have been overwhelmed with compliments and congratulations. Prince Albert
and the Queen both wrote to him.

August 28th. The Queen is gone to Ireland, and Lord Granville with her, who is afterwards to attend her to Balmoral. This
is new, because hitherto she has always had with her either the
Premier or a Secretary of State. Granville is to be relieved when
circumstances admit, but at present there is no other arrangement
feasible. Aberdeen and Clarendon are both kept in town till
the question is settled. Newcastle got leave to go to Clumber for
his boys' holidays, and Her Majesty does not desire to have
[*Palmerston*].

When I heard Granville was to go with her, I thought it so
desirable that if possible so marked a slight should not be put on
Palmerston that I spoke to Graham about it and suggested to
him to speak to Aberdeen and get him to prevail on the Queen to
have Palmerston in his turn. He said he thought like me that it
was a pity, but he did not believe anything would make her have
him at Balmoral, as her antipathy to him was not the least diminished nor her resentment for what she considered his bad be-
havior to herself. Her dislike of him is in fact of very long
standing, and partly on moral, partly on political grounds. There
are the old offences when he was at the Foreign Office, which
sunk deep in her mind, and besides this the recollection of his
conduct before her marriage, when in her own palace he made
an attempt on the person of one of her Ladies, which she very
justly resented as an outrage to herself. Palmerston, always enter-
prising and audacious with women, took a fancy to Mrs. Brande
(now Lady Dacre) and at Windsor Castle, when she was in waiting and he was a guest, he marched into her room one night. His
tender temerity met with an invincible resistance. The Lady did
not conceal the attempt and it came to the Queen's ears. Her
indignation was somehow pacified by Melbourne, then all powerful and who on every account would have abhorred an esclandre
in which his colleague and brother-in-law would have so discred-
itably figured. Palmerston got out of the scrape with his usual

luck; but the Queen has never forgotten and will never forgive it.

November 15th. The Queen told Clarendon an anecdote of Palmerston, showing how exclusively absorbed he is with *foreign* politics.[32] Her Majesty has been much interested in and alarmed at the strikes and troubles in the North, and asked Palmerston for details about them, when she found he knew nothing at all. One morning, after previous enquiries, she said to him, 'Pray, Lord Palmerston, have you any news?' To which he replied, 'No, Madam, I have heard nothing; but it seems certain *the Turks have crossed the Danube.*'

J*anuary 15th,* 1854. I have never yet noticed the extraordinary run there has been for some weeks past against the Court, more particularly the Prince, which is now exciting general attention, and has undoubtedly produced a considerable effect throughout the country. It began a few weeks ago in the press, particularly in the 'Daily News' and the 'Morning Advertiser,' but chiefly in the latter, and was immediately taken up by the Tory papers, the 'Morning Herald' and the 'Standard,' and for some time past they have poured forth article after article, and letter after letter, full of the bitterest abuse and all sorts of lies. The 'Morning Advertiser' has sometimes had five or six articles on the same day all attacking and maligning Prince Albert. Many of these are very vague, but the charges against him are principally to this effect, that he has been in the habit of meddling improperly in public affairs, and has used his influence to promote objects of his own and the interests of his own family at the expense of the interests of this country; that he is German and not English in his sentiments and principles; that he corresponds with foreign princes and with British Ministers abroad without the knowledge of the Government, and that he thwarts the foreign policy of the Ministers when it does not coincide with his own ideas and purposes. He is particularly accused of having exerted his influence over

[32] [*He was at this time Home Secretary.*]

this Government to prevent their taking the course which they ought to have done with regard to Turkey, and of having a strong bias towards Austria and Russia and against France. Then it is said that he is always present when the Queen receives her Ministers, which is unconstitutional, and that all the papers pass through his hands or under his eyes. He is accused of interfering with all the departments of government, more particularly with the Horse Guards, and specifically with the recent transactions and disagreements in that office, which led to the retirement of General Brown, the Adjutant-General. Then he and the Queen are accused of having got up an intrigue with foreign Powers, Austria particularly, for getting Palmerston out of office last year; that she first hampered him in the Foreign Office, by insisting on seeing his despatches before he sent them off, and then that she compelled John Russell to dismiss him on the ground of disrespectful conduct to herself, when the real reason was condescension to the wishes of Austria, with which Power the Prince had intimately connected himself. Charges of this sort, mixed up with smaller collateral ones, have been repeated day after day with the utmost virulence and insolence by both the Radical and the Tory journals. For some time they made very little impression, and the Queen and Prince were not at all disturbed by them; but the long continuance of these savage libels, and the effect which their continual refutation has evidently produced throughout the country, have turned their indifference into extreme annoyance. I must say I never remember anything more atrocious or unjust. Delane went to Aberdeen and told him that immense mischief had been done, and that he ought to know that the effect produced was very great and general, and offered (if it was thought desirable) to take up the cudgels in defence of the Court. Aberdeen consulted the Prince, and they were of opinion that it was better not to put forth any defence, or rebut such charges in the press, but to wait till Parliament meets, and take an opportunity to repel the charges there. One of the papers announced that a Liberal member of Parliament intended to bring the matter forward when Parliament meets, but I do not expect he will make his appearance. At present nobody talks of anything else, and those who come up from distant parts of the country say that the subject is the universal topic of discussion in country towns and on railways. It was currently reported in the Midland and Northern counties, and actually stated in a Scotch paper, that Prince Albert had been committed to the Tower, and there were people found credulous and foolish enough to believe it. It only shows how much malignity there is amongst the masses, which a profligate and impudent mendacity can stir up, when a plausible occasion is found for doing so, and how 'the mean are gratified by insults on the high.' It was only the other day that the Prince was extraordinarily popular, and received wherever he went with the strongest demonstration of public favour, and now it would not be safe for him to present himself anywhere in public, and very serious apprehensions are felt lest the Queen and he should be insulted as they go to open Parliament a fortnight hence.

January 29th. The attacks on the Prince are subsiding, except from the 'Morning Advertiser,' which goes doggedly on in spite of its lies being exposed. John Russell told me the other day that soon after the Queen's marriage she asked Melbourne whether the Prince ought to see all the papers and know everything. Melbourne consulted him about it, and he thinks that he consulted the Cabinet, but is not quite sure of this. However, Melbourne and Lord John (and the whole Cabinet if he did consult them) agreed that it was quite proper she should show him and tell him everything, and that was the beginning of his being mixed up in public affairs. Why he did not then begin to be present at her interviews with her Ministers I do not know, but that practice began when Peel came in, and Lord John said he found it established when he came back, and he saw no objection to it. He told me last night that the Queen had talked to him about the present clamour, which of course annoyed her, and she said, if she had had the Prince to talk to and employ in explaining matters at the time of the Bedchamber quarrel with Peel, that affair would not have happened. Lord John said he thought she must have been advised by somebody to act as she did, to which she replied with great candour and naïveté, 'No, it was entirely my own foolishness.' This is the first time I have heard of her acknowledging that it was 'foolishness,' and is an avowal creditable to her sense. Lord John said, when Lord Spencer was consulted on the matter he replied, 'It is a bad ground for a *Whig* Government to stand on, but as gentlemen you can't do otherwise.'

February 2nd. The run upon the Prince was carried on equally by the 'Morning Herald' and the 'Morning Advertiser' till within ten days of the meeting of Parliament, when the former was stopped; the latter never ceased. I have heard it surmised more than once that these attacks proceeded from Paris, and were paid for by the Emperor Louis Napoleon, but I never could believe it. The other day I met M. Alexandre Thomas at dinner at Marble Hill, and we came to town together. He told me he had no doubt the abuse of the Prince was the work of the Emperor, and paid for by him. It did not make much impression on me at the moment; but now, putting all these things together, I cannot help partaking in the opinion that the whole thing has been got up, managed, and paid for by Louis Napoleon, Walewski, and Palmerston. In the first place I believe Palmerston to be capable of anything, and to be excessively reckless, daring and vindictive. Indeed, it is difficult to see what *interest* he can have in taking such a course; and if he really has done it, it must be to gratify his hatred of the Court and in hatred of the Orleans's as well.

February 9th. Nobody now thinks of anything but of the coming war[33] and its vigorous prosecution. The national blood is up, and those who most earnestly deprecated war are all for hitting as hard as we can now that it is forced upon us.

March 29th. The die is cast, and war was declared yesterday. We are already beginning to taste the fruits of it. Every species of security has rapidly gone down, and everybody's property in stocks, shares, &c., is depreciated already from twenty to thirty per cent. I predict confidently that, before many months are over,

[33] [*The Crimean War.*]

people will be as heartily sick of it as they are now hot upon it. Nobody knows where our fleets and armies are going, nor what they mean to attempt, and we are profoundly ignorant of the resources and power of Russia to wage war against us.

April 2nd. The debates in both Houses were marked by great bitterness on the part of the Opposition, by Derby in one House, and by Disraeli and Layard in the other. The war fever is still sufficiently raging to make it impossible for any man who denounces the war itself to obtain a patient hearing. Nobody ventures to cry out against it but Bright in the House of Commons, and Grey in the House of Lords, but already I see symptoms of disquietude and alarm. Some of those who were most warlike begin to look grave, and to be more alive to the risks, difficulties, and probably dangers of such a contest. I cannot read the remonstrances and warnings of Bright without going very much along with him; and the more I reflect on the nature of the contest, its object, and the degree to which we are committed in it, the more uneasy I feel about it, and the more lively my apprehensions are of our finding ourselves in a very serious dilemma.

May 3rd. The death of Lord Anglesey, which took place a few days ago, has removed one of the last and the most conspicuous of the comrades of the Duke of Wellington, who all seem to be following their commander very rapidly. I have lived with Lord Anglesey for so many years in such intimacy, and have received from him such constant kindness, that I cannot pass over his death without a brief notice.

A more gallant spirit, a finer gentleman, and a more honourable and kindhearted man never existed. His abilities were not of a very high order, but he had a good fair understanding, excellent intentions, and a character remarkably straightforward and sincere. In his youth he was notoriously vain and arrogant, as most of his family were, but as he advanced in age, his faults and foibles were diminished or softened, and his virtues and amiable disposition manifested themselves the more. He distinguished himself greatly in the command of the cavalry in Sir John Moore's retreat, but was not employed in the Duke's army during the subsequent years of the Peninsular war. In the Waterloo campaign he again commanded the cavalry, not, as was supposed, entirely to the Duke's satisfaction, who would have preferred Lord Combermere in that post. He lost a leg at the battle of Waterloo; for this wound Lord Anglesey was entitled to a very large pension, of which he never would take a shilling. He was a great friend of George IV., and exposed himself to unpopularity by taking the King's part in the Queen's trial; but their friendship came to an end when Lord Anglesey connected himself with the Whig party, and when he went to Ireland as Lord Lieutenant he deeply offended the King by his open advocacy of the Roman Catholic cause in 1829. The Duke of Wellington, then Minister and about to give up the Catholic question, quarrelled with Lord Anglesey and recalled him. For some years past they had not been on very friendly terms. Lord Anglesey was jealous of the Duke, and used to affect to disparage his capacity both as a general and a statesman, and this political difference completed their mutual estrangement. These hostile feelings did not, however, last long; Lord Anglesey had a generous disposition, and was too fair and true to do permanent injustice to the Duke. I do not know how the reconciliation between them was brought about, but their temporary alienation was succeeded by a firm and lasting friendship, and the most enthusiastic admiration and attachment entertained by Lord Anglesey towards the Duke. For many years before the death of the latter, the two old warriors were the most intimate friends and constant companions, and every vestige of their former differences and antipathies was effaced and had given way to warm sentiments of mutual regard. When the regiment of Guards became vacant, King William sent for Lord Anglesey and announced to him that he was to have it, he of course expressed his acknowledgements; but early the next morning he went to the King and said to him that he felt it his duty to represent to him that there was a man worthier than himself to have the regiment, that Lord Ludlow had lost his arm at their head, and that he could not bear to accept that to which Lord Ludlow was so justly entitled. This remonstrance, so unselfish and honourable, was accepted, and the regiment was conferred on Lord Ludlow.

September 11th. I went to The Grove on Friday, but was brought up on Saturday by gout, and detained in London ever since. We had much talk about a variety of things. The Prince is exceedingly well satisfied with his visit to the Emperor. The Queen wrote this to Clarendon and said, "This prolonged absence is very trying to the Queen." Four days absence! H.M. thinks nothing of taking her Ladies from their husbands and families for months together, nor of the *trials* of those whose husbands are sent to the Baltic or the Euxine, certainly not to return for many months, perhaps not at all. Such is the personal selfishness and unreasonableness of people who have been accustomed never to be thwarted in any of their desires and to have everything their own way; and yet she has a strong sense of duty in great things and is generally ready to yield to advice.

London, September 19th. At The Grove again last week, where as usual I heard a great deal of miscellaneous matters from Clarendon. I asked him what the Prince had told him of his visit to Boulogne, and what his opinion was of the Emperor. This is the substance of what he said as far as I recollect it: The Prince was very well satisfied with his reception; the Emperor took him in his carriage *tête à tête* to the great review, so that they conversed together long and without interruption or witnesses. The Emperor seems to have talked to the Prince with more *abandon* and unreserve than is usual to him. The Prince was exceedingly struck with his extreme apathy and languor (which corresponds with what Thiers told me of him) and with his ignorance of a variety of matters which it peculiarly behoved him to know. The Emperor said that he felt all the difficulties of his own position, and enlarged upon them with great freedom, particularly adverting, as one of them, to the absence of any aristocracy in France. The Prince, in reply to this, seems to have given him very judicious advice; for he told him that any attempt to *create* an aristocracy in France resembling that of England must be a failure, the conditions and antecedents of the two countries being so totally dissimilar; that he might confer titles and distinctions to any amount, and so surround himself with adherents whom he had obliged, but that he had better confine himself to that and not attempt to do more. When they parted, the Emperor said he hoped it would not be the last time he should have the pleasure of seeing His Royal Highness, to which the Prince replied that he hoped not, and that he was charged by the Queen to express her hope that he would pay her a visit at Windsor, and give her an opportunity of making the Empress's acquaintance, to which the Emperor responded 'he should be very glad to see the Queen at Paris.' This *insouciant* reception of an invitation which a few months before he would have jumped at is very unaccountable, but it meant something, for it was evidently a *mot d'ordre*, because when the Prince took leave of Marshal Vaillant, he said he hoped he would accompany the Emperor to Windsor, where, though they could show no such military spectacle as the Emperor had shown him, they would do what they could, to which Vaillant replied, 'We hope to see Her Majesty the Queen and Your Royal Highness at Paris.' There seems no disposition at present to give him the Garter which is supposed to be the object of his ambition, and which Walewski is always suggesting.

October 2nd. It seems that there was some misunderstanding as to the invitation given by the Prince to the Emperor at Boulogne, and the latter gives a very different account of what passed from that given by the Prince. The Emperor says that when he took leave of the Prince, he said, 'I have not been able to give you such a reception as I could have wished, but you see I am only occupying an hotel; if you will come to Paris, where I should be delighted to receive the Queen, I could give her and yourself a more fitting reception;' and then, he says, the Prince invited him to Windsor, which he only seems to have taken as a civility unavoidable under the circumstances. It is impossible to say which account is the true one, but I rather believe that of the Emperor to be correct. Clarendon wrote this to the Queen, whose answer I saw; she said the intention was to make the invitation something between a cordial invitation and a mere civility, which the Emperor might avail himself of or not, according to his convenience.

October 20th. Ever since the news came of the battle of the Alma, the country has been in a fever of excitement, and the newspapers have teemed with letters and descriptions of the events that occurred. Raglan has gained great credit, and his march on Balaklava is considered a very able and judicious operation. Although they do not utter a word of complaint, and are by way of being fully satisfied with our allies the French, the truth is that the English think they did very little for the success of the day, and Burghersh told some one that their not pressing on was the cause (and not the want of cavalry) why the Russian guns were not taken. The French, nevertheless, have been well disposed to take the credit of the victory to themselves.

Burghersh tells two characteristic anecdotes of Raglan. He was extremely put out at the acclamations of the soldiers when he appeared amongst them after the battle, and said to his staff as he rode along the line, in a melancholy tone, 'I was sure this would happen.' He is a very modest man, and it is not in his nature any more than it was in that of the Duke of Wellington to make himself popular with the soldiers in the way Napoleon used to do, and who was consequently adored by them. The other story is that there were two French officers attached to headquarters, very good fellows, and that the staff were constantly embarrassed by the inveterate habit Raglan had of calling the enemy 'the French.' He could not forget his old Peninsular habits.

November 14th. Yesterday morning we received telegraphic news of another battle, from which we may expect a long list of killed and wounded. The affair of the 25th,[34] in which our light cavalry was cut to pieces, seems to have been the result of mismanagement in some quarter, and the blame must attach either to Lucan, Cardigan, Captain Nolan who was killed, or to Raglan himself. Perhaps nobody is really to blame, but, if any one be, my

[34] [*The Charge of the Light Brigade.*]

own impression is that it is Raglan. He *wrote* the order, and it was his business to make it so clear that it could not be mistaken, and to give it conditionally, or with such discretionary powers as should prevent its being vigorously enforced under circumstances which he could not foresee, or of which he might have no cognisance.

The Grove, December 31st. The last day of one of the most melancholy and disastrous years I ever recollect. Almost everybody is in mourning, and grief and despair overspread the land. At the beginning of the year we sent forth an army amidst a tumult of joyous and triumphant anticipation, and everybody full of confidence and boasting and expecting to force the Emperor Nicholas in the shortest possible time humbly to sue for peace, and the only question was, what terms we should vouchsafe to grant him, and how much of his dominions we should leave him in possession of. Such presumptuous boasting and confidence have been signally humbled, and the end of this year sees us deploring the deaths of friends and relations without number, and our army perishing before the walls of Sebastopol, which we are unable to take, and, after bloody victories and prodigies of valour, the Russian power hardly as yet diminished or impaired.

M*arch 11th, 1855.* Clarendon was much pleased with his visit to the Emperor,[35] who talked to him very frankly and unreservedly about everything. They lit their cigars and sat and talked with the greatest ease. He said the Emperor spoke to him about the English press, and all he said was sensible and true; that he was aware that a free press was a necessity in England, and as indispensable as the Constitution itself, and that he had hitherto believed that the editors of the principal newspapers had the good of their country at heart, and always acted from conscientious motives; but that he could no longer entertain that opinion.

35 [Louis Napoleon.]

The press during the past months, and the 'Times' particularly,[36] had done an incalculable amount of mischief to England and to the alliance between us. The effect produced by their language in Germany was most injurious, and of service only to Russia. When the English papers talked of their own country in the way they did, of its degradation and disgrace, its maladministration, the ruin of its military power, and the loss of all that makes a nation great and powerful, though he (the Emperor) knew what all this meant, and how much or how little of truth there was in such exaggerated statements, yet in France they were generally believed.

April 20th. The visit of the Emperor has been one continued ovation, and the success of it complete. None of the Sovereigns who have been here before have ever been received with such magnificence by the Court or by such curiosity and delight by the people. Wherever and whenever they have appeared, they have been greeted by enormous multitudes and prodigious acclamations. The Queen is exceedingly pleased with both of them; she thinks the Empress very natural, graceful, and attractive, and the Emperor frank, cordial, and true. He has done his best to please her, talked to her a great deal, amused her, and has completely succeeded. Everybody is struck with his mean and diminutive figure and vulgar appearance, but his manners are good and not undignified. He talked a very long time to Lord Derby on Tuesday at Windsor and to Lord Aberdeen on Wednesday. This last was very proper, because he had a great prejudice against Aberdeen, and fancied he was his enemy, which Aberdeen knew. When he was invested with the Garter, he took all sorts of oaths—old feudal oaths—of fidelity and knightly service to the Queen, and he then made her a short speech to the following effect:— 'I have sworn to be faithful to Your Majesty and to serve you to the best of my ability, and my whole future life shall be spent

[36] [In justice to the conductors of the "Times" it must be said that although the language of the paper was violent and extremely annoying to the Government and its Allies, yet it was by the power and enterprise of the press that the deplorable state of the army was brought to the knowledge of the public and even of Ministers themselves.]

in proving the sincerity with which I have thus sworn, and my resolution to devote myself to your service.' The fineness of the weather brought out the whole population of London, as usual kept in excellent order by a few policemen, and in perfect good humour. It was a beautiful sight last night when the Royal and Imperial party went to the Opera in state; the streets lit by gas and the houses illuminated and light as day, particularly opposite the Travellers' Club, where I was. I am glad the success of the visit has been so great, and the contentment of all the parties concerned so complete, but it is well that all will be over tomorrow, for such excitement and enthusiasm could not last much longer, and the inconvenience of being beset by crowds, and the streets obstructed, is getting tiresome.

Paris, June 26th. Yesterday morning arrived an invitation to dine at the Tuileries the same evening. I went there, was ushered into a room with eight or ten men in it, none of whom I kr ew except Count Bacciochi, whom I had met at Fould's the day before —three in uniform, the rest in plain clothes. A man, whom I suppose to be the *aide de camp de service,* came forward to receive me and invited me to sit down. Presently the same or another man came and said 'Milord' (they all milorded me), 'vous vous mettrez à table, s'il vous plaît, à côté de l'Empereur à sa droite.' I was then taken into the next room, which adjoins the cabinet of the Emperor. In a few minutes His Majesty made his appearance; he immediately came up to me, bowed very civilly, and asked me the usual questions of when I came to Paris, etc. In a minute dinner was announced and we went in. As we walked in he said to me, 'L'Impératrice sera bien fâchée de ne vous avoir pas vu.' At dinner, which did not last above twenty-five minutes, he talked (a sort of dropping conversation) on different subjects, and I found him so easy to get on with that I ventured to start topics myself. After dinner we returned to the room we had left, and after coffee, seeing me staring about at the portraits, he said all his family were there, and he told me who they all were and the history of these portraits, which, he said, had made the tour of the world.

After this he asked me to sit down, which I did at a round table by his side, and M. Visconti on the other side of me, and then we had a conversation which lasted at least an hour and a half on every imaginable subject. It was impossible not to be struck with his simplicity, his being so natural and totally without any air or assumption of greatness, though not undignified, but perfectly *comme il faut,* with excellent manners, and easy, pleasant, fluent conversation. I was struck with his air of truth and frankness, and though of course I could not expect in my position and at this first interview with him that he should be particularly expansive, yet he gave me the idea of being not only not reserved but as if, when intimate, he would have a great deal of *abandon.* I do not know that he said anything wonderfully striking, but he made a very favourable impression on me, and made me wish to know more of him, which I am never likely to do.

Paris, July 9th. I meant to have left Paris last night, but, an invitation arriving to dine with the Emperor at St. Cloud today, I put off going till tomorrow.

July 10th. I dined at Villeneuve l'Étang. We went to the Palace of St. Cloud in Cowley's carriage, where we found an equerry and one of the Emperor's carriages, which took us to Villeneuve. A small house, pretty and comfortable enough, and a small party, all English—Duke and Duchess of Hamilton, Lord Hertford, Lord and Lady Ashburton, General Torrens and his *aide de camp,* Cowley and myself, the Duc de Bassano, Comte de Montebello, the *aide de camp de service,* and M. Valabrègue, *écuyer,* that was the whole party. The Emperor sat between the two ladies, taking the Duchess in to dinner. It lasted about three quarters of an hour, and as soon as it was over His Majesty took us all out to walk about the place, see the dairy and a beautiful Bretonne cow he ordered to be brought out, and then to scull on the lake, or *étang,* which gives its name to the place. There were a number of little boats for one person to scull and one to sit, and one larger for two each; the Emperor got into one with the Duchess, and all the rest of the people as they liked, and we passed about half an hour on the water. On landing, ices, etc., were brought, and the carriages came to the door at nine o'clock, a *char à banc* with four *percherons* and postillions exactly like the old French postboy, and several other open carriages and pair. The two ladies got into the centre of the *char à banc*, Cowley, Hertford, and I were invited to get up before, and the Emperor himself got up behind with somebody else, I did not see who. We then set off and drove for some time through the woods and drives of Villeneuve and St. Cloud, and at last, at about ten o'clock, we were set down at the Palace. There we all alighted, and, after walking about a little, the Emperor showing us the part which Marie Antoinette had built and telling some anecdotes connected with Louis XVIII. and Louis Philippe, and the Château, he shook hands with all of us very cordially and dismissed us. His Majesty got into the *char à banc* and returned to Villeneuve, and we drove back to Paris. When we were walking about the court of the Château (it was quite dark) the sentinel challenged us—'Qui va là?' when the Emperor called out in a loud voice, 'L'Empereur.'

Of course, in this company there was nothing but general conversation, and I had no opportunity of having any with His Majesty; but he was extremely civil, offering me his cigars, which I declined, and expressing anxiety that I should not catch cold. He made the same impression on me as before as to his extreme simplicity and the easiness of his intercourse; but I was struck with his appearance being so very *mesquin,* more than I thought at first.

London, August 21st. The Queen as usual has had magnificent weather for her Paris visit, and all has gone well there except that unluckily she arrived after her time at Boulogne and still more at Paris, consequently the Emperor was kept waiting at Boulogne, and the whole population of Paris, which turned out and waited for hours under a broiling sun, was disappointed, for they arrived when it was growing dark. However, in spite of this, the scene appears to have been very fine and animated. Clarendon, who is not apt to be enthusiastic, writes so to Palmerston, and tells him that Marshal Magnan said he had known Paris for fifty

years, and had never seen such a scene as this, not even when
Napoleon returned from Austerlitz.

September 5th. I saw Clarendon one day last week for a short
time, but had no opportunity of hearing the details of his sojourn
at Paris. He said the Queen was delighted with everything and
especially with the Emperor himself who, with perfect knowledge of women, had taken the surest way to ingratiate himself
with her, by making love to her. This it seems he began when he
was in England, and followed it up in Paris. As his attentions
tickled her vanity without shocking or alarming her modesty, and
the novelty of it (for she never had any love made to her before)
made it very pleasant, his success was complete. After his visit
the Queen talked it all over with Clarendon, and said "It is very
odd; but the Emperor knows everything I have done and where
I have been ever since I was twelve years old; he even recollects
how I was dressed, and a thousand little details it is extraordinary
he should be acquainted with. "Le coquin," thought I (said
Clarendon to me), "he has evidently been making love to her"—
and he continued in much the same tone at Paris much to her
delight. She has never before been on such a social footing with
anybody, and he has approached her with the familiarity of their
equal positions, and with all the experience and knowledge of
womenkind he has acquired during his long life, passed in the
world and in mixing with every society."

September 17th. The Prince of Wales was put by the Queen
under Clarendon's charge, who was desired to tell him what to
do in public, when to bow to the people, and whom to speak to.
He thinks the Queen's severe way of treating her children very
injudicious and that the Prince will be difficult to manage, as he
has evidently a will of his own and is rather positive and opin-
ionated, and inclined to lay down the law; but he is clever and
his manners are good. One day in the carriage some subject was
discussed, when the Prince said something which Clarendon
contradicted, to which he replied, "At all events that is my
opinion," when Clarendon said "Then Y.R.H.'s opinion is quite
wrong," which seemed to surprise him a good deal. Another day

he told him what he ought to do or say and added that the Queen
had commanded him so to instruct H.R.H., who said that he was
aware of it, the Queen having told him so herself. He said that
the Princess Royal was charming, with excellent manners, and
full of intelligence. Both the children were delighted with their
séjour, and very sorry to come away. When the visit was drawing
to a close, the Prince said to the Empress that he and his sister
were both very reluctant to leave Paris, and asked her if she could
not get leave for them to stay there a little longer. The Empress
said she was afraid this would not be possible, as the Queen and
the Prince would not be able to do without them; to which the
boy replied, 'Not do without us! don't fancy that, for there are
six more of us at home, and they don't want us.'

London, November 12th. I saw Disraeli and had some talk
with him. He told me that he had now nothing whatever to do
with the 'Press,' and that the series of articles in that paper on the
war and in favour of peace were all written by Stanley. He said
he had received a letter from Stanley to this effect: 'My dear
Disraeli,—I write to you in confidence to tell you that I have been
offered and have refused the Colonial Office. As it is due to Lord
Palmerston to keep his offer secret, I have told nobody of it but
yourself and my father, and I beg you not to mention it to anybody.' On receiving this he said he began to concoct an answer
in his mind of rather a sentimental kind, and conveying his approbation of the course he had taken, but before he put pen to paper
he got the 'Times' with Stanley's letter to Sir — —, which was
tantamount to a disclosure of the whole thing, on which he wrote
instead, 'Dear Stanley,—I thank you for your letter, but I had already received your confidential communication through your
letter to Sir — —.'

December 17th. This morning the two new volumes of Macaulay's History came forth. The circumstances of this publication are, I believe, unprecedented in literary history; 25,000
copies are given out, and the weight of the books is fifty-six tons.
The interest and curiosity which it excites are prodigious, and
they afford the most complete testimony to his immense popular-

ity and the opinion entertained by the world of his works already published. His profits will be very great, and he will receive them in various shapes. But there is too much reason to apprehend that these may be the last volumes of his history that the world will see, still more that they are the last that will be read by me and people of my standing. Six years have elapsed since the appearance of the first volumes, and these two only advance about ten years. He announced at the outset that he meant to bring down the history of England to a period within the memory of persons still living, but his work has already so much expanded, and of course will do so still more from the accumulation of materials as he advances, that at his present rate of progress he must live much beyond the ordinary duration of human life, and retain all his faculties as long, to have any chance of accomplishing his original design; and he is now in such a precarious state of health that in all human probability he will not live many years. It is melancholy to think that so gifted an intellect should be arrested by premature decay, and such a magnificent undertaking should be overthrown by physical infirmities, and be limited to the proportions of a splendid fragment. He is going to quit Parliament and to reside in the neighbourhood of London.

December 21st. The poet Rogers died two days ago at the age of 93. I have known him all my life, and at times lived in a good deal of intimacy with him, but for some years past he had so great an aversion to me that I kept away from him and never saw anything of him. He was an old man when I first made his acquaintance between thirty and forty years ago, or probably more. He was then very agreeable, though peculiar and eccentric; he was devoured by a morbid vanity, and could not endure any appearance of indifference or slight in society. He was extremely touchy, and always wanted to be flattered, but above all to be listened to, very angry and mortified when he was not the principal object in society, and provoked to death when the uproarious merriment of Sydney Smith or the voluminous talk of Macaulay overwhelmed him and engrossed the company; he had a great friendship nevertheless for Sydney Smith, but he never liked

Macaulay. I never pretended, or could pretend, to be a rival to him, but I was not a patient and attentive listener to him, and that was what affronted him and caused his dislike to me as well as to anyone else of whom he had the same reason to complain. His voice was feeble, and it has been said that his bitterness and caustic remarks arose from the necessity of his attracting attention by the pungency of his conversation. He was undoubtedly a very clever and accomplished man, with a great deal of taste and knowledge of the world, and he was the last survivor of the generation to which he belonged.

The Grove, December 26th. Here are letters from Seymour at Vienna describing his good reception there, gracious from the Court, and cordially civil from the great society, especially from Metternich who seems to have given the *mot d'ordre*. Metternich talked much to Seymour of his past life and recollections, complimented him for his reports of conversations with the Emperor Nicholas, and said that many years ago the Emperor had talked to him (Metternich) about Turkey in the same strain, and used the same expression about 'le malade' and 'l'homme malade,' when Metternich asked him 'Est-ce que Votre Majesté en parle comme son médecin ou comme son héritier?'

March 10th, 1856. This morning I went to St. Germains to see a stag hunt in the forest—a curious sight, with the old-fashioned *meute;* the officers, and those privileged to wear the uniform, in embroidered coats, jackboots, and cocked hats; piqueurs on horseback and foot with vast horns wound round their bodies; the costume and the sport exactly as in the time of Louis XIV., rather tiresome after a time. The old château is a melancholy *délabré* building, sad as the finishing career of its last Royal inhabitant. These recollections come thick upon one—Anne of Austria and the Fronde, Louis XIV. and Mademoiselle de la Vallière—for here their lives began. When the Queen was here she insisted on being taken up to see Mademoiselle de la Vallière's apartment, to mark which some slight ornaments remain. Here too James II. held his dismal Court and came to his unhappy and bigoted end. After it ceased to be a palace, it became successively a prison, a school, and a barrack, and now the Emperor has a fancy to restore it.

April 1st. News of peace reached London on Sunday evening, and was received joyfully by the populace, not from any desire to see an end of the war, but merely because it is a great event to make a noise about. The newspapers have been reasonable enough, except the 'Sun,' which appeared in deep mourning and with a violent tirade against peace.

June 1st. The state of affairs with America becomes more and more alarming.[37] Grey told me the other night that he had had a long conversation with Dallas, whose tone was anything but re-assuring as to the prospect of peace; and yesterday I met Thack-eray, who is just returned from the United States. He thinks there is every probability of the quarrel leading to war, for there is a very hostile spirit, constantly increasing, throughout the States, and an evident desire to quarrel with us. He says he has never met with a single man who is not persuaded that they are entirely in the right and we in the wrong, and they are equally persuaded if war ensues that they will give us a great thrashing; they don't care for the consequences, their riches are immense, and 200,000 men would appear in arms at a moment's notice. Here, however, though there is a great deal of anxiety, there is still a very general belief that war cannot take place on grounds so trifling between two countries which have so great and so equal an interest in remaining at peace with each other. But in a country where the statesmen, if there are any, have so little influence, and where the national policy is subject to the passions and caprices of an

[37] [In consequence of the dispute with the American Government on the subject of Foreign Enlistment, Mr. Crampton, the British Minister, was or-dered to leave Washington on May 28th. He arrived in England on June 15th; but Lord Palmerston stated in the House of Commons that the dismissal of Mr. Crampton did not break off diplomatic relations with the United States, as Mr. Dallas remained in this country. It is remarkable that within a few months or even weeks two British Ministers received their passports from foreign governments and were sent away—a very uncommon occurrence!]

ignorant and unreasoning mob, there is no security that good
sense and moderation will prevail. Many imagine that matters
will proceed to the length of a diplomatic rupture, that Crampton
will be sent away and Dallas retire in consequence, and that
then by degrees the present heat will cool down, and matters be
amicably arranged without a shot being fired. I feel no such confidence, for if diplomatic intercourse ceases numerous causes of
complaint will arise, and as there will be no means left for mutual and friendly explanation and adjustment, such causes will be
constantly exaggerated and inflamed into an irreconcileable
quarrel. Matters cannot long go on as they now are without the
public here becoming excited and angry, and the press on both
sides insolent, violent, and provoking, and at last, going on from
one step to another, we shall find ourselves drifted into this odious
and on both parts suicidal contest, for there is not a blow we can
strike at America and her interests that will not recoil on us and
our own. It has often been remarked that civil wars are of all
wars the most furious, and a war between America and England
would have all the characteristics of a civil and an international
contest; nor, though I have no doubt that America is in the wrong,
can I persuade myself that we are entirely in the right on either
of the principal points in dispute. We have reason to congratulate
ourselves that the Russian war is over, for if it had gone on and all
our ships had been in the Baltic, and all our soldiers in the Crimea, nothing would have prevented the Americans from seizing
the opportunity of our hands being full to bring their dispute with
us to a crisis.

June 7th. The American horizon is rather less dark. Nothing is
yet known as to Crampton's dismissal, and Dallas does not believe
it. The Danish Minister at Washington writes over here that he
thinks the clouds will disperse and there will be no serious
quarrel.

August 4th. History is full of examples of the slight and
accidental causes on which the greatest events turn, and of such
examples the last war seems very full. Charles Wyndham told
me that nothing but a very thick fog which happened on the

morning of Inkerman prevented the English army being swept from their position and totally discomfited. The Russians could see nothing, lost their own way, and mistook the position of the British troops. Had the weather been clear so that they had been able to execute their plans, we could not have resisted them; a defeat instead of the victory we gained would have changed the destiny of the world, and have produced effects which it is impossible to contemplate or calculate.

J*anuary 28th*, 1857. Two remarkable deaths have occurred, one of which touches me nearly, that of Madame de Lieven. Madame de Lieven came to this country at the end of 1812 or beginning of 1813 on the war breaking out between Russia and France. Pozzo di Borgo had preceded the Lievens to renew diplomatic relations and make arrangements with us. She was at that time young, at least in the prime of life, and though without any pretensions to beauty, and indeed with some personal defects, she had so fine an air and manner, and a countenance so pretty and so full of intelligence, as to be on the whole a very striking and attractive person, quite enough so to have lovers, several of whom she engaged in succession without seriously attaching herself to any. Those who were most notoriously her slaves at different times were the present Lord Willoughby, the Duke of Sutherland (then Lord Gower), the Duke of Cannizzaro (then Count St. Antonio), and the Duke of Palmella, who was particularly clever and agreeable. Madame de Lieven was a *très grande dame*, with abilities of a very fine order, great tact and *finesse*, and taking a boundless pleasure in the society of the great world and in political affairs of every sort. People here were not slow to acknowledge her merits and social excellence, and she almost immediately took her place in the cream of the cream of English society, forming close intimacies with the most conspicuous women in it, and assiduously cultivating relations with the most remarkable men of all parties. These personal *liaisons* sometimes

led her into political partisanship not always prudent and rather
inconsistent with her position, character, and functions here. But
I do not believe she was ever mixed up in any intrigues, nor even,
at a later period, that she was justly obnoxious to the charge of
caballing and mischief-making which has been so lavishly cast
upon her. She had an insatiable curiosity for political information,
and a not unnatural desire to make herself useful and agreeable
to her own Court by imparting to her Imperial masters and mistresses all the information she acquired and the anecdotes she
picked up. Accordingly while she was in England, which was
from 1812 to 1834, she devoted herself to society, not without
selection, but without exclusion, except that she sought and habit-
ually confined herself to the highest and best. The Regent, afterwards George IV., delighted in her company, and she was a
frequent guest at the Pavilion, and on very intimate terms with
Lady Conyngham, for although Madame de Lieven was not very
tolerant of mediocrity, and social and colloquial superiority was
necessary to her existence, she always made great allowances for
Royalty and those immediately connected with it. She used to be
a great deal at Oatlands, and was one of the few intimate friends
of the Duchess of York, herself very intelligent, and who therefore
had in the eyes of Madame de Lieven the double charm of her
position and her agreeableness. It was her duty as well as her
inclination to cultivate the members of all the successive Cabinets
which passed before her, and she became the friend of Lord
Castlereagh, of Canning, the Duke of Wellington, Lord Grey,
Lord Palmerston, John Russell, Aberdeen, and many others of
inferior note, and she was likewise one of the *habitués* of Holland
House, which was always more or less neutral ground, even when
Lord Holland was himself a member of the government. When
Talleyrand came over here as Ambassador, there was for some
time a sort of antagonism between the two embassies, and particularly between the ladies of each, but Madame de Dino (now
Duchesse de Sagan) was so clever, and old Talleyrand himself
so remarkable and so agreeable, that Madame de Lieven was
irresistibly drawn towards them, and for the last year or two of

their being in England they became extremely intimate; but her greatest friend in England was Lady Cowper, afterwards Lady Palmerston, and through her she was also the friend of Palmerston, who was also well affected towards Russia, till his jealous and suspicious mind was inflamed by his absurd notion of her intention to attack us in India, a crotchet which led us into the folly and disaster of the Afghan war. In 1834 the Lievens were recalled, and she was established at St. Petersburg in high favour about the Empress, but her *séjour* there was odious to her, and she was inconsolable at leaving England, where after a residence of above twenty years she had become rooted in habits and affections, although she never really and completely understood the country. She remained at St. Petersburg for several months, until her two youngest children were taken ill, and died almost at the same time. This dreadful blow, and the danger of the severe climate to her own health, gave her a valid excuse for desiring leave of absence, and she left Russia never to return. She went to Italy, where M. de Lieven died about the year 1836 or 1837, after which she established herself in Paris, where her salon became the rendezvous of the best society, and particularly the neutral ground on which eminent men and politicians of all colours could meet, and where her tact and adroitness made them congregate in a sort of social truce.

I do not know at what exact period it was that she made the acquaintance of M. Guizot, but their intimacy no doubt was established after he had begun to play a great political part, for his literary and philosophical celebrity would not alone have had much charm for her. They were, however, already great friends at the time of his embassy to England, and she took that opportunity of coming here to pay a visit to her old friends. The fall of Thiers' Government and Guizot's becoming Minister for Foreign Affairs of course drew Madame de Lieven still more closely to him, and during the whole of his administration their alliance continued to be of the closest and most intimate character. It was an immense object to her to possess the entire confidence of the French Minister for Foreign Affairs, who kept her *au courant* of all that was going on in the political world, while it is not surprising that he should be irresistibly attracted by a woman immensely superior to any other of his acquaintance, who was fully able to comprehend and willing to interest herself about all the grand and important subjects which he had to handle and manage, and who associated herself with a complete sympathy in all his political interests. Their *liaison*, which some people consider mysterious, but which I believe to have been entirely social and political, grew constantly more close, and every moment that Guizot could snatch from the Foreign Office and the Chamber he devoted to Madame de Lieven. He used to go there regularly three times a day on his way to and his way from the Chamber, when it was sitting, and in the evening; but while he was by far her first object, she cultivated the society of all the most conspicuous and remarkable people whom she could collect about her, and she was at one time very intimate with Thiers, though his rivalry with Guizot and their intense hatred of each other eventually produced a complete estrangement between her and Thiers.

The revolution of 1848 dispersed her friends, broke up her salon, and terrified her into making a rather ludicrous, but as it turned out wholly unnecessary, escape. She came to England, where she remained till affairs appeared to be settled in France and all danger of disturbance at an end. She then returned to Paris, where she remained, not without fear and trembling, during the period of peril and vicissitude which at length ended, much to her satisfaction, with the *coup d'état* and the Empire. Guizot had returned to Paris, but constantly refused to take any part in political affairs, either under the Republic or with the new government of Louis Napoleon. This, however, did not prevent Madame de Lieven (though their friendship continued the same) from showing her sympathy and goodwill to the Imperial *régime*, and her salon, which had been decimated by previous events, was soon replenished by some of the ministers or adherents of the Empire, who, though they did not amalgamate very well with her old *habitués*, supplied her with interesting information, and subsequently, when the war broke out, rendered her very essential service. When the rupture took place all the Russian subjects were ordered to quit Paris. She was advised by some of her friends to disobey the order, for as she was equally precluded from going to England, the circumstances in which this order placed her were indescribably painful and even dangerous, but she said that however great the sacrifice, and though she was entirely independent, she was under so many obligations and felt so much attachment to the Imperial family that, cost her what it might, she would obey the order, and accordingly she repaired to Brussels, where for a year and a half or two years she took up her melancholy and uncomfortable abode. At last this banishment from her home and her friends, with all the privations it entailed, became insupportable, and she endeavoured, through the intervention of some of her Imperialist friends, to obtain leave of the French Government to return to Paris, either with or without (for it is not clear which) the consent of her own Court. The Emperor Napoleon seems to have been easily moved to compassion, and signified his consent to her return. No sooner did this become known to Cowley and the English Government than they resolved to interpose for the purpose of preventing her return to Paris, and Cowley went to Walewski and insisted that the Emperor's permission should be revoked. The *entente cordiale* was then in full force, nothing could be refused to the English Ambassador, and Madame de Lieven was informed that she must not come back to Paris. She bore this sad disappointment with resignation, made no complaints, and resolved to bide her time. Some months later she caused a representation to be made to the French Government that the state of her health made it impossible for her to pass another winter at Brussels, and that she was going to Nice, but as it was of vital importance to her to consult her medical adviser at Paris, she craved permission to proceed to Nice *viâ* Paris, where she would only stay long enough for that purpose. The permission was granted. She wrote me word that she was going to Paris to remain there a few days. I replied that I was much mistaken in her if once there she ever quitted it again. She arrived and was told by her doctor that it would be dangerous in her state to continue her journey. She never did proceed further, and never did quit Paris again. The Government winked at her stay, and never molested or interfered with her. She resumed her social habits, but with great caution and reserve, and did all she could to avoid giving umbrage or exciting suspicion. It was a proof of the greatness of her mind, as well as of her prudence and good temper, that she not only testified no resentment at the conduct of Cowley towards her, but did all she could to renew amicable relations with him, and few things annoyed her more than his perseverance in keeping aloof from her. From the time of her last departure from England up to the death of Frederic Lamb (Lord Beauvale and Melbourne) she maintained a constant correspondence with him. After his death she proposed to me to succeed him as her correspondent, and for the last two or three years our epistolary commerce was intimate and unbroken. She knew a vast deal of the world and its history during the half century she had lived and played a part in it, but she was not a woman of much reading, and probably at no time had been very highly or extremely educated, but her excessive cleverness and her *finesse d'esprit* supplied the want of education, and there was one book with which her mind was perpetually nourished by reading it over and over again. This was the 'Letters of Madame de Sévigné,' and to the constant study of those unrivalled letters she was no doubt considerably indebted for her own epistolary eminence, and for her admirable style of writing, not, however, that her style and Madame de Sévigné's were at all alike. She had not (in her letters at least) the variety, the abundance, or the *abandon* of the great Frenchwoman, but she was more terse and epigrammatic, and she had the same graphic power and faculty of conveying much matter in few words.

Nothing could exceed the charm of her conversation or her grace, ease, and tact in society. She had a nice and accurate judgement, and an exquisite taste in the choice of her associates and friends. It has been the fashion here, and the habit of the vulgar and ignorant press, to stigmatise Madame de Lieven as a

mischievous intriguer, who was constantly occupied in schemes
and designs hostile to the interests of our country. I firmly believe
such charges to be utterly unfounded. She had resided for above
twenty years, the happiest of her life, in England, and had imbibed a deep attachment to the country, where she had formed
many more intimacies and friendships than she possessed anywhere else, and to the last day of her life she continued to cherish
the remembrance of her past connexion, to cultivate the society
of English people, and to evince without disguise her predilection
for their country. She had never lived much in Russia, her connexion with it had been completely dissolved, and all she retained of it was a respectful attachment to the Imperial family,
together with certain sympathies and feelings of loyalty for her
native country and her Sovereign which it would have been
unnatural and discreditable to disavow. Her well-known correspondence with the Imperial Court was only caused by the natural anxiety of those great persons to be kept *au courant* of social
and political affairs by such an accomplished correspondent, but
I do not believe she was ever employed by them in any business
or any political design; on the contrary, she was rather distrusted
and out of favour with them, on account of her being so denatu-
ralised and for her ardent affection for England and the English.
Russia was the country of her birth, France the country of her
adopted abode, but England was the country of her predilection.
With this cosmopolite character she dreaded everything which
might produce hostile collision between any two of these countries. She was greatly annoyed when the question of the Spanish
marriages embittered the relations between France and England,
but infinitely more so at the Turkish quarrel, and the war which
it produced. Those who fulminated against her intrigues were, as
I believe, provoked at the efforts she made, so far as she had any
power or influence, to bring about the restoration of peace, an
unpardonable offence in the eyes of all who were bent on the
continuation of the war. She lived to see peace restored, and
closed her eyes almost at the moment that the last seal was put to
it by the Conference of Paris. Her last illness was sudden and

short. Her health had always been delicate, and she was very nervous about herself; an attack of bronchitis brought on fever, which rapidly consumed her strength, and brought her, fully conscious, within sight of death; that consummation, which at a distance she had always dreaded, she saw arrive with perfect calmness and resignation, and all the virtues and qualities for which the smallest credit was given her seem to have shone forth with unexpected lustre on her deathbed. Her faculties were bright and unclouded to the last, her courage and presence of mind were unshaken, she evinced a tender consideration for the feelings of those who were lamenting around her bed, and she complied with the religious obligations prescribed by the Church of which she was a member with a devotion the sincerity of which we have no right to question. She made her son Paul and Guizot leave her room a few hours before she died, that they might be spared the agony of witnessing her actual dissolution, and only three or four hours before the supreme moment, she mustered strength to write a note in pencil to Guizot with these words: 'Merci pour vingt années d'amitié et de bonheur. Ne m'oubliez pas, adieu, adieu!' It was given to him after her death.

April 4th. The fate of Bright, Cobden, and Co. exhibits a curious example of the fleeting and worthless nature of popular favour. They who were once the idols of millions, and not without cause, have not only lost all their popularity, but are objects of execration, and can nowhere find a parliamentary resting place. No constituency will hear of them. The great towns of Lancashire prefer any mediocrities to Bright and Cobden. It seems that they had already ceased to be popular, when they made themselves enormously unpopular, and excited great resentment, by their opposition to the Russian War, the rage for which was not less intense in Manchester and all the manufacturing district than in the rest of the kingdom. This great crime, as it appeared in the eyes of their constituents, was never pardoned, and their punishment was probably determined while the war was still going on. As the favour of Cobden fell, so that of Palmerston rose, and his visit to Manchester a few months ago

raised the favour to a pitch of enthusiasm. When Cobden therefore originated the China motion, he no doubt gave great offence, and he sealed his own condemnation. Bright has been long
abroad, and has done nothing lately that any one could take umbrage at, but his opposition to the war has not been forgotten
or forgiven, and when Cobden appeared at Manchester as his
representative, and made a very able speech in his behalf, it is
highly probable that his advocacy was in itself fatal to his re-
election. It seems quite clear that another man, Sir Elkanah
Armytage, lost his election at Salford solely because he was
strongly supported and recommended by Cobden.

May 1st. George Anson[38] writes to me from India that there is
a strange feeling of discontent pervading the Indian Army from
religious causes, and a suspicion that we are going to employ our
irresistible power in forcing Christianity upon them. It is not true,
but the natives will never be quite convinced that it is not, as long
as Exeter Hall and the missionaries are permitted to have *carte
blanche* and work their will as they please in those regions.

May 10th. [On] the death of Lady Ashburton[39] Milnes has
written a short, but very fair and appropriate notice for the
'Times' newspaper, which of course was intended as a eulogy, and
not as a *character*, with the bad as well as the good that could
be said of her. Lady Ashburton was perhaps, on the whole, the
most conspicuous woman in the society of the present day. She
was undoubtedly very intelligent, with much quickness and
vivacity in conversation, and by dint of a good deal of desultory
reading and social intercourse with men more or less distinguished, she had improved her mind, and made herself a very
agreeable woman, and had acquired no small reputation for ability and wit. It is never difficult for a woman in a great position and
with some talent for conversation to attract a large society around
her, and to have a number of admirers and devoted *habitués*.

[38] [General Anson was at this time Commander-in-Chief in India.]
[39] [Harriet Mary, eldest daughter of the sixth Earl of Sandwich, was
married in 1828 to William Bingham Baring, afterwards second Baron Ashburton. Her hospitality made Bath House and the Grange the centres of a
brilliant literary society.]

Lady Ashburton laid herself out for this, and while she exercised hospitality on a great scale, she was more of a *précieuse* than any woman I have known. She was, or affected to be, extremely intimate with many men whose literary celebrity or talents constituted their only attraction, and while they were gratified by the attentions of the great lady, her vanity was flattered by the homage of such men, of whom Carlyle was the principal. It is only justice to her to say that she treated her literary friends with constant kindness and the most unselfish attentions. They, their wives and children (when they had any), were received at her house in the country, and entertained there for weeks without any airs of patronage, and with a spirit of genuine benevolence as well as hospitality. She was in her youth tall and commanding in person, but without any pretension to good looks; still she was not altogether destitute of sentiment and coquetry, or incapable of both feeling and inspiring a certain amount of passion. The only man with whom she was ever what could be called *in love* was Clarendon, and that feeling was never entirely extinct, and the recollection of it kept up a sort of undefined relation between them to the end of her life. Two men were certainly in love with her, both distinguished in different ways. One was John Mill, who was sentimentally attached to her, and for a long time was devoted to her society. She was pleased and flattered by his devotion, but as she did not in the slightest degree return his passion, though she admired his abilities, he at last came to resent her indifference, and ended by estranging himself from her entirely, and proved the strength of his feeling by his obstinate refusal to continue even his acquaintance with her. Her other admirer was Charles Buller, with whom she was extremely intimate, but without ever reciprocating his love. Curiously enough, they were very like each other in person, as well as in their mental accomplishments. They had both the same spirits and cleverness in conversation, and the same quickness and drollery in repartee. Her faults appeared to be caprice and a disposition to quarrels and *tracasseries* about nothing, which, however common amongst ordinary women, were unworthy of her superior understanding. But during her last illness all that was bad and hard in her nature seemed to be improved and softened, and she became full of charity, good-will, and the milk of human kindness. I was once very intimate with her, but for a long time past our intimacy had dwindled into ordinary acquaintance.

June 28th. The Queen has made Prince Albert 'Prince Consort' by a patent ordered in Council, but as this act confers on him neither title, dignity, nor privileges, I cannot see the use of it. He was already as high in England as he can be, assuming the Crown Matrimonial to be out of the question, and it will give him no higher rank abroad, where our acts have no validity.

September 6th. They have made some Peers, of whom the most conspicuous is Macaulay, and I have not seen or heard any complaints of his elevation.

While Macaulay is thus ascending to the House of Peers, his old enemy and rival Croker has descended to the grave, very noiselessly and almost without observation, for he had been for some time so withdrawn from the world that he was nearly forgotten. He had lived to see all his predictions of ruin and disaster to the country completely falsified. He continued till the last year or two to exhale his bitterness and spite in the columns of the 'Quarterly Review,' but at last the Editor (who had long been sick of his contributions) contrived to get rid of him. I never lived in any intimacy with him, and seldom met him in society, but he certainly occupied a high place among the second-rate men of his time; he had very considerable talents, great industry, with much information and a retentive memory. He spoke in Parliament with considerable force, and in society his long acquaintance with the world and with public affairs, and his stores of general knowledge made him entertaining, though he was too overbearing to be agreeable. He was particularly disliked by Macaulay, who never lost an opportunity of venting his antipathy by attacks upon him, and his severe review of Boswell's *Life of Johnson* almost broke Croker's heart.

Hatchford, November 8th. The most interesting event during the last few days is the failure of the attempted launch of the big ship (now called 'Leviathan),' and it is not a little remarkable that all the *great* experiments recently made have proved failures. Besides this one of the ship, there was a few weeks ago the cracking of the bell (Big Ben) for the Houses of Parliament, and not long before that the failure of the submarine telegraph in the attempt to lay it down in the sea. The bell will probably be replaced without much difficulty, but it is at present doubtful whether it will be found possible to launch the ship at all, and whether the telegraphic cable can ever be completed.

Frognal, November 14th. The news of the capture of Delhi and the relief of Lucknow excited a transport of delight and triumph, and everybody jumped to the conclusion that the Indian contest was virtually at an end. Granville told me he thought there would be no more fighting, and that the work was done. I was not so sanguine, and though I thought the result of the contest was now secure, I thought we should still have a great deal on our hands and much more fighting to hear of before the curtain could drop. But I was not prepared to hear the dismal news which arrived to-day, and which has so cruelly damped the public joy and exultation. It appears that Havelock is in great danger and the long suffering garrison of Lucknow not yet out of their peril, for the victory of Havelock had not been complete, the natives were gathering round the small British force in vast numbers, and unless considerable reinforcements could be speedily brought up, the condition of the British, both military and civilians, of men, women, and children, would soon again be one of excessive danger.

November 17th. As if we had not embarrassments enough on our hands, America is going to add to them, for President Buchanan, who hates England with a mortal antipathy, threatens to repudiate the Clayton-Bulwer Treaty upon the pretence that we have not abided by its conditions, and if he proposes to the Senate to declare it null and void, the Senate will do so at his bidding. This would be a flagrant violation of good faith, and of the obligations by which all civilized nations consider themselves

bound. If this event happens, it will place us in a very perplexing
dilemma, especially after Palmerston's absurd bravado and confident boastings of our power, for we are not in a condition to
enable us to take a high line corresponding with that lofty language, and we shall have to eat humble pie and submit to the
affront. Hitherto all other nations and governments have behaved
to us as well and as respectfully as we could desire, and far more
than we deserve; but if America bullies us in one instance, and
we are found pocketing the affront, it is by no means improbable
that other governments will begin to take advantage of our weakness, and adopt towards us a conduct injurious to our interests
or a tone galling to our pride.[40]

November 25th. Clarendon told me of a conversation he had
recently had with the Queen *à propos* of Palmerston's health,
concerning which Her Majesty was very uneasy, and what could
be done in the not impossible contingency of his breaking down.
It is a curious change from what we saw a few years ago, that
she is become almost affectionately anxious about the health of
Palmerston, whose death might then have been an event to be
hailed with satisfaction. Clarendon said she might well be solicitous about it, for if anything happened to Palmerston she would
be placed in the greatest difficulty. She said that in such a case
she should look to *him,* and expect him to replace Palmerston,
on which Clarendon said he was glad she had broached the subject, as it gave him an opportunity of saying what he was very
anxious to impress upon her mind, and that was the absolute
impossibility of his undertaking such an office, against which he
enumerated various objections. He told her that Derby could not
form a Government, and if she had the misfortune to lose Palmerston, nothing remained for her to do but to send for John Russell
and put him at the head of the Government. She expressed her
great repugnance to this, and especially to make him Prime Min-

---

[40] [These apprehensions were unfounded. Mr. Buchanan did not seek to
abrogate the Clayton-Bulwer Treaty with reference to the eventual construc-
tion of a passage through the Isthmus of Central America, and the neutral
character of that undertaking, which is now said to be in progress by the
Canal of Panama, has remained unchanged to the present time.]

ister. Clarendon then entreated her to conquer her repugnance, and to be persuaded that it would never do to offer him anything else, which he neither would nor could accept; that the necessity was to have a man who could lead the House of Commons, and there was no other but him; that Lord John had consented to take a subordinate office under Lord Aberdeen, who was his senior in age, and occupied a high position, but he would never consent to take office under him (Clarendon), and the proposal he would consider as an insult. For every reason, therefore, he urged her, if driven to apply to him at all, to do it handsomely, to place the whole thing in his hands, and to give him her full confidence and support.

December 2nd. B—— showed me the Draft of the Queen's Speech this evening after dinner. Cobbett in his Grammar produces examples of bad English taken from Kings' Speeches, which he says might be expected to be the best written, but generally are the worst written documents in the world. It would be difficult to produce any former Speech more deplorably composed than this one. Long sentences, full of confusion, and of which the meaning is not always clear, and some faults of grammar for which a schoolboy would be whipped. B—— was so struck by one I pointed out that he said he would beg Palmerston to alter it. If this Speech escapes severe criticism and ridicule I shall be much surprised, as I am already that George Lewis, who has so lately been a literary critic, and is a correct writer himself, should have allowed it to pass in its present shape, and indeed the sentence he himself put in about his own business is as bad as any other part of it.

December 31st. Met Clarendon last night, talked about the Hanoverian jewel question; that the Queen and Prince were desperately annoyed at the award, which they thought unfair. The Prince asked Clarendon whether Parliament could not be applied to to make good the jewels, which were the very ones the Queen had always worn; and that the dignity of the Crown required she should be properly furnished with such ornaments. C. told him it was out of the question, that the Government could not make any such application to Parliament, and that it was far better for *them* (the Court) that it should not be done; that her popularity was in great measure owing to her own judicious conduct and abstinence from that extravagance which had marked the reign of George IV; that nobody cared whether she was attired in fine pearls or diamonds, and would rather rejoice to see her without them than she should wear them when they belonged to somebody else, or that substitutes were supplied by funds raised by taxation. So they gave it up, as he says they are always ready to do when a matter is fairly put before them. But he said the Queen was very anxious to know Lord Lyndhurst's opinion upon the award, so last night I went to his house and asked him, telling him the reason why. He said he had no doubt the award was correct; that in their case the jewels were divided into two categories: first, those which came from George II and were undoubtedly Hanoverian; and secondly, those which George III had given Queen Charlotte. They had heard Counsel on both sides, and neither side chose to produce the will of George III, which they never had before them, so that they were in a difficulty about these latter stones. Tindal died the day they were to have met to draw up the award. He and Lyndhurst were agreed, Langdale doubted. Lyndhurst said he had no doubt if they had had King George III's will, as Wensleydale and his Commission had, they should all three have agreed, and to the same award.

January 23rd, 1858. On arriving in town yesterday, I received a visit from Disraeli, who said he had come to consult me *in confidence,* and to ask my opinion, by which his own course would be very much influenced. I was not a little surprised at this exordium, but told him I should be glad to hear what his object was, and that he was welcome to any opinion he wished for from me. He then began a rather hazy discourse, from which I gathered, or at least thought I gathered, that he thinks the present state of affairs very serious, and the position of the Government very precarious; that he is meditating on the possible chances there may be for him and his party in the event of Palmerston's fall, and knowing that some sort of coalition with some other party would be indispensable to form any other Government, an idea had crossed his mind that this might be practicable with some of the most moderate of the Whigs, especially with the younger ones, such as Granville and Argyll, and he wished to know if I thought this would be possible, and whether I could be in any way instrumental in promoting it, and if I did not think so what my ideas were as to the most advisable course in order to avert the threatened Reform, and to give the country a better Government than this. This, with a great deal of verbiage and mixed with digressions about the leading men of the present day, seemed to me to be the substance and object of his talk. He professed to speak to me of his own sentiments without disguise, and with entire confidence about everything, but I cannot call to mind that he imparted to me anything of the slightest interest or importance. It would be difficult and not very interesting to write down our somewhat vague and *décousu* conversation, but I told him that I knew very little of the dispositions of any of the men he alluded to, but I did not believe they any of them would be parties to any such combination as he looked to, or separate from their present colleagues.

February 2nd. The Indian question has for the moment been superseded by the French question as it may be called, that is, by the storm which is raging in France against this country, its institutions and laws, in reference to the assassination plot of January 14.[41] It is well known that the French Government had

---

[41] [It was known in France that the explosive bombs with which Orsini had attempted the life of the Emperor Napoleon were manufactured in England, and that some of the accomplices of that conspirator were still in this country, where the law could not reach them for a crime committed abroad. These facts called forth a strong hostile feeling, and England was accused of harbouring assassins. On January 20 Count Walewski addressed a remonstrance to the British Government, which remained unanswered, and on January 23 Count Persigny spoke in strong language to a deputation from the City of London.]

been urging our Ministers to adopt measures or to pass laws against the refugees and their machinations in this country; but while this question was under discussion, we were astounded by a speech made by Persigny in reply to an address from the City, and still more by the publication in the 'Moniteur' of certain addresses from corps or regiments of the French army to the Emperor, full of insult and menace to this country. These offensive manifestations naturally excited great indignation here, and the Press did not fail to hurl back these insults, and to retort with interest upon the persons from whom they had proceeded or who had permitted their appearance. On Sunday I spoke to Clarendon on the subject. He is very much annoyed and embarrassed by this posture of affairs as might be expected, but more than this he is very much alarmed, more than I think he need be. I said it seemed to be that the Emperor had forgotten his usual good sense, and that he who knows this country ought to have felt that if he wishes to have anything done here, he is taking the most effectual means to prevent it by permitting the military addresses to appear in the 'Moniteur,' since in the present state of the Press this is tantamount to their being published by the Government itself. I said I could not believe that these hot and enthusiastic expressions were to be taken entirely as proofs of a passionate attachment to the Emperor's person, but that these were outbreaks of that hatred of England which sometimes slumbered, but never died. He said the Emperor felt that his alliance with this country was indispensable to him, and regretted sincerely the displays of feeling in France, but that he did not dare to repress the sentiments evinced by the army. He added that he had not blamed Morny, who could not say less than he did without being denounced by the Chamber as an inadequate exponent of its sentiments. The French, seeing how all our force is absorbed in our Indian war, think they may treat us as they please, and Clarendon fancies that if any accident were to befall the Emperor, any Government that might be able to establish itself would go to war with us as the best means of ingratiating itself with the nation and of being able to establish itself. He says they can march 50,000 men at a moment's notice to Cherbourg, where there is an abundance of war steamers ready to transport them across the Channel, while we have no soldiers and no ships to defend us in case of such a storm suddenly bursting. George Lewis says that Clarendon is haunted with this apprehension, which he does not share in the slightest degree.

Though there is some truth in this account of the Emperor's position, I cannot believe that he might not have kept matters more quiet in France than he has done. There can be no doubt that our international relations are upon a very unpleasant and perilous footing, and that the evil is not corrected by the fact of the two Courts being on friendly terms, by proofs of friendship in the shape of handsome bridal gifts from the Emperor and Empress to the Princess Royal. We are going to do something to soothe the French; but as it will, I believe, be no more than to make that a felony which is now only a misdemeanour, it may be doubted if this will satisfy or appease them.

February 11*th*. I never remember Parliament meeting with much greater curiosity and excitement. The situation of the Government is generally regarded as so precarious, and the revolution in Palmerston's popularity and therefore his power is so extraordinary, that everybody is expecting some great events will occur, and the hopes of all who wish for a change and who expect to profit by it are reviving. The bill brought in by Palmerston on Tuesday for the purpose of punishing conspirators and with a view to satisfy the exigency of the French Government made a great stir. The leave to bring it in was carried by a large majority, thanks to the Conservatives, but its success was principally owing to the Emperor's apology arriving just before the debate began. This pacified most of those who were enraged at the publications in the 'Moniteur.'

Perhaps the most serious reflexion to which this matter gives rise is the suspicion that the conduct of the Emperor Napoleon betrays either some strange infirmity in his faculties, or something so unsound and dangerous in the state of France, as to be pregnant with possible consequences it is frightful to contemplate. All that he has been doing, or has allowed to be done of late, is indicative of a change; for the moderation and prudence, together with firmness and decision, which have hitherto formed his best claim to the admiration and approbation of this country seem to have completely deserted him. The penal laws enacted or to be enacted in France are considered as the inauguration of a reign of terror, and there is rapidly growing up the same sort of feeling about the French Empire that there is here about the Palmerston Government. Nobody pretends to foresee what will happen, but everyone thinks that the state of France is rendered more combustible, and that any spark may produce an explosion. Those who are most attached or most favourable to the Imperial Government are the most alarmed, and, when they dare speak out, express the greatest regret and alarm at all that is passing in France.

June 22nd. Among the events of last week one of the most interesting was the Queen's visit to Birmingham, where she was received by the whole of that enormous population with an enthusiasm which is said to have exceeded all that was ever displayed in her former receptions at Manchester or elsewhere. It is impossible not to regard such manifestations as both significant and important. They evince a disposition in those masses of the population in which, if anywhere, the seeds of Radicalism are supposed to lurk, most favourable to the Conservative cause, by which I mean not to this or that party, but to the Monarchy and the Constitution under which we are living and flourishing, and which we may believe to be still dear to the hearts of the people of this country. This great fact lends some force to the notion entertained by many political thinkers, that there is more danger in conferring political power on the middle classes than in extending it far beneath them, and in point of fact that there is so little to be apprehended from the extension of the suffrage, that universal suffrage itself would be innocuous. Amongst the concessions of last week was the passing of Locke King's Bill for abolishing a property qualification, which was done with hardly any opposition. There can be no doubt that the practice was a mere sham, and that a property qualification was very often a fiction or a fraud, and such being the case, that it was useless to keep up the distinction; but it struck me, though I do not find that it occurred to anybody else, that the abolition might sooner or later have an indirect influence upon the question of the suffrage, for it may be urged, not without plausibility, that if it be held no longer necessary that a representative should have any property whatever, there is great inconsistency in requiring that the elector should have a certain amount of property to entitle him to vote.

June 26th. Then there is a grand mess about the Jew question, which is hung up in a sort of abeyance in consequence of Derby's not being able to come down to the House of Lords. From the moment that Derby took upon himself to announce his abandonment of the contest, which he did not frankly and fully, but sulkily and reluctantly, he seems to have half repented of what he did, and to have permitted all sorts of difficulties while his subordinates and some of his colleagues have interposed to prevent or delay the final settlement. It is difficult to believe that he himself ever cared a straw about the Jew question, or that his opposition had any motive except that of pleasing the bigoted and narrow-minded of his party. His good sense saw that the moment was come when surrender was the best policy if not an absolute necessity, and having given utterance to this conviction, no doubt to the enormous disgust of many of his followers, it was his interest to get rid of the question as quickly as possible, and dismiss what as long as it remained on the *tapis* in any shape was a source of disagreement and ill-humour between him and his party. It is marvellous, therefore, that so clever a man should have acted so foolish a part as he has done. Having disgusted his own party by his concession, he is now disgusting everybody else by his hesitation and pusillanimity in carrying it out, and, with an absence of dignity and firmness which is utterly unworthy of the high position he holds, he has permitted his Chancellor and some half-dozen subordinate members of his Government to do all they can to thwart the settlement of the question, and prolong the exclusion of the Jews. Instead of taking the matter into his own hands, he has permitted a sort of little conspiracy to go on, which is exceedingly likely to bring about a collision between the two Houses, and to raise a flame in the House of Commons the consequences of which may be more serious to the Government than any one contemplates. Lyndhurst, whose wise head is provoked and disgusted to the last degree at all these proceedings, has bitterly complained of them, and at the way in which they have treated him, and the bill he drew up for the express purpose of putting an end to the dilemma.

July 9th. After all Derby ran true to the Jew Bill, and if he did it in an awkward way, allowances must be made for him and for his difficulties with his party, who are full of chagrin at being compelled to swallow this obnoxious measure. It is on the whole better that the bulk of them should have voted in conformity with their notorious opinions, as it made no difference as to the result, and has a better appearance than if they had whisked round at Derby's bidding.

July 13th. After an ineffectual attempt on the part of the Opposition to get rid of the 'reasons' of the Lords, the Jew Bill has passed, Granville and Lansdowne protesting against the absurdity of the conduct of Derby with regard to it.

November 4th. I hear the Queen has written a letter to the Prince of Wales announcing to him his emancipation from parental authority and control, and that it is one of the most admirable letters that ever were penned. She tells him that he may have thought the rule they adopted for his education a severe one, but that his welfare was their only object, and well knowing to what seductions of flattery he would eventually be exposed, they wished to prepare and strengthen his mind against them, that he was now to consider himself his own master, and that they should never intrude any advice upon him, although always ready to give it him whenever he thought fit to seek it. It was a very long letter, all in that tone, and it seems to have made a profound impression on the Prince, and to have touched his feelings to the quick. He brought it to Gerald Wellesley in floods of tears, and the effect it produced is a proof of the wisdom which dictated its composition.

December 12th. [*Clarendon*] told me a curious story about our young Princess of Prussia, in which he had been confidentially consulted. It is worth recording as affording a peep behind the curtain of the royal stage. As far as I remember it was to this effect:—When C. was at Berlin, Stockmar came to him and said, 'I want to talk to you on a very important matter and to invoke your aid. It relates to "this poor child here." Her mother is behaving abominably to her; and unless a stop can be put to her conduct I know not what may be the consequences, for she is not in good health, and she is worried and frightened to death.' The Queen wishes to exercise the same authority and controul over her that she did before her marriage; and she writes her constant letters full of anger and reproaches, desiring all sorts of things to be done that it is neither right nor desirable that she should do, and complaining of her remissness in writing to her sisters or to Miss Hilliard, and of her forgetting what is due to her own family and country, till the poor child (as S. called her) is made seriously ill, and put in a state dangerous to her in her actual condition.

Stockmar entered into various details as to the Queen's exigencies and her unkind and imprudent conduct; and said he was going to write to H.M. and tell her the whole truth in a style to which she was little accustomed, and such a letter as she probably had never had in her life before; but that a viva voce communication would do more than any letter, and he wanted C. to go to the Prince as soon as he got home and speak to him on this subject; and if he consented to this Stockmar would tell the Queen that he had imparted everything to C., who would be ready to communicate with H.M. upon it. C. said he might make any use he pleased of him, but asked what the Prince had been doing all this time, and why he had allowed such a state of things to go on. S. replied that the P. could do nothing; that he was completely cowed, and the Q. so excitable that the P. lived in perpetual terror of bringing on the hereditary malady, and dreaded saying or doing anything which might have a tendency to produce this effect. C. did not arrive in England till some weeks after this conversation; but in the meantime Stockmar's letter had been received, and immediately after C.'s arrival he was sent for to Windsor. The Prince saw him first; told him the Q. would not allude to the subject, but that he wished to go into it thoroughly with C., and to speak with perfect openness upon it. He entered upon this occasion into many details concerning the education of his children, and expressed something like regret or doubt about what he called the 'aggressive' system that the Q. had followed towards them. C. said 'Y.R.H. must permit me to express my thoughts with freedom, or I had better not say a word to you on the subject.' The P. acquiesced, when he resumed by a strong protestation against the word 'aggressive,' as totally inapplicable to any sound system of education. 'I' (he said) 'have six children, and after all our children are much like Royal Children and require the same treatment. Now we have never used severity in any shape or way, never in their lives had occasion to punish any of them, and we have found this mode of bringing them up entirely successful.' The P. said to C. what Stockmar had before said, that he had always been embarrassed by the alarm he felt lest the Q.'s mind should be excited by any opposition to her will; and that in regard to the children the disagreeable office of punishment had always devolved upon him. Clarendon said all that he had promised Stockmar he would in backing him up. The P. listened very complacently to all he said, and when he went away the next day they both took leave of him in a manner which showed that they had taken all he had said in very good part, and left him with the impression that he had done much good. He told me that the Prince himself, in spite of his natural good sense, had been very injudicious in his way of treating his children, and that the Prince of Wales resented very much the severity which he had experienced.

The Queen it seems was never really fond of the Princess Royal because she thought her ugly; and unlike most mothers who think their children better looking than they are, the Q. was always finding fault with her daughter's looks, and complaining of her being ugly and coarse, very unjustly, and in which C. said he had often contradicted her Majesty. Royal marriages are in almost all cases affairs of diplomatic arrangement, in which the Parties have seldom seen each other before they are contracted; but in no private station was there ever a more complete love match than that of the Pss. Royal. No negotiation had ever taken place, no communication between the respective Parents. The young Prince went to Balmoral resolved to see what the Pss. was like, and if he did not find her attractive to retire without making any sign, and never more to return to England. But after a week passed in her society he fell over head and ears in love with her; and one day out walking on the hills he asked her whether she could like him enough to leave her Family and Country and become his wife. The sentiment was mutual, and she at once replied in the affirmative. She was only fourteen and a mere child. When she got home she was terrified at what she had done and went in great agitation and in floods of tears to confess to her Parents what she had done, which she seemed to think would be considered a great crime. She found herself forgiven, and from that moment the engagement was concluded; but the Q. and P. regretted that they had suffered her to be exposed to such temptation and to become contracted in marriage before she was out of the nursery. The P. told C. they never would again permit any nursery courtships, and they now are putting a veto on a similar project with regard to Pss. Alice.[42] The Queen of the Netherlands is dying to have her for her son,[43] and entreated C. the other day at Stutgard to help to bring it about; but the Q. will not allow any steps to be taken for that purpose, though as the young man is about the best Protestant parti to be had, it will probably come to pass sooner or later.

[42] Princess Alice (1843–78), second daughter of Queen Victoria; married Louis, Grand Duke of Hesse, 1862.
[43] William, Prince of Orange (1840–79), eldest son of William III of Holland; never married.

January 31st, 1859. Dined with Lord Salisbury on Saturday at the Sheriffs' dinner, when I met all the Cabinet, except Malmesbury, Hardwicke, and John Manners. Derby told me a curious thing. An experiment was made of the possible speed by which a telegraphic message could be sent and an answer got. They fixed on Corfu, made every preparation, and sent *one word*. The message and return were effected in six seconds. I would not have believed this on any other authority.

Derby told me that the Princess Royal's accouchement was near turning out fatally, though nobody knows it and, as he believes, the Queen herself has never been apprised of the danger her daughter was in. The labor lasted thirteen hours and the child got twisted in the womb and came out with his bottom foremost.[44]

June 12th. After a not very remarkable debate, the division yesterday morning gave a majority of thirteen to the Opposition, which was more than either side expected. Derby resigned at eleven o'clock, and the Queen immediately after marked her sense of his conduct by sending him an extra Garter in an autograph letter. Much to his own surprise she sent for Granville (and for nobody else) and charged him with the formation of a Government. What passed between Her Majesty and him I know not, but he accepted the commission and has been busy about it ever since. How he is to deal with Palmerston and Lord John, and to make such a project palatable to them I cannot imagine. What the Queen has done is a very significant notice to them of her great reluctance to have either of them at the head of affairs, and it cannot but be very mortifying to them to be invited to accept office under a man they have raised from the ranks, and who is young enough to be son to either, and almost to be grandson of the elder of the two. Nor will the mortification be less, after they have both so publicly avowed their expectations

[44] [*The child was Kaiser Wilhelm, deposed after World War I.*]

that one or other of them must be sent for, and their having, in what they consider a spirit of self-sacrifice, consented to serve under each other, but without ever saying or dreaming that it could be necessary to say they would take office under any third party. Nobody, indeed, has ever thought of the possibility of any but one of them being called upon by Her Majesty, and the only question has been which it would be.

June 13th. Lord Granville told me yesterday evening what had passed, and that his mission was at an end, and Palmerston engaged in forming a Government. The account of it all appears in the 'Times' this morning quite correctly. Granville was rather disappointed, but took it gaily enough, and I think he must have been aware from the first of the extreme difficulty of his forming a Government which was to include these two old rival states-men. Palmerston had the wisdom to accede at once to Granville's proposal, probably foreseeing that nothing would come of Gran-ville's attempt, and that he would have all the credit of his com-plaisance and obtain the prize after all. The transaction has been a very advantageous one for Granville, and will inevitably lead sooner or later to his gaining the eminence which he has only just missed now, which would have been full of difficulties and future embarrassments at the present time, but will be compara-tively easy hereafter. Lord John's conduct will not serve to in-gratiate him with the Queen, nor increase his popularity with the country.[45]

June 26th. All the time that the formation of the new Govern-ment was going on I was at a cottage near Windsor for the Ascot races, and consequently I heard nothing of the secret proceed-ings connected with the selection of those who come in, and the exclusion of those who belonged to Palmerston's last Government, nor have I as yet heard what passed on the subject. The most remarkable of the exclusions is Clarendon's, who I was sure, when

[45] [It was the refusal of Lord John Russell to serve under Lord Granville which rendered the formation of a Cabinet by that statesman impossible. At the same time Lord John Russell expressed his willingness to serve under Lord Palmerston on condition of his taking the department of Foreign Affairs.]

the Foreign Office was seized by John Russell, would take nothing else; and of the admissions, Gladstone's, who has never shown any good will towards Palmerston, and voted with Derby in the last division. This Government in its composition is curiously, and may prove fatally, like that which Aberdeen formed in 1852, of a very Peelite complexion, and only with a larger proportion of Radicals, though not enough, it is said, to satisfy their organs, and Bright is displeased that he has not been more consulted, and probably at office not having been more pressed upon him. It is still very doubtful whether Cobden will accept the place offered to him.

June 27th. Yesterday I went to Kent House, where I found Clarendon and his sister alone, and we had a long talk, in the course of which he told me all that had passed (especially with regard to himself) about the formation of the Government. Although he spoke very good-naturedly about Granville and his abortive attempt, I saw clearly that he thought Granville had been in the wrong to undertake it, and that he ought at once to have told the Queen it was impossible, and have declined it. Though Palmerston had given a qualified consent to act with him, it was with evident reluctance, and he had guarded it by saying it must be subject to his approbation of the way in which the Government was composed. Lord John's consent was still more qualified, and he annexed to it a condition which at once put an end to the attempt. This was, as I had suspected, that he should be leader of the House of Commons. To this Palmerston refused to agree, and so the whole thing fell to the ground. Granville, by Clarendon's advice, at once reported his failure to the Queen, gave her no advice as to whom she should send for, and of her own accord she sent for Palmerston.

Previously to this, and I think before the vote, Palmerston and Clarendon had discussed the probability of Palmerston's forming a Government, when Palmerston told him he should expect him to return to the Foreign Office. As soon as Palmerston had been with Her Majesty, he went off to Pembroke Lodge, and saw Lord John; told him all that had happened, and that he would of course take any office he pleased. Lord John said, 'I take the Foreign Office.' Palmerston said he had contemplated putting Clarendon there again, enumerating his reasons and Clarendon's claims, but that if he insisted on the Foreign Office as a right, he must have it. Lord John said, 'I do insist on it,' and so it was settled.

I ought to have inserted that when Palmerston and Clarendon talked the matter over at first, Clarendon begged him not to think of him, and that if, as was probable, John Russell desired the Foreign Office, he *must* give it him, for if he did not, or even made any difficulty, an immediate breach would be the consequence, and John Russell would get up a case against Palmerston which would be very embarrassing. Palmerston at first said he should certainly insist on Clarendon's not being put aside to please Lord John, but in the end Clarendon persuaded him not to adhere to that resolution.

Dublin, August 24th.   Yesterday in the morning a review in the Phœnix Park, after which Bagot took me to Howth Castle, which I was curious to see, but it is not very remarkable, though very ancient. It has a modernised appearance, and is a comfortable house, said to be the oldest *inhabited* house in Ireland, and one of the towers of fabulous antiquity. I remarked that the hall door was left open, according to the traditional obligation. One of the Ladies St. Lawrence told me the story as follows: An old woman, 'the Granawhile,' came to the castle and asked for hospitality or alms, and was refused and driven away. She was the wife of a pirate. On the seaside she found the young heir with his nurse, whom she seized and carried off. Afterwards she brought the boy back, and consented to restore him on condition that henceforward no beggar should be refused admittance, that the hall door should be kept continually open, and that at dinner a place should be kept and a plate laid for any stranger who might appear. The beggars are kept away by not being admitted through the lodge gates; the hall door is open, but there is another door behind it, and the vacant place has by degrees fallen into disuse. I know not how old the story is, but there is enough to show that it had a foundation of some sort, and that it retains a relic in the customs of the family. On returning to Dublin I went to see Trinity College, and the beautiful museum erected a few years ago. Dublin is, for its size, a finer town than London, and I think they beat us hollow in their public buildings. We have no such squares as Merrion Square, nor such a street as Sackville Street.

London, December 25th. Disraeli raised himself immensely last year, more, perhaps, with his opponents and the House of Commons generally than with his own party, but it is universally acknowledged that he led the House with a tact, judgement, and ability of which he was not before thought capable. While he has thus risen, no rival has sprung up to dispute his pre-eminence. Walpole and Henley are null, and it is evident that the party cannot do without Disraeli, and whenever Parliament meets he will find means of reconciling them to a necessity of which none of them can be unconscious, and I have no doubt that whenever any good opportunities for showing fight may occur the whole party will be found united under Disraeli's orders.

J*anuary 2nd*, 1860. The death of Macaulay is the extinction of a great light, and although every expectation of the completion of his great work had long ago vanished, the sudden close of his career, and the certainty that we shall have no more of his History, or at most only the remaining portion of King William's reign (which it is understood he had nearly prepared for publication), is a serious disappointment to the world. His health was so broken that his death can hardly create any surprise, but there had been no reason lately to apprehend that the end was so near. I have mentioned the circumstance of my first meeting him, after which we became rather intimate in a general way, and he used frequently to invite me to those breakfasts in the Albany at which he used to collect small miscellaneous parties, generally including some remarkable people. I don't think he was ever so entirely agreeable as at his own breakfast table, though I shall remember as long as I live the pleasant days I have spent in his society at Bowood, Holland House, and elsewhere. Nothing was more remarkable in Macaulay than the natural way in which he talked, never for the sake of display. 'Don't you remember?' he was in the habit of saying when he quoted some book or alluded to some fact to listeners who could not remember, because in nineteen cases out of twenty they had never known or heard of whatever it was he alluded to. I do not believe anybody ever left his society with any feeling of mortification, except that which an involuntary comparison between his knowledge and their own ignorance could not fail to engender. For some years past I had seen little or nothing of Macaulay. I have often regretted the total cessation of our intercourse, but what else could be expected from the difference of our habits, pursuits, and characters? I have only recently read over again the whole of his 'History of England' with undiminished pleasure and admiration, though with a confirmed opinion that his style is not the very best, and that he is not the writer whom I should be most desirous to imitate.

London, February 22nd. I returned to town on Monday. The same night a battle took place in the House of Commons, in which Gladstone signally defeated Disraeli, and Government got so good a majority that it looks like the harbinger of complete success for their Treaty and their Budget. Everybody agrees that nothing could be more brilliant and complete than Gladstone's triumph, which did not seem to be matter of much grief to many of the Conservative party, for I hear that however they may still act together on a great field-day, the hatred and distrust of Disraeli is greater than ever in the Conservative ranks, and Derby himself, when he heard how his colleague had been demolished, did not seem to care much about it. They say that he betrays in the House of Commons a sort of consciousness of his inferiority to Gladstone, and of fear of encountering him in debate.

February 26th. On Friday night Gladstone had another great triumph. He made a splendid speech, and obtained a majority of 116, which puts an end to the contest. He is now *the* great man of the day, but these recent proceedings have strikingly displayed the disorganised condition of the Conservative party and their undisguised dislike of their leader. A great many of them voted with Government on Friday night, and more expressed satisfaction at the result being a defeat of Disraeli.

London, November 13th. At the end of three months since I last wrote anything in this book, I take my pen in hand to record my determination to bring this journal (which is no journal at all) to an end. I have long seen that it is useless to attempt to carry it on, for I am entirely out of the way of hearing anything of the slightest interest beyond what is known to all the world. I therefore close this record without any intention or expectation of renewing it, with a full consciousness of the smallness of its value or interest, and with great regret that I did not make better use of the opportunities I have had of recording something more worth reading.

Index

Abercromby, James, 92
Aberdeen, 4th Earl of, 16, 20, 237, 295, 297, 306, 317, 329, 342
Adair, Sir Robert, 12, 248
Addington, Henry (Viscount Sidmouth), 268
Adelaide, Queen (to William IV), 41, 44, 62, 65, 97, 106–7, 110, 112, 116, 123–24, 126–28, 130–31, 173–74
Alava, Don Miguel Ricardo de, 66
Albemarle, Lord, 110, 115, 140
Albert, Prince (Consort), 162 n, 167, 168–70, 173, 176, 178, 185, 196, 202–3, 208, 214, 216, 242–43, 253, 257–59, 261–62, 289, 296–99, 302–4, 326, 329, 337–39
Alexander I, Emperor of Russia, 66–67, 206–7
Alexander II, Emperor of Russia, 211–14
Allen, Dr., 104
Allen, John, 77, 182, 201–2
Althorp, Viscount, 60, 92, 200
Alvanley, Lord, 21, 96–97; obituary, 259–61
Amyot, Thomas, 22
Anglesey, 1st Marquis of, 21, 133–34, 213; obituary, 300–1
Angoulême, Duc de, 80 n
Angoulême, Duchesse de, 79 n, 80 n
Anne of Austria, 313
Anson, George, 223, 258, 324
Arbuthnot, George, 200, 222
Arbuthnot, Mrs., 17–18, 286
Argyll, 8th Duke of, 331

Armytage, Sir Elkanah, 324
Arnold, Dr. Thomas (of Rugby), 100
Ashburton, Lady, 308; obituary, 324–26
Ashburton, Lord, 174, 190, 308
Ashley, Lord, 151, 179
Auckland, Lord, 69
Augusta, Princess, 44, 131, 176
Augusta, Princess Royal, 227
Austen, Jane, 90
Austin, Charles, 188, 189
Austin, Mrs., 209, 239

Bacciochi, Count, 307
Bachelor (attendant of William IV), 127
Bagot, Lord, 343
Baring, Sir Francis (Baron Northbrook), 73–74, 190
Barnes, Thomas, 184, 223–24
Barrot, Odilon, 230–31
Bassano, Duc de, 308
Batchelor (valet de Chambre to George IV), 16
Bath, Lady, 9
Bathurst, Lord, 14, 15–16, 18
Beauclerck, Major, 83
Beaufort, Duchess of, 156
Beauvale, Lady, 227, 228, 292–93
Beauvale, Lord (Frederick Lamb), 216, 228, 277; obituary, 291–92; 321
Beckett, Thomas à, 90
Bedford, Duchess of, 173–74
Bedford, Duke of, 173, 202, 222, 264

Belfast, George, Earl of, 43
Belgioso, Princess, 181
Bentinck, George, 11
Berri, Duc de, 80 n
Berry, Agnes, 209
Berry, Mary, 208–9; obituary, 290–91
Bessborough, Lady, 251
Birch, Mr., 258
Blanc, Louis, 241, 282
Blessington, Lady, 145–47, 148, 282–84
Blessington, Lord, 282
Bonaparte, Napoleon, 3, 4, 52, 132, 206–7, 286
Borgo, Pozzo di, 316
Boswell, James, 22
Bressano, Princess, 31
Bridge, Mr. (silversmith), 49
Bright, John, 300, 323, 342
Broglie, Duc de, 236, 237, 238–39
Brougham, Lord, 10, 56, 58, 61, 63–64, 88, 91, 93, 95–96, 99, 101–3, 114–15, 145, 155, 158, 165–66, 168, 189, 201, 283, 292
Brown, General, 297
Brownlow, Lord, 44
Brummell, George ("Beau"), 259
Brunnow, Count von (Russian Ambassador), 211–12, 263
Buchanan, James, 327, 328 n
Buckingham, James Silk, 83
Buller, Charles, 145, 195, 325
Buller, James, 38
Bulwer-Lytton (Lord Lytton), 145, 148, 283
Burdette, Sir Francis, 59–60
Burdett Coutts, Miss, 225
Burghersh, Lord, 304
Burke, Edmund, 12, 94–95, 248–49, 260
Burke, Richard, 12, 248
Buol, Count Karl von, 276
Burrell, Peter (Baron Gwydir), 7
Buxton, Fowell, 63
Byng, Frederick ("Poodle"), 86
Byng, Sir John, 24, 66
Byron, Lord, 24–25, 145, 250 n

Cairne, Captain, 141
Cambridge, Duchess of, 131
Cambridge, Duke of, 176–77, 212
Cambridge, Princess of, 131

Canning, George, 10, 37, 48, 50, 52–53, 54, 58, 66, 91–92, 120, 200, 218, 248, 317
Cannizzaro, Duchess of, 180–82
Cannizzaro, Duke of (Count St. Antonio), 180–81, 316
Canterbury, Archbishop of, 126
Cardigan, Lord, 304
Carhampton, Lord, 278–79
Carlile, Richard, 139
Carlisle, Lord, 11
Carlyle, Thomas, 325
Carnot, Hippolyte, 241
Caroline, Queen to George IV, 149
Castlereagh, Viscount, 52, 58, 317
Cavaignac, Louis Eugène, 247
Cavendish, Lord George, 248
Cavendish, Henry Frederick, 128
Cayla, Madame du, 19–20
Cetto, Baron August von, 263
Charlotte, Princess, 6, 120
Charlotte, Queen to George III, 330
Chatham, 1st Earl of (Pitt the Elder), 90–91, 166, 199, 218
Chesterfield, Earl of, 41
Chesterfield, 4th Earl, 20, 100
Cholmondeley, Lord, 169
Chorley, Henry, 145
Chrysostom, St. John, 183
Clanricarde, Lady, 214
Clarence, Duke of, 14–15
Clarendon, 4th Earl of (George Villiers), 178–79, 214, 261–63, 265, 295, 296, 302–3, 305, 309–10, 325, 328–30, 332–33, 337–39, 341–43
Clinton, Lady, 173–74
Clinton, Robert, 18th Baron, 43
Cobbett, William, 64–65, 83, 329
Cobden, Richard, 276, 323–24, 342
Coleridge, Samuel Taylor, 89
Combermere, Lord, 301
Condé, Prince and Princess de, 80 n
Conroy, Sir John, 111, 124–26, 130, 159–60, 162–63
Conyngham, Lady, 9, 16, 19, 317
Conyngham, 1st Marquis, 38, 111, 116, 126, 128
Cowley, 1st Earl of, 308–9, 320–21
Cowper, Earl of, 78
Cowper, Lady, 49, 130, 166, 250 n, 318
Cowper, William, 91

Crabbe, George, 89
Crampton, Sir John, 314 n, 315
Creevey, 23–24, 88
Croker, John Wilson, 72, 168, 193, 225, 326
Cumberland, Duke of (King of Hanover), 14–15, 20, 21–22, 26, 40–41, 205–6, 242

Dacre, Lady (Mrs. Brande), 295
Dallas, George Mifflin, 314 n, 314–15
Damer, Dawson, 96–97
D'Aremberg, Pierre, 236
Davies, Scrope, 259
Dawson, Miss, 258
Deffand, Madame du, 290
Delane, John, 184 n, 297
Delessert, M., 234
Denison, Lady Elizabeth, 9
Denman, 1st Baron, 64
Derby, 14th Earl of, 83–84, 88, 101, 300, 306, 328, 335–36, 340, 342, 345
D'Escars, Duc, 19
D'Escars, Duchesse, 19
Devonshire, 6th Duke of, 210, 214
Dickens, Charles, 218
Dino, Madame de, 70
Disraeli, Benjamin, 128, 222, 224, 289–90, 300, 311, 330–31, 344–46
D'Orsay, Count, 145, 148, 166; obituary, 281–84
Dorset, Duke of, 104
Douro, Lady, 258
Douro, Lord, 45
Duchâtel, Madame, 238
Duchâtel, M., 230, 234
Duff Gordon, Sir Alexander, 209
Duff Gordon, Lady, 209, 218 n
Dumas, Alexandre (Père), 237 n
Duncannon, 1st Baron, 85, 93, 155, 182, 210
Drummond, Henry, 101
Dudley, Lord, 278
Duncombe, Thomas, 73, 75, 95, 96, 195
Dundas, Robert (2nd Viscount Melville), 188–89
Durazzo, Madame, 27
Durham, Lord, 145, 223–24

Eden, Robert (Bishop of Bath and Wells), 138–39

Edward III of England, 90
Edward VII. See Prince of Wales
Egerton, Lady Frances, 129
Egerton, Francis (1st Earl of Ellesmere), 218
Egremont, 3rd Earl of, 43, 77–78, 87–88, 249–50
Eldon, 1st Earl of, 18, 58, 269
Ellenborough, 2nd Baron, 15, 64, 190
Ellice, Edward (the Elder), 292
Ellis, Agar, 50
Emily, Princess, 155
Errol, Lord, 41, 42, 178
Erskine, Lady Augusta, 65, 104–5
Esterhazy, Prince Nicholas, 131
Esterhazy, Prince Paul, 46–47, 179
Eugénie, Empress, 293–94, 306, 307, 311

Faithfull, George, 83
Falck, Baron Anton, 46
Falmouth, 1st Earl of, 17
Ferrari, Madame, 27
Feodora, Princess, 162 n
Fisher, John (Bishop of Rochester), 198
FitzAlan, Lord, 131
Fitzclarence, Adolphus, 65, 97, 106–8, 110, 124, 173, 196, 207
Fitzclarence, Augustus, 62, 65
Fitzclarence, Frederick, 62
Fitzclarence, George (1st Earl of Munster), 38, 42, 56, 62, 93, 124
Fitzgerald, Hamilton, 158, 160
Fitzherbert, Mrs., 42, 67, 109–10
Fitzpatrick, Richard, 12
Fitzroy, Charles, 98
Flahault, Auguste Comte de, 243
Flahault, Madame de, 104
Foley, 259
Fondi, Princess, 31
Forster, John, 145
Fox, Charles James, 12, 76, 79, 144, 248
Fox, Mrs. C. J., 144
Fox, Miss, 202
Francis, Emperor of Austria, 243–44
Franklin, Benjamin, 66
Fullerton, Lady Georgiana, 239

Garrick, David, 76
George II, 155, 210, 330

George III, 3–4, 8, 20, 89–90, 194, 268, 330

George IV: as Regent, 6; as King, 8, 9–10, 11–12, 13, 15–16, 18, 19–22, 23, 26, 37–38; funeral, 39–40; 46–47, 91, 109–10, 112, 119, 120, 127, 194, 228, 301, 317

George, Prince of Denmark, 168

Girardin, Emile, 231

Gilbert, Davies, 73

Gladstone, William E., 291, 294–95, 342, 345–46

Glastonbury, Lord, 211

Gloster, Duchess of (18th century), 209

Gloucester, Duchess of, 131, 167, 177

Goderich, Viscount, 11, 58

Gordon, 258

Gore, Sir John, 41

Gore, Lady, 41

Gosset, Sir William, 243

Goulburn, Henry, 72, 82, 89

Grafton, 4th Duke of, 11

Graham, Sir James, 229, 295

Grammont, Duc de, 79 n–80 n

Grant, Charles, 27

Grant, Sir Robert, 27, 58

Granville, Lady, 103–4, 239

Granville, Lord, 213, 214, 279, 295, 327, 331, 336, 340–42

Grassini, Josephine, 286

Gregorio, Cardinal, 29

Grenville, Thomas, 197–98, 199, 211

Greville, Henry, 276

Grey, Sir Charles, 98

Grey, 2nd Earl, 18, 51, 61, 62, 63–64, 68, 74, 84, 88, 100, 101, 104, 116, 128, 200, 244, 252, 287, 317

Grey, 3rd Earl, 300, 314

Grey, Lady, 128

Grisi, Giulia, 99

Guiccioli, Countess, 24, 283

Guizot, Francois, 174, 230–31, 233–38, 239–40, 318–19, 323

Guizot, Madame, 237

Halford, Sir Henry, 3–4

Hamilton, Duke and Duchess of, 308

Hanover, King of. See Duke of Cumberland

Hardinge, 1st Viscount, 17, 65–66

Hardwicke, 4th Earl of, 340

Hardy, Sir Thomas, 83

Harewood, Lord, 149

Harrowby, 1st Earl of, 15, 214

Hastings, Lady, 149, 155, 160

Hastings, Lady Flora, 147, 148–50, 155–57, 158–60, 253

Hastings, Lord, 43, 61, 147, 148, 160

Havelock, Sir Henry, 327

Hawes, Sir Benjamin, 195

Head, Sir Edmund, 209

Heathcote, Sir Gilbert, 184

Henley, Joseph, 344

Henry II of England, 90

Henry VII of England, 198

Hertford, Lady, 192

Hertford, 3rd Marquis of, 191–94

Hertford, 4th Marquis of, 308–9

Hildyard, Miss, 258

Hill, Lord, 56

Hill, Lord Arthur, 30

Hilliard, Miss, 337

Hobhouse, John Cam (Baron Broughton), 152

Hodges, Colonel, 96–97

Hohenlohe, Ernest, Prince of, 162 n

Holland, Lady, 76–77, 101, 182–83, 201–2, 211; obituary, 220–21

Holland, Lord, 69, 75–76, 89, 101, 145, 166; obituary, 177; 182, 201–2, 317

Holmes, Billy, 95

Hook, Walter, 136

Horner, Francis, 201

Howe, Lord, 41

Howick, Viscount. See Grey, 2nd Earl

Hume, Dr. John Robert, 96

Hume, Joseph, 263

Huskisson, William, 49–51, 53

Huskisson, Mrs. William, 49

Ingestre, Lady Sarah, 156

Inglis, Sir Robert Harry, 57, 73

Irving, Washington, 25–26

James II of England, 314

Jeffrey, Francis, Lord, 86, 201

Jekyll, Joseph, 211

Jerrold, Douglas, 218

Jersey, 5th Earl of, 18, 40

Jocelyn, Robert, Viscount, 221

John, Archduke of Austria, 243

Johnson, Dr. Samuel, 22–23, 76

Jordan, Mrs., 120

Keate, Doctor, 227
Kemble, Charles, 76
Kemble, Fanny, 25
Kent, Duchess of, 105–8, 110–11, 115, 122, 124–26, 128, 129–31, 138, 143, 148–50, 159–63
Keppel, Sir William, 9
Klopstock, Friedrich, 90
Knighton, Sir William, 13, 16, 110
Kolowrath, Count Francis, 243
Kossuth, Louis, 276–77

Lamartine, Alphonse Marie de, 236–37
Lamb, Lady Caroline, 250 n
Landor, Walter Savage, 145
Lansdowne, Lord, 11, 93, 112, 114–15, 167, 189, 214, 252, 262, 263–64, 336
Landseer, Sir Edwin, 283
Langdale, Charles, 330
Laval, Duc de, 46
Layard, Sir Austin Henry, 300
Ledru-Rollin, Alexandre, 241
Leeds, Duke of, 11, 41
Legge, 30
Lehzen (Letzen), Baroness, 113, 126, 158, 162, 163, 173, 196
Leigh, George, 67
Leiningen, Charles Frederick, Prince of, 162 n
Le Marchant, Sir Denis, 223–24, 244
Leopold, King of the Belgians, 112, 131–32, 162 n, 224, 242
Leslie, Professor, 86
Letzen. See Lehzen
Leveson, Francis, 57–58
Lewis, George, 209, 329, 333
Lewis, Matthew Gregory ("Monk"), 85
Lhuys, Drouyn de, 263–64
Lieven, Madame de, 9, 124–25, 233–36, 243, 292; obituary, 316–23
Lilford, Lady, 202
Litchfield, Lady, 156
Liverpool, Lord, 8, 120, 154, 169, 222, 269
Locock, Doctor, 178
Londonderry, 3rd Marquis, 60–61, 245
Lopes, Sir Massey, 51
Loughborough, Lord, 89–90

Louis XIV of France, 313
Louis XVIII of France, 79 n–80 n, 309
Louis Napoleon. See Napoleon III
Louis Philippe, King of France, 47, 132, 230–38, 239–40, 241–42; death, 275–76; 283, 309
Lucan, Lord, 304
Ludlow, Lord, 301–2
Ludwig I, King of Bavaria, 242
Lushington, Sir Henry, 85
Luttrell, Henry, 10, 25, 76, 100, 144; obituary, 278–79
Lyndhurst, Lord, 60, 73, 167, 171, 283, 330, 336
Lyndhurst, Lady, 51
Lyttelton, Lady, 294
Lytton, Lord. See Bulwer-Lytton

Macaulay, Thomas Babington, 69–70, 86, 101–3, 136–37, 182–83, 188–89, 209–10, 311–12, 313, 326; death, 344–45
Macaulay, Zachary, 102
MacGregor, M., 10
Mackintosh, Sir James, 24
Macready, William Charles, 145, 148, 283
Mahon, Charles Patrick, 128
Maitland, Sir Thomas (General), 174–75
Malibran, Madame Maria Felicia, 99
Malmesbury, 3rd Earl of, 340
Maltzahn, Count, 292
Mann, Horace, 208
Manners, Lord John, 340
Mansfield, Lord, 60
Marescalchi, Mme. de, 67
Marie Antoinette, Queen of France, 309
Marlborough, Sarah, Duchess of, 187–88
Marlborough, 1st Duke of, 46, 157, 206–7
Marriott, Captain, 145
Matuscewitz, Count André, 45, 283
Mazarin, Cardinal, 197
Melbourne, 2nd Viscount, 70, 75, 85, 89, 91–93, 99–100, 113–14, 119, 121–22, 124, 125, 127–28, 130, 137–38, 139, 141–44, 147–48, 149–50, 151–56, 161–62, 170, 171, 173,

178–79, 182, 186–87, 196, 197, 204, 214, 218 n, 221–22, 228–29; obituary, 249–56; 275, 291, 295, 298
Mellish, Sir George, 187
Melville, 2nd Viscount, 16
Metternich, Prince von, 242, 243–44, 292, 313
Mildmay, Sir Henry, 259
Mill, James, 57
Mill, John Stuart, 325
Milnes, Richard Monckton, 281, 324
Minto, Lord, 105
Molé, Comte, 231, 235
Montebello, Comte de, 308
Montgomery, Alfred, 165 n
Monti, Vincenzo, 67
Montijo, Mme. de, 293
Montpensier, Duc de, 231, 236
Montrose, Duchess of, 156
Montrose, 4th Duke of, 38, 156
Moore, Sir John, 300
Moore, Thomas, 24–26, 85–86, 100, 145, 188
More, Sir Thomas, 183
Morny, Duc de, 332
Morpeth, Viscount (6th Earl of Carlisle), 152, 182
Motteux, John, 66
Mount Charles, Lord, 13, 40, 42
Moxon, Edward, 224
Münchhausen, Baron, 128
Munro, Sir Thomas, 183
Munster, 1st Earl of. See Fitzclarence, George
Murray, Sir George, 206

Napier, Admiral (Captain), 105
Napoleon III (Louis Napoleon), 145, 278, 280, 282–84, 293–94, 299, 302–4, 305–7, 308–9, 319–20, 331 n, 332–33
Narischkin, Madame, 20
Neumann, Baron Philip von, 179
Newcastle, 4th Duke of, 21
Newcastle, 5th Duke of, 295
Nicholas, Emperor of Russia, 305
Nolan, Captain, 304
Normanby, Lady, 152
Normanby, Lord, 136, 144, 153, 170
North, Lord, 15, 60, 89, 91

Northumberland, Duchess of, 111, 113, 169
Northumberland, Duke of, 169
Norton, Caroline (the Hon. Mrs.), 218 n

O'Connell, Daniel, 83, 96–97; death, 224–25
O'Connell, Morgan, 96, 261
O'Connor, Feargus, 249
Orleans, Duc de, 207
Orléans, Duchesse de, 232, 234, 238
Orsini, Felice, Count, 331 n
Orsini, Princess, 29
Osborne, Lord Sidney, 259
Ossulton, Lord, 128, 129

Pagès, Garnier, 241
Paget, Lord Alfred, 165 n
Paget, Clarence, 170
Palmella, Duke of, 316
Palmerston, Viscount, 58, 93, 103–4, 174, 179–80, 187, 195, 214, 228, 241, 244, 261–62, 263–66, 276–77, 279–81, 291–92, 295–96, 297, 299, 314 n, 317–18, 328, 329, 333, 340–43
Palmerston, Lady (earlier Lady Cowper), 170, 254, 291
Paxton, Sir Joseph, 211
Payne, John, 259
Peel, Jonathan, 95
Peel, Sir Robert, 58, 60, 72, 74–75, 81–82, 83, 93, 95, 97, 101, 112, 114–15, 119, 151–55, 167, 168, 186, 190–91, 194–96, 200, 204–5, 222–23, 226, 228, 245, 248, 255; obituary, 266–75; 287, 298
Peel, Sir Robert (the elder), 222
Perceval, Rev. A. P., 136
Perceval, Spencer, 89, 100–1, 268–69
Persigny, Duc de, 332
Piscatory, M., 236, 239
Pitt, William (the younger), 79–80, 211, 218, 268–69
Plunket, 1st Baron, 18
Pole, Sir Charles, 42
Porson, Richard, 197–98
Portland, 3rd Duke of, 248
Portman, Lady, 149–50, 158
Portman, Lord, 149
Pretender, the Old, 206

Princess Alice (Grand Duchess of Hesse), 339
Princess Royal of England (Crown Princess of Prussia), 333, 337–40
Prussia, Friedrich, Crown Prince of, 339

Queen Maria Amelia (wife of Louis Philippe), 231–33, 239

Radnor, Lord, 95
Raglan, Lord. See Somerset, Lord Fitzroy
Ranke, Leopold von, 209–10
Richmond, 3rd Duke of, 89–90, 248
Richmond, 5th Duke of, 11–12, 60, 62
Richmond, Margaret, Countess of, 198
Ridsdale, Parson, 78
Robarts, Abraham, 94
Robinson, Sir George, 69
Robinson, Sir Thomas, 90
Rockingham, 2nd Marquis of, 248
Roebuck, John Arthur, 83
Rogers, Samuel, 10, 76, 85, 100, 189, 278–79; obituary, 312–13
Rolfe, Baron, 182
Rolle, Lord, 135
Romney, Lady E., 78
Ros, Henry, 19th Baron de, 23, 25, 66, 96
Rosebery, Lord and Lady, 128
Rothschild family (in Frankfort), 203–4
Russell, Charles, 243, 249
Russell, Lord John, 57, 65, 66, 73, 92, 101, 122, 148, 150–53, 168, 179, 182, 184, 186, 187, 188, 195, 214, 225, 228, 240, 244, 256, 257–58, 262–63, 264–66, 274, 276–77, 280–81, 297–99, 317, 328–29, 340–43
Russell, Lady Wriothesley, 249
Russell, Lord Wriothesley, 202, 249

St. Aulaire, M. de, 214
Salisbury, Lord, 340
Santa Cruz, Marchioness of, 293
Sartorius, Admiral, 105
Saxe-Coburg, Duchess of, 173
Saxe-Coburg, Ernest, Duke of, 162 n

Saxe-Coburg, Ferdinand, Prince of, 162 n
Saxe-Weimar, Duchess of, 62
St. Cyr, Marshal Gouvion de, 289
Scott, Sir Walter, 24, 26
Sefton, Earl, 21, 43, 49, 63–64, 68
Sefton, Lady, 64
Selwyn, George, 155
Sévigné, Madame de, 90, 321
Seymour, George Hamilton, 313
Shaftesbury, 7th Earl of, 61
Shafto, Mr., 165 n
Sharpe, Sutton, 190
Shelburne, 2nd Earl of, 248
Shuttleworth, Kay, 198
Siddons, Mrs., 25
Sidney, Sir Philip Charles, 42
Smith, Robert ("Bobus"), 90, 211
Smith, Sydney, 86, 201; obituary, 215–16; 260, 278, 312
Smith, Vernon, 195
Smithson, Sir H., 78
Somerset, Lady Fitzroy, 260
Somerset, Lord Fitzroy (Lord Raglan), 66, 140–41, 304–5
Somerville, Mrs., 90
Southey, Robert, 51, 56–57
Spencer, John, 188
Spencer, 3rd Earl, 188, 200, 216–18, 243, 299
Spring Rice, Thomas, 1st Baron Monteagle, 89, 92
Staël, Madame de, 67, 90
Stanley, Edward John ("Ben"), 153
Stanley, Lord. See 14th Earl of Derby
Stanley, Lord, 15th Earl of Derby, 311
Stephen, James, 101–2, 136–37
Stewart, Dugald, 201
Stockdale, Mr., 4
Stockmar, Baron, 337–38
Strachan, Lady, 192
Strathaven, Lord, 40
Stuart, Sir Charles, 3
Stuart, Dudley, 276, 281
Sussex, Duke of, 14, 40, 42, 44, 114
Sutherland, Duke of, 174, 316
Sutton, Manners, 73

Talleyrand, Charles Maurice, 66, 68, 70, 77, 79–81, 104; obituary, 132–33; 206–7, 317

Tavistock, Lord, 73, 157–59
Tavistock, Lady, 62, 158
Taylor, Sir Henry, 57, 89, 91
Taylor, Sir Herbert, 98
Taylor, Watson, 43
Temple, Lord, 199
Tennyson, Charles (M.P.), 59–60
Thackeray, William Makepeace, 191 n, 314
Thiers, Louis Adolphe, 235–36, 289, 318–19
Thomas, Alexandre, 299
Thomson, Poulett, 81
Thurlow, Lord, 89–90
Thurn and Taxis, Princess of, 206
Thynne, Lord John, 134–35
Townshend, "Tommy," 91, 211
Tredcroft, Mrs., 78
Trench, Col. Frederick William, 225
Torrington, Lord, 99
Turner, J. M. W., 78

Vaillant, Marshal, 303
Valabrègue, M., 308
Vallière, Mademoiselle de la, 313
Van de Weyer, Sylvain, 214
Victoria, Queen: as Princess, 105, 106–7, 111, 113; as Queen, 113–16, 119, 123–28, 128–31, 134; coronation, 136; 137–38, 139–40, 141–44, 147, 150–55, 156, 158–65, 166–68; wedding, 168–70; 171–72, 174, 175–76, 178, 185–87, 194, 195–96, 204–5, 207–8, 212, 214, 216, 221–22, 223, 225, 228–29, 242–43, 251, 252–55, 257–58, 261–62, 264–65, 275, 280–81, 294, 295–96, 297–98, 302–3, 306, 309–10, 313, 326, 328–30, 334, 336–41
Vigny, Alfred de, 145
Villiers, Charles, 57
Villiers, George, 61, 138
Vincent, Baron Karl, 206–7
Visconti, M., 308
Visconti, Madame, 181
Voltaire, 26
Vyvyan, Sir Richard, 59–60

Walden, Howard de (Lord), 11
Wales, Prince of (future Edward VII), 202, 223, 227–28, 294, 310–11, 336–37
Walewski, Count, 280, 299, 303, 320, 331 n
Walpole, Horace (Lord Orford), 208–9, 290
Walpole, Spencer, 344
Wellesley, Gerald, 336
Wellesley, Lord, 165 n
Wellington, Duke of, 4, 14, 16–18, 19–22, 24, 38, 39–40, 45, 47–48, 49–51, 52–55, 58, 59, 67, 72, 73–75, 84, 91–94, 95–96, 101, 110, 114–16, 120, 131, 133, 134, 135, 140–41, 149, 150–55, 157, 159–65, 167–68, 170, 171–72, 185, 187, 194, 206–7, 212, 225, 242, 245, 267, 269–70; obituary, 284–89; 300–1, 304, 317,
Wensleydale, Lord, 330
Westmoreland, Lord, 3
Wetherell, Sir Charles, 57
Wharncliffe, Lord, 60, 104, 153, 198
Whewell, William, 189
Whiting, attendant of William IV, 127
Wilhelm, Kaiser, 340 n
William IV, 43–47, 55–56, 59–61, 65, 67, 74–75, 92, 97–98, 99, 104–9, 110–11, 112–13, 116; obituary, 119–22; 125, 127, 131, 210, 217, 252, 271, 301
Willoughby, Lord, 135, 169, 316
Winchelsea, 9th Earl, 16–18, 99, 104
Windham, William, 22–23
Wilberforce, William, 84
Wolfe, James, 199
Wolsey, Cardinal, 183
Worcester, Lord, 96
Wordsworth, William, 57, 89
Würtemberg, King of, 43–45
Wykeham, Miss, 120
Wyndham, Charles, 315

Yarmouth, Lord, 194
York, Duke of, 6–7, 10, 12, 37, 120
York, Duchess of, 5–7, 317

Zichy-Ferraris, Countess, 192–93

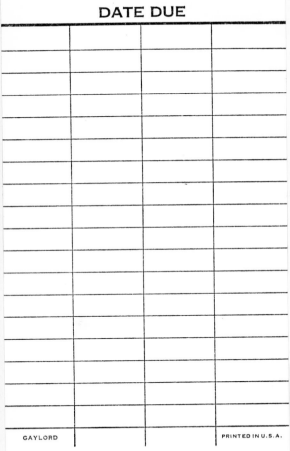

DATE DUE

GAYLORD			PRINTED IN U.S.A.